The Great Books

The Great Books

A Journey Through 2,500 Years
of the West's Classic Literature

Anthony O'Hear

Wilmington, Delaware

O'Hear, Anthony.

   The great books : a journey through 2,500 years of the West's classic literature / Anthony O'Hear. — 1st U.S. ed. —Wilmington, Del.: ISI Books, c2009.

     p. ; cm.
     ISBN: 978-1-933859-78-1

     Originally published: Cambridge, UK : Icon, 2007, under title: The great books: from The Iliad and The Odyssey to Goethe's Faust : a journey through 2,500 years of the West's classic literature.
     Includes index.

     1. Best books. 2. Literature. 3. Classical literature. I. Title.

PN511 .O34 2009   2008928732
011.73—dc22   0902

ISI Books
Intercollegiate Studies Institute
Post Office Box 4431
Wilmington, DE 19807-0431
www.isibooks.org

Manufactured in the United States of America

For Chris Woodhead, fellow pilgrim, fellow reader

Contents

List of Illustrations

To read great books does not mean one becomes "bookish"; it means that something of the terrible insight of Dostoyevsky, of the richly-charged imagination of Shakespeare, of the luminous wisdom of Goethe, actually passes into the personality of the reader; so that in contact with the chaos of ordinary life certain free and flowing outlines emerge, like the forms of some classic picture, endowing both people and things with a grandeur beyond what is visible to the superficial glance.

—John Cowper Powys

Author's Preface

For one person to write a book on the "great books" may seem the height of presumption, and from one point of view it probably is. After all, distinguished scholars have spent lifetimes working on each of the books considered here, without in any sense exhausting the richness of what they have to offer.

But there is scholarship and there is enthusiasm. This is a book written by an unashamed enthusiast. I love these books, and I return to them again and again. I want most of all to communicate to others something of the enthusiasm I have, and to help new readers journey through territories that to us in the twenty-first century are increasingly difficult to penetrate. Maps are needed, and this is a large part of what I am trying to supply. I hope that with what is provided here my readers will quickly go on to be readers of Homer, of Aeschylus, of Virgil, of Dante, of Milton and the rest, and that they will be able to read these great books with delight and enjoyment, as well as gaining from them illumination, insight, and wisdom.

This book is a book about great books, and also about the way in which earlier works in the tradition influence later works and are continually referred to in them, often indeed in ways which throw light on the earlier works themselves. However, we have also selected a number of illustrations for the book, and in the text I occasionally refer to music. I hope in these ways to suggest that many of the books being considered here have entered Western culture in ways way beyond the literary. They are in a wide sense part of our heritage, and have influenced and been reflected in that heritage in manifold ways through the centuries. It is further testimony to the organic nature of a culture and its development that some of the translations used here are themselves classic works of English literature: Pope's translations of Homer, Dryden's of Virgil, and Arthur Golding's of Ovid.

There are many modern editions of the works we consider here, and it is neither necessary nor appropriate to recommend any particular ones, save to say that many series of texts, such as the Oxford World's Classics, Penguin Classics, and Everyman's Library, contain helpful introductions and notes to the individual works. It is also worth pointing out here that, as translations often follow their own enumeration of lines and passages (and in some cases there is no standard system of line numbering anyway), we have not included line numbers in this book until we reach some of the later works, where doing so is both unambiguous and helpful. Nevertheless, there are enough pointers in this book to enable readers to find passages quoted or referred to easily enough in whatever edition is being used.

This is not an academic book in today's sense of academic book, nor is it intended as a work of original scholarship. Nevertheless, I hope that what I have written will stand up to scholarly scrutiny. This would doubtless be a vain hope had not a number of friends more expert than I in various of my authors cast their critical eyes over the relevant chapters. It is with great gratitude that I record here my thanks to David Taylor, Edward Dowler, Michela Massimi, Natasha O'Hear, David Moses, Inma Alvarez, Thea O'Hear and Roger Hausheer. Some of these friends will find that the occasional phrase or sentence or suggestion of theirs has strayed into the final text, and David Taylor has kindly allowed me to use some of his translations of Sophocles. I hope that those who have helped me so generously will not feel that I have abused their goodwill.

I have also to thank João Carlos Espada, Director of the Institute of Political Studies (Instidudo de Estudos Politicos) at the Catholic University of Portugal, for without him this book would not exist. I would never have embarked upon it had I not had a conversation with him in a Lisbon restaurant in 2003. We were talking about some vague plans Roger Scruton and I had then had for giving a lecture course on great books in London. "Come and give it here," said João. My doubts about giving such a course on my own, about giving such a course in Portugal, and about giving it in Portugal in English were quickly swept aside; so in the autumn and spring of 2004–05 I found myself as Calouste Gulbenkian Visiting Professor at the Catholic University of Portugal teaching a course entitled "The Tradition of the Great Books." I have to thank both João and the Calouste Gulbenkian Foundation for making this possible, and also for my audiences in Lisbon whose responses and comments made me think that developing the lectures into a book might be worthwhile.

I should also mention that an earlier version of the Epilogue was originally given as a lecture that the Prince of Wales invited me to give at his Educational Summer School in Buxton in 2004, and was then repeated as a public lecture at the Calouste Gulbenkian Foundation in Lisbon in 2005. I am grateful for both these opportunities to try out my thoughts. Finally I would to thank Peter Pugh, Duncan Heath and Lucy Leonhardt at Icon Books; Peter for taking the project on in the first place, Duncan for his meticulous editing of my manuscript, and for the many improvements he has made to it, and Lucy for picture research.

Introduction

"These fragments I have shored against my ruins." Thus T. S. Eliot wrote at the end of *The Waste Land*. The fragments are fragments from the literature of the past. Eliot contrasted the wholeness of past eras in our heritage with what he saw as the fracturing of feeling, sensibility and belief in his own day, the 1920s, a time of public and, for Eliot himself, personal collapse.

Eliot wrote in the expectation that his readers would have some inkling of the texts he was referring to, as did his contemporaries Ezra Pound and James Joyce who also filled their works with references to the great works of the past. This expectation may have had a degree of disingenuousness about it, particularly when, as was often the case with Pound, the references were to highly obscure events and texts. Nevertheless, when Pound transcribed a fragment of Book Ten of Homer's *Odyssey* and presented it as his First Canto, he could reasonably have relied on most of his readers recognizing what he was doing, just as a couple of generations earlier Tennyson's readers would have understood what he was up to in his poem "Ulysses," and may even have recognized that the Ulysses/Odysseus figure he was imagining owed as much to Dante as to Homer.

No longer. At the start of the twenty-first century, even for educated people, Homer, Greek tragedy, Virgil, Ovid and Dante no longer form an instantly recognizable cultural background, as once they did. Their absence from modern sensibility means in turn that we miss a great deal in writers closer to our time and language, such as Milton, Racine, Goethe, and even Chaucer and Shakespeare. These more modern writers, too, can seem forbidding to generations unschooled in entering worlds and cultures remote from their own. And we do not realize that even though the Greek and Roman classics and the medieval world are truly remote from us, our own minds and feelings are stocked with themes and attitudes rooted in those classics. So a journey through the ancient classics is a journey of discovery, to be sure, but it is also a journey of self-discovery (which was part of what Eliot and Pound were getting at in their superficially forbidding works).

To admit that the great books of the past may be difficult for today's readers is emphatically not to say that these books are not in all kinds of ways rewarding, once the initial hurdle of unfamiliar background and myth is overcome. It is one of the main aims of this book to help today's readers to read Homer and the rest not just with profit, which is certainly there, but even more with enjoyment, fascination, and pleasure on all sorts of levels, from the most sublime to the most earthy. It would be an exaggeration to say that someone who has not read the books we are about to examine is a stranger to the human condition; but there is certainly much about our condition, and particularly our condition as Westerners, that he or she will not be aware of.

Mentioning our condition as Westerners suggests a necessary qualification of our aim in this book. It is not claimed here that the only great books of the world are those within the Graeco-Roman Christian tradition. There are doubtless great books from Persia, from the Indian sub-continent, from China, from Japan and from other places besides, and doubtless we could read some of these books with benefit. But they have not fed into our thought and traditions in the same way as Homer and those works in some form of descent from Homer, the works we are to look at here.

Homer and the rest are not all the great books there are, but that they are great books can hardly be in dispute. Some might quarrel with omissions from our list, and we might agree that some books we have not included have as much merit as some of the ones we have included. And, with the exception of Goethe's *Faust, Part Two*, we have not included works from the nineteenth and twentieth centuries, partly on the grounds of space and partly because, for the most part, works from the past 200 years do not have the particular difficulties of background and reference of those from earlier times. However, the books we are to study have all survived the toughest test of all, the test of time.

In the words of the philosopher David Hume (from 1757):

The same Homer, who pleased at Athens and Rome two thousand years ago, is still admired at Paris and at London. All the changes of climate, government, religion, and language have not been able to obscure his glory. Authority or prejudice may be able to give a temporary vogue to a bad poet or orator; but his reputation will never be durable or general. When his compositions are examined by posterity or foreigners, the enchantment is dissipated and his faults appear in their true colours. On the contrary, a real genius, the longer his works endure, and the more wide they are spread, the more sincere is the admiration which they meet with.[1]

That the works on our list of great books should be on that list is no decision of ours. They are there because they have appealed in many different times and places, and also because they have influenced the writers who have followed them. In that sense, they are cornerstones of our literary and cultural heritage, and there are continuities of theme and influence which run through our selection, and which will guide our commentary.

We start with Homer's *Iliad,* his account of the Trojan War, and we end with Goethe's *Faust, Part Two.* Artificial or not, there is a sort of symmetry about this, for Homer's tale begins with the abduction of Helen of Troy and Goethe's conjures up visions of the same Helen. Over and above the personality of Helen, we might be led by the symmetry to see what Goethe calls the "eternal feminine" running through much of our story, the feminine as creative force, but also at times as leading to destruction.

Homer's myth refers back to the judgment of Paris, when one of the princes of Troy chooses the goddess of love above the goddesses of marriage and of wisdom. He wins Helen for himself—and plunges Troy into war. In the fallout from the war, Agamemnon the leader of the Greeks incurs the mortal enmity of a woman, his wife, and pays the price. Odysseus, another of the Greeks, spends ten years travelling back to the wife he has left, a tale enlivened by amorous and other dalliances en route. In the Greek tragedies we look at, we see the maiden Antigone putting family piety before political necessity and the mother of the King of Thebes more responsive than her son to the call of Dionysus, the god of nature, wine, and frenzy.

In Homer, the Greeks defeat the Trojans, destroy Troy, and enslave their women. But in *The Aeneid,* the Roman Virgil's myth, the outcome is reversed. Aeneas the Trojan escapes from Troy and wanders until he finds what eventually becomes Rome. He escapes from the mad love of Dido the Carthaginian queen to wed the daughter of the King of the Latins. In Ovid, Virgil's near contemporary, we find a host of stories of the power and attraction of love, from the most profane to the most faithful.

A different atmosphere enters with Saint Augustine, for whom sexual love is the root of corruption. But in Dante's *Divine Comedy,* as deeply a Christian work as Augustine's *Confessions,* the creative love of a woman for the poet incarnates divine wisdom itself and leads Dante to the beatific vision, arguably the most sublime of all interpretations of the eternal feminine. By contrast, Milton, Pascal and Racine take a more Augustinian view of femininity, by turns seductive and destructive, a theme we also find in Shakespeare's *Hamlet* (though much of the fault there is Hamlet's own). Chaucer and Cervantes take us down their own by-ways, but we end with Goethe, for whom a synthesis of Gretchen, Helen, the Christian Marys of the Gospels and the nymph Galatea rising from the waves is the source of life, creativity, compassion and redemption.

It would be absurd to pretend that there is a single theme running through all our great books, and also far too reductive an approach to the books themselves. But as our sketch of the eternal feminine might suggest, there are criss-crossing and overlapping currents, and also (as we will emphasize) many references in the later works to earlier ones, which at the same time throw light on the earlier ones. No doubt we could also develop sketches of the way in which the themes of war, peace, social order, nature, piety, crime and punishment, forgiveness, homecoming, work, and much else besides move in and out of focus in our great books, and also how our own attitudes to these and other things are rooted in these earlier treatments of which we are no longer fully aware.

We hope that in reading our great books, readers of today will come to enjoy what they read, and at the same time gain a less fragmentary sense of their own cultural roots.

Homer

Any survey of the "great books" must begin with the ancient Greeks. Not only are their works monumental in themselves: for the cultures influenced by the Greeks, Greek art and literature is the fountainhead of so much later work. The philosopher A. N. Whitehead once remarked that all Western philosophy consists of footnotes to Plato. It would not be difficult to make a similar point about Greek literature. This will become evident over and over again as we make our journey from Homer to Goethe, through Roman and European thought and literature. But just because—even to those initially unacquainted with them—there will be a sense of familiarity when we look at Homer and Greek tragedy, and also at Greek sculpture, architecture and philosophy, there is also a danger. In approaching the ancient Greeks we must never forget how different they are from us, and how far their world and its atmosphere are from ours.

At first sight, there is a striking absence among the ancient Greeks of what we would call the Christian virtues, those of humility and concern for the underdog. Pride and even a degree of ruthlessness are admired by the Greeks—although, as we will see, among their writers, including Homer himself, there are forceful criticisms of these attitudes once we get beneath the surface. Then, to the Greek mind, fate, sometimes seen as the caprice of the gods, is implacable, unsoftened by thought of redemption. The Greeks did not value equality, despite their invention of democracy. Nor until comparatively late on was critical reasoning regarded as desirable; indeed, as we will see, in Homer's character Thersites it was regarded as thoroughly undesirable. And forcing those who would rather not do so to think about what they were doing helped to bring about Socrates' death.

Then there were the gods and the mysteries. Some have argued that in Homer and in the tragedies the gods do not cause things to happen that would not have happened anyway. The gods, in other words, represent forces which are already within us. But even if we accept this, to the vast majority of the Greeks in classical times the gods were ever-present. Or rather, the Greeks lived in an atmosphere in which there was a union in which the divine, the human, the animal, and the material all meshed. In the words of George Seferis, the great modern Greek poet, in Homer "the whole world is a woof of 'umbilical cords'; the earthly, the heavenly world, animals, plants, the hearts of men, good, evil, death, life—that ripen, vanish, and flower again."[2] The Greek gods were not Christian gods or saints. They were more like contending forces of nature, but forces with minds and intentions of their own, interweaving with ours. Even the abstract philosophy of the Greeks is far from ours. Whitehead's remark may have some truth, but the Plato studied by philosophers of today is a Plato who is almost a colleague or contemporary of ours, with our mentality. The fact that all his thought is framed in a mystical myth of the transmigration of souls between this world and another more perfect world, more real than ours, to which we aspire whether we recognize it or not, is typically overlooked as too embarrassing even to notice, let alone to take seriously.

Finally, there are the myths. As Matthew Arnold said of the Athenian playgoer entering the theater, "the terrible old mythic story on which the drama was founded stood, before he entered the theater, traced in its bare outlines on the spectator's mind; it stood in his memory, as a group of statuary, faintly seen at the end of a long and dark vista."[3] Homer and the tragedians took their audiences on journeys during which they saw the statuary afresh, maybe in new and dramatic lights. But the core and even the detail of what they were showing their audiences, the audiences already knew. The Greeks lived and breathed these myths, which formed the basis of their religion and of their self-understanding. The relationship between the ancient Greek poets and their audiences, then, was quite different from that between modern writers and their audiences, and also from that between modern audiences (for whom the myths are not part of a universal inheritance) and the ancient Greeks.

We have two works traditionally attributed to Homer. Despite emerging from a rich literary tapestry which would include the poems of Hesiod and the Homeric hymns, the works attributed to Homer himself are, equally traditionally, regarded as the starting points of Western literature. There is *The Iliad,* a poem of epic struggle among heroes, and also of war and peace. There is *The Odyssey,* the archetypal tale of quest and homecoming, and also of righteous revenge.

We do not know whether both poems were written by the same author, or even whether there was a poet called Homer. We do not know when either poem was written or, more probably, orally composed. There seems to have been a standard written text used in festivals in Athens from about 550 B.C., but it is generally supposed that the originals, whether written or not, were composed much earlier, maybe dating from the eigth century B.C. These "originals" themselves are thought to have been based on centuries of earlier oral tradition, with bardic recitation and embroidering of myths emerging from the depths of time.

We do not need to go any further into the question of "Homer" here, save perhaps to remark that each of the poems reveals within itself an impressive unity of theme, treatment and language. How far the two poems are similar in style, and hence conceivably the work of the same voice, remains a matter of dispute.

What is clear, though, is that the classical Greeks themselves—those in the sixth and fifth centuries B.C.—regarded the connected tales as deriving from a much earlier period, maybe from as far back as the middle of the second millennium B.C. The classical Greeks were aware of what they called Cyclopean architecture in places like Mycenae and Tyrins, colossal fortified palaces they believed to have been constructed by giants, surrounded by equally colossal tombs filled with rich grave goods. The world that these places testified to was a feudal world. It was dominated by powerful kings of immense wealth, surrounded by their knights and households of women-folk and also by armies of lesser soldiers and slaves. This world was marked by constant warring and fighting, and this is what Homer describes. We can never know whether there was a Trojan War, fought between a combined force of Achaeans (Greeks) against Troy in what is now north-western Turkey. But since the nineteenth-century archaeologists, led by the great Heinrich Schliemann, have revealed that there were great palaces and fortifications and tombs dating from the second millennium in just the places Homer said they were, including Mycenae and Troy themselves.

The Iliad

The epic poem which is the foundation of Western literature was probably composed in the form we have it around 700 B.C. Its theme is the mythical ten-year war between the states of Greece and the great city of Troy, set sometime in the second millennium B.C. The war was caused by the abduction of the beautiful Helen, wife of the King of Sparta, by Paris, one of the Trojan princes. The Iliad focuses on just four days of the war, now in its ninth year. The Greeks are encamped outside Troy, unable to take it; the Trojans are unable to dislodge the Greeks; and Achilles, the greatest of the Greek warriors, is angry. The Iliad is, as Homer tells us, the tale of the wrath of Achilles, and what that wrath brings about. Unsparing and without illusion, Homer shows the pity of war against the background of the great and luxurious civilization of Troy; but we know from the start that the city is doomed by an implacable fate, as delivered partly by means of the interference of the quarrelling Olympian gods. Ultimately, though, no human, Trojan or Greek, is victorious; all are victims of this war. The possibility of redemption is suggested only by the meeting between Priam and Achilles at the end of The Iliad. *Priam, the King of Troy, is desolate at the death of Hector, his son and Troy's best and only hope, at the hands of the remorseless Achilles. For just a few moments Achilles and Priam ponder their own fragility in mutual recognition of their common humanity.*

The Iliad is about the Trojan War, a war between the combined forces of Greece and the Asiatic state of Troy, whose city is the fabulously rich Ilium (hence *Iliad*). But it is about only one incident in that war, in all four days of battle and a few weeks surrounding those days. The war itself, as Homer tells us, lasted for ten years overall, and its origins went back further still.

We could begin with the judgment of Paris, even though Homer himself makes but passing reference to the story. Paris, a prince of Troy, though living at the time as a shepherd, is asked to judge between the three great goddesses of Olympus (where the gods live) as to which is the most beautiful: Hera, the wife of Zeus, the king of the gods, and herself the patron of marriage and motherhood; Athene, the goddess of wisdom, of the arts and of military power; and Aphrodite, the goddess of love (who is Venus in Latin). Paris chooses Aphrodite, and he gets both his reward and the undying hatred of Hera and Athene.

Paris's reward is to gain the love and the body of Helen, the most beautiful woman in the world. It comes about this way. Helen is the result of the coupling of her mother Leda with Zeus disguised as the famous swan— hence the countless images of Leda and the Swan in classical and later art. By the time Paris comes on the scene, Helen is the wife of Menelaus, the King of Sparta. Paris goes to visit Menelaus in Sparta. With the assistance of Aphrodite, Paris and Helen fall in love. They elope back to Troy, where they live as man and wife.

In order to avenge his shame and the abuse of his hospitality, Menelaus and the rest of the Greek kings, led by Agamemnon (his brother and King of Mycenae), declare war on Troy. A great fleet is assembled, but before it can leave Agamemnon has to sacrifice his daughter Iphigenia to secure a fair wind. (The sacrifice of Iphigenia is not mentioned by Homer, but it becomes prominent in other classical texts, including Aeschylus's *Oresteia*, as we will see later. It is also worth noting that Clytemnestra, Agamemnon's wife who hates him over Iphigenia, is the half-sister of Helen.)

The Greeks' force includes Odysseus, the wily King of Ithaca famous for his cunning; Nestor, the wise old ruler from Pylos; the two Ajaxes; Idomeneus, the King of Crete; Achilles, the greatest fighter of all (who was tricked into going by Odysseus); Patroclus, Achilles' closest friend; and many others drawn from all over Greece. This force lands on the coast of Troy, near Ilium. During the campaign they attack a temple sacred to the sun god Apollo, patron of music and prophecy. They carry off Chryseis, the daughter of Apollo's priest, as booty for Agamemnon, so earning that cruel god's hostility. By contrast, Poseidon, the god of the sea, is pro-Greek because the Trojans never paid him for building the walls of Troy. The gods and goddesses are thus taking an interest in the battle below, lining up on one side or the other.

The campaign goes on inconclusively for nine years, the Trojans refusing to come out and fight a full battle, and the Greeks (who are called Achaeans in Homer) camped on the shore, unable to take the city. It is at this point, in the tenth year of the war, that *The Iliad* itself begins. Its twenty-four Books cover just four days on the conflict, but in them the whole story is suggested.

Book One opens with Homer invoking the muse, the goddess of poetic inspiration:

> Achilles' wrath, to Greece the direful spring
> Of woes unnumber'd, heavenly goddess, sing!
> That wrath which hurl'd to Pluto's gloomy reign
> The souls of mighty chiefs untimely slain;
> Whose limbs unburied on the naked shore,
> Devouring dogs and hungry vultures tore.
> Since great Achilles and Atrides [Agamemnon] strove,
> Such was the sovereign doom, and such the will of Jove [Zeus].
> (All translations from *The Iliad* are those of Alexander Pope (1715–20).)

Thus the opening of *The Iliad*. Its subject and the mainspring of all its action are indeed the wrath of Achilles. The Achaeans are afflicted with plague, which they believe is caused by Apollo's anger over the abduction of Chryseis. Urged by Calchas, their priest, and backed up by Achilles, Agamemnon is forced to return Chryseis to her father. In return and to avoid losing face, Agamemnon insists that Achilles give him Briseis, Achilles' own prize and bed-slave. Intervention by the goddess Athene prevents Achilles from killing Agamemnon on the spot and Briseis is seized. A distraught and furious Achilles withdraws himself, Patroclus and his Myrmidon troops from the war.

Achilles calls on his mother, the sea-nymph Thetis, to let the Trojans win. Thetis, who once saved Zeus when long ago he was in danger from the combined forces of Hera, Poseidon and Athene, goes to Olympus to entreat Zeus. Her arms around his knees, she prays him to let the Trojans have the upper hand at least until the Greeks pay back Achilles, and Zeus agrees. Hera, enemy of the Trojans and also of Zeus's amours, is furious, but peace between them is restored by Hephaestus, the lame smithy god. Hephaestus reminds Hera and the other immortals of what happens to those who oppose Zeus, who, by this time, is powerful enough to command all the others. It is not worth the gods fighting over the fate of mere mortals. At this reminder of Zeus's power, the gods desist from quarrelling and set about feasting and carousing, laughing at the crippled Hephaestus bustling around the hall filling their glasses.

On earth, meanwhile, at the start of Book Two Agamemnon is sent a dream by Zeus, convincing him that the Greeks will win. But when day breaks, and Agamemnon calls a general council, the Greeks themselves start to rush back to their ships. Odysseus lambasts them, and the council reconvenes. It will already be clear that honor and shame and military prowess are the dominant motives in the Homeric world. In a voice not heard again until, perhaps, Socrates, Thersites, a common soldier, injects some common sense into the discussion: Has Agamemnon not got enough spoils and women from the war already? Let us, cowards as we are, leave Agamemnon here:

> Hence let us fly, and let him waste his store
> In loves and pleasures on the Phrygian shore.
> We may be wanted on some busy day
> When Hector comes . . .

And look how he has treated Achilles, a much better man than he. For his pains Thersites is thrashed by Odysseus, who, along with Nestor, urges battle. The Greek army gathers, while the Trojans arm and leave the city. Homer catalogues both forces. We are now in Day One of the four days of battle.

Day One of the Battle

At the start of Book Three the armies meet to engage in battle, and Paris proposes that he has single combat with Menelaus in order to bring the war to an end. Helen is alerted to the duel and comes to the battlements. Strangely perhaps, she is admired, even loved, by Priam, the King of Troy and the Trojan elders—the gods, not she, are responsible for the war, says Priam. Helen points out some of the Greek heroes to Priam. In the duel Menelaus begins to overwhelm Paris, but Aphrodite rescues Paris and—in a passage of highly charged erotic power—takes him back to Ilium, to the delights of the bed of an initially reluctant Helen.

In Book Four, Athene and Hera plot the destruction of Troy. Athene persuades Pandarus, a Trojan archer, to shoot at Menelaus. She deflects the arrow, but it has its desired effect. The temporary truce is broken. Battle now starts in earnest. Roared on by Agamemnon, praising some, castigating others, the Greeks have the better of things at first. In Book Five, Diomedes, a young Greek hero, urged on by Athene, wreaks havoc among the Trojans, forcing a partial retreat.

> Thus from high hills the torrents swift and strong
> Deluge whole fields, and sweep the trees along
> Through ruin'd moles the rushing wave resounds
> O'erwhelms the bridge, and bursts the lofty bounds . . .
> So rag'd Diomedes, boundless in his ire,
> Drove armies back, and made all Troy retire.

Pandarus fires an arrow at him, but again it fails to kill, only rousing Diomedes the more, like a lion attacking a herd of sheep:

> He foams, he roars; the shepherd does not stay,
> But trembling leaves the scattering flocks a prey.
> Heaps fall on heaps; he bathes the ground with blood,
> Then leaps victorious o'er the lofty mound.

In his rampage, he kills Pandarus and injures Aeneas, one of the greatest of the Trojan leaders, who is also the son of Aphrodite. Aphrodite rescues her son, and Diomedes now oversteps himself, stabbing Aphrodite herself. He is warned by Apollo, who, with Ares, the god of war, is starting to intervene on behalf of the Trojans. Hector, the greatest and noblest of the Trojans, begins to take a hand as well, and the Greeks are driven back. Hera and Athene rally the Greeks, and Diomedes, protected by Athene, wounds Ares, who returns to Olympus to complain to Zeus.

In Book Six, the battle swings back towards the Greeks. Diomedes' remorseless slaughter of Trojans continues, interrupted only when he and Glaucus, a Trojan, come to a chivalrous agreement based on earlier family ties. Conversations between those engaged in killing and being killed, often hostile and contemptuous, but often too moderated by a grudging respect for the courage and virtue of one's opponent, are a feature of the Homeric narrative. Hector, meanwhile, returns to Ilium to make the women of Troy attempt to appease Athene through a sacrifice, unsuccessfully as it turns out. We are shown Ilium in all its grandeur, the benefits of the peace and civilization in the great city in stark contrast to the carnage on the plain below. Hector has poignant meetings with his mother Hecabe and with Helen. Helen is abject:

> Would heaven, 'ere all these dreadful deeds were done,
> The day that show'd me to the golden sun
> Had seen my death! Why did not whirlwinds bear
> The fatal infant to the fowls of air?
> Why sunk I not beneath the whelming tribe
> And mid the roarings of the water died?

But failing that, would that "I had been wife to a better man." Hector urges her to persuade Paris to rejoin the battle.

Hector, meanwhile, goes on to talk to his own wife, Andromache, and to see Astyanax, his infant son. Andromache is desperate for Hector to remain in Ilium, directing the fighting from there. But bound by the code of honor, Hector cannot be a coward, even though he knows well that the day will come when Troy is destroyed along with Priam and his mother and all Troy's warriors and glories. But worse still:

> Thy griefs I dread:
> I see the trembling, weeping captive led
> In Argive [Greek] looms our battles to design,
> And woes of which so large a part was thine!

He sees Andromache, in other words, taken as a slave by the Greeks. Hector then goes to take the child, but the child is frightened by his father's armour and helmet. Hector removes his helmet, kissing and dandling Astyanax, praying to the gods that his son be no less excellent than his father in strength and in battle. Heavy with foreboding, Hector leaves Andromache and Astyanax, and with Paris returns to the battle.

Inspired by the gods, Hector decides to issue a challenge to a Greek to engage in single combat (Book Seven). Menelaus volunteers, but is dissuaded, and the greater Ajax, the biggest and strongest of the Greek heroes, steps forward. The duel is inconclusive. Hector and Ajax exchange gifts, parting as friends. Night begins to fall. In the Greek camp Nestor advises the Greeks to announce a truce the next morning, to collect their dead and to build a defensive wall and ditch around the ships, all of which they proceed to do. In Ilium too there is talk of putting an end to the war, though Paris refuses to give up Helen. At dawn the Trojans offer the Greeks all that Paris brought to Troy—except Helen. Urged on by Diomedes, the Greeks reject this with a roar. A short truce will allow the dead to be gathered, washed and cremated, after which the war will start again.

Day Two of the Battle

At the start of Book Eight, Zeus warns the gods against further interference on the plain below, after which the clash of arms and screams of men and horses begin again. In a Greek advance Diomedes kills Hector's charioteer, but is himself held up by a thunderbolt from Zeus right in front of his chariot. The Greeks are routed by Hector and pushed back to the ditch around their ships. Hera and Athene attempt to intervene on behalf of the Greeks, but are warned off by Zeus, who tells them that the Trojans will continue to have success until Patroclus is killed and Achilles returns to the battle. Night comes on before Hector and the Trojans can destroy the Greek ships. Full of hope that at long last the Greeks are to be driven from their land, the Trojans camp out on the plain with a thousand camp fires lighting the plain and Troy itself:

> The long reflections of the distant fires
> Gleam on the walls, and tremble on the spires.
> A thousand piles the dusky horrors gild,
> And shoot a shady lustre o'er the field.
> Full fifty guards each flaming pile attend,
> Whose umber'd arms, by fits, thick flashes send.
> Loud neigh the coursers o'er their heaps of corn
> And ardent warriors wait the rising morn.

In the Greek camp, Agamemnon, despairing, suggests that they leave (Book Nine), but he is rebuked by Diomedes. Nestor suggests that they attempt to conciliate Achilles and bring him back into the war. A mission consisting of Odysseus, Ajax and Phoenix, Achilles' old tutor, goes to Achilles. But Achilles is adamant. He rejects all gifts and entreaties. He will not fight again until the Trojans are attacking him and his own ships. Odysseus has to report that Achilles is angrier than ever. Diomedes says the Greeks should forget Achilles and that Agamemnon himself should lead them into battle the next morning.

Agamemnon and Menelaus are deeply worried (Book Ten). They cannot sleep, and call a council of the Greek chieftains. As a result Diomedes and Odysseus volunteer to go to the Trojan camp, to spy. On the way they find a Trojan spy, Dolon, coming the other way. They interrogate and kill him. Acting on Dolon's information, they advance to the Trojan camp, killing a band of sleeping Thracians and their king, and stealing their famous horses, which they bring back to the Greeks in triumph.

Day Three of the Battle

At the start of Book Eleven, Agamemnon arms and leads out the Greeks. He is a lion in battle, remorselessly spearing Trojans and hacking them to pieces. The Trojans are driven back to the gates of Ilium, but Hector then rallies the Trojans, and gradually things turn their way. Agamemnon's charge is stopped when he himself is wounded and has to retreat. Hector himself kills nine Greeks. Diomedes and Odysseus kill seven Trojans, and although Diomedes drives Hector off, he is wounded by an arrow from Paris. Odysseus and Menelaus are also wounded. Ajax kills five Trojans, but is himself forced back. Patroclus is sent by Achilles to find out what is going on. Nestor urges him to enter the battle himself, in Achilles' armour.

The fighting has now reached the ditch around the Greek ships, but the Trojans cannot cross it by chariot (Book Twelve). They will have to storm it on foot. Zeus, though, sends them an omen. An eagle flies overhead with a snake in its talons. In a desperate lunge, the snake bites the eagle. In agony, the eagle drops the snake. The Trojan priest reads this as meaning that the Greeks will slaughter many Trojans if they breach the ditch, and that they should retreat. Hector contemptuously rejects this advice, and the Trojans storm on. Prominent are the two Ajaxes, desperate in defense of the Greeks, and Sarpedon, a Trojan, who is also a son of Zeus by a mortal woman. Sarpedon breaches the Greek wall. After an intense struggle, Hector is the first man through, smashing a gate in the wall.

At the start of Book Thirteen the Trojans reach the Greek ships, and Zeus turns away in the belief that no gods will break his edict. But Poseidon does, firing up the Greeks, among them the two Ajaxes and Idomeneus. Hector, leading the Trojan onslaught, is held up. In the fierce fighting many die. The advantage begins to swing back to the Greeks as the Trojans are out-maneuvered. As Hector attempts to regroup the Trojans, he and Ajax taunt each other.

With Agamemnon, Odysseus and Diomedes all wounded, and the ships under threat, spirits are low in the Greek camp (Book Fourteen). Poseidon, disguised as an old man, exhorts Agamemnon to rouse himself from despair, and Hera too decides to take a hand. Her method is not disguise as a human, but a full-on seduction of Zeus, to keep his attention away from Troy. She tricks Aphrodite into giving her an appropriately named aphrodisiac to administer to Zeus. She engages the god Sleep to help her, and the spell begins to work. . . . Wrapped in a golden cloud that Zeus himself calls up, they begin to make love on one of the peaks of Mount Ida, near to Troy itself:

> His eager arms around the goddess threw.
> Glad Earth perceives, and from her bosom pours
> Unbidden herbs and voluntary flowers;
> Thick new-born violets a soft carpet spread,
> And clustering lotos swelled the rising bed,
> And sudden hyacinths the turf bestow,
> And flamy crocus make the mountain glow,
> There golden clouds conceal the heavenly pair,
> Steeped in soft joys, and circumfused with air;
> Celestial dews, descending o'er the ground,
> Perfume the mount, and breathe ambrosia round.
> At length with love and sleep's soft power oprest,
> The panting thunderer nods, and sinks to rest . . .

With Zeus thus overcome by sleep and love, Poseidon fires up the Greeks. The greater Ajax fells Hector with a boulder. Hector is withdrawn by his men. The Greeks are rampant and, as Book Fifteen begins, the Trojans are retreating, pursued by the Greeks.

Zeus wakes up, furious at Hera's trick. He will get Apollo to cure Hector of his wounds and Poseidon called off. But he also foretells the entry of Patroclus into the battle, and the deaths of his own son Sarpedon and also of Patroclus and of Hector himself at the hands of Achilles. From then on the Greeks will eventually triumph, capturing Ilium itself. Hector, revived by Apollo, re-enters the battle. There is terrible slaughter. The Greeks are driven back to the ships once more, resistance really coming only from Ajax as the Trojans start to fire the ships.

As this is going on, in Book Sixteen we see Patroclus persuading Achilles to let him, in Achilles' armour, lead Achilles' troops, the Myrmidons, into the battle to save the Greeks. Achilles assents, but warns him not to attempt to do more than save the ships. He is not, in the flush of victory, to go on to Ilium itself. When the Trojans see the Myrmidons—warriors like flesh-eating wolves—led, as they believe, by Achilles himself, they panic and are driven back. Many Trojans are killed, including twelve by Patroclus himself. One of these is Zeus's son Sarpedon. But not even Zeus can save him against Fate:

> How many sons of gods, foredoom'd to death,
> Before proud Ilion must resign their breath!

II

Sarpedon, killed by Patroclus, calls on the Trojans to save his armour from the Greeks, but

> The fates supprest his lab'ring breath
> And his eyes darken'd with the shades of death:
> Th' insulting victor with disdain bestrode
> The prostrate prince, and on his bosom trod:
> Then drew the weapon from his panting heart,
> The reeking fibres clinging to the dart:
> From the wide wound gush'd out a stream of blood,
> And the soul issu'd in the purple flood.

In the end, as the fight rages, the Greeks strip Sarpedon of his armor, but Apollo rescues the body. Patroclus and the Greeks drive on, right up to the walls of Ilium. At Apollo's behest, Patroclus himself withdraws a little, though continuing to fight. Eventually he is wounded both by a blow from Apollo, knocking off his helmet, and a spear thrown by a Trojan. Hector moves in for the kill. He is taunted by the dying Patroclus as being only the third of his attackers and as having only a short time to live before he is himself killed by Achilles.

The Greeks, led by Menelaus, attempt to defend Patroclus' body and Achilles' armor (Book Seventeen). But Hector leads a Trojan assault and captures the armor, putting it on himself. For this he is pitied by Zeus: his supremacy will be short-lived and he will have no homecoming. Both sides redouble their efforts, with Aeneas prominent among the Trojans, who once more begin to dominate. A mist forms around the body of Patroclus, where the fighting is the most intense. Menelaus, encouraged by Athene, manages to drag Patroclus' body back to the Greek side. Eventually, under cover from the two Ajaxes, Menelaus and Meriones, another of the Greeks, begin to bear the body off the battlefield.

Achilles is now informed of Patroclus' death (Book Eighteen). From now on, Achilles will hold center stage. A black cloud of grief engulfs him, and he lets out a terrifying cry which his mother Thetis hears in the depths of the sea. Sorrowfully, Thetis warns him that his own death will follow on Hector's, if that is the road he wishes to take. It is. Not even Herakles could escape his fate, and I must win glory too! Back on the battlefield Hector is close to recapturing Patroclus' body. Achilles goes to the ditch and, crowned by Athene with a golden cloud, raises a tremendous shout. The Trojans are terrified and withdraw, but Hector unwisely rejects the chance to go back into Ilium itself. The Trojans, the fools, as Homer says, will stay on the plain. As night falls, Achilles and the Greeks mourn and tend the body of Patroclus. Meanwhile

Thetis persuades Hephaestus to use all his skill to make new armor and a splendid new shield for Achilles. The shield is decorated with fantastic scenes depicting the earth, sea, sky and heavens; then two towns, one with scenes of a wedding and a court in session, the other under siege from a great army and the ensuing battle; also pastoral scenes of ploughing, reaping and grape-gathering, with herds of cattle and flocks of sheep and farm buildings; and then one of youths and maidens dancing, with a large crowd round about them and a singer of tales with his lyre; and finally, round the whole edge of the shield, the mighty stream of Ocean.

Day Four of the Battle

Achilles, with his new armor, summons the Greeks to hear him apologise to Agamemnon (Book Nineteen). Agamemnon says that the quarrel arose because he was blinded by Zeus and Ate (Folly), his eldest daughter. Odysseus mediates further. The Greeks feast before resuming battle, and Achilles and Agamemnon end their feud. Briseis, returned to Achilles, and Achilles himself mourn Patroclus. Achilles arms for the battle. Xanthus, one of his horses, prophesies his eventual fate, which fires up Achilles even more.

In Book Twenty, Zeus removes the ban on interference by the gods. Hades (the underworld) is nearly split open by the sound of the gods on the war-path. As the two armies race towards each other, Aeneas, inspired by Apollo, challenges Achilles; he is worsted, but rescued by Poseidon (this is because Aeneas's lineage is beloved of Zeus and destined to be saved by Aeneas, and Zeus would be angered were Aeneas snuffed out). As Achilles' bloody rampage begins, Apollo warns Hector not to take Achilles on, rescuing him by means of a dense mist when Achilles catches sight of him. Achilles' rampage gathers pace, as an inhuman fire; Achilles' horses trample on the shields and bodies of the slain, as Achilles presses on:

> All grim with dust; all horrible with blood;
> Yet still insatiate, still with rage on flame:
> Such is the lust of never dying fame!

The Greeks pursue the Trojans to the river Scamander (Book Twenty One), and Achilles cuts them in two, one half driven across the plain towards Ilium, the other into the river itself. Lycaon, one of Priam's fifty sons, begs for mercy, embracing Achilles' knees and recalling an earlier encounter when they broke bread together. He receives no pity from Achilles:

> The great, the good Patroclus is no more!
> He, far thy better, was foredoom'd to die . . .

Sudden, his broad sword display'd,
And buried in his neck the reeking blade.
Prone fell the youth; and panting on the land
The gushing purple dyed the thirsty sand.
The victor to the stream the carcass gave
And thus insults him floating on the wave:
'Lie there Lycaon! Let the fish surround
Thy bloated corpse, and suck thy gory wound.
There no sad mother shall thy funerals weep,
But swift Scamander roll thee to the deep,
Whose every wave some watery monster brings
To feast unpunish'd on the fat of kings,
So perish Troy and all the Trojan line!
Such ruin theirs and such compassion mine.'

Many others are cut down by Achilles in similar style. Then the god of the Scamander himself, angered by the slaughter, turns on Achilles in a mighty flood, uprearing and rushing on him to drown him. Achilles is saved by the intervention of Hera, who gets Hephaestus to staunch the flow of water and dry the plain with a supernatural fire. After this, the gods start to fight among themselves, Athene against Ares and Aphrodite, Poseidon against Apollo, Hera against Artemis, the sister of Apollo and goddess of the hunt. Priam, meanwhile, seeing the rout of the Trojans, opens the gates of Ilium. The Greeks are held back by Agenor, a Trojan warrior, and then Apollo who impersonates Agenor, leading Achilles away from the city gates.

With all the Trojans in the city, Hector remains outside (Book Twenty Two). Achilles, released from his deception by Apollo, is on the warpath. Priam and Hecabe implore their son to come in behind the walls, but he refuses to retreat. He has to face Achilles. They meet, and Achilles chases Hector as a hawk pursues a dove. Three times the pair circle the walls of Ilium. Zeus and Apollo withdraw their protection from Hector, and Athene now takes a hand, impersonating Deiphobus, Hector's favourite brother. Together they will face Achilles. Spear thrusts are exchanged, but Hector then realizes "Deiphobus" has vanished. He is on his own, and he knows that Athene has tricked him. He falls on Achilles, brandishing his sword. As he charges, Achilles drives his spear through Hector's neck, unprotected by armor. Showing no mercy, Achilles fixes Hector's body by the ankles and drags him behind his chariot round the city and off to the Greek ships. Priam and Hecabe lament, but Andromache, ignorant of the fight, is preparing a hot bath for her man. "Foolish one," says Homer in a rare personal comment, "she knew not that he was now beyond the reach of baths, and that Athene had laid him low by the hand of Achilles." She finds out soon enough. With the wriggling worms eating Hector, the Trojans' only real defense, the fate of Astyanax is at best one of servitude and oppression.

In Book Twenty Three, as night falls on the Fourth Day of the battle, the Greeks withdraw to their camp. The body of Hector is flung face down beneath the funeral pyre of Patroclus. During the night Achilles is visited by Patroclus's shade, who tells him that he, Achilles, will die at Troy too, and begs that they should be buried together. Achilles reaches out to embrace him, but there is nothing to grasp. The next morning Patroclus' pyre is burned, his bones placed in a golden vessel to wait for Achilles' death. There is human sacrifice here, too, Achilles killing twelve noble Trojans, to be burned on Patroclus's pyre. The Greeks feast and have games to celebrate Patroclus: chariot-racing, boxing, wrestling, foot races, armed combat, discus, archery and javelin. As would be expected, competition is fierce and contentious.

Achilles withdraws to his camp, and frets for eleven days (Book Twenty Four). He attempts to mutilate Hector's unburied corpse, but Aphrodite and Apollo preserve the body. On the twelfth day, the gods send Thetis to tell Achilles to relent. The messenger goddess Iris is sent to Priam, to tell him to go to Achilles with a ransom, to plead for the body. Against Hecabe's advice he goes, guided at night through the Greek lines by the god Hermes. Achilles is amazed to see Priam, but Priam reminds Achilles of his own father. This is often seen as the finest moment of *The Iliad*, the implacable Achilles at last recognizing the humanity of his enemy, and Priam at the same time seeing Achilles, too, as a fellow suffering human being.

Together they weep, Priam for Hector and Achilles for his father and for Patroclus. Achilles accepts the ransom, and Hector's body is prepared, out of sight of Priam, in case, Achilles thinks, seeing the body would provoke the old man to anger, provoking in its turn the wrath of Achilles himself. They eat, and agree to an eleven-day truce to allow Hector's burial and funeral games. As Priam leaves, Achilles begins to sleep for the first time since Patroclus's death, the fair-cheeked Briseis by his side. Priam, with Hermes, transports Hector's body back to Ilium. Cassandra, Priam's ill-fated prophetess daughter, cries out to the Trojans to welcome back their hero, the glory of the city and the people. Andromache, Hecabe and Helen all lament the greatest and noblest of the Trojans. Eleven days later, Hector is burnt on a great funeral pyre, his bones buried in a grave mound. There is a magnificent funeral feast in Priam's palace:

> A solemn, silent, melancholy train
> Assembled there . . .

And sadly shar'd the last sepulchral feast.
Such honours Ilion to her hero paid
And peaceful slept the mighty hero's shade . . .
. . . and so ends *The Iliad* of Homer.

The Sequel

Troy is not taken in *The Iliad;* though, with the death of Hector, we know it will be. Part of Homer's genius is that, in a sense, no more needs to be said. Nevertheless, incidents from the later history of Troy feature importantly in the literature following *The Iliad,* not least *The Odyssey* itself. So we will give a brief summary of the most significant of these.

Odysseus, disguised as a beggar, makes his way into Troy. There he meets and speaks to Helen, who tells in *The Odyssey* how she washed him and promised not to reveal him to the Trojans. In return Odysseus reveals the Greeks' plans, which please her because she is longing to return home, having recovered from the madness that Aphrodite visited on her. While in Troy, Odysseus steals the Palladium, a black stone, sacred to Athene and the "luck" of Troy, on which Troy's safety depended. He also kills a number of Trojans.

The war continues in desultory fashion. Paris brings the Amazons to fight on the Trojan side, but they are defeated by Achilles and Ajax. Achilles also kills the Ethiopian Memnon, but is then himself killed by an arrow in his foot, fired by Paris. Odysseus recovers Achilles' body, but both he and Ajax claim the armor for themselves. Odysseus prevails. Ajax goes mad, killing a flock of sheep and then himself.

Odysseus and Diomedes sail to Lemnos to pick up the archer Philoctetes, whom the Greeks had cruelly abandoned there ten years earlier on their way to Troy. Reluctantly Philoctetes comes with them, and one of his arrows kills Paris.

Odysseus now plots the trick of the Wooden Horse. The Greeks appear to sail away, leaving on the beach a huge wooden horse, ostensibly a peace offering for the theft of the Palladium. In fact it is filled with Greek soldiers. Laocoön, the priest, and Cassandra warn the Trojans that it is a trick. But Laocoön and his sons are killed by a great sea snake, sent by Poseidon, and Cassandra had been condemned by Apollo, whom she has refused, to foresee the future but not to be believed. Helen suspects there are Greeks inside the horse and tries talking to them, but they keep silent. Believing the Greeks to have gone for good, the Trojans drag the horse into Ilium with great rejoicing. In the night, with the Trojans tired and drunk from their merry-making, the horse opens and the Greeks come out. They open the gates of the city for the Greek army which, under cover of night, has returned, the fleet having simply hidden off-shore behind an island.

Ilium is destroyed, its men slaughtered. Astyanax is thrown over the battlements, to prevent the appearance of another Hector. Helen, who has taken up with Deiphobus after the death of Paris, is spared by Odysseus. She returns to Sparta with Menelaus. Andromache is abducted by Neoptolemus, the son of Achilles, and Cassandra by Agamemnon.

We will look later at the fortunes of some of those who escaped the burning city, including Odysseus, Agamemnon, Menelaus, Helen, and Aeneas.

Themes from *The Iliad*

To us in the twenty-first century, the gods are anything but god-like. They are childish, they quarrel, they fight, they seduce each other and humans, they bear resentments, they laugh at disability (specifically at Hephaestus). Nor are they immune to the ravages of fate. Even Zeus cannot protect his favored son Sarpedon against Patroclus.

Complaints of this sort against the Homeric gods are not new. As early as the sixth century B.C., the agnostic philosopher Xenophanes was speaking of the gods behaving in ways which universally cause shame among human beings. Plato in *The Republic* (c. 375 B.C.) took the Homeric descriptions of the gods to be so disgraceful as to require censorship of such tales in an ideally regulated society. A little po-faced, perhaps; would we want to lose the account of Zeus and Hera's love-making or that of Thetis supplicating Zeus on behalf of her son? Zeus, too, does understand the poignancy of the fate of at least some of the humans, a fate he cannot in the end deflect.

But the gods lack a crucial dimension of existence by virtue of the one respect in which they differ from us. The immortals are condemned by their immortality to an existence of frivolity, at least as compared to the scenes enacted below on the plain of Troy. Sarpedon, in fighting heroically and dying bravely, is morally more worthy than Zeus on Olympus. It is this crucial difference as much as anything which led Longinus in the first-century A.D. to write that "as far as possible Homer made the humans in the Trojan War gods, and the gods human." And we can add to this the fact that, despite some muttering and dissent, in the end the immortals simply accept Zeus's commands, not because they agree with them or respect him, but simply because he is more powerful. There is nothing in Olympus like Hector bravely accepting his fate, let alone anything comparable to Milton's Satan rebelling against God (if that is to be regarded as noble).

Of the human characters, Agamemnon is flawed, but still magnificent. He is the Lord of Men, and a lion in battle. On the other hand he is indecisive, vain, and deceitful, and shown to be all these things. But, Thersites apart, the Greeks recognize him to be their leader, and some of his failings arise from the difficulties inherent in leadership. In Plato's *Republic* his nobility is marked by his being reincarnated as an eagle.

Achilles is the hero of *The Iliad,* or so he has been taken by generations of readers, not least by Alexander the Great. Knowing that his own life will be short, he is magnificent in his indifference to fate and to others, in his god-like isolation and in his rage. He inspires deep affection and loyalty, amounting almost to love, from those who know him: Patroclus, his Myrmidons, and even arguably Briseis. On the field of battle he is elemental, almost a force of nature. He is, of course, supremely brave, but also supremely pitiless, not least in his sacrifice of the twelve Trojan youths at the funeral of Patroclus. At least he is pitiless until he recognizes his own suffering and humanity in acknowledging the suffering and humanity of Priam. That it is Achilles, of all people, who takes the old man's hand and weeps with him in their mutual sorrow is what raises *The Iliad* itself to a level way beyond what could have been anticipated before that point, and what, as we will see, provides a puzzling contrast with the end of Virgil's *Aeneid.*

Hector has some claim to being the most noble character in *The Iliad.* He is depicted as the guardian of "chaste wives and little children." He fights not because he wants to, but because he has to on behalf of his family and his people; and, lacking Achilles' arrogance, he may be even braver. On the other hand, in the fighting he is as merciless as anyone else, as Patroclus finds to his cost. The Trojans respect and follow him, but he is not a wise leader. On two occasions on the Third Day of the battle, success and thought of final victory go to his head. He refuses good advice, which leads directly to the Trojans' downfall. That, though, may have come anyway, because Hector is the great warrior he is only in the absence of Achilles. His leave-taking of Andromache and Astyanax is unbearably poignant, as are his death and his courage in finally turning to face Achilles when he knows all is lost.

Andromache is the most tragic figure in *The Iliad.* She is the embodiment of virtuous womanhood and motherhood, in contrast to Helen. She, more than anyone else, shows what the Trojans were fighting for, a life of peace and civilized existence for all, but particularly for children and women. But, as we know—and as she knows—this cannot be, and as a woman her fate is entirely dependent on the actions of others.

The Iliad is, as Simone Weil put it in a marvelous essay, a poem (the poem) of might.[4] It shows what war does to men and women. War turns women into booty and men into things; either killing machines or victims. We see this phenomenon again and again in *The Iliad.* To what once were men, spears lance beneath the brows, down to the eyes' roots, skulls are cracked to splinters, brains are splattered beneath helmets, shrieking heads tumble in the dust, spears skewer men through the groin and guts, livers split, stabbed hearts judder in their last throes, until blood stains the dust of the plain and night blinds men's eyes; these victims once were men, often individuated by Homer and captured in a few brief phrases, phrases which often recall the homes, the families, the flocks and the fields they never again will see. Meanwhile, their butchers, the killing machines, vaunt and taunt—of the main characters, Patroclus alone a partial exception—their own humanity as much lost in the orgy of slaughter as that of their victims.

It is indeed a world far from hot baths, described without flinching by Homer. In this world, as we have said, men become things and women booty. All, victors and victims alike, lose their essential humanity, in which—like Achilles and Priam at the end—each recognized the vulnerable and morally inviolable humanity of the other. In the killing frenzy, by contrast, all are dehumanized, turned into animals or other forces of inhuman nature. Hence the characteristic Homeric imagery: the Greeks as cattle before the assault of a murderous lion when Hector routs them; the Trojans like uprooted trees swept by the wind as in a forest fire, the force of nature in this instance Agamemnon.

There is something deep in this portrayal of men and women in the condition of war as subject to purely natural forces. For there is a strong strain of thought about political reality which says that all that really rules in the affairs of men is the law of force, conceived as a law of nature. This strain of thought may be found in Hobbes, but it was not foreign to the classical Greeks. In a notorious incident in the Peloponnesian War (in 416 B.C.) the Athenians tell the islanders of Melos to submit to superior force or pay the penalty. According to the historian Thucydides, the Athenians tell the Melians that "our opinion of the gods and our knowledge of men leads us to conclude that it is a general and necessary law of nature to rule whenever one can. This is not a law we made ourselves, nor were we the first to act upon it when it was made. We found it already in existence, and we shall leave it to exist forever among those who come after us." And they add that were the positions reversed, the Melians would act in exactly the same way themselves.

In a way, in *The Iliad* we see the operation of the law of force as a law of nature. But there is more to it than that, for, as Weil also points out, the destruction of Troy and of the civilized world it encompassed was an atrocious crime. The founding myth of Greece portrays a primal crime. Deep down, and belying the "official" morality of pride and honor, far from glorying in it, the Greeks were haunted by it, and from it they derived a profound sense of human misery. Without sentimentality, *The Iliad* also portrays the misery and evil of human existence far from hot baths. And it also portrays the precariousness of victory, the constant reversals of fortune in war, and the short life of those who vaunt over their victims.

> While the immortals know no care, as Achilles says to Priam,
> Two urns by Zeus's high throne have ever stood,
> The source of evil one, and one of good;
> From thence the cup of mortal man he fills
> Blessings to these, to those he distributes ill;
> To most he mingles both; the wretch decreed
> To taste the bad unmix'd, is curs'd indeed;
> Pursued by wrongs, by meagre famine driv'n,
> He wanders, outcast both of earth and heaven.
> The happiest taste, not happiness sincere;
> But finds the cordial draught is dash'd with care . . .

Zeus's evil gifts are the lot of us all, as Achilles says. Homer shows us such are the lot of victors and victims alike.

Over the centuries, some have read *The Iliad* as a poem of the magnificence of heroism and war. Magnificence of this sort there is, certainly on the surface. We have to remember that the society Homer is describing is a radically aristocratic-cum-feudal one, in which leaders command as much by personal bravery, example and power as by more political or legalistic means. They gain allegiance from their vassals by their own example, by leading from the front. In such societies, loss of face is the worst thing that can happen to a man—or at least to a leader.

Not for nothing is the action of *The Iliad* motivated by the losses of face of both Agamemnon and Achilles. And not only is courage in battle the supreme Homeric test for a man; as we see in the case of Hector, the gentler arts of civilization depend on the willingness of men of supreme courage and nobility to be ready to kill and be killed, and also to exemplify the type of magnificence Homer shows us. So if the Homeric heroes are killing machines, they are not just killing machines, as is shown by the respect they sometimes show each other even in killing or death, and which is shown supremely in the reconciliation of Achilles and Priam. Their bravery, and the meaning of their bravery and even their arrogance, arises from a type of society which requires such attitudes, and which requires them for the preservation of its not necessarily ignoble form of life, however undemocratic and distant from ours that may be.

As to the deeper meaning of *The Iliad,* inherently critical of the characteristic Greek aristocratic pride of life, Simone Weil comes near the mark.

"There is no picture of human destitution more pure, more bitter and more poignant than *The Iliad*. The contemplation of human misery in its truth implies a very high spirituality." But the human misery in its truth which *The Iliad* portrays is not confined to the misery of battle or caused by battle. It is the far more general misery of fate itself, that symbolized in Zeus's two urns, that mixture of good and evil, and ultimately of death, which is the lot of us all, in whatever circumstances. This notion of fate was also elaborated by the Greeks as a thread wound around a man from his birth, prefiguring the great realities of existence, and the unavoidable destiny of each individual: riches, troubles, homecoming and, above all, death. Fate, in all sorts of ways, is the everpresent backdrop to *The Iliad*.

The gods of ancient Greece are not, as we have seen, all-powerful, but whether or not the gods are subject to unavoidable fate need not detain us here, because what they are not subject to is death. Homer and the Greek tragedians (and *The Iliad* supremely, for the reason Weil gives) look at the fate of men—and women—unflinchingly, without illusion, without sentimentality, without evasion, without romantic self-vaunting bombast, but also without despair. *Pace* Weil sees in Homer and the tragedians intimations of Christianity, this is not a Christian attitude, because Christianity offers us redemption from fate; but it is an attitude which deserves the accolade of high spirituality. And Weil is surely right when she says at the end of her essay on *The Iliad,* encapsulating its deeper message below the superficial grandeur of the heroism it so vividly portrays, that "only he who knows the empire of might and who knows *not* to respect it, is capable of love and justice."

The Odyssey

The second epic attributed to Homer tells of the adventures of the cunning Odysseus, one of the Greek heroes at Troy, in his ten-year voyage from Troy back to his own kingdom of Ithaca. Odysseus is continually forestalled in his homecoming by Poseidon, the god of the sea, whom he has offended. After many incidents—seafaring, military, magical and amorous—he ends by losing all his ships and all his men. His wife Penelope is meanwhile a prisoner in her own palace, besieged by a horde of suitors seeking her hand in marriage and feasting at Odysseus's expense. Guided by the goddess Athene, Odysseus does return to Ithaca to wreak a terrible revenge on the suitors. The Odyssey *is the archetypal tale of homecoming; but that raises the question, taken up by later writers, as to whether the wily, energetic and restless Odysseus could in this world ever really be at home.*

Whether or not *The Odyssey* was composed by the author of *The Iliad*, it does form a partial sequel to *The Iliad*, in the sense that its theme is the journey taken by Odysseus after he and the other Greeks left Troy. In *The Odyssey*, apart from Odysseus himself, we meet various characters from *The Iliad*, including Helen and Menelaus and the shades of Agamemnon, Achilles and Ajax. It is easy to see the Odysseus in the two poems as the same character, though he is naturally far more center-stage in the sequel. And just as in *The Iliad* the action is focused on a short episode in a much larger story, of which we are made aware, so in *The Odyssey* the action is concentrated on the events immediately preceding and following Odysseus's return to his island of Ithaca, though in the course of the narrative we learn much of his wanderings in the previous ten years.

Having said that Odysseus is center-stage in *The Odyssey*, by a stroke of storytelling genius on Homer's part, we do not at first meet Odysseus. We learn that he has been away from his home and kingdom for twenty years, and that many there assume that he will never return, to their advantage. The first part of the poem has Telemachus (the son whom Odysseus never really knew, having left Ithaca when he was a tiny baby) and us, the readers, embarking on a search for the lost king.

The Odyssey opens with the gods on Olympus discussing Odysseus's predicament. It is now twenty years since the fleet set sail for Troy, and ten years since its fall. Except Odysseus, all have made it home or are dead. Odysseus longs to get home to his wife and family, but is being held on the island of Ogygia by the nymph Calypso, who wants to marry him. He is also being persecuted by Poseidon, because, as we shall see, Odysseus has blinded his son, the Cyclops Polyphemus. But Poseidon is temporarily absent, and Athene, Odysseus's protector, pleads for him. Zeus agrees that she should go to Ithaca to encourage Telemachus, now a young man, to go and seek news of Odysseus.

This she does, impersonating Mentes, a mortal, an old friend of Odysseus. The situation in Ithaca is bad. Penelope, Odysseus's faithful wife and Telemachus' mother, is being besieged by one-hundred and eight "suitors," local nobles who are sitting around in the palace all day feasting and revelling at Odysseus's expense, ostensibly seeking her hand in marriage. Penelope is holding them off by saying that she will marry none of them until she has completed a funeral shroud for Odysseus's father Laertes, who is still alive, but retired to the country. She weaves by day, and unravels by night as the suitors feast off the fat of Odysseus's estate. Fired up by Athene, Telemachus confronts the suitors, telling them they have to leave.

But they will have none of it. They know the trick Penelope is playing on them and have no intention of leaving. They will stay until Penelope accepts one of them. Particularly obnoxious are the arrogant and bullying Antinous and the oleaginous and scheming Eurymachus. Derided by the suitors, though supported by Mentor, an old friend of Odysseus, Telemachus sets sail in search of news of his father.

He goes first to Pylos, to visit King Nestor. He is well received and hears a lot from Nestor about the ill-fated departure of the Greeks from Troy, about a quarrel between Menelaus and Agamemnon, about the fleet being scattered, about the terrible fate which awaited Agamemnon at home—being murdered by his wife and her paramour—and about much else besides, but nothing about what eventually happened to Odysseus. But they might know at Sparta, so Nestor's son Peisistratus will take Telemachus there.

Telemachus is recognized by Helen and Menelaus as Odysseus's son, and Helen tells Telemachus about Odysseus entering Troy as a beggar and meeting her. All speak well of Odysseus and of his endurance and resolution, and Menelaus tells Telemachus of a prophecy he heard on his own long and indirect voyage back to Sparta. Odysseus is alive, but a disconsolate prisoner on Calypso's island, without a boat or means of escape. Telemachus determines to return to Ithaca. Meanwhile on Ithaca, to Penelope's dismay, the suitors are plotting to ambush Telemachus on his return and kill him.

Zeus now sends Hermes to instruct Calypso to release Odysseus. She goes to find him, and the first we see of Odysseus, he is pensive on the lonely beach

> With streaming eyes in briny torrents drown'd,
> And inly pining for his native shore;
> For now the soft enchantress pleased no more;
> For now, reluctant, and constrain'd by charms,
> Absent he lay in her desiring arms,
> In slumber wore the heavy night away,
> On rocks and shores consumed the tedious day;
> There sate all desolate, and sighed alone,
> With echoing sorrows made the mountains groan,
> And roll'd his eyes o'er all the restless main,
> Till, dimmed with rising grief, they stream'd again.
> (All translations from *The Odyssey* are those of Alexander Pope, assisted
> by William Broome and Elijah Fenton (1725–26))

Upset as she is by the gods' edict, Calypso wishes Odysseus happiness, but warning him that he will still have many trials to face, and chiding him that Penelope cannot be compared to her in face or form. She also reminds him that she has offered—and he is refusing—the offer of eternal life and youth if he were to stay with her. With Calypso's help he makes a boat and sails off, only to be wrecked by Poseidon. For two days he clings to a beam from the wreckage, finally landing on an island, where he shelters and falls asleep.

This is the island of the Phaeacians (possibly Corfu), ruled by Alcinous. Alcinous has a daughter, Nausicaa, one of the most delightful creations in ancient literature. Nausicaa is roused by Athene to go and do some laundry in a river near to the palace. When this is finished, her maids start playing ball: "along the skies, / Toss'd and retoss'd, the ball incessant flies. / They sport, they feast; Nausicaa lifts her voice, / and warbling sweet, makes earth and heaven rejoice." Just as Artemis the huntress seeking boar and deer in the woods and mountains outshone her companion nymphs, so "With equal grace Nausicaa trod the plain, / And shone transcendent o'er the beauteous train." When it is time for them to go, Nausicaa herself throws the ball; one of the others misses it—and they all cry out, awakening Odysseus:

> What sounds are these that gather from the shores?
> The voice of nymphs that haunt the sylvan bowers,
> The fair haired Dryads of the shady wood
> Or azure daughters of the silver flood?

Chivalrously taking care to hide his nakedness with a bough, he emerges, frightening off all the girls, except Nausicaa herself. Odysseus throws himself on her mercy, and she leads him to the city, taking care that they should not actually arrive together so as to preserve her good name.

As instructed by Nausicaa, Odysseus makes his way to Alcinous's palace; he goes in with Athene's help, and finds Alcinous and Arete, his queen. Embracing Arete's knees, Odysseus pleads for help on his journey home. This Alcinous agrees to do, after Odysseus has explained that he is not a god, and how, after his captivity on Ogygia, he ended up where he is. Alcinous would like to have Odysseus as a son-in-law, but will not detain him, after they have entertained him with games, singing, and feasting the next day.

In the morning, after sacrifices, the games duly take place, with Odysseus—with no false modesty—beating them all with the discus. After dancing and feasting, at Odysseus's request, the bard Demodocus begins to sing of the Wooden Horse of Troy. As he sings, Odysseus's "griefs renew, / Tears bathe his cheeks, and tears the ground bedew; / As some fond matron views in mortal flight / Her husband falling in his country's right." But only Alcinous actually observes this. He commands Demodocus to desist, and demands that Odysseus explain why he is so moved.

Odysseus reveals himself and—both to us and the Phaeacians—recounts his adventures since leaving Troy, all the time insisting that there is nothing dearer to him than Ithaca, his own country and home. After leaving Troy,

Odysseus and his men sack Ismarus, the city of the Cicones. But instead of quickly making off with the women and booty they have seized, his fools of men stay on, and many of his companions are killed by reinforcements brought in. After that, passing Cythera, they come to the land of the lotus-eaters. Eating this fruit destroys all ambition or desire to return, and numbers succumb. The rest sail on to the country of the Cyclopes, one-eyed giants, a fierce, uncivilized people without laws, ships or trade, but living in a land of plenty. Odysseus and twelve of his companions go ashore, to the cave of the Cyclops Polyphemus, in the hope of a friendly reception.

But when the giant comes in with his flocks, he traps the men inside and eats two of them. The next morning he drives his flock out and leaves, but not before sealing the mouth of the cave with a huge boulder. During the day, Odysseus sharpens a huge piece of wood in the cave into a stake. At night, the Cyclops returns with his flocks. Odysseus plies the Cyclops with wine, and tells him that his name is Nobody. After announcing that he will eat Nobody last, the Cyclops topples over drunk. Odysseus heats up the stake and drives it through his single eye, blinding him with terrible pain. His cries arouse his fellow Cyclopes, but in answer to their queries as to who has attacked him, Polyphemus replies "Nobody," and they go away. Next morning the blinded Polyphemus stands in the door of the cave, feeling for anyone attempting to leave. Odysseus and his men tie themselves under the bellies of the rams, and, as Polyphemus feels only the backs of his animals as they leave the cave, escape back to the ships. But Odysseus, from the sea, cannot resist deriding Polyphemus and revealing who he really is. Polyphemus, unavailingly hurling boulders at the ships, swears that his father Poseidon will take revenge on Odysseus. If he ever gets home, it will be with none of his men.

The Ithacans come next to the island of Aeolus, keeper of the winds, where they spend a happy month. When they leave, Aeolus gives them sacks of wind to blow them along, but Odysseus's men open the sacks, thinking they are full of gold and silver, and they are blown back to Aeolia. They are cursed by Aeolus, and sail on to the land of the Laestrygonians, giants who massacre all the men in Odysseus's squadron, except those on his own ship, which is the only one to escape. They come next to the island of the sorceress Circe. They divide into two groups to search for provisions, and one group find themselves at Circe's house. She turns all of them into pigs, except one who escapes to tell what has happened. The god Hermes now appears to Odysseus, giving him a magic herb to protect him from Circe's spells. Odysseus goes to Circe, and is saved from being turned into a pig, but has to share Circe's bed, which he does in great luxury. Circe turns the pigs back into men. They all stay on the island in comfort and plenty for a year. At the end of this time, they yearn for home, and Circe lets them go, though telling Odysseus he will have to go down into Hades (the underworld) to consult the prophet Tiresias. As they leave Circe's palace, Elpenor, a young sailor, gets drunk, climbs on the roof and falls off, killing himself.

As instructed by Circe, Odysseus and his men sail to the land of the Cimmerians, a sunless land of mist and fog. They sail up the River Oceanus until they reach the entrance to Hades. There they make sacrifice, and the souls of the dead start pouring out. The first they recognize is Elpenor, who upbraids them for not having given him proper burial. Then Odysseus meets Anticleia, his mother, and Tiresias. Tiresias tells him that they will have a hard time of it on the way back to Ithaca. On no account are they to touch the flocks of the Sun-god on the island of Thrinacie. If they do, only Odysseus will ever reach home. When he does, he will find—and kill—the suitors in his palace. After that he must make one last journey to a people who know nothing of the sea, who mistake an oar, which Odysseus will be carrying, for a winnowing fan. He must make sacrifice there to Poseidon, before himself dying a gentle death, far from the sea. Odysseus then questions his mother about Penelope and Telemachus, and his father Laertes. All yearn for Odysseus's return, and Odysseus tries, but fails, to embrace his mother's shade. There follows a procession of other famous women, including Antiope, the mother of the founders of Thebes, Epicaste (Jocasta), Oedipus' mother, and Leda. After the women have been chased off by Persephone, queen of Hades, there comes Agamemnon, vitriolically comparing the iniquity of his wife (who had him and Cassandra murdered) with the virtue of Penelope. Then come Achilles and Patroclus. Achilles speaks:

> Talk not of ruling in this dolorous gloom,
> Nor think vain words (he cried) can ease my doom.
> Rather I'd choose laboriously to bear
> A weight of woes and breathe the vital air,
> A slave to some poor hind that toils for bread,
> Than reign the sceptered monarch of the dead.

Odysseus gives Achilles news of the valour of Neoptolemus, Achilles' own son, in the front of the action in the last days of Troy. But the shade of Ajax refuses to acknowledge Odysseus or accept his apology. Odysseus also sees King Minos, the judge of the dead, Orion the great hunter, and Tityus, Tantalus, and Sisyphus, all being tortured eternally for defying the gods, and finally the mighty Herakles, who salutes his mortal visitor.

They go back to Circe's palace, to give Elpenor proper burial, and Circe warns them about the Sirens and Scylla and Charybdis, all of which they will have to pass. Odysseus avoids the Sirens, who drag men down to destruction by the sweetness of their song, by plugging the ears of his men with wax and by lashing himself to the mast, so that he can both hear their song and be prevented from responding to it. Scylla is a monster who catches sailors from their ships to eat them, and Charybdis is a terrible whirlpool, on either side of a narrow strait. Scylla snatches six of Odysseus's comrades, but the ship gets through the straits, after which they find land and shelter. But it is Thrinacie, and while Odysseus is asleep, his men kill the Sun-god's cattle. When they sail off again, the ship is destroyed by a storm and all the men but Odysseus drown. Odysseus stays on what is left of the ship, and lashing mast and keel together, he manages to get back past Scylla and Charybdis. After nine days and nights on the raft, he lands on Ogygia, where he is received kindly by Calypso and is to remain for seven years.

After Odysseus finishes his account there is silence. Alcinous then invites all to feast and sacrifice to Zeus before they send Odysseus off with a ship and crew. This they do, setting Odysseus down in Ithaca, but the return voyage is not without incident. Enraged by what has happened, Poseidon turns the ship into stone off the Phaeacian coast. Odysseus is met by Athene in Ithaca, who warns him about the suitors, and, for protection, transforms him into an old beggar. She tells him to go to the hut of Eumaeus, a loyal old swineherd.

When he reaches the hut, the dogs snap and snarl at him. Eumaeus chases them away, and welcomes the old beggar without realizing who he is, at the same time praising Odysseus and vilifying the suitors. Odysseus pretends to be a refugee from Crete, who had been to Troy with Idomeneus, but has suffered many misfortunes since his return. Eumaeus and the beggar eat, after which Odysseus is given a bed and Eumaeus goes to watch his boars through the night.

In Sparta, Athene visits Telemachus, telling him it is time to return. Sailing back from Pylos, he picks up a prophet, Theoclymenus, and takes him with him to Ithaca. In Eumaeus' hut, Eumaeus and Odysseus eat their evening meal. Eumaeus dissuades Odysseus from going to the palace, and tells of his own adventures. Reaching the coast, Telemachus gets himself dropped off, sending Theoclymenus and the crew to sail on to the harbor and the palace.

The next morning, as Eumaeus and Odysseus are having breakfast, Telemachus appears. He is embraced by Eumaeus with expressions of affection and relief that he is safely back. Eumaeus goes to the palace to tell Penelope the good news secretly. While he is away, Athene gets Odysseus to reveal himself to Telemachus. Swearing Telemachus to secrecy, the two plot revenge. In the palace the suitors hear that Telemachus has returned and plot his capture and possible death.

Telemachus makes for the town, followed separately by Odysseus and Eumaeus. In Penelope's hall, Telemachus and his mother are joined by Theoclymenus, who says that Odysseus is back, planning revenge on the suitors. En route for the palace, Odysseus is insulted by Melanthius, a disloyal herdsman, who continues to dog his steps after he has reached the palace. Once there, Odysseus is recognized by Argos, his hunting dog of twenty years earlier, who dies having seen his master one last time. Odysseus enters the palace and is insulted by the suitors. Penelope is intrigued by the beggar and asks to see him.

Odysseus is insulted by Irus, another beggar, and the suitors force the two to fight. Odysseus wins. Penelope now announces to the suitors that, as Telemachus is a man, and with Odysseus gone, and as Odysseus had instructed if he failed to return, the time for re-marrying is near. The suitors still refuse to leave and continue to insult Odysseus—Antinous and Eurymachus as always to the fore.

At night, with the hall empty of suitors, Odysseus and Telemachus start hiding the suitors' weapons. Penelope comes down and upbraids Melantho, one of her maids and the mistress of the suitor Eurymachus, for continuing to insult the beggar Odysseus. For the first time Odysseus and Penelope begin to converse. Pretending to be a Cretan, Odysseus tells her something of Odysseus's wanderings and assures her that he is still alive. Penelope orders Eurycleia, Odysseus's old nurse, to wash him, and she recognizes her master from an old hunting scar on his thigh. Odysseus fiercely enjoins her to secrecy. In somber mood, Penelope tells Odysseus how she intends to choose her new husband. She will set up a shooting competition in which the winner will be the one who can shoot an arrow from Odysseus's bow through twelve axe-heads set up in a row.

The next morning, Odysseus is encouraged by Athene. The hall is prepared for feasting and the contest. Eumaeus brings in a loyal cowherd, Philoetius. The suitors begin to revel and plot against Telemachus, insulting both him and Odysseus. Theoclymenus foretells their fate, but they take no notice, continuing to feast.

Penelope now announces the competition. Telemachus sets up the axes and tries to string the bow himself, failing narrowly. As the suitors attempt—and fail—to string the bow, Odysseus reveals himself to Eumaeus and Philoetius, bringing them into the plot. He also tells Eurycleia to bolt the doors of the hall. After Eurymachus has failed to string the bow, Antinous suggests a pause. Odysseus steps forward, asking to be given a chance. Antinous is furious, but Telemachus and Penelope insist. Commanded to leave by Telemachus, Penelope retires to sleep, her eyes full of tears for Odysseus. To the derision of the suitors, Odysseus picks up the bow, and then,

28

to their dismay, strings it and shoots a single arrow through all twelve axes, after which he tears off his rags, and, emptying a full quiver of arrows at his feet, shoots Antinous through the neck. There is uproar as Odysseus reveals himself, continuing to fire arrows at the suitors, Eurymachus receiving the second blow. Telemachus and the others bring in the hidden arms, but so does Melanthius, arming the suitors. On his second journey, as Telemachus and Odysseus hold off the suitors, he is caught and tied up by Eumaeus and Philoetius. Athene then takes the form of Mentor. With her help, and bit by bit, the suitors are all hacked down:

> All steeped in blood, all gasping on the ground.
> So, when by hollow shores the fisher-train
> Sweep with their arching nets the roaring main,
> And scarce the meshy toils the copious draught contain,
> All naked of their element, and bare,
> The fishes pant, and gasp in thinner air;
> Wide o'er the sands are spread the stiffening prey
> Till the warm sun exhales their soul away.

Only the herald and a bard are spared, while a dozen disloyal serving maids are executed and the treacherous Melanthius is terribly mutilated before being killed.

Eurycleia is sent to tell Penelope the news, but she cannot believe her. She is still doubtful even after Odysseus himself has appeared. By a stratagem worthy of Odysseus himself, Penelope tricks Odysseus into divulging the secret of the marriage bed that Odysseus himself had constructed years earlier, a secret known only to the two spouses and a single maid of the time, now long dead. At this, Penelope's unbelieving heart is convinced, and

> Touch'd to the soul the king with rapture hears,
> Hangs round her neck, and speaks his joy in tears.
> As to the shipwreck'd mariner, the shores
> Delightful rise, when angry Poseidon roars:
> Then, when the surge in thunder mounts the sky,
> And gulf'd in crowds at once the sailors die:

And, recalling Odysseus's own fate:

> If one, more happy, while the tempest raves,
> Outlives the tumult of conflicting waves,
> All pale, with ooze deformed, he views the strand,
> And plunging forth with transport grasps the land:

The ravish'd queen with equal rapture glows,
Clasps her loved lord, and to his bosom grows.
Nor had they ended till the morning ray,
But Pallas held backward the rising day,
The wheels of night retarding, to detain
The gay Aurora in the wavy main;
Whose flaming steeds, merging through the night,
Beam o'er the eastern hills with streaming light.

Odysseus eventually speaks of the last journey prophesied by Tiresias, and then they lay themselves down to love and to further talk about all that has happened, until sleep comes upon them.

In the morning Odysseus leaves to visit his father and to repair the depredations that the suitors wreaked on his estate and flocks by raids of his own. The suitors meanwhile are escorted by Hermes, squealing like bats, to "the dusky land of dreams / . . . where souls unburied dwell / In ever flowing meads of asphodel." Down there Agamemnon and Achilles hear of Odysseus's triumph. Agamemnon once more praises Penelope's fidelity. On earth, Odysseus is reunited with Laertes, his father. Meanwhile the families of the suitors want revenge on Odysseus. Athene joins Odysseus as Mentor one last time. After a brief scuffle between Odysseus and Telemachus and their attackers, which has the attackers turning on their heels, with Zeus she restores peace in Ithaca.

Themes from *The Odyssey*

The Odyssey is lighter in tone and color than *The Iliad,* the battle in Odysseus's palace and the loss of all Odysseus's companions on the voyage notwithstanding. Odysseus's wanderings may be long, circuitous and at times directionless—for him—but we, the audience, know they are coming to an end. Also each new landing, grim as some of them might be, ushers in a new and interesting adventure. *The Odyssey* also has a single identifiable hero, whose cause against the suitors—in contrast to the causes of the heroes of *The Iliad*—is assumed by Homer and all his readers to be righteous. We may feel that their punishment, and even more that of the maids, is excessive for the crime they have committed, but there is never any doubt that they deserve some punishment; and such are the pace of the second half of *The Odyssey* and its mounting tension that it is hard even for modern readers not to rejoice at the outcome of the battle. To put it bluntly, in *The Odyssey* what we see is the eventual triumph of good people (Penelope, Telemachus, Eumaeus) after years of apparently hopeless oppression and insults from bullies and tyrants.

As to Odysseus himself, in his travels he may not be entirely admirable. He is certainly opportunistic at times, cunning and callous at others, and he does not always seem too concerned at the fate of his companions, all of whom die on the journey while he alone survives. Though he weeps for the foolish Elpenor, there is little of the poignancy at the deaths of his mainly nameless companions which we are made to feel in *The Iliad* about so many of those who fall on the plain of Troy. And Odysseus's companions are foolish and disobedient. They cut the strings of the flasks of the winds, they slaughter the flocks of the Sun-god, they get turned into swine, they stay among the lotus-eaters.

Nor, despite his impressive and thought-provoking refusal of an immortal life with Calypso (thought-provoking especially after his encounter with Achilles' shade), are we convinced that a desire to return to Ithaca is always Odysseus's only motive. Penelope's fidelity is never in doubt at any level, where Odysseus's fidelity might charitably be described as long-term, constant at a deep level despite episodic and not always or entirely unwelcome interruptions on the surface. This, along with his wiliness and his at times picaresque adventures, makes him a more interesting hero. After all, a completely single-minded homecoming which brooked no delay or distraction would hardly be worth writing about, let alone reading about. This does, of course, raise the question posed by Dante in the *Inferno,* Canto XXVI, and taken up by Tennyson in his poem "Ulysses." Can we really believe that the Odysseus depicted in *The Iliad* and *The Odyssey* would ever be content to sit in Ithaca with Penelope, gradually handing over the reins of power to Telemachus? Homer does not quite ask us to believe this; there is still the question of the mysterious last voyage enjoined on him by Tiresias. In Dante, Odysseus (or Ulysses as he calls him) is put into the Eighth Circle of Hell, as one of the great false counselors. But Dante sees him as noble too. He has Odysseus, ever the wanderer, ever the searcher for knowledge and for new experience, sailing off beyond the pillars of Hercules, into the Atlantic ocean, beyond the inhabited world, to meet his final, noble doom, and the theme of Odysseus as the eternal searcher is further elaborated by Tennyson.

Mention of Dante and Tennyson reminds us that, even more than *The Iliad*, *The Odyssey* has provided a rich source of inspiration for subsequent writers. There is, famously, James Joyce's somewhat clunking attempt to transpose its details to the streets of Leopold Bloom's Dublin in *Ulysses,* and Virgil's consummate homage to Homer in *The Aeneid* (to which we will shortly be turning). Out of a thousand other examples, we could mention here the reading of Odysseus's reception in Eumaeus' hut—surely in itself one of the most moving testaments in world literature to the superiority of simple peasant virtue to all the trappings of wealth and fame—in Goethe's

The Sufferings of the Young Werther. Werther himself, having been rebuffed in polite society, drives away to watch the sun setting from the top of a hill, while reading "that beautiful passage in Homer where Ulysses is entertained by the hospitable swineherd," and is, as we all are, deeply moved.

Werther also refers to Odysseus's talk of "the immeasurable sea and the boundless earth," reminding us that in Homer the Romantics found a rich source of inspiration, with his acute sensitivity to the forces of nature and to the interweaving of the human, the natural and the divine. *The Odyssey* is a tremendous tale, riveting still in its tension, in its beauty, in its density of detail, in its richness of incident and in the sheer mastery of the telling and construction. But it is more than that. There is in it a sense of fate and destiny, numinous, even religious, suggested by Homer in the divine interventions and the visits to the underworld—which are surely not just literary devices. This sense of mystery and transcendence is wonderfully evoked for us today by Seferis in his poem *Stratis Thalassinos among the Agapanthi* (Stratis the Sailor being an Odysseus figure in many of Seferis' poems):

> The first thing God made is the long journey
> that house there is waiting
> with its blue smoke
> with its aged dog
> waiting for the homecoming so that it can die.
> But the dead must guide me . . .
> (Translation by Edmund Keeley and Philip Sherrod (Jonathan Cape, 1973).)

As, of course, they and the gods guide Odysseus.

Greek Tragedy

Greek tragedies were performed in ancient Greece from the late 6th century B.C. and subsequently as civic and religious events. They may have been in a deep sense entertaining, but they were not entertainment, or at least not merely entertaining. In Athens, where the form began, tragedies were part of the Great Festival of Dionysus which had grown up in the mid-sixth-century B.C.

The basic form of tragedy seems to have involved a chorus enacting a heroic story, with music and dancing, and later with a small number of actors playing the key roles. The focus of most tragedy was the struggle of men with forces beyond human power, in the words of Sophocles, "the encounters of man with more than man." And, as the stories would usually have been well known to the audiences, the point of the drama was very much the way the dramatist approached the old tale, the themes his presentation brought out, and the feelings and reaction his work evoked in the audience before him.

By the mid-fifth century the festival lasted up to seven days, and, as well as plays, it included religious processions involving both actors and audience. The audiences could consist of as many as 17,000 spectators, an extraordinary number when one considers that the free adult male population at the time numbered not more than 40,000. According to Maurice Bowra there was a sense in which Greek tragedy was, within obvious limitations, intensely democratic, like Athens itself. He wrote that the unique character of Attic (Athenian) poetry stemmed "from the Athenian democracy itself. Tragedy was performed with religious solemnity . . . before a vast, critical, amazingly intelligent audience. Such a performance was, in every sense, a public event."

The plays which were put on were chosen by scrutineers, and the three different authors selected each year were involved in a competition for the three prizes awarded annually. Each of the chosen authors would have his own day, during which he would put on a trilogy of tragedies, followed by a "satyr" play, a sort of comedy. As well as having religious connotations, the plays would often refer more or less explicitly to contemporary events. No doubt these contemporary references and audience reaction to them played a role in the judging.

In Greek tragedy, the Chorus is often the main collective character, representing both participants in the drama (such as the old men of Argos in *Agamemnon* or the Furies in *The Eumenides*) and the supposed reaction of the audience to the events unfolding before it. The Chorus thus both pushes the action on and comments on it. In this latter role it was crucial in incarnating the reaction of the community to the events unfolding before it.

In *The Birth of Tragedy out of the Spirit of Music*[5] the philosopher Nietzsche offered the following fanciful account of Greek tragedy and the role of the Chorus. Tragedy has its origins in song, says Nietzsche ("tragedy" in Greek meaning "goat-song"). According to Nietzsche, the song in question is the Dionysian song of eternal pain. (Remember that it was at the festival of Dionysus that the tragedies were performed.) Dionysus was a god of nature, particularly of wine and of frenzy, who had been torn to pieces by his followers, losing his individuality and returning to an original state of oneness with nature. His followers seek a similar fate, initially through the frenzied rites associated with the god, but also through participating in tragedy.

For Nietzsche, Dionysus represented particularly the pain and suffering inherent in existence itself. So the Chorus, which is also the audience and its collective voice, sings its song of eternal sorrow, and dreams. But in its dream it conjures up images for itself of heroes and gods, divine images inspired by the god Apollo, which through their transcendent beauty somehow enable us—the Chorus/audience—to come to terms with the pain of existence. For their very beauty is conditioned by the fact that they stare into the Dionysian abyss, but remain beautiful. In the Dionysian rite, which is the theater, these images are, of course, the actors on the stage, part of our collective dream, representations of Agamemnon, Oedipus, Antigone and the rest. We see and participate in their beauty and their suffering, and are reconciled to fate.

All this is entirely fanciful as history or literary analysis. But it does, I think, in its poetic way, tell us something of the spirit of Greek tragedy and of its quasi-religious meaning and function. Sitting on a hillside even today in one of the vast semi-circular theaters of ancient Greece, open to the stars above and with the atmosphere redolent of the country around, watching an ancient tragedy unfold before a host of other spectators all focused on the action, one can feel something of what Nietzsche was evoking. You can also be cut to the quick, as I was in the ancient theater of Elis in the Peloponnese, when I saw the scene in Euripides' *The Trojan Women* in which the body of

Astyanax is brought on to the stage on Hector's shield after Odysseus and the Greeks have thrown the child from the battlements of Troy. In a setting like that, it is possible to feel very close to the ancient myths and their power. You can also feel the truth of the terrible old saying, repeated at the start of Sophocles' *The Women of Trachis:* "You cannot know a man's life before the man / has died, only then can you call it good or bad."

Nietzsche also takes up a theme prominent in Aristophanes' comedy *The Frogs* (405 B.C.), which features a contest between Aeschylus, the leading dramatist of the old school, and Euripides, the last of the great tragedians. As it moved from Aeschylus to Euripides, Greek tragedy became somewhat less hieratic and mythical, and if not less religious in a broad sense, certainly less reverential to the gods. It became more argumentative, more human and more like the sort of thing which could be put on in a modern theater today. In *The Frogs,* Euripides is represented as claiming to have taught the common people to speak, "democracy in action" he calls it, something to which the Aeschylus of the play reacts with horror. His heroes aren't the idlers, swindlers, crooks and women of low character whom we now see on the stage: the dramatist's duty is not to offer people a mirror of themselves or to help them to argue like barrack-room lawyers, but to elevate them, to show them something higher.

According to both Aristophanes and Nietzsche, in Aeschylus's plays there is a sense of myth and of an unquestioned cosmic order. The shared symbolic order is taken for granted, whereas in Euripides we have characters arguing all the time about the propriety of what is going on, reasoning critically about it. Nietzsche allies this lawyerly spirit which he finds in Euripides to the questioning by Socrates of established doctrines and pieties. He wrote that Socrates was the revenge of Thersites, the common soldier at Troy who dared to question the propriety of Agamemnon's leadership. Certainly the Olympian gods could not seriously survive the assault on their morals and behavior by Plato, no doubt inspired by Socrates, his teacher and idol. And in Euripides' plays the heroes of Homeric myth are not shown to be merely no better than the rest of us; they are not treated in a more heroic or elevated fashion either. In a sense they are us, raising just the sorts of questions and making just the sorts of observations we might make, only in a different historical setting.

Aeschylus's *Oresteia: Agamemnon*

Aeschylus's Agamemnon *is the first in the trilogy of plays known as The* Oresteia *(originally performed in Athens in 458 B.C.). Agamemnon, the victorious leader of the Greeks at Troy, returns to his home city of Mycenae after his ten-year absence. But it is not triumph which awaits him, but a savage death at the hands of his wife Clytemnestra, who has long plotted revenge on her husband for having earlier sacrificed the life of their daughter Iphigenia to speed the Greeks on their voyage to Troy. In the later plays, Orestes, the son of Agamemnon and Clytemnestra, spurred on by his sister Electra, kills Clytemnestra in a second revenge killing. He is then pursued to Athens by the Furies, loathsome half-bird, half-woman creatures dedicated to avenging blood crimes like matricide. But in Athens the goddess Athene intervenes against the Furies to replace the endless cycle of primitive retribution and private revenge and counter-revenge with a system of justice based on public law and public courts. Orestes is pardoned and the Furies are transformed into the Kindly Ones, spirits presiding over the conduct of civilized law.*

Aeschylus was born in 525 B.C. and died in 456 B.C. He wrote over seventy plays, seven of which have survived, including the Oresteian trilogy, the only complete trilogy that still exists, which was put on in 458 B.C. Aeschylus fought in the Persian wars, and was in the battle of Marathon (490 B.C.), a defining moment in the history of Greece in general and of Athens in particular, in which a tiny Athenian force defeated a huge Persian army. In his play *The Persians,* the mainspring of the action is the battle of Salamis (480 B.C.), where the largely Athenian navy defeated the Persians in a victory regarded as a triumph of civic and democratic spirit. Interestingly, in his play Aeschylus presents the point of view of the defeated Persians, and it is a tragedy: he is too humane and too deep to succumb to any shallow triumphalism, and we can only speculate about what Aeschylus's own attitude would have been to the barbarism that Athens itself wreaked on opponents after his death. Nevertheless, in common with his compatriots, Aeschylus did see the victories of the Athenians over the Persians as the triumph of a society of free men over despotism, and this spirit is reflected in his plays, as is Bowra's description of Attic poetry. In *The Oresteia* above all we see a celebration by Aeschylus of Athenian institutions, in which force, blind revenge, and blood debt give way to a rational, humane, and democratic rule of law.

Agamemnon is the opening play of the trilogy, and the darkest, apparently without hope of the redemption which eventually comes at the end. The play takes place outside the great palace at Argos (Mycenae), a place whose ruins still evoke awe. The whole citadel, in the mountainous landscape of southern Greece, is surrounded by a colossal Cyclopean wall, which one enters through a great gate decorated in the wall above by two rampant lionesses carved into the stone. The palace itself is now flattened, but it must have been extensive and sumptuously decorated. And there are great tombs, once filled with treasures and gold, inside and outside the citadel itself. When *Agamemnon* opens, a watchman is looking out to the mountains to see if there is any sign of Agamemnon's return from Troy, for which he had left ten years earlier. But to grasp fully what *The Oresteia* is about, and the extent of the crimes and slaughter always in the background, we have to go back further still in the mythic story, three generations before Agamemnon.

The ancestor was Tantalus, whose shade Odysseus met in Hades. He had fed the flesh of his son Pelops to the gods, for which he was condemned to have water and food forever within sight but out of grasp. Pelops was, however, restored to life, and set out to win the hand of Hippodameia, and rulership of part of what we now call the Peloponnese. This he did by killing her father Oenomaus in a chariot race fixed by Myrtilos, the charioteer, who caused a wheel to come off Oenomaus' chariot; but Pelops failed to give Myrtilos his reward, killing him instead, and was cursed. (There is a superb sculpture of this incident from the pediment of the Temple of Zeus at Olympia, remarkably well preserved in the Olympia museum.) The curse soon begins to work. Pelops and Hippodameia have two sons, Atreus and Thyestes. Thyestes seduces Atreus's wife and claims his throne. Atreus banishes him, but, in an act of apparent reconciliation, calls him back for a banquet. But the food he is served is the flesh of two of his sons. Another curse ensues, as Thyestes flees into exile with Aegisthus, his third son. Atreus's sons are Agamemnon and Menelaus, and they marry Helen of Sparta and her half-sister Clytemnestra. On Helen's abduction by Paris, Agamemnon and Menelaus sail to Troy, as we know, but Agamemnon has to sacrifice his daughter Iphigenia to get a fair wind. Clytemnestra hates Agamemnon for this, and takes Aegisthus as her lover while Agamemnon is away in Troy. When the play opens she is awaiting Agamemnon's return and the opportunity to enforce the punishment she has prepared for him.

Why, we wonder, are the Greeks so obsessed with these tales of hereditary guilt, of curses ringing down the generations and of terrible crimes like infanticide, murder, and deception? *The Oresteia* is an attempt to break the cycle of blood and revenge which is its motive force.

Even in translation, it is possible to see that *The Oresteia* as a whole, and *Agamemnon* in particular, consists of poetry of a very high order: condensed, multiply layered, frequently ambiguous, inexhaustible in meaning and symbolism. It exudes atmosphere even when meaning is elusive. It evokes the whole history of the house of Atreus and of the Trojan War. There is a way in which the play is static—we know what is going to happen, or if we do not we are given continual hints in advance; nevertheless, in the imaginative re-presentation of the events it describes, we participate in them ourselves.

And despite (or because of) the fact that we know what is going to happen, the tension can become close to unbearable.

Returning to the palace of Atreus in Argos, the watchman on the roof sings of Troy and of that woman—with a man's will (Clytemnestra, of course). At long last, after ten years of waiting, he sees light in the east, a beacon which signifies that Agamemnon is on his way. The Chorus of the old men of Argos now sings of Troy, of the Greek fleet, and of the young who died, and of a Fury who will avenge. Clytemnestra—for she will be the Fury for the young daughter who dies, just as the sons of Atreus were for Paris's crime—moves around, putting incense on the altar fires.

The old men recall an omen at Aulis, where Iphigenia was sacrificed. Two eagles swoop on a pregnant hare, killing it and her unborn young. Typically the Chorus, all the time singing the refrain "Cry, cry for death, but good win out in glory in the end," (Translation by Robert Fagles, Viking Penguin, 1990) fails to understand the omen's full significance; though they do say that Artemis, goddess of the hunt and protector of the unborn, hates the eagles' feast, which they see as a warning against the desecration of Troy by the victors. For the eagles are Agamemnon and Menelaus, but the eagles' feast is surely somewhat closer to home: that forced on Thyestes. And who is the she who hates the eagles' feast? Is it Artemis or is it really Clytemnestra? For we next hear of a child-avenging Fury, the child now surely Iphigenia. And then a great hymn to Zeus, at once agnostic as to Zeus's nature, but recalling Zeus's own predecessors as sovereign gods (both violently overthrown by their successors) and the destiny laid down for us humans, that of suffering into truth:

> Zeus—if to The Unknown
> That name of many names seem good,
> Zeus, upon Thee I call.
> Thro' the mind's every road
> I passed, but vain are all,
> Save that which names thee Zeus, the Highest One.
> Were it but mine to cast away the load,
> The weary load, which weighs my spirit down.
> He that was Lord of old,
> In full-blown pride of place and valour bold,
> Hath fallen and is gone, even as an old tale told!
> And he that next held sway,
> By stronger grasp o'erthrown
> Hath passed away!
> And whoso now shall bid the triumph chant arise

To Zeus, and Zeus alone,
He shall be found the truly wise.
'Tis Zeus alone who shows the perfect way
Of knowledge: He hath ruled,
Men shall learn wisdom, by affliction schooled.
In visions of the night, like dropping rain,
Descend the many memories of pain
Before the spirit's sight; through tears and dole
Come wisdom o'er the unwilling soul . . .
(All other translations from Aeschylus are those of E.D.A. Morshead
(1909).)

Man must suffer to be wise; maybe better, endure to be wise. In Greek, with assonantal effect, *to pathei mathos:* by suffering (*pathos*) comes understanding (*mathos*), learning through endurance, the harsh discipline of submission to the fate destined for us by Zeus, or whatever we call the force behind the cosmic moral order.

And suddenly the Chorus appears to realise the impending crisis. It sings in sixty poignant and dramatic lines of the appalling death of Iphigenia, a sweet virgin beauty roughly slaughtered by priests on an altar, all denying her the pity her eyes demanded. But what comes next? They cannot see it, they cannot say—except that justice will be done.

Clytemnestra now speaks of how the light is racing over the mountains in a string of beacons from Troy to Argos; how, after the mourning of the women of Troy, at long last the Greeks have had their first good night's sleep in years. Let no new disaster strike those now at last returning, but (ominously) with the return "my fair hopes are changed to fairer joys."

The second Chorus has a net laid over the towers of Troy, anticipating another net of murderous intent. Nothing can avoid the blow of Zeus and the demand of Justice. Paris's crime is again referred to, and the way Helen brought destruction with her as dowry. Menelaus's plight is graphically described: "woe for the bride-bed, warm / Yet from the lovely limbs, the impress of the form / Of her who loved her lord a while ago," and his hands find her not; but the people are muttering that all the death which ensued is for another man's wife. . . . In the midst of this meditation comes news of a herald and armed men approaching. But can it be true?

The herald rushes in. Prepare for Agamemnon's triumphal return. We had a long and terrible time, but it is all over now; let Argos receive her general home and give thanks to Zeus for victory. Clytemnestra enters, overjoyed at the day. With dramatic irony she announces that she will prepare all she needs to give the king the best welcome home. He will find her as the day he left her, faithful as a watchdog to his home:

> His foemen's foe, in all her duties leal,
> Trusty to keep for ten long years unmarried
> The store whereon he set his master-seal.
> Be steel deep-dyed, before ye look to see
> Ill joy, ill fame, from other wight, in me!

The herald then admits that the Greek fleet has been blown apart by a storm shortly after leaving Troy. Menelaus's ships have been separated from the rest (a story Menelaus himself takes up in *The Odyssey* when Telemachus visits him in Sparta). Of the rest, all but Agamemnon's ship have sunk, the Aegean sea blooming with corpses, "flecked with flowers of death." And all this hell and so much more, the Chorus takes up; and they sing also of Helen the destroyer, a lion cub brought up by a shepherd, who eventually turned on the shepherd and his house, she who came to Troy as "a spirit as of windless seas and skies, a gentle phantom-form of joy and wealth" becoming a curse descending on all the pride of Priam and all of Troy.

Agamemnon enters in his chariot, followed by his spoils of war and Cassandra. He is hailed by the Chorus, and is pompous and self-righteous in response. It was just revenge, and the Argive lion glutted itself on Trojan blood.

Clytemnestra now speaks to the Chorus, telling of her love for Agamemnon and of the long wait and all the rumors of his death, and of how many times she despaired of this moment, wavering between life and death. Her fears, she tells Agamemnon, explain why their child is not there to welcome him—but the child she is referring to here is not Iphigenia, but Orestes, their son, sent for safety (she says) to Phocis. As for her, her eyes have been sore with weeping, but now she invites the conquering hero to walk on a carpet of purple silk, so his feet will not touch the earth. Agamemnon demurs. Such an honor is for the gods alone. Clytemnestra now draws Agamemnon on, into her trap. Appealing to his vanity, she asks what would Priam have done had he been in Agamemnon's position? And in this war of ours, over this cloth, it becomes the victor to give the woman her victory.

Agamemnon is defeated by Clytemnestra's stronger will. He falls into her trap. He commits the sin of hubris, a mere mortal usurping what belongs to the gods. Agamemnon begins to step down on to the tapestry, and Cassandra is revealed. He pauses to enjoin compassion on her. Clytemnestra urges him on:

A Sea there is—and who shall stay its springs?
And deep within its breast, a mighty store,
Precious as silver of the purple dye,
Whereby the dipped robe doth its tint renew.
Enough of such, O king, within thy halls
There lies, a store that cannot fail, but I—
I would have gladly vowed unto the gods
Cost of a thousand garments trodden thus,
(Had once the oracle such gift required)
Contriving ransom for thy life preserved.
For while the stock is firm the foliage climbs,
Spreading a shade, what time the dog-star glows;
And thou, returning to thy hearth and home,
Art as a genial warmth in winter hours
Or as a coolness when the lord of heaven
Mellows the juice within the bitter grape.
Such boons and more doth bring into a home
The present footstep of its proper lord.
Zeus, Zeus, Fulfilment's lord! My vows fulfil,
And whatsoe'er it be, work forth thy will!

Purple is, of course, the color of blood; the inexhaustible sea may also be the sea of the feud of the house of Atreus, the ransom for thy journey's end and the staining of the purple dye not that suspected by Agamemnon; the bitter unripe grape is the virgin daughter, its mellowing by the lord of heaven sacrifice of Agamemnon himself, who is the proper lord presently stepping up for sacrifice, while the coolness in the house is that of death itself. Oblivious, Agamemnon walks on, Clytemnestra exulting, calling on Zeus, the master of fulfilment, to fulfil her vows and his will. The Chorus sings of foreboding and of blood staining the earth. Clytemnestra addresses Cassandra, commanding her to enter the palace to participate in the cleansing sacrifice which is being prepared within. To Clytemnestra's contempt, Cassandra appears not to understand.

Struck with horror, Cassandra begins to invoke Apollo. Gradually she recounts the bloody history of the house of Atreus, the murdered children, the sodden limbs on which their father fed, and now a worse crime still: the treacherous welcome of the cleansing sacrifice. She sees death's new weapon, a hunting net, the king trapped in the sacred bath, and her own fate, which she distinguishes from that of Philomela. (Philomela, in a tale we will examine when we look at Ovid's *Metamorphoses,* was at least transformed by the gods into a nightingale after she had fed their son to her wicked husband Tereus.)

Cassandra sees the home of Argos as haunted by the Furies, foul bird-like female deities with snakes around their breasts, whose role is to pursue offenders, particularly those who have spilt blood unjustly. In this house here "they sit within, they chant the primal curse, each spitting hatred on that crime of old." After recounting the fate of Troy, she begins to spell out to the Chorus exactly what is going to happen. Because Thyestes ate his brothers, Aegisthus, a coward lion, has been in Argos plotting against him who trod down Troy, together with the false she-dog who has just cried out with joy at the conqueror's safe return. The Chorus say they understand about Thyestes, but not the rest: "'Tis Agamemnon's doom thou shalt behold," says Cassandra, and she too will be destroyed. But because of her refusal of Apollo's love, Apollo's curse prevails once again. The Chorus refuses to believe her, just as the Trojans did earlier.

She invokes Apollo, who gave her part of his own foresight and has brought her from Troy to die in the death-reeking place. She will never be disbelieved again, and after her death a third will come to avenge her cause, a son to kill his mother and avenge his father:

> And now why mourn I, tarrying on earth,
> Since first mine Ilion has found its fate
> And I beheld, and those who won the war
> Pass to such issue as the gods ordain?
> I too will pass and let them dare to die!
> Portal of Hades, thus I bid thee hail!
> Grant me one boon—a swift and mortal stroke,
> That all unwrung by pain, with ebbing blood
> Shed forth in quiet death, I close mine eyes.

She goes to the door of the palace, but cries and turns back, choking at the stench of murder. Invoking revenge on her and Agamemnon's murderers, she goes in:

> Ah state of mortal man! In time of weal,
> A line, a shadow! And if ill fate fall,
> One wet sponge-sweep wipes all our trace away—
> And this I deem less piteous of the two.

Cries break out from within, as Agamemnon is killed, stabbed in the bath. Clytemnestra, sword in hand, throws open the doors, revealing the body of Agamemnon wrapped in a purple cloak, and also that of Cassandra.

Clytemnestra makes it clear that it was she who had struck Agamemnon three times, having cast round him a great net as if catching a fish. She exults as the cornfield exults when its seed bursts forth in the spring. She is upbraided by the Chorus, but she brushes them aside contemptuously. He killed his daughter, whom my pain brought forth, for a spell to stop a wind. He was ripe for punishment. The Chorus once more upbraids Helen, but Clytemnestra will have none of it. Helen did not order the fighting, nor was her fault the only one. She, Clytemnestra, did this murder, but it is just part of the feud and vengeance which haunts the house of Atreus, and she dwells again on the lovely Iphigenia. The Chorus is at a loss. Where does Right or Justice lie in all of this—"who in the end can know?"—but a murderer must die. Clytemnestra concurs. Agamemnon is the murderer, and now let the cycle of killing stop.

Aegisthus appears for the first time. He recalls his father's banquet, and his curse on the house of Pelops on learning the truth. This is the origin of the present deed, which he had long planned. The Chorus insults him for his cowardice in not going to Troy and also for letting his woman do the work, but he threatens them and draws his sword. Clytemnestra steps in, urging all to accept Fate. The Chorus raises the possibility of Orestes' returning. Clytemnestra insists that she and Aegisthus now have the power and together will enforce order in the house.

The Choephori (the Libation Bearers) and *The Eumenides* (the Kindly Ones)

In the second and third parts of *The Oresteia,* we gradually emerge from the night of *Agamemnon.* Indeed, the rest of the trilogy can be seen as an attempt to resolve the conundrum posed at the end of *Agamemnon,* where Clytemnestra asks that the cycle of crime, killing and revenge in the cursed household should stop with the ritualistic slaughter of Agamemnon. But, as the Furies say early on in *The Eumenides,* what we have at the end of *Agamemnon* is (in Robert Fagles' translation): "Guilt both ways, and who can call it justice?" For all her justification, Clytemnestra's crime—for it is a crime in the manner of its doing if in nothing else—still calls out for vengeance (or is it justice?). And in *The Choephori* this is what she gets, at the hands of yet another member of the cursed family, Orestes, her and Agamemnon's son.

The Choephori takes place seven years after Agamemnon's death. Under the rule of Clytemnestra and Aegisthus, the people are sullen. Agamemnon remains buried, without honors, outside the city walls. When the play opens, Orestes has been brought back from Phocis by Hermes the messenger god, acting for Apollo, as Cassandra foretold. He is standing by Agamemnon's grave as Electra, his sister, who has never come to terms with her father's death, and some slave women come to offer libations. (They are the libation bearers of the title.) Overcoming initial doubt on Electra's part, Electra and Orestes recognize each other, and in the recognition sing that Zeus is with them now. Encouraged by the Chorus of slave girls, they begin a lament by their father's grave, summoning up his spirit and the spirit of revenge The Chorus reports that Clytemnestra has been haunted by a dream of a snake at her breast. Eventually Orestes and Pylades, a friend, go to the palace, disguised as foreign traders. They are not recognized, and tell Clytemnestra that Orestes has died in Phocis. Aegisthus goes to question the "messengers," but they kill him. Clytemnestra and Orestes, who is now revealed, confront each other. Clytemnestra offers Orestes her breast, appealing to his pity and his sense that she is his mother, but to no avail. Before he kills her, she warns him, nevertheless, that the Furies have been appointed by the gods to avenge matricide. After the deed, Orestes attempts to justify himself; but even as he does so, the Furies gather to repay this new pollution.

The Eumenides opens in Delphi, at the Delphic oracle in the temple of Apollo. The priestess goes in to see who is waiting inside, but she comes out screaming. He is a man polluted with blood he has shed, surrounded by Furies. The curtain opens and we see Apollo and Hermes, with Orestes before them, with the twelve Furies asleep around him. Apollo sends Orestes under the guidance of Hermes to Athens to seek Athene's help. When he goes off, the shade of Clytemnestra rouses the Furies to their task. Apollo tells the Furies to go to Athens too.

In the temple of Athene, both Orestes and the Furies state their positions before the statue of the goddess. The Furies insist here, as they do all through, that if they did not pursue law-breakers, Law itself would fail. Athene arrives from Troy. She hears the two sides. The Furies drive out murderers and a mother's murder can never be just. Orestes admits to matricide, but insists that it was just retribution; and further that Apollo would have punished him if he had failed in his duty. Athene states that as the case is so grave she will set up a court of twelve of her wisest citizens to hear it. When the court convenes, Orestes insists that his deed was just and was done at Apollo's command, but the Furies insist again that a mother's murder is worse than that of a husband, because the mother gives you life.

Apollo now takes over Orestes' defense with a sequence of astonishingly poor arguments, by turn blustering and casuistical, ending with the claim that man, not woman, is the source of a child's life. (He refers here to Athene herself, born fully adult from the head of Zeus.) Athene now calls for the jurors to vote, counseling them to find a mean between anarchy and tyranny, balancing fear of the law and of its enforcement (which must never completely go) with reverence for its sanctity.

The votes are even, and Athene, as her father's child swayed by Apollo's last point, gives the casting vote in favor of Orestes. Orestes goes free, though not, it needs to be emphasized, guilt-free, pledging eternal friendship between Athens and Argos. Apollo goes with him. The Furies, naturally, are outraged: "Woe on you, younger gods! The ancient right / Ye have over-ridden, rent it from my hands." In their shame they want vengeance. Gradually, though, Athene placates them. She invokes the goddess Peitho (Persuasion) to soothe them, and to moderate their harshness with humanity and understanding. Henceforth, under the tutelage of Zeus and Peitho, they will be revered in Athens, and no house will prosper which does not have their favor.

The Furies—now the Eumenides, the Kindly Ones, with Athene as their leader—will now guard Athens and its people and uphold its laws. There will be an end to civil war and to the endless cycles of revenge and reprisals of a life for a life, replaced now by regeneration, humanity, and joy. The persuasion of democracy and of the institutions of law and the jury court will supplant the dominance of force (and by the time Aeschylus was writing, Peitho was the goddess of democracy). The trilogy ends with a torchlight procession from the theater to the shrine below the Areopagus, where the Kindly Ones are also still the spirits of awe and dread, upholding the law which makes civilized life possible.

Conclusion

The end of *The Oresteia* is, of course, the reworking of the ancient myth so as to represent the founding of the Athenian institutions of courts and rational, humane deliberation, with Argos/Mycenae displaced. Nevertheless, the house of Atreus remains its focus and its mainspring. It is a house running with blood. Murder, deception, infanticide (twice), cannibalism, adultery, gamicide, regicide, matricide and the crime of Troy itself: all are part of its history and of the cycles of vengeance which ensue.

Are all cities founded on such crimes? Is there any civilization not founded on original rapine and slaughter? How can such origins be overcome? And is there any case of significance in which the plea "Guilt both ways, and who can call it justice?" might not be heard?

The answer we are given in *The Oresteia* is probably "yes" to the first two questions: what we call civilization is indeed founded on acts of original criminality. But (third question) vengeance cannot be the answer, for the very reasons explored with such compelling existential force in *The Oresteia*. That is not civilization, but simply a continuation of the original crime. Life in such conditions will be for all concerned an oscillation between anarchy and tyranny. In either case, the powerful win by sheer power. Humanity goes to the wall.

Civilization does need Furies. The Furies are right about that, even if, as the Chorus observes at the end of *The Eumenides,* once they are accepted, their wrath is tempered. Even before that, though, they have much the better of the arguments in *The Eumenides.* But we do not need the loathsome creatures of the night who sit on the roof of Atreus's palace and who pursue Orestes. They must retain their awesomeness, but as Kindly Ones. Pursuit of personal vengeance must give way to the rule of law, individual revenge to public law and political institutions. Vendettas and personal retribution must be replaced by impartial courts which will be able to staunch the cycle of blood through the exercise of reason, and humanity, and, in a sense, resolve the dilemma posed by the need for revenge and its exercise. More generally, a society with institutions based on discussion, reason and humanity is preferable to ones in which rule is by force and the arbitrary decisions of one man or a few. How, though, can such ideals be secured? *The Oresteia* does not tell us.

The trilogy was first performed in 458 B.C., which was when Athenian power and civilization were in the ascendant—and *The Oresteia* was indeed a major element of that rise. Yet all too soon after Aeschylus, Athens became involved in a long, terrible and enervating war with Sparta (which she eventually lost). During this war, in the year 416 B.C., the Athenians—who had no doubt themselves participated in Aeschylus's plays—perpetrated a crime as terrible and as inexcusable as that of Troy itself, and as barbaric as anything the Persians did in Aeschylus's youth. Because the islanders of Melos insisted on neutrality in Athens' war with Sparta, all the men were slaughtered, the women and children enslaved and the island itself handed over to Athenian settlers. While this could be regarded as representing a failure of the institutions that Aeschylus was celebrating at the end of *The Eumenides*—for the Athenian assembly actually voted in favor of the massacre of the Melians—Aeschylus could quite reasonably reply that all this shows is that good institutions on their own are not enough. While good institutions are certainly an advance on private law and private justice, their success depends on their being run by men of good will, which was not the case in Athens in 416 B.C.

In the famous "Melian Dialogue" in Book Five of his *History of the Peloponnesian War,* Thucydides has the Athenians arguing prior to the slaughter that, in relations between states, the one necessary law of nature is to rule whenever one can. As the weaker power, the Melians owe it to themselves to submit to the one which is stronger. There would be no disgrace in giving way in such circumstances to the greatest city in Greece, especially when favorable terms are being offered. The Melians refuse the terms, with the consequences just mentioned. We will never know for certain what the author of *The Persians* and *The Oresteia* would have made of the Melian Dialogue. It is, though, safe to speculate that in his plays Aeschylus provides material enough to counter the stance that his compatriots took then in both word and deed.

Sophocles' Theban Plays: *Antigone*

Sophocles lived from 496 B.C. until 406 B.C. He was from the generation after Aeschylus and that before Euripides, although his career overlapped with that of Aeschylus. Sophocles actually took the prize for tragedy in 468 B.C., defeating Aeschylus. His death, however, was in the same year as that of Euripides. The plays we have of Sophocles are mostly later than the earliest surviving work of Euripides, and his last play, *Oedipus at Colonus,* was first produced after his and Euripides' death.

Sophocles' tone, though, is different from either Aeschylus or Euripides. It is sparer than either, more tragic, more implacable even than Aeschylus. It is far less argumentative than Euripides, and less concerned with normal human feelings and reactions. There is in Sophocles no sense of anything but the necessity of fate. Fate comes to seem religiously necessary in a vision of life which is, humanly speaking, as bleak as could be. At the end of *The Women of Trachis,* after terrible events which have little to do with anything that those who have suffered have deserved, Sophocles says this:

> You see the great indifference of the gods
> to these things which have happened,
> who begat us and are called our fathers
> and look on such sufferings.
> What is to come no one can see,
> but what is here now is pitiable for us
> and shameful for them,
> but of all men hardest for him
> on whom this disaster has fallen.
> Maiden, do not stay in this house:
> you have seen death and many agonies,
> fresh and strange,
> and there is nothing here that is not Zeus.
> (Translation by Bernard Williams (University of Chicago Press, 1993).)

What happens on earth is pitiable for us humans, who cannot avoid it, but shameful for the gods, who begat us and are called our fathers; but . . .

there is nothing here which is not Zeus. This is the lesson of those who have looked into the abyss but who have seen no redemption. It is the very opposite of the optimistic rationalism of much modern philosophy, the thought that if we understand the cause of something, even of something bad, and its necessity, that itself helps us to live through it. That is not the sense of "there is nothing here that is not Zeus." What we have here is necessity, to be sure, but as far as the events described are concerned, an unconsoling necessity.

All this, of course, raises the question as to the point or purpose of tragedy like Sophocles.' What do we gain from watching it? Traditionally (after Aristotle), it has been said that one's emotions are purged by watching the terrible events recounted on the stage—this is the concept of *catharsis,* a sort of cleansing, which makes tragedy sound like a sort of psychotherapy, after taking which one will feel better. It would be odd if one "felt better" after hearing of Oedipus gouging out his eyes, or perhaps, more precisely, one would be odd if that were one's reaction. But what might not be odd would be the sense that one could look on the cruellest workings of Zeus, and not be complicit in them, even in a perverse sense enjoying them (as typically happens in film presentations of such things, and may indeed be true of the revenge dramas of the Jacobeans); but rather through the stark and terrible beauty of the work of the dramatist look on them in their full truth, and yet not despair. Nietzsche said that we have art so that we do not perish from the truth: art can allow us to grasp the truth, objectively and unsentimentally, and yet not perish from it. Something like this is the effect of Greek tragedy in all its absence of redemptive consolation, and, above all, the effect of Sophocles.

The Theban Plays

Sophocles' Theban Plays do not constitute a trilogy like Aeschylus's *Oresteia.* They were written over a considerable span of years, and not in order. The earliest, *Antigone,* which deals with the latest events in the story, dates from around 442 B.C. *Oedipus the King* is from the 420s B.C., while *Oedipus at Colonus* was produced posthumously around 401 B.C.

However, all three plays deal with a continuous sequence of events in Thebes, focusing on Oedipus and his blighted family. As with *The Oresteia,* to understand the action we need to go back to the earlier history of the house, in this case that of Thebes.

The city of Thebes was founded under the direction of the Delphic oracle by Cadmus, who slew a dragon and then, as instructed, sowed the dragon's teeth in the ground. The teeth sprang up as giants, who immediately fought each other until only five remained. With Cadmus, and under him, these five founded Thebes. Cadmus's son was Polydorus, though he also had daughters in the form of Semele, who was loved by Zeus and produced Dionysus, and Agave, who became the mother of Pentheus. (This female line of Cadmus will become important when we look at Euripides' *Bacchae*.)

Polydorus' son was Labdacus, and Labdacus produced Laius. Laius married Jocasta, and they had a son. Laius and Jocasta were told by the Delphic oracle that their son would kill his father and marry his mother. To avoid this fate, they give the baby boy to a shepherd with instructions that he is to be abandoned on a mountain, with his feet pinioned to stop him crawling to safety. But the shepherd takes pity on the baby and gives him to another shepherd, from neighboring Corinth, to bring up as his own.

This the Corinthian shepherd does, but after a while he gives the child to the king and queen of Corinth, Polybus and Merope, who are childless. They bring the boy up as their own. They call him Oedipus ("swollen-footed," the result of his being tethered to the mountain). When Oedipus grows up, he is taunted about his parentage. He goes to Delphi to find out from the oracle who his parents are. The oracle tells him that he is fated to kill his father and marry his mother. Distraught, he flees, vowing never to return to Corinth so as to avoid this catastrophe.

He comes to a crossroads in the mountains, where he has an argument with another traveler. They fight and Oedipus kills his opponent. He walks on, and comes to the city of Thebes, which is in turmoil. The city is suffering from a plague foisted on them by the Sphinx, a monster sitting outside the city who destroys those who cannot answer her riddle. (What is it which has four legs at dawn, two legs at midday and three legs at dusk? The answer is man.) In addition, the King of Thebes has recently been killed.

Oedipus, though, solves the riddle, and frees the city from the Sphinx and the plague lifts. As a reward he is given the widowed queen as his bride. Together they have four children: Eteocles, Polynices, Ismene and Antigone. Thebes has fifteen years of prosperity, but then famine and pestilence afflict the city again.

It is at this point that *Oedipus the King* begins. Creon, the brother of Jocasta the queen, has been sent to Delphi to consult the oracle once more, so as to rid the city of this new plague. The oracle says that the killer of Laius must be brought to justice. The blind seer Tiresias is brought in by Oedipus, but remains silent. Oedipus insults him, and Tiresias tells him that the killer he is seeking is himself, and that he, Oedipus, is committing a sin by living with Jocasta. Oedipus suspects that Creon is behind all this—which Creon denies—and banishes him.

After this, everything unravels inexorably and with great speed. Jocasta tells Oedipus of the original prophecy, and about how the baby was abandoned and Laius killed by robbers on the road. This, though, does not wholly reassure Oedipus, who wants to know more about the killing at the crossroads. He sends for a witness to the killing. A messenger then arrives with the apparently good news that Polybus, Oedipus's supposed father, has died peacefully in old age. But the messenger also reveals that he was the Corinthian shepherd who was actually given the baby Oedipus by the Theban shepherd and brought him to Corinth.

Jocasta realizes the truth, and warns Oedipus against pursuing the matter further. But he insists that the Theban shepherd be found: he must know the truth and who he is. The second shepherd arrives and all is made plain to Oedipus. Jocasta, meanwhile, has hanged herself. On seeing her body, Oedipus, distraught, snatches the brooches from her dress and drives them into his eyes time and again. He rails against his pollution—all human infamy, as he puts it, in one crime confounded. Creon reappears, to take over. Ismene and Antigone, the young daughters of Oedipus and Jocasta, are led in, and Oedipus, blind and broken, seeks banishment. But Creon insists that they await a divine sign. The Chorus comments, in the version by W. B. Yeats (1928):

> Make way for Oedipus. All people said
> "That is a fortunate man";
> And now what storms are beating on his head?
> Call no man fortunate that is not dead.
> The dead are free from pain.

Oedipus the King is the quintessential tragedy: spare, inexorable, every effort of human beings to avoid the divinely inspired inevitable fruitless, simply making the inevitable more certain, every opening of hope actually yet another step on the road to doom. There is also the role of hidden or gradual self-knowledge and the connection between them, and the suffering which then ensues.

In his *Poetics* less than a century later, the philosopher Aristotle saw the play as exemplifying much of what he took to be the essence of tragedy: a noble hero, marred by a tragic flaw or error (in Oedipus's case, impetuous pride); a scene of recognition, a change from ignorance to knowledge in which the world of the hero is shattered; and finally, the reversal of fortune through an event which has the consequence opposite to the one expected (in this case, the effect of the messenger's testimony). All these things contribute to the pity which Aristotle saw as the typical effect of tragedy on an audience. The action, too, conforms to the classical ideal of unity of time and place: the events seen on the stage all happening in one place, in one continuous action. And there is also the relationship between Oedipus and his real parents, on which a whole school of psychology has been erected.

By contrast to the horrors of *Oedipus the King, Oedipus at Colonus* is elegiac and religious in a very obvious sense. Many years after the terrible events in Thebes, the blind and aged Oedipus, now in perpetual exile, is wandering around Greece, led by Antigone. Polynices has gone to Argos, where he has married the daughter of the king, and is preparing to lead a military action against Thebes. This is because he and Eteocles had seized power from Creon, but had then fallen out themselves, Eteocles emerging as the winner. Ismene is also in Thebes, waiting for better news.

When the play opens, Antigone and Oedipus have reached a grove on the outskirts of Athens, sacred to the Eumenides. The elders who care for the grove are hostile to Oedipus's presence, but go to seek advice from Theseus, the King of Athens. Ismene appears, with the bad news about the impending war between Polynices and Eteocles. Creon is also on his way, seeking Oedipus's return because of an oracle which says that Thebes must be Oedipus's last resting place. Theseus arrives, and Oedipus declares that he will give Athens the gift of his body. Theseus promises to protect Oedipus.

Creon then enters, demanding Oedipus's return. Oedipus refuses, because when he wanted to go, Thebes would not let him; now they want him only for their own purposes. Creon then gets his soldiers to take Antigone away, saying they have already seized Ismene. But when he starts to leave himself, he is prevented by the return of Theseus, who holds him until the daughters are returned. When they return, Theseus leaves, and the Chorus sings the wisdom of the ancient wood-god Silenus: the best of all things is not to be born, not to be; but the second best is to die soon. And Oedipus is a rock on which the billows of adversity break.

Polynices now turns up, seeking Oedipus's blessing for his expedition. Oedipus curses both brothers: may they kill each other. Antigone pleads with Polynices to desist, unsuccessfully. But before he goes, he asks the sisters to bury him if necessary.

A great storm brews up. It is the sign of the time of Oedipus's death. Theseus is summoned, and Oedipus tells him that he will die in a secret, hallowed place, known to Theseus alone, to ensure the safety of Athens. He takes leave of Antigone and Ismene on the brink of a chasm. He is called by a divine voice, accompanied only by Theseus. No one but Theseus sees what happens, whether Oedipus is lifted away by the gods, or goes down into the earth. What is certain is that, at the end, he died without pain, more wonderfully than any other man. Theseus comforts Antigone and Ismene, and sends them back to Thebes. They will try to staunch the bloodshed there.

There are those who think that *Oedipus at Colonus* is Sophocles' masterpiece. There is about it a mystery and a sense of transcendence, and also of a resolution beyond suffering. Its ending is extraordinarily beautiful, in the literal sense awesome; but sad, too, beyond the gore and horror of *Oedipus the King*. As Antigone puts it:

> I never knew how great the loss could be
> Even of sadness; there was a sort of joy
> In sorrow, when he was at my side.
> Father, my love, in your shroud of earth
> We too shall love you for ever and ever.
> (Translation by E. F. Watling (Penguin, 1947).)

Antigone

Sophocles' Antigone, which dates from 441 B.C., is the classic depiction of the tension which exists between pure morality, as represented by Antigone, and the compromises demanded by public policy, as represented by Creon, her uncle. Antigone is the daughter of Oedipus, the tragic King of Thebes who attempts to outwit fate but succeeds only in enacting his destiny by killing his father and marrying his mother, the very fate he wants to avoid. After Oedipus's death, Antigone disobeys Creon, who is now ruler of Thebes, by insisting on the primacy of familial and religious piety over political necessity, and she herself is condemned to death. The story of Oedipus is told by Sophocles in two earlier plays (Oedipus the King and Oedipus at Colonus), which, together with Antigone, make up his Theban Plays.

Before the play opens, Polynices has attacked and entered Thebes with his allies and troops from Argos and elsewhere, and pitted the so-called Seven against Thebes against seven chosen Theban warriors. In the fighting, Eteocles and Polynices kill each other, and Creon emerges as undisputed ruler of Thebes. In an effort to assert his authority, he commands that Eteocles be buried with full honors, but that Polynices be left outside the city, unburied, his soul thereby unable to find rest. To Greek eyes, this is not only a disgrace in itself, but also an affront to the piety which the gods demand the dead should be shown. But, orders Creon, anyone who disobeys his command will himself be sentenced to death.

The play opens with the sisters Antigone and Ismene discussing Creon's edict. Antigone tries to persuade Ismene to help her bury Polynices, but Ismene dares not: "we are women; it is not for us to fight against men." Antigone is scornful. Is Ismene prepared to defy the holiest laws of heaven by leaving her brother unburied? The exchange ends with Antigone telling

Ismene to leave her alone with her own madness and her honorable death. Does she, even then, will death? Ismene replies:

> Then go, if you will have it . . .
> You go on a fool's errand!
> Lover true
> To your beloved, none the less, are you!
> (Translation by Sir George Young (1888).)

Antigone, then, is by worldly standards a fool, a pure fool, but, poignantly, also capable of inspiring affection and love.

The Chorus, with typical insensitivity, sings jubilantly of the defeat of Polynices and the sun now dawning the brightest ever on Thebes. Zeus has struck the proud man down. Creon now enters, and in a fine speech explains both his policy to keep Thebes safe from her enemies, and the way in which the differential treatment being accorded to Eteocles (the patriot, burial with honors) and Polynices (the enemy, left to be eaten by dogs and vultures) will help to promote peace and loyalty in Thebes. A sentry rushes in, full of fear. Polynices' body has been covered with earth. The Chorus mutters that this might be an act of the gods. Creon will have none of it. Discontented elements in the city, wanting to undermine the law, have paid people to do this. The perpetrator must be discovered and brought before him.

The Chorus now sings one of Sophocles' most powerful hymns:

> In this world are many wonders,
> None more wonderful than man.
> He can sail the stormy ocean:
> Through the deep his way he'll plan.
> Mother Earth to him must offer
> Year by year her rich supply.
> As he toils with beasts of burden,
> Nothing can his will deny.
> All that lives on earth or heaven,
> All that dwells beneath the sea,
> He can capture with his cunning.
> Nothing from his grasp can flee.
> On the mountainside he chases,
> Hunting lions to their den.
> Horse and cattle learn to heed him.
> And all accept the rule of men.
> Man has learnt the gift of language:
> Fast as wind his speed of thought.

Shelters, houses, towns and cities,
All by man's great skill are wrought.
His the power that knows no limit;
His the cure for every ill.
He has conquered every danger.
Death alone defeats us still.
(Translation by David Taylor.)

With these thoughts in our minds of man's ability to do everything except escape death, Antigone is brought in, escorted by two soldiers. The sentry says that they had cleaned the corpse of its covering. A storm had then brewed up, after which they saw Antigone standing by the now uncovered body, screaming like an angry bird who returns to find its nest emptied of its chicks. She then picked up more earth and started making offerings to the dead.

Creon charges her with breaking the edict. Antigone tells him that the order did not come from Zeus or the gods of the underworld. Justice knows no such law, and Creon, being only a man, has no power to overrule the edict of the gods. She knows that she will have to die for this, but could not have left her mother's son lie unburied. The Chorus comments that she has her father's stubborn pride. Creon replies that the most obstinate spirit is often the soonest to snap. He orders Ismene to be fetched. Antigone asks him why he is delaying having her killed, adding that the people would say that what she did was honorable. When Creon denies this, Antigone says that they dare not tell Creon what they really think. Creon says that he cannot give equal honor to the good and to the bad, and that an enemy is still an enemy, even when dead. Antigone: "I was made for fellowship in love, not fellowship in hate." Creon: "Then get you down thither, and love, if you must, the dead! No woman while I live shall order me."

After this extraordinarily quick and pointed exchange, Ismene is brought in. She insists to Creon that she was part of the plot, but Antigone denies her any part in it, and taunts her: Creon is the one Ismene loves, and her choice was life, while mine was death. Creon says that both are mad, and Ismene asks him in turn whether he is prepared to kill his son's bride (for Antigone is engaged to marry Haemon, Creon's son). Creon is predictably dismissive— there are other fields for Haemon to plough. The sisters are taken away.

The Chorus sings another great hymn. Happy are those who do not know the taste of evil, but the house of Labdacus is cursed from one generation to the next. Zeus lives on high Olympus in great brilliancy, but one law is unchangeable: "Nothing great / Enters the life of man without suffering." And for the man chased by the avenging power, the time is short before suffering comes.

Haemon enters. Initially he appears to side with Creon. He will be bound by Creon's guidance. Creon tells him that Antigone is an enemy. Traitors cannot be tolerated: "obedience is due / To the State's officer in small and great, just and unjust commandments." This obedience keeps order in the city and saves the lives of hundreds. Maybe, though, Creon has overplayed his hand, for Haemon now begins to tell him that in the city there are murmurings of pity and whispers of support for Antigone. For Creon to think his is the only wisdom shows a shallow spirit and an empty heart. The wisest man knows how and when to give way, like a sailor tacking and slackening the sails before the wind.

Creon is indignant. Is he to take lessons from a person of Haemon's age or from the populace of Thebes? He is king, and responsible only to himself. Haemon retorts that Creon would make an excellent king alone in an empty land. Haemon insists that he is pleading the cause of Creon and himself, as well as that of Antigone; but if Antigone dies, she will not die alone. Creon orders Antigone to be brought in to be condemned to death, and Haemon storms out. Antigone's sentence is to be walled up in a cave with enough food to acquit him of the guilt of her blood: a peculiarly slow and horrible death, of course.

The Chorus now sings of the power and madness of love, which spares neither god nor man, splitting families and houses and consuming everyone. Aphrodite works her will on all. Antigone enters. Death will be her dowry. She laments the cold tomb in which she is to hover, between life and death, and also the curse of the house of Labdacus and the shame of her parents. The way that lies before her has neither funeral hymn nor wedding march: "Day's hallowed orb on high / I may no longer see; / For me no tears are spent, / Nor any friends lament the death I die" (translation by Sir George Young). Creon roughly orders her to be taken away. Antigone says that she will go to her grave, to be welcomed by those members of her family who have gone before her there: her mother, her father and Polynices. She has buried all of them, and she has done for Polynices what she could not do for husband or son. Now because of Creon's command, she will have neither husband nor son. But what law of heaven has she broken? What god can save her now? She is going because she honored the things which should be honored. As she goes, the Chorus sings of those from mythology who have died in prison.

The blind Tiresias is led in, and upbraids Creon. He hears of birds in vicious combat. From the sacrifice he has made rank juices ooze. The blood of Oedipus is on the altars, there is a blight on Thebes which is Creon's doing. Creon must relent, and give up his will. Creon (like Oedipus earlier in the saga) accuses Tiresias of seeking his own advantage. Tiresias replies with a terrible prophecy. Creon's son will die; there are two debts for Creon to pay, one for the unburied Polynices and one for Antigone whom he has entombed. This cannot be altered. It all follows necessarily from Creon's deeds.

Hearing this, Creon finally relents, and orders the freeing of Antigone. The Chorus sings of the beauty of Thebes, but then a messenger enters (once again telling us of violent and bloody deeds which have happened off-stage, "ob-scene"). Creon was once an enviable man, who saved his country from its enemies. But no more. Haemon has killed himself. Creon's wife Eurydice enters, and the messenger tells her that Creon had gone to give Polynices proper burial, before going to the cave where Antigone was immured. But when he got into the mouth of the cave he found Antigone hanged with her own dress, and with Haemon clinging to her. Haemon spat at Creon and stabbed himself with his own sword, embracing the dead Antigone as he too died. Creon enters with the body of Haemon: "thou art sped for a fault that was mine, not thine." But that is not the end of it, because he now finds that Eurydice too has killed herself, cursing him the slayer. Creon is led away: "Cast me out, no other than a man undone." It was unintended, but his fate is too heavy for him. The Chorus has the last word:

> The greatest part of happiness is wisdom;
> Divine laws man ought always to uphold.
> To boastful tongues sure punishment will follow,
> And wisdom we learn only when we're old.
> (Translation by David Taylor.)

Themes from *Antigone*

According to some commentators, including notably the philosopher Hegel, *Antigone* is Greek tragedy in its purest form, not so much guilt both ways (and who can call it justice?), but irreconcilable right both ways and who can deny either or bring them together? For Hegel, both Antigone and Creon are right, equal and opposing forces, in his system of thesis and antithesis in collision. Antigone represents the female, the private, the inward and the subjective, the sanctity of the family and primeval piety, as expressed in the everlasting law of the gods, the ancient gods of the underworld, a law whose origin no one knows; Creon stands for the male, the public arena, public and political law, and the necessity of the state. At the level at which each is operating there can be no resolution. Resolution—in Hegel's terms, synthesis—is possible only by some melding of the public and the private which is beyond the consciousness of either protagonist in the play to effect, though in the play the audience is itself raised to a higher state of consciousness in which both thesis and antithesis can be seen as limited.

No doubt this is a healthy corrective to the modern sentimentality that conflict resolution is always possible between people of good will. For, on the face of it, neither Antigone nor Creon is unjustified, and both are sincere in their beliefs and actions. The conflict arises because Antigone is following the law of the gods and also of family piety, while Creon is following the law of man and his loyalty is to the city and its good ordering. The tragedy is that both are right, but that the two laws and the two loyalties, in this extreme situation, clash head-on. There can be no compromise which will leave either position intact. In Greek tragedy, it could be said, the pathos is precisely that there is no overarching deity or code, such as the Christian God, which can adjudicate between the conflicting rights, and the upshot is that whatever is done, though right from one point of view, will be wrong from another equally valid perspective. Our tragedy—and not just Antigone's—is that, as human beings, we have to live with conflicting sets of values.

There is undeniably something of this in *Antigone.* There is a degree of even-handedness in Sophocles' treatment of the two protagonists, or at least on the validity of their respective positions. Or perhaps more accurately, from the materials that Sophocles presents us with, it would be possible to construct an even-handed treatment, in which reasons of state—not, of course, to be minimized in a situation such as that of Thebes of recent invasion and potential civil war—would be nicely balanced by reasons of divine law and family (and let us not forget the havoc that Antigone's terrible family has wreaked on the hapless citizens of Thebes). Also it could be pointed out that Antigone's flaws nicely balance those of Creon. If Creon is heartless to Haemon, so is Antigone to Ismene. If Antigone will not listen to Creon, nor will Creon to Antigone. Above all, if Antigone is self-willed (Oedipus's daughter indeed), as the Chorus tells her before she is led to her tomb—determined to follow what she sees as a divine command—so is Creon, fit only to rule a deserted land alone—as Haemon tells him.

Nevertheless, most modern readers will still probably feel that Antigone ultimately has the better of the argument or is at least the better human being. She may be a fool, but she is a pure fool, her values are categorical and her courage when under pressure and faced with death is unflinching. Even if there is a slight hint that she may will her death, her integrity is complete and her love unwavering. Compared to her, Creon looks messy, and his reasons full of evasion and sophistry even. Moreover, as the play progresses, Creon is offered ways out of the impasse, particularly by Haemon. Haemon, in saying that Creon would make a good ruler in a deserted land, surely echoes the democratic feeling of the audience of Sophocles, as well as our sense today.

There is also more than a hint of petulance in Creon's angry response to Tiresias. In short, unsettling as this may be to the philosophical straitjacket of Hegel and his followers, in Sophocles' play does civil order really depend on unyielding enforcement of his edict about Polynices and on the breaking of Antigone? Although Antigone sees herself as divinely motivated, does not her predicament and Sophocles' play reveal a fundamental lack of humanity in Creon? Should a civilised society not have room for a humane reading of its laws and decisions? Would order in Thebes really be undermined were Creon to relent and show the humanity Haemon asks of him? For Creon, the cost of not having space of this sort is the destruction of all that is most dear to him, and personal ruin and disgrace. Nor should we forget what the Chorus has reminded us of in speaking of Aphrodite: that it is love—that of Antigone for Polynices, and that of Haemon and Antigone together—which Creon in his rage denies and tramples down.

The truth of the matter is that in order to get a drama of any conviction or tension Sophocles had to give Creon some case, which he certainly does, giving him about the best case he could. But it is not just for modern audiences—predisposed to applaud conscientious objectors, particularly if they are women—that Antigone is in the right. For Sophocles (and his audience) human laws are secondary to divine ones, and Creon, for inferior reasons of state, is placing what is in effect political expediency above religious piety. In the play he is denounced by Tiresias the divine prophet (as Oedipus had been earlier), and he is also punished for his wickedness. Antigone's unshakable conviction in her rectitude has, for Sophocles and the Greeks, an unshakable foundation in divine law which, unlike the man-made law of Creon and other rulers, can never be unjust. *Antigone* is not just a case of the individual conscience against the collective *raison d'état,* though it does contain that in it. Ultimately Sophocles' play is about divine law against the merely human (although of course in this case the divine law seems to uphold basic human sentiment), and Antigone's stature derives from that. As such it would be quite anachronistic to see the play as presenting a case of competing plural values, between which there could be no decision. This might be how we tend to see such conflicts, but it is not how Sophocles and the Greeks saw it, and there is little justification in Sophocles' work for such a view.

Euripides: *The Bacchae*

Euripides was born in 484 B.C. and died in 406 B.C. He took himself into exile in 407 B.C., which is when he wrote *The Bacchae*. In all he wrote ninety-two plays, many during the course of the Peloponnesian War against Sparta and her allies, which lasted intermittently from 431 to 404 B.C. This ended in defeat and disaster for Athens, which during the course of the war witnessed oscillations between oligarchic dictatorship and an increasingly disorderly democracy. Nearly all the plays of Euripides which we have come from the period of the war.

Many of Euripides' plays can be seen as providing sharp commentaries on contemporary events. For example, *The Women of Troy*, *Orestes* and *Iphigenia in Aulis* are all about war, and predominantly antiwar. *The Women of Troy* is also seen by some as being anti-men too. *Medea* portrays a woman badly wronged, and if she wreaks horrific revenge on Jason, her tormentor, she is by far the strongest character in the play. That Euripides' audience understood many of his plays as bearing contemporary reference is indicated by the fact that *The Women of Troy*, clearly an outstandingly powerful drama, but also clearly warning against the cruelty of war and also against hubris in the conduct of victory, failed to win the first prize for tragedy in 415 B.C. This was just after Athens had conducted the massacre on the neutral island of Melos, and just before she launched a grandiose expedition to Sicily with great optimism (wholly misplaced, as it turned out).

Apart from hostility to war in some of his plays, the prevailing tone of much of Euripides' writing is skeptical, almost Sophistical in spirit. The Sophists were skilled philosophers who tended to use their skills in constructing arguments and in teaching others how to win arguments; the upshot of their activity was to introduce a degree of relativism and skepticism into public discourse, because in practice they demonstrated that anything could be either defended or attacked by argument, depending on one's starting point.

There is no reason to suppose that Euripides was himself a relativist or a Sophist, but his style owes something to Sophistical methods. In his plays, in contrast to those of Aeschylus, the traditional values, hierarchies and myths are not taken as unquestioned. We have already noted that Aristophanes represents Euripides as having given ordinary people and their feelings a voice, and in many of his plays there is an emphasis on free speech, on hearing both sides of the argument (quite unlike Odysseus's treatment of Thersites in Homer), and even on occasion on the superiority of equality over monarchy and tyranny. In contrast to Sophocles, in Euripides we are not normally enjoined simply to accept fate. By Euripides' day, the spirit of the time had become more questioning, more rationalistic, less accepting of ancient hierarchies and values, and, along with the Sophists and (as we will see) with Socrates too, an important element in this change of spirit was the writing of Euripides.

The Bacchae

*Euripides' The Bacchae (produced only after the poet's death) de-
picts the eternal tension between cool rationality and the irrational
and poetic forces which lurk within us. Pentheus, the King of Thebes,
accuses Dionysus, a god who represents passion, music, nature, and
intoxication, of leading astray the women of Thebes. He hates Dionysus, but is also fascinated by him. He attempts to imprison him, with
catastrophic results.*

In general terms, we may see something in it of despair at the follies of a
people and of their rulers. But far from being wholly rationalistic or full
of legalistic sophistry, *The Bacchae* seems to be advocating within limits a
return to our natural roots, to instinct and to forces anterior to civilization,
and which civilization papers over at its peril. It shows us that the tension
between reason and instinct exists not just in society as a whole, but also in
each individual, and particularly in individuals who deny that it does exist
in them.

There is also in *The Bacchae* the theme of religious mystery. So-called
mystery cults were indeed a feature of classical Greece (and of Rome, too).
Alongside the civic ceremonies and devotions, there were more hidden cults
which attracted large numbers of devotees. Like the mysteries at Eleusis, just
outside Athens, to which many Athenians belonged, these cults often involved some identification of the individual believer with the god. At Eleusis
the believer would go down under the earth with Persephone (who was also
known as Kore and was the daughter of the corn-goddess Demeter). They
would in spirit enter Hades where Persephone had been abducted by Pluto,
the god of the underworld, and come up again into the upper world, as Persephone did in her myth, reborn into new life, just as the seed planted in the
winter re-emerges as a crop or flower in the spring. The initiate shared the
pain and triumph of the god, and the hope of a happy existence after death
in the underworld, but secretly. People who revealed the secrets of Eleusis
were killed. Aeschylus himself had to flee when believers thought he had revealed some of their cult in one of his plays. The cult which forms the focus
of *The Bacchae* is murderous and destructive, far more so than the Eleusinian
mysteries, though also pregnant with intimations of new life.

The Bacchic cult centres on Dionysus (who is called Bacchus in Latin,
and also sometimes in Greek), the patron god of tragedy itself, as we have
seen. In *The Bacchae*, Dionysus is ultimately a destructive force, though initially in the play he is a beautiful, fascinating and reconciling spirit, enabling
his followers to come to terms with their instincts and with nature as a whole.
To start with, his followers revel in wine, music, dance, and group feeling

and integration. But then, after he is opposed and held by the authorities, he and his followers turn to violence, hunting and tearing animals to pieces and eating them raw; and before the final scene of awful recognition, there is a murderous orgy of violence and savagery.

The question which *The Bacchae* raises is how to reconcile instinct with reason; and how to cope with the strain of civilization without either lapsing into a desiccated rationalism, paradoxically fascinated with what it would suppress, or throwing civilization over altogether in a brutal pandemonium of instinct.

The play opens in the palace of Pentheus at Thebes. The ruling family is the same family as Oedipus,' but a few generations earlier. As well as Polydorus (Oedipus's great-grandfather), Cadmus, the founder of Thebes, had several daughters, including Agave, the eldest, and Semele. Semele was loved by Zeus, and became pregnant by him. She was killed by a lightning bolt from Hera, who was jealous, but the infant in her womb was brought to birth by Zeus in his own thigh. This was Dionysus. Agave married a mortal man, and their son was Pentheus. When the play starts, Pentheus is King of Thebes.

Dionysus appears, disguised as a mortal man. By his mother's monument, he recounts Semele's death and his own origins and upbringing. He has been travelling in the East, setting up his rites there, and now he has come to Thebes, his first mission in Greece. He says that Semele has been dishonored by her sisters, who have been saying that Dionysus was her son by a mortal lover, and that she had been killed by Zeus (not Hera) for claiming falsely that Zeus was the father of Dionysus. Because of this insult to his mother, Dionysus has caused the women of Thebes to go into the mountains as his disciples. But Pentheus has forbidden his worship in Thebes. He, Dionysus, will lead his women against the city. Thebes will have to learn a lesson.

The Chorus of Dionysus's followers, known variously as Bacchants (or Bacchanals), Corybantes, or Maenads, now sings of the delights of their worship and of Dionysus's birth and upbringing. Zeus kept him hidden from Hera, and when he was born he had the horns of a bull. Zeus wreathed snakes around his head, and his followers do the same as they dance through the mountains, clad in skins torn from animals and carrying garlands of ivy, sprays of fir and branches of oak and ash. Invoking natural forces and instincts, and also Eastern rituals, beyond the constraints of the Greek city, they exhort the women of Thebes to join the throng in trance and in dance:

> On the mountains wild 'tis sweet
> When faint with rapid dance our feet;
> Our limbs on earth all careless strewn,

To quaff the goat's delicious blood,
A strange, a rich, a savage food.
Then off again the revel goes,
O'er Phrygian, Lydian mountain brows,
Evoe! Evoe! Leads the road,
Dionysus's self the maddening God!
And flows with milk the plain, and flows with wine,
Flows with the wild bees' nectar dews-divine;
And soars, like smoke, the Syrian incense pale—
The while the frantic Bacchanal
The beaconing pine-torch on her wand
Whirls around with rapid hand,
And drives the wandering dance about,
Beating time with joyous shout
And casts upon the breezy air
All her rich luxuriant hair;
Ever the burden of her song
"Raging, maddening, haste along
Dionysus's daughters . . ."
(All translations from *The Bacchae* are those of Henry Hart Milman
(1865))

On the mountain, there are ecstasy and divine possession, and these fascinate those below in Thebes.

Tiresias, the ancient prophet, and Cadmus, the old King of Thebes, now appear. The two old men, already garbed like Bacchants, will go on to the mountain. Age is no bar to mingling in the rite, though Euripides presents them as undignified and even comic figures.

Pentheus arrives, railing against the recent events. He has thrown some of the Maenads into prison, claiming that they are promiscuous, devotees rather of Aphrodite than of Dionysus. He will imprison the rest, too, including his mother Agave and her sisters Ino and Autonoe. But his immediate target is the stranger, the oriental conjuror with golden locks and eyes moist with Aphrodite's fire, who is whipping up enthusiasm in Thebes, and who, he insists, is not Dionysus, who was destroyed by the thunderbolt which killed Semele.

He lambasts Tiresias and Cadmus for their lack of the dignity of age. Tiresias replies by speaking of mankind's two primal needs: food, given to us by Demeter; and wine, given to us by the son of Semele, who, rescued by Zeus, is even now on the crags of Delphi to the north. In the dances that he and his followers undertake, contrary to the fears of Pentheus, the chaste are not made unchaste. They should all be made welcome in Thebes. Cadmus warns against offending the gods, reminding Pentheus of the fate of Actaeon, Autonoe's son and his own cousin, who was torn to pieces by his own hounds for offending Artemis.

When the old men try to wreathe Pentheus in ivy to get him to join them on the mountain, he drives them away, ordering the capture of the womanly man who is leading the women astray so that he may stone him to death.

The Chorus laments Pentheus's blaspheming of the god who brings peace and joy. Pride and lawlessness will bring us down. Dionysus's gifts are those of love and peace, and his enemy the man who rejects these for a life of foolish austerity.

Dionysus is now brought before Pentheus. The soldiers say that he made no resistance, but that the women Pentheus had captured have walked miraculously free of their prison and made for the glens to dance and revel. Pentheus interrogates Dionysus, who tells him that he is a Lydian, instructed by Zeus in new mysteries. Now widespread in the East, these are superior in morals, though different in custom from those in Thebes. They are performed mainly at night, because night promotes solemn awe. Pentheus is angry and unimpressed. He will cut Dionysus's hair and remove his thyrsus (his symbolic stick of reed with ivy twisted round it, referred to in the Chorus we have just quoted). Dionysus warns Pentheus that he is insulting the god and that the god will come to his aid. Dionysus is taken off to the stables.

The Chorus calls on Dionysus to rescue his followers from the anger of Pentheus, and to "quell the bloody tyrant in his pride." Dionysus responds with a voice from within, as son of Zeus and Semele. He summons up an earthquake, and Pentheus's palace begins to shake. On Semele's monument, the blaze flames up. The palace crashes down and Dionysus appears. He tells his women to rise up and that Pentheus had captured him only in his mind. In his delusion he had tied up a bull, while Dionysus watched. When the flames leaped up and the palace started to crumble, Pentheus ran around in a panic. He struck with his sword at a phantom, thinking it was Dionysus, and then saw the stable a heap of rubble with Dionysus walking out.

Pentheus now upbraids Dionysus. He tells him that he is "wise in all wisdom save in that thou should'st have," to which Dionysus retorts: "In that I should have, wisest still am I." A herdsman enters from the mountains where he saw Bacchants streaming out of the city, led by Agave, Ino and Autonoe. At first they rested modestly under the trees, but once awakened by Agave, they loosened their garments, and some suckled young animals. They wore garlands of ivy and of oak leaves and flowers. When they struck the earth and rocks with their thyrsi, water, milk, wine and honey flowed. Some shepherds gathered to watch them. As the women began to dance the Bacchic dance, the men jumped out to catch them. But the women turned on them, and the men fled. The women then began to attack the flocks, tearing the animals to pieces, limb from limb with their hands. The band of women then destroyed two villages, themselves untouched by any spears or weapons thrown at them, but wounding any in their way with their thyrsi. They then returned to the mountain to cleanse themselves of the stains of their exploits with water from the fountains that the god had earlier produced for them, and by being licked by snakes.

At this report, Pentheus speaks of Bacchic arrogance, and orders war against the Bacchanals. Dionysus warns him not to take up arms against a god. He will bring the women down himself without force. This offer Pentheus angrily rejects, calling for his arms. Dionysus then makes to Pentheus the fatal suggestion that he, Pentheus, has a strange desire to see the women, to which Pentheus accedes. Dionysus agrees to take him; he will have to dress as a Bacchant. As he leaves, walking through Thebes in female dress, Dionysus foretells his fate: to be torn to pieces by his own mother.

The Chorus sings of the joy of a fawn playing who has jumped free of the huntsman's net; and also of the law of heaven hunting down the impious man. Musing on fate and ambition, it concludes:

> Some mortals end in bliss
> Some have already fled away:
> Happiness alone is his
> That happy is today.

Dionysus comments on the madness of he who would see what he should not see. Pentheus is dazed and deluded. He is completely in the hands of the god, who begins to lead him to the mountain. He tells him his mother will take him aloft in her hands. Pentheus: "'Tis my desert"; Dionysus:

> Thou art awful!—awful! Doomed to awful end!
> Thy glory shall soar up to the high heavens!
> Stretch forth thine hand, Agave! Ye her kin,
> Daughters of Cadmus! To a terrible grave
> Lead I this youth! Myself shall win the prize—
> Bromius and I; the event will show the rest.

The Chorus sings of the Maenads dancing in ecstasy and about to be maddened by the madman spying on their rites, unrecognized by his mother who thinks of him as born to a lioness or a Gorgon. The Chorus calls on justice, invoking Dionysus to hunt the hunter:

Come Dionysus, come 'gainst the hunter of the Bacchanals,
Even now, as he falls
Upon the Maenads fatal herd beneath,
With smiling brow
Around him throw
The inexorable net of death.

A messenger, who was also Pentheus's attendant on the mountain, now enters to announce Pentheus's death. With Dionysus, the two of them had climbed into the mountain. In a valley they had found the women working peacefully and singing. But Pentheus could not see them, so he bent an ash tree down and rose on it as it sprang back up. He could now see the Maenads, but they could also see him on top of the tree. Maddened by Dionysus, the women pulled down the ash, to stop the intruder revealing their mysteries. His mother was the first to fall on him, but despite his plaints she failed to recognize him, thinking him an animal. In her frenzy, and strengthened by the god, she ripped out an arm from his shoulder, her sisters his other limbs, throwing them all around the mountain. Agave then put his severed head on her thyrsus and led the whole band of women down to Thebes. At this, Agave herself enters, in triumph. She sings that she has killed a lion cub and that soon her son Pentheus will lead the praise of Thebes to her exploit. In her madness, still calling for her son, she boasts that she and her women have with their bare hands done what huntsmen need weapons to do.

A chastened Cadmus now enters. With Tiresias, he has seen his daughters' terrible deeds, and has brought back the scattered remains of Pentheus's body. Agave, though, still exalting in her triumph, upbraids him for his sullenness. To return her to sanity, in a terrible scene of recognition and reversal, Cadmus forces his daughter to look at the "lion" she has in her hands. She realizes at last that it is Pentheus's head. Cadmus tells her that, in the very place where Actaeon, her nephew, had been torn to pieces by his dogs, she had done the same to her son. Pentheus had gone, Cadmus says, to mock the god; and Agave, with the whole city, was maddened. "Dionysus hath destroyed us!," Agave cries. Cadmus says that, like Agave herself and her sisters, Pentheus refused to worship Dionysus. All were then caught up in "one dread doom":

O if there be who scorneth the great gods,
Gaze on this death, and know that there are gods.
Agave becomes once more a mother, piteous and sorrowful: "O thou hard god! Was there no other way to visit us?"

Dionysus gives judgment on them all. All this has happened because Thebes refused to recognize his birth; only in Thebes, city of his birth, is he not honored. Cadmus and his wife will be turned into snakes, fated to destroy much until they blasphemously attack Apollo's shrine, after which they will be taken to the Isles of the Blest. Agave and her sisters are condemned to exile.

Themes from *The Bacchae*

As already suggested, some of Euripides' works can be seen as criticizing the gods and their actions and edicts, and this is definitely true of *The Bacchae*. Dionysus may be right at a certain level, but what he brings about is not right, and when Agave recognizes what she has done she is distraught; nor is Pentheus altogether wrong in his attitude to the women and the oriental stranger who seems to be leading them astray. Nor, to take a more minor passage, is Euripides particularly kind to the follies of Cadmus and Tiresias, who resemble a pair of aging hippies.

The ancient Greeks were very conscious of the fragility of civilization, and of the ever-present threat of the inhuman, the wildly instinctual, the irrational. A characteristic and pervasive theme in their art and story telling is the struggle between (civilized) men and gods, on the one hand, and inhuman, semi-human or animalistic forces on the other: Odysseus versus the Cyclops, lapiths (men) versus centaurs, gods versus giants, Greeks (at Troy) versus Amazons (who are seen as wild and monstrous women), heroes versus monsters of all sorts. Light is always on the one side, and dark on the other.

In this context, *The Bacchae* may seem to represent a partial reversal. Is there not in it a critique of civilization and of reason? Are not the glens and meadows of the mountains more attractive than the city? Are the Bacchants not advocating a desirable peacefulness and proximity to nature? We have, though, to be cautious here. Certainly there are aspects of the Bacchic life which seem to represent a desirable harmony with nature. But that is more in the first half of the play. Later the women are destroyers of all that is maternal, precious and peaceful. Dionysus is eventually revealed as implacable, vengeful, and murderous. He is as terrible as anything in Aeschylus. It is true that his implacability is partly in response to Pentheus's aggression. But the response is, to put it mildly, excessive and terrible. And it seems clear from the start that Dionysus always intended to punish Thebes. We should, I think, be cautious of reading back our own nature romanticism into Euripides' text.

Having made these points, though, it is also true that Euripides is warning us against closing our mind to the need we have for the type of experience that Dionysus represents: wine, obviously, but also music, dance, unity with nature, and submersion in its beauty and grandeur, and group celebration of religious mysteries. The bad effects, portrayed so vividly in *The Bacchae,* arise precisely when Dionysus is driven out of the city. It is then that his worship takes on clandestine, irregular and vicious forms. More generally, should not *The Bacchae* be seen as Euripides' dreadful warning against the likely effects of crazy religions, crazed practices and divinities of dubious provenance—a kind of plea for rationalism, in other words?

An interpretation of *The Bacchae* as an argument for a rationalistic attitude to life and religion would be to tilt things too far in that direction. Euripides seems acutely aware of the contradictions in his theme and also in us. We are complicated, even contradictory beings, both rational and instinctual, creatures of intellect but also of passion. What we need, as Plato also argued, is not to suppress any part of our nature, but to bring the various elements into harmony—the rational side in charge, maybe, but not so as to suppress or deny other elements of ourselves. And Dionysus, for all his literally awful destructiveness, is by no means wholly unattractive in Euripides' play, or wholly wrong. Far better, Euripides may be telling us, to welcome Dionysus into the city and into our hearts, than to deny him and attempt to suppress what he stands for. He is, after all, a god, and a god recognized by the Greeks, and worthy of worship. Significantly, and in an almost contemporary spirit, Euripides is careful to show Pentheus's rigidity against Dionysus as stemming from a repressed fascination with the women and what they are doing, even to the extent of agreeing to dress like them, to dress as a woman. He actually wants to see them and to know, but cannot admit this to himself.

All this may be what Euripides is telling us, in a play of awesome beauty and terror. But it cannot be said that he provides any solution to the dilemma he raises. How can Dionysus be admitted into the city without unleashing disorder? Or, from the other point of view, how can a rational and civilized conduct of human affairs make room for the instinctual and the non-rational? We must not suppress our irrational, passionate side, but if we allow it to take us over, the consequences will be dire. But what, in any concrete situation, will this doubtless wise advice mean, what course of action will it suggest?

Euripides might say, with Pascal, that the heart has its reasons, which reason does not know—but that is more like a diagnosis of the problem than a resolution of it. It is surely not coincidental, though, that Euripides produced this late masterpiece when Athens was going though its darkest period, deeply unsettled by the strains that its formerly peerless civilization had brought to bear on it. In a sense, *The Bacchae* remains highly relevant to our situation in the twenty-first century, following a century in which darker and more irrational forces, both political and personal, have been much to the fore. It would be trite, but nonetheless true, to say that we have made little progress on the way to resolving the conflicts and dilemmas that Euripides confronts us with in *The Bacchae*.

Plato and the
Death of Socrates

The philosopher Socrates was condemned to death by the people of Athens in 399 B.C. His crime was that he had corrupted the young of the city and introduced strange gods, thereby undermining the religion of the city. In his account of Socrates' Apology (to the Athenian Court) and in three other short dialogues, Socrates' devoted disciple Plato shows how Socrates rebutted these charges. While Plato's dialogues illustrate just how his teacher might have infuriated some of his right-thinking contemporaries, they also show why Socrates believed that the good man can never be harmed, and also why death itself, at the right time and in the right spirit, is to be welcomed. Death, for Socrates and Plato, is but a stage through which the soul may ascend to a higher form of existence than that of our current state of embodiment on earth.

Socrates was Plato's mentor and inspiration, and in his day one of the most noted figures in Athens. He was born in 469 B.C. and died, as a result of a death sentence imposed on him by the city, in 399 B.C. He had fought with courage and distinction in the early phase of the Peloponnesian War, but during the second half of his life he gained fame or notoriety as a philosopher. Unlike the Sophists—itinerant teachers of argument and rhetoric—he took no money for what he did. Nor, unlike the Sophists, was he interested in enabling those he taught just to win arguments. He was interested in truth, and more specifically, in finding out what the foundations were for various positions. His method was to question and to get his interlocutors themselves to question things they thought they knew. In the questioning, he would often reduce those to whom he was speaking to a state of confusion and even incoherence. His own stated position was that he had been told by the Delphic oracle that he was the wisest of men; but, after thought and enquiry, he concluded that his wisdom consisted in realizing that what he knew was that he did not know. While Socrates himself may have been content to admit his ignorance, this was not necessarily true of his victims, so to speak.

By many, Socrates was loved and admired. Unfortunately for him, some of his admirers included notorious members of the aristocratic party in Athens, such as Alcibiades, Athens' most brilliant general who had actually fought against Athens for a time during the Peloponnesian War, and also people who had been involved in the various oligarchic dictatorships which from time to time had replaced democracy in Athens during the war. So Socrates gained some powerful enemies, both by reason of his own deflating behavior and by reason of his friendships. His enemies accused him of corrupting the young (because he seemed to encourage skepticism and also to show up the ignorance of senior people in Athens) and also of irreligiousness (because, though in a deep sense religious, he questioned the virtue and even the existence of the Olympian gods). In 399 B.C., during a period of democratic rule, Socrates' enemies took the chance to have him tried on both these charges before the Court of Athens, a democratic jury consisting of 501 citizens, chosen each year by lot.

Socrates himself wrote nothing, but he was much written about: by Aristophanes, the comic playwright and a friend; by Xenophon, the historian; and above all by Plato, his greatest pupil and disciple. Plato was born in 429 B.C. and died in 347 B.C. He was an aristocrat by birth, and relations of his were prominent in the dictatorship of 404 B.C. If Plato had not been hostile to democracy already, the trial and death of his beloved Socrates would surely have made him so. After Socrates' execution, until his own death, he wrote a long series of dialogues, philosophical conversations in which Socrates is usually the main protagonist, and in which we can often see vivid examples of Socratic demolition of those who think they know. The Socrates of the Platonic dialogues is, though, a problem for scholars. Not only do we not know with any certainty the ordering of the dialogues in time, but in the dialogues, despite an underlying consistency, "Socrates" is portrayed as holding differing philosophical views. We often simply do not know which of the theses that "Socrates" advances are those of the historical Socrates and which are those of Plato.

This problem need not worry us here, because what we are going to do is to consider (Plato's) *Apology of Socrates*—Plato's account of the speech that Socrates gave to the jury in 399 B.C—and, more briefly, *Euthyphro*, *Crito*, and *Phaedo*, dialogues which describe the events before and after the speech, including Socrates' death in prison as a result of drinking the poison hemlock, which he had been condemned to do. Although these dialogues themselves date from different periods, collectively they build up a coherent and moving portrait of Socrates the man, and of his ideas.

In the short dialogue *Euthyphro*, Socrates is pictured on his way to his pre-trial hearing. He is joined by Euthyphro, a young man, also on his way to the court. Socrates tells Euthyphro that he is accused of corrupting the young and also of the impiety of inventing new gods and of failing to acknowledge the old ones. As an explanation of what might underlie the latter charge, Euthyphro refers to Socrates speaking of his being visited by a supernatural voice, something which becomes important later. On being asked by Socrates what he is doing in court, Euthyphro tells him that he is on his way to prosecute his own father for manslaughter. Apparently a laborer working for Euthyphro's father had killed a slave in a fight. Euthyphro's father threw the offender into a ditch and left him there, tied up, until he got some advice from officialdom on what to do about him. The man in the ditch died of neglect before any advice came back.

Perhaps surprisingly, Socrates evinces no concern for the dead laborer, but instead presses Euthyphro as to whether he isn't being impious in prosecuting his father. Euthyphro replies by pointing out that Zeus himself, the most righteous of the gods, had put his own father (Kronos) in chains because he had swallowed his sons, and Kronos had done a similar thing to his father Ouranos for a similar reason. This, though, fails to move Socrates. It is partly because he finds it hard to accept such stories about the gods that he is being called to trial. He asks Euthyphro whether he really believes that the gods engage in civil war, quarrels and all the scandalous things that poets and artists portray them as doing. Euthyphro apparently does accept all this, so Socrates begins to probe with him the nature of piety.

Euthyphro's first stab is that piety is what pleases the gods. Socrates counters by pointing out that different things please different gods (as Euthyphro has tacitly admitted in his example of Zeus, Kronos and Ouranos); but even if they did all dislike something, would that make it impious? Or would it be rather that the reason they all disliked it was because it was impious in itself (and independently of their liking or disliking it)? This is the crux of the argument.

It is in fact a profound question, which in one form or another has puzzled theologians and religious thinkers ever since. (For if we say that what makes something good or pious is something separate from the gods loving it, we seem to be implying that there are criteria of goodness independent of God, to which His will is subject, and by which we as humans can judge God. This of course is what Socrates is doing in the case of the Olympians— and finding them wanting—but to many religious people there is something blasphemous about our subjecting God to our standards of goodness or in thinking that there is in the universe a Good separate from God to which God should bow. On the other hand, to make goodness simply what God likes or desires or creates seems to make it arbitrary, with the sorts of difficulties Socrates raises apropos the Olympians if God or a god desires something which to us seems abhorrent, and with goodness too immediately connected to whatever God happens to will.)

Not surprisingly, Euthyphro can make little headway on the profound question, and falls back on defining piety as the service of the gods. But, says, Socrates, why do they need service from us? Does it do them any good? Euthyphro is reduced to saying that our service is pleasing to the gods, and we are back where we started. Socrates chides him for initiating the manslaughter charge if he does not know what piety is, and attempts to detain him to continue the investigation. Euthyphro, defeated, storms off in a huff: he has urgent business to attend to. Socrates comments that this is a great shame, because if he had been able to learn what piety was from Euthyphro, he might be able to escape his own accusers and also live better for the rest of his life.

Euthyphro, short as it is, is fascinating on many levels. It shows the Socratic gadfly in operation, and how annoying it might be to the self righteous, particularly in a time of national crisis. It demonstrates Socrates' attitude to the Olympian gods, and shows why he might have been accused of impiety by the righteous. It raises a genuine question of great importance, which has exercised religious and other thinkers ever since. And it also shows us how the Homeric world-view and the lapidary certainties of an Aeschylus could hardly survive intact after Socrates.

In his *Apology,* Socrates addresses the Athenian Court to defend himself against the twin charges of the impiety of inventing new gods and of corrupting the young. He begins his defense by distancing himself from the ridiculous figure portrayed by Aristophanes in his comedy *The Clouds* (a kind of eccentric who speculates ludicrously about the heavens). He also insists that he never took payment for teaching. He then refers to the saying of the Delphic oracle that there is no one wiser than Socrates, and how this troubled him. It set him on the task of finding someone who was wiser than himself—so as to refute the oracle. He started interrogating those with a reputation for wisdom, and also others such as poets and craftsmen. What he discovered was that, though these people thought they knew all sorts of things, they could never explain what it was they were supposed to know. He at least knew his own ignorance. What the oracle must have meant was that the wisest of men is he who, like Socrates, acknowledges his own ignorance.

All this questioning, which he saw as being divinely commanded, which he has continued ever since, has made him poor and also unpopular. Unpopularity was compounded by the fact that young people started to listen to his cross-questioning; his victims began to hit back by accusing him of the normal charges against the philosopher, of atheism and the like. He is also accused of corrupting the young, though Meletus, his prime accuser, has never actually shown any interest in his teaching. Meletus also needs to establish whether Socrates believes in no gods or in gods different from those of the state. He, Socrates, cannot be an atheist, because he believes in supernatural activities—and hence must believe in gods producing them. (The Court would have been aware here of Socrates' famous invocations of his *daimon,* a supernatural voice which at times of crisis prevented him from making a wrong choice. But we must also note that Meletus, who simply accepts what Socrates says at face value, is extremely slow on his feet here: for the charge of impiety is not that Socrates is an *atheist,* but that he is inventing *new* gods.)

Socrates now turns to the question of why he has continued to do things which have brought him hostility and the danger of the death penalty. He refers first to Achilles in *The Iliad,* avenging Patroclus, as honor demanded, even though he knew it would lead to his death, and then to his own confronting the possibility of death in the battles he fought in. When one is doing what one knows one has to do, one should not be moved by fear of death—for we are ignorant about whether death is a blessing or an evil, but we know what we have to do. Even if he were to be offered acquittal were he to give up his questioning, he could not, as this is what his God commands. (Notice that Socrates' God is singular, not Christian exactly, but not the Zeus of Olympus either.) He goes on to say that no greater benefit has ever befallen Athens than his divinely-inspired care of their souls.

This last remark, of course, produces uproar. But Socrates goes on. It is far worse to put an innocent man to death than to be put to death. If they get rid of him, they won't easily find a replacement. God has appointed him to be a gadfly to stimulate a lazy, large thoroughbred horse into action. If you slap me down, he says, you can go on sleeping to the end of your days.

Socrates now goes on to explain why he has not taken part in politics or public life. He has been prevented from doing so by his supernatural voice or daimon. He has held office only once, and that was when he was elected to the Council, when he voted against an unconstitutional proposal to execute the naval commanders of Arginusae (a notorious incident in the Peloponnesian War in 406 B.C.). When under the Oligarchs in 404 B.C. he was ordered to fetch Leon of Salamis for execution, he simply stayed at home. He has never acted unjustly, and he has never had any secret doctrine. People enjoy listening to him, because they like to see those who claim to be wise being shown up for what they are. But he has always acted in obedience to the commands of God. If he has corrupted the young, let his accusers ask the fathers of his supposed victims, many of whom are in court. They will find none to speak against him. He will, though, not deign to produce his children weeping before the jury, for such pathetic scenes would disgrace the city. The jury should decide where justice lies, and on that alone.

The jury brings in a verdict of guilty (by 280 votes to 221), and Meletus asks for a sentence of death.

In response, Socrates says that he will propose an alternative sentence. As he has never cared for money or any other rewards, but has simply tried to do in private what is best for all of them individually, as a public benefactor, he should, like a victor in the Olympic Games, be given free dinners for life. He will accept neither imprisonment nor banishment, nor will he agree quietly to mind his own business. He will never stop discussing goodness and all the other topics he is interested in, for that would be to disobey God: the unexamined life is not worth living. He would, though, accept a fine, which he could afford, of 100 drachmas, or 3,000 drachmas to be put up for him by his friends.

Unsurprisingly, this apparent arrogance does not help his cause. Socrates is sentenced to death by 360 votes to 141 for the fine, a bigger margin than on the original verdict.

In his concluding speech, Socrates says that his condemnation is due to his refusal to weep before the jury and to say things which he would have regarded as unworthy. To those who condemned him, he prophesies that the verdict will do far more harm to Athens in the form of future criticism than it does to him, an old man and close to death anyway. To those who voted for him, he says that all through the day and throughout his speech his daimon never opposed him. The sentence actually appears to him to be a blessing. Death is either extinction, with no further experience, a dreamless sleep, which must be a boon; or it is removal to the place where all the dead are gathered, which would be a state of unimaginable happiness. Death we must look forward to with confidence, for the good man can never be harmed, either in life or in death. His fate is not a matter of indifference to the gods. As for himself, the time has come to be released from the cares and distractions of this life. He bears no grudge against his accusers, though they did wrong in (falsely) believing they were harming him. He asks only that his sons should not be brought up after he is dead to prefer money to the good. He is going to death and the others to life, but which prospect is better, only God can know.

The dialogue *Crito* takes place after Socrates' trial, when he is in prison waiting for the time when he will have to take the hemlock, the poison which will kill him. A friend, Crito, tries to persuade Socrates to escape from prison and go into exile (which would have been possible). Crito says that Socrates owes it to his friends and to his young children to escape. Socrates refuses. The important thing is not to live, but to live well, and this means above all doing no wrong. In order to justify this refusal, Socrates imagines a dialogue between himself and the Laws and Constitution of Athens. If he were to leave in the circumstances Crito is advocating, he would be injuring the Laws. In fact he has an implicit contract with the Laws. They have nurtured him and given him everything; moreover, he has never shown any inclination to leave Athens, not even to go to Sparta or Crete, places he admired, and not even at his trial. So he has always accepted their authority, in return for the benefits they have accorded him. If he were to run away, he would be doing something dishonorable in itself, and he would enter his place of exile as an enemy of their Constitution as well. His death sentence is not the work of the Laws themselves, but of his fellow men; nevertheless to leave as a fugitive, though it might give him a few short years of life, junketing disgracefully in Thessaly perhaps, would be to repay wrong with wrong and to break his agreements and contracts with the Laws. This would be to injure himself, his friends, his country and the Laws themselves, and this would not be looked upon kindly by the laws which obtain in the next world. So, the Laws conclude, do not take Crito's advice, but rather ours.

Socrates does, of course, take the advice of the Laws. The dialogue *Phaedo* is an account of his last hours in prison and his death, ostensibly by one Phaedo, who (unlike Plato himself) was actually there. It is as long as the other three dialogues put together, and contains a large amount of detailed and at times difficult philosophical argument, attempting in the main to show that death is a blessing rather than a curse. Here we will simply sketch its main themes as they bear directly on Socrates' own death.

Socrates, speaking to his disciples who are gathered in his cell, initially rejects suicide as being insulting to the gods. Nevertheless, a philosopher should be cheerful when faced with death, for death is the release of the soul from the body and from distraction such as diseases, love, desire, fancies of all sorts, and wealth. Dying is the profession of the true philosopher; the true aim of the moral life is the purgation of emotion and desire, from which bodily existence holds us back. Someone scared of death shows that he loves not wisdom but the body.

Having sketched the philosophical attitude to death, Socrates goes on to offer a number of proofs of the immortality of the soul. None is particularly convincing as a proof, but together they build up the Socratic/Platonic picture of the self and the soul. This is based on the belief that we human beings have fallen into the material world as immaterial souls from a perfect realm. A sign of this is that we have knowledge of perfect things, such as absolute beauty and absolute equality. Such things are not to be found in our imperfect experience, but only in approximations to the perfect, so when we appeal to such notions we are recollecting memories of the perfect world from which we came. Our pre-existing souls will continue to exist after death, because they themselves are constant and invariable and invisible. After life, good souls may go back into the realm of divine freedom, while those who are not good will return to the world of bodily bondage and pleasure and pain. Obviously, from this perspective, for the good man death is not to be feared; he should welcome it, like the swans who sing more sweetly when they sense the approach of death.

Socrates and his companions consider the idea that the soul might be like the invisible attunement of the strings of a musical instrument, or like that which adjusts or harmonizes the parts of a physical body. But attunement and harmonization cannot exist independently of what is tuned or harmonized, so if this is what the soul is, it cannot do without bodily existence, and it will cease to exist when the body dies. We should focus rather on thinking of the soul as grasping an ultimate standard of reality—which takes us back to the recollection argument; and also as that which governs and directs the body.

At this point in the discussion, Socrates engages in a passage of intellectual autobiography. When he was young, he had a passion for physical science, and trying to find out the causes of phenomena. But he discovered (unlike the Socrates of *The Clouds*) that speculation of this sort was confusing and unsatisfactory. He had some hope when he discovered that the philosopher Anaxagoras said that Mind was the cause of order and everything which exists, Mind being that which produces and arranges everything in the way that it is best for it to be. But his hopes were quickly dashed when he discovered that actually Anaxagoras made no use of Mind in his explanations, instead proposing as causes air, ether, water, and other absurdities. This would be like saying that the reason why Socrates is here in his prison is because his sinews and bones had caused it. By Dog!, he says, he fancies these sinews and bones would have been in the neighborhood of Megara or Boetia long ago, did he not think that it was right and more honorable to submit to his country's punishment than take off away from here.

What Socrates is looking for with the physical world, as well as in the case of his own actions, are explanations which will show what it is best to do and why it is good that things are as they are. We would say that these are not the sorts of explanations that scientific enquiry will uncover—and Socrates would no doubt agree, which is why he says that he is uniquely unfitted for that type of enquiry. He is looking for explanations in terms of some ultimate Goodness which forms everything, including us, and draws us to It by means of spiritual knowledge and desire. We must consider not the things which Anaxagoras and the scientists speak of, but the real, ultimate causes of Beauty, Goodness, Magnitude, and so on, which the good and beautiful things and the quantities of things on earth participate in and reflect. In our own existence, the function of the soul is to make the body alive, and as such its essence must be to be alive itself; so it is imperishable and cannot die.

If our souls are immortal, we must not neglect them, or they will have wickedness clinging to them. Socrates concludes his discussion of the soul by developing a myth. We are living in a hollow in the earth (rather like someone living at the bottom of the sea), which means that we do not have a good perspective on what is above. On death, our souls go to various places, depending on our behavior in life. The worst ones are plunged into Tartarus, the earth's deepest chasm, from which they never emerge. Some, though, whose crimes are curable, are cast out eventually to be purified, as are those whose lives are neutral. But those who have lived well pass up into the earth's surface, while those who have lived lives of philosophic perfection pass upward beyond the earth's surface, where they live without bodies, going into places ever more beautiful and magnificent. Socrates insists that the myth is not exact, but the drift of it is clear enough. The time has come for him to make his journey.

He urges his followers to keep their spirits up, and goes off to bathe. His wife and his children and other women-folk arrive. He talks to them and dismisses them. The prison guard comes in, apologizing for what he has to do, and departs in tears. Socrates urges no delay, and the hemlock is brought in. He drinks it, and his followers begin to cry and wail. Socrates upbraids them: to avoid such a scene was his reason for sending the women away. As the poison begins to work, Socrates, as his final word, tells Crito to offer a cock to Aesculapius (the god of healing, to whom sacrifice is made by those who have been healed). After that he falls dead and they close his mouth and eyes.

There is much that can and should be said about Socrates, his death and Plato. His death is the philosophical equivalent of a religious martyrdom, Socrates a martyr to free speech and free enquiry. So indeed has he often and classically been taken. But, as I. F. Stone has argued in his brilliant book *The Trial of Socrates,*[6] things may not be quite as clear-cut if we examine them more closely. Why, for example, in *Crito* do the Laws of Athens speak of Sparta and Crete as being places Socrates admired (for their laws and order), but which were hardly bastions of liberty and free enquiry? Was it pure coincidence that Alcibiades, for many Athenians a highly suspect figure and actually a traitor, had been so close to Socrates? What did Socrates do to oppose the dictatorships in Athens, apart from going home when he was supposed to be fetching Leon of Salamis for his execution? Why had some of the key aristocrats involved in the 404 B.C. oligarchic seizure of power been close to Socrates? And, particularly in the speech in which he asked for dinners for life or a trivial fine, did not Socrates treat the court and the democratic faction aligned against him with contempt? Did he not actually desire his condemnation and death?

None of this, though, shows that Socrates was actually opposed to democracy, and even less to free enquiry. Nor can it remove the stain on Athens and its democracy, which Socrates predicted, nor the shame involved in it being the very institutions which Aeschylus celebrated as the height of humanism which condemned Socrates. Nor does making out a partial defense of Socrates' accusers show that he would have espoused the highly illiberal regimes that Plato advocated in some of his dialogues. What it does suggest is that for Socrates the cure of the soul, rather than politics, was of prime importance. Socrates wanted men to turn their attention away from this world and its concerns to the Good beyond, from which we originally came and to which it is our proper destiny to return. From this perspective, time taken away from the philosophic life was bound to be time wasted, at best. Socrates may not have been anti-democratic, but there is a strong sense in which he is anti-political and, to that extent, uncivic.

Nietzsche, as already mentioned, saw Socrates as, along with Euripides, the force which killed off the ancient myths and values of classical Greece. They did, but in different ways. In a more profound sense, though, Socrates may have killed off the tragic spirit. For that spirit sees good men being harmed by the gods and by their fate. They may (may) learn wisdom thereby, but they are harmed, and the wisdom is a terrible and disconsolate one: best not to be born at all; and if born, best to die soon. But for Socrates the good man cannot be harmed, and, if death is a desirable state, it is not non-existence which is wanted but a higher state to which we can realistically aspire, and in the light of which death appears as a cure. This is not a tragic message at all, nor is it one which would justify seeing Socrates as a secular humanist before his time (as is common today). To its critics (such as Nietzsche) the message is life denying; but to its adherents it is the most beautiful vision of all.

Virgil and *The Aeneid*

The Aeneid, *the great epic of Rome and of the Roman Empire, was virtually complete when the poet died unexpectedly in 19* B.C. *In it Virgil essays his own* Odyssey *and* Iliad *(in that order), and also reverses the outcome of the Trojan War. For Aeneas, his hero, is a prince of Troy, mentioned many times by Homer, and famous for his bravery and his leadership. In a Roman myth which Virgil draws on and embellishes, under divine guidance Aeneas flees the burning city in order to found what eventually becomes Rome. After many wanderings around the Mediterranean, including a famous dalliance at Carthage with Dido, its unhappy queen, Aeneas finds the place in Italy where he is to establish the new Troy (Aeneas's* Odyssey*). There he fights an epic war (his* Iliad*), so as to unite the Trojans and the indigenous Latins, now seen together as the forebears of Rome, of which Aeneas has detailed premonitions. Troy/Rome, in Virgil's hands, thus wins out over Homer's Greeks.* The Aeneid *is a glorification of Rome, of the mission of the empire it is to become, and also of Augustus, the first Emperor, a personal friend of Virgil. But beneath the glittering surface, Virgil's treatment of his theme is more complicated and more equivocal. And did the dying poet want his work destroyed, as a persistent legend dating from the time of his death has it?*

Virgil (Publius Vergilius Maro) was born near Mantua in 70 B.C. and died in Brindisi in 19 B.C. He lived through a tumultuous period of Roman history: civil war in 49 B.C., the death of Pompey (48 B.C.), the assassination of Caesar (44 B.C.), the defeat of Brutus and Cassius (42 B.C.), the defeat of Antony (29 B.C.), and the accession to power of Octavian, Caesar's great-nephew and adopted heir, in 27 B.C., now styled as Augustus and the first of the Roman Emperors.

Virgil's own background was rural and agricultural, and this is reflected especially in his early poetry, which celebrates pastoral life and our roots in the natural world. Significantly for later ages—and, as we will see, for Dante—in one of these early poems, the fourth of his *Eclogues*, Virgil speaks of the return to earth of the Virgin, the goddess personifying Justice, and of the First-born of a new Golden Age, a child of the gods, at whose birth creation rejoices. Maybe Virgil wrote the poem as a celebration of peace after years of war, and also of Octavian's marriage in 40 B.C.; but later readers have been struck by its hints of the prophet Isaiah and of the Christian message.

The Aeneid itself was started in 29 B.C., in part as a praise of Octavian. The poet is known to have read Books Two, Four and Six at least to the Emperor, as Octavian had become. In 19 B.C. Virgil thought that he had three years more of work on the poem, but it was not to be. Returning from a trip to Athens with Augustus, he died on landing in Italy. It was widely believed subsequently that he wanted the manuscript of *The Aeneid* burned. Whether this is true or not, it was actually published, on the order of Augustus, by Virgil's friends Varius Rufus and Plotius Tucca, and they published it in the state in which Virgil left it, with sixty lines incomplete and a number of minor inconsistencies. The story of Virgil's wish that *The Aeneid* be suppressed forms the basis of Hermann Broch's masterpiece *The Death of Virgil*,[7] in which the dying Virgil wrestles with his past, his supposed sycophancy in his masterpiece, and his own refusal of love.

The story of Virgil's intention to suppress *The Aeneid* raises fascinating questions, not least about the morality of the action of Varius and Tucca in publishing it against the last wish of its dying author. In the circumstances, should we be reading it? Leaving aside this question, though, we can say that *The Aeneid* is indeed a celebration of Rome, its history and mission, and of Augustus. But it is much more than that.

The Aeneid is a tour de force, combining and reversing both *The Iliad* and *The Odyssey,* and shadowing both of Homer's epics in many details. In *The Aeneid*, the Trojans become the victors, because Aeneas, the Trojan prince who is the hero of *The Aeneid* and who is mentioned by Homer in *The Iliad* (as we have seen), founds the race of Latins/Romans, who are in a sense the new Trojans. In the first half of *The Aeneid* we hear the story of Aeneas's own *Odyssey*, in this case his wandering from the burning city of Troy to his new home in Latium. In the second half of *The Aeneid*, Aeneas and his Trojan followers, in their own version of *The Iliad*, fight a war not to preserve their existing home, but to secure a new one.

In a number of places in *The Aeneid,* such as the speech of the Greek hero Diomedes in Book Eleven, the post-Troy travails of the Greeks are dwelt on. But so, of course, are the Trojans' own, especially in Book Two, in which

Aeneas himself tells the story of the fall of Troy—and here *The Aeneid* Book Two parallels the section of *The Odyssey* in which Odysseus tells his story of Troy to the Phaeacian court. After Troy has fallen, Aeneas in his travels is pursued and harried by the wrath of Juno (who is the Greek Hera; in this chapter we will give the Greek equivalents of the Roman gods where this is needed for clarification). Juno hates the Trojans and their successors because of the judgment of Paris and also because the beautiful boy Ganymede, whom Jupiter (Zeus) loves and smuggled into Olympus as a cup-bearer for the gods, is, like Paris, a Trojan prince. Juno's anger impels the whole story, just as Achilles' wrath does in *The Iliad*. Similarly, just as Athene protects Odysseus and Telemachus in *The Odyssey,* so does Venus (Aphrodite) protect Aeneas, who is actually her child by the mortal man Anchises. Then, as Odysseus goes down to Hades to speak to the dead, so does Aeneas, who also, like Achilles, has a shield made for him by Vulcan (Hephaestus) at the request of his divine mother. And when Aeneas is off the field of battle, things go badly for the Trojans just as they did for the Greeks in the absence of Achilles.

All these references and parallels to Homer which Virgil makes in *The Aeneid* are intentional, and there are many others too. Even the source of the legend of Aeneas is Homeric. In *The Iliad,* on the Trojan side, Aeneas is second only to Hector in strength and valour, even taking on Achilles in single combat; and when Poseidon (Neptune), fearing for the outcome, rescues Aeneas from Achilles, he prophesies that Aeneas and his descendants will come to rule Troy; but at the same time Hera (Juno) professes undying hatred of Aeneas and of Troy, prophesying that Troy will be consumed by Greek fire.

In a sense, both Homeric prophecies came true, according to the legend worked up over the centuries. Troy was indeed destroyed, as we know. But, in the legendary accounts, Aeneas leads his father Anchises, his son Ascanius, his followers, and the Trojan gods out of the burning city. Eventually, what is left of Aeneas's band reaches Hesperia (Italy), where they settle in Latium. They build the city of Lavinium and found a second settlement called Alba Longa, which they and their descendants rule for 300 years. Aeneas himself, though as the son of Venus a doughty warrior, is a man of peace and piety, in contrast, say, to his descendant Romulus, the founder of Rome itself, who appeared several centuries later. This, anyway, is the legend Virgil worked up into *The Aeneid*.

With all this burden of memory and of the model of Homer having to be reworked and overturned and even transcended in favor of the Trojans/Romans, *The Aeneid* can seem less spontaneous and more self-conscious than either *The Iliad* or *The Odyssey*. In Friedrich Schiller's famous distinction, expounded in his essay of 1795 entitled "On Naive and Sentimental Poetry," [8]

Homer is the naive artist, with an immediate and unreflective truthfulness and feeling for nature. Virgil (in terms of the distinction) is sentimental, self-conscious and reflective; in Schiller's terms he is seeking nature rather than being nature (though it must be conceded that Virgil does have a strong sense for nature and also a facility for metaphor which rivals that of Homer). It is, though, impossible at times not to feel that there is in Virgil a sense of control, and almost of contrivance, in his reworking of the themes he finds in Homer, and also in the admittedly masterly way he weaves the whole of Roman history and pre-history into his narrative. But this sense never completely overwhelms genuine poetic and dramatic feeling, as was recognized by Virgil's audience right from the start. Virgil's younger contemporary Propertius said of *The Aeneid*, with possibly only slight exaggeration, considering Virgil's masterly construction and powers of synthesis (to say nothing of his language): "Something greater than *The Iliad* is coming to birth."

In Virgil, genuine and profound feeling does emerge, often. Moreover, his triumphalism regarding Rome's destiny is somewhat tempered. Roman virtue, severe, modest, pious and courageous, is as important for Virgil as is Roman might. Aeneas is constantly portrayed as pious, and also as being driven by divine command to found a new Troy in Italy. But the new Troy lacks the opulence of the old Troy and indeed of Carthage: Roman severity again. Nor is Aeneas insensitive to the loss he inflicts in the pursuit of his divine mission on some of those he fights, or as it is presented by Virgil, has to fight. Further, as we will see, hanging over the eventual triumph of Aeneas there is both a sense of loss in general—of Troy, of his father, of many of his comrades—and, more personally and particularly, of Carthage.

For, unwittingly from the point of view of Aeneas himself, but as all of Virgil's Roman readers of *The Aeneid* will have appreciated, Aeneas visits on Carthage at the hands of the Romans the very same fate as Troy itself had suffered at the hands of the Greeks. As a result of the perpetual enmity between the Romans and the Carthaginians which (according to Virgil) Dido instituted after Aeneas had betrayed and left her, Carthage was itself razed to the ground by the Romans in 146 B.C. And, to continue the theme of the desolation of loss, of the very pain of existence itself, it is when Aeneas himself first arrives in Carthage and sees painted on the walls of the temple scenes from the battle of Troy that he utters the words, almost untranslatable, but standing in a way for one feeling which the whole of *The Aeneid* profoundly evokes: "Sunt lacrimae rerum et mentem mortalia tangunt."

In Robert Fitzgerald's version (using sixteen words where Virgil uses seven):

> . . . they weep here
> For how the world goes, and our life that passes
> Touches their hearts.

Or perhaps, more literally, "the world is tinged with tears and mortality touches the mind." The sense is conveyed in either case, but in neither Virgil's consummate and telling construction and brevity.

The Aeneid

The first six books of *The Aeneid* are Virgil's re-casting of *The Odyssey*, and tell of Aeneas's voyage from Troy to Italy.

Book One opens with a ringing invocation, in which many of the themes of the poem are laid out:

> Arms and the man I sing, who, forc'd by fate
> And haughty Juno's unrelenting hate,
> Expell'd and exil'd, left the Trojan shore.
> Long labours, both by sea and land, he bore,
> And in the doubtful war, before he won
> The Latian realm, and built the destin'd town;
> His banish'd gods restor'd to rites divine,
> And settled sure succession in his line,
> From whence the race of Alban fathers come,
> And the long glories of majestic Rome.
> (All translations from *The Aeneid* are those of John Dryden (1697))

Juno, the lover of the Greeks and of Carthage, is full of anger towards Aeneas. After seven years of voyaging—just when Aeneas is at last skirting the coast of Sicily en route for the west of Italy, the intended destination—she gets Aeolus, the god of the winds, to raise a dreadful storm. Neptune calms the sea, and seven out of the original twenty ships land on the shore of ancient Libya (now Tunisia) in North Africa. Aeneas reminds his followers that they have braved Scylla and the Cyclops, and that they are destined by Jupiter to found a colony in Latium. But inwardly he is in despair.

Venus now entreats Jupiter on behalf of her son. Jupiter reassures her of his commitment to the promised destiny, and pronounces the first of the several prophecies in *The Aeneid* on the destiny of Rome, right down to the triumphs and peace won by Julius Caesar. He also sends Mercury (Hermes) to prepare the Carthaginians to welcome the Trojans.

In a passage highly reminiscent of *The Odyssey*, Venus now appears to Aeneas, who is exploring the land around, in the form of a Tyrian girl. She tells him the story of Dido, formerly of Tyre and married to Sychaeus. Her brother Pygmalion murdered Sychaeus for his wealth and Dido escaped along the coast, close to what is now Tunis, and set about founding the new city of Carthage, of which she is queen. Aeneas recognizes his mother, who hides him and his companion in a cloud so that they can enter Carthage secretly.

When they do, they find a great and beautiful city being built. No doubt thinking how far he is from his destiny, Aeneas says: "Thrice happy you whose walls already rise." (For Virgil's Roman readers, the irony here would be unmistakable: the thrice happy people here celebrated by Aeneas will eventually be as happy as were Priam and his family when their great city was razed to the ground.) In the center of the city is a magnificent temple dedicated to Juno, and on its walls he sees the scenes from the Trojan War which provoke the lament we have already referred to. Aeneas's companions, whom he thought lost in the storm, meanwhile enter the city and are made welcome by Dido, who recalls their fame and their misfortunes. Aeneas now reveals himself in all his beauty and majesty as the son of Venus. Dido is captivated already and asks to see Ascanius (or Iulus), Aeneas's son. But Venus, aware that Carthage is Juno's city and that Aeneas's destiny is elsewhere, has plans to destabilize the situation and the city. She substitutes her own son Cupid for Ascanius. Dandling Cupid on her knee, as the whole party feasts, Dido falls completely victim to the madness of love:

> Th' unhappy queen with talk prolong'd the night,
> And drank large draughts of love with vast delight;
> Of Priam much enquir'd, of Hector more . . .

She entreats Aeneas to tell her about the war and about his flight, his wanderings and his woes.

Book Two has Aeneas recounting the fall of Troy. The Greeks left their wooden horse on the shore, and feigned to sail away. The Trojans, cooped up so long in the city, issued in a throng, "like swarming bees." The priest Laocoön, though, warns them of the trickery of the Greeks and of Ulysses (Odysseus), and launches a spear into the side of the horse. At this point Sinon, a captive Greek, is brought in. He says that he hates the Greeks and has deserted because they wanted to use him as a sacrifice to appease Apollo (as they did with Iphigenia to get to Troy in the first place). They have now gone away to consult oracles in Argos over Ulysses' theft of the Palladium; meanwhile they have left the wooden horse in reparation. It is all lies, of course. But when Laocoön is about to sacrifice a bull on the altar, he and his sons are strangled by two huge sea snakes, sent by Neptune to avenge the priest's assault on the horse. The Trojans, maddened by joy, drag the horse into the city, oblivious to the fate of Laocoön and deaf to Cassandra's warnings. In the night, the Greek fleet returns and the men in the horse open the gates of Ilium. As Aeneas sleeps, the ghost of Hector appears to him, foretelling the ruin of Troy and ordering Aeneas to leave the city, taking with him its gods, to found a new city over the sea. Troy is torched, after savage fighting in which Aeneas takes part. Cassandra is dragged out of the shrine, and her fiancé Coroebus killed in the fighting, as are the other Trojan warriors, and then the aged Priam, killed by Achilles' son Pyrrhus. Aeneas wants to kill Helen, the author of all this misery, but he is restrained by his mother:

> Not Helen's face, nor Paris was in fault;
> But by the gods was this destruction brought—

—particularly by Neptune, Juno and Minerva (Pallas Athene), under the eye of Jupiter. Aeneas nevertheless resolves to fight on, but a sacred fire which plays around the face of his son and a thunderbolt from Zeus convince him to obey the gods. He takes Ascanius by the hand and his father Anchises, who has the hearth-gods, on his back, and he tells his wife Creusa (who is Hector's sister) and their servants to meet them at the shrine of Ceres, outside the city. In the chaos Creusa is lost, though her ghost appears, telling Aeneas of his destiny to travel for many years and then found a city in Latium by the Tiber. He returns to the city to gather as many of the survivors as he can.

Book Three contains the account of Aeneas's sea-borne wanderings around the Mediterranean. Outside the burning wreck of Ilium, he and his followers build a fleet. They sail out and first land in Thrace. There they find a plant oozing and dripping with blood. They find that it is above the corpse of Polydorus, a Trojan on a mission from Priam, killed for the gold he was carrying. They give him decent burial, and sail on from the ill-omened spot, next reaching Delos, where Aeneas is told to settle in Crete. But on arrival there his own gods tell him that this is not the place. They must go on to Hesperia, and Anchises remembers that Cassandra too had said this. They are blown off course in a storm, landing in the Strophades where they encounter Harpies, vile half-woman half-bird creatures, who defile and be-smirch the Trojans' food. They attempt vainly to fight them off, and Celano, the leader of the Harpies, tells them that for this offense they will have to undergo famine before they reach Italy. They sail on, past several islands to the west of Greece, including Zachynthus and Ithaca, finally reaching a town on the mainland, where they celebrate with games.

Sailing on to Chaonia, they discover that Pyrrhus (Neoptolemus) has been killed by Orestes, and that Andromache, whom Pyrrhus has carried off from Troy, is now living as the wife of Helenus, a surviving son of Priam. Andromache contrasts her fate as a captive unfavorably with that of Polyx-ena, Priam's virgin daughter who died at Troy. She asks after Ascanius, and

Helenus arrives, showing them his land—a miniature Troy, Aeneas thinks. After a few days of ease, Aeneas consults Helenus, who is also a seer. He is told that when he reaches Italy he will know that they have found the right place when they see beneath an oak tree a sow with a litter of 30 snow-white piglets. But before they reach the appointed place, they will face many trials, including Greeks on the west coast of Italy, Scylla and Charybdis (in the straits between Italy and Sicily) and a visit to the dead. Andromache bids them farewell, saying that Ascanius reminds her of Astyanax, and on they go westwards. Avoiding Greek territory on the west of Italy, they land briefly to make sacrifice on the Italian coast. They sail on towards Sicily. They see Charybdis, the terrible whirlpool, and land on the Cyclops' island (Sicily) where they pick up Achaemenides, a Greek left behind from Ulysses' expedition. As he is telling the Trojans what happened before, Polyphemus himself appears, frightening them away. Avoiding Scylla, they land at Drepanum (in Sicily), where Anchises dies, and at this point Aeneas's account ends. (It was after this that they were blown off course to the coast of North Africa.)

Book Four is the account of the love of Dido for Aeneas, which in a way reflects that of Calypso for Odysseus, but far more tragically. After hearing Aeneas's account of his travels, Dido is sleepless. Her sister Anna encourages her. She has been faithful to the memory of Sychaeus and has turned down suitors from Africa, including Iarbas; but now with a Trojan ally what greatness will accrue to Carthage! Dido roves around her kingdom, "sick with desire." She shows Aeneas the city, but its building is now neglected as her love takes up all her attention. In heaven, Juno and Venus discuss the situation. Juno sees the love of Dido as a way of detaining Aeneas in Carthage, in a way falling into Venus' trap, and arranges a storm when Dido and Aeneas go hunting the next day, so that they will take shelter in a cave . . . which is what happens. During the storm, Dido and Aeneas are separated from the rest of the party, and take refuge in their cave:

> The queen and prince, as love or fortune guides,
> One common cavern in her bosom hides.
> Then first the trembling earth the signal gave,
> And flashing fires enlighten all the cave;
> Hell from below, and Juno from above,
> And howling nymphs, were conscious of their love.
> From this ill-omen'd hour in time arose
> Debate and death, and all succeeding woes.
> The queen whom sense of honour could not move,
> No longer made a secret of her love,

But call'd it marriage, by that specious name
To veil the crime and sanctify the shame.

Dido calls it marriage, but Aeneas never does, although they spend the winter together, "wasted in luxury," Dido "forgetful of her fame and royal trust, dissolv'd in ease, abandoned to her lust." And nor could the love be secret. Iarbas, the rejected suitor, hears of it and prays to Jupiter, who sends Mercury (Hermes) to remind Aeneas of Italy. The god finds Aeneas engaged in building work in Carthage. Warned off strictly, Aeneas tells his men to prepare the fleet in secret. But Dido guesses what is going on, and before Aeneas can speak to her, she begs him to stay, invoking their love and "marriage." Aeneas insists that they were not married, and claims that he is not leaving willingly, but forced by fate and the command of the gods. This enrages Dido, who accuses him of treachery. She says she will hold him back no longer but will come to haunt him in the future. Aeneas continues to prepare the fleet. With one last effort, Dido sends Anna to implore Aeneas to stay just a little longer, but she is rebuffed.

Dido determines on suicide. She tells Anna that she has a spell to bring Aeneas back, ordering her to make a pyre in the palace and to lay on it Aeneas's arms and clothes. At night she firms up her resolve; meanwhile Aeneas, visited again by Mercury, orders his fleet to sail before it is light. In the morning, distraught, Dido reflects: Could she not have served Ascanius as a feast for his father? Could she not have killed the Trojan? She calls on Juno and the Furies for revenge, and addresses her own people:

Now, and from hence, in ev'ry future age,
When rage excites your arms, and strength supplies the rage,
Rise some avenger of our Libyan blood,
With fire and sword pursue the perjur'd brood:
Our arms, our seas, our shores, oppos'd to theirs:
And the same hate descend on all our heirs.

(The avenger is Hannibal, of course, but we and Virgil are aware that Hannibal's wars led in the end to the total destruction of Carthage by the Romans.) Dido climbs her pyre, and stabs herself with her sword. Anna is distraught at Dido's deception, but climbs the pyre and takes her dying sister in her arms. Juno sends Iris to take her soul to the shades below.

In Book Five, as the Trojans leave Carthage, they see the blaze of Dido's funeral pyre. They do not know what it is, but they are full of foreboding over the fate of Dido. They are driven by storm to Sicily, where they are welcomed in the city of Eryx, where the Trojan Acestes is king. It is one year after the death of Anchises, and they perform funeral rites for him; a huge snake glides harmlessly around the altar and the funeral gifts. There follow the funeral games (as after the funeral of Patroclus): a ship race, running, boxing, archery and a parade of boys on horseback. During the games, Juno persuades the women in Aeneas's party to set their ships on fire—they are tired of seven years' fruitless wandering since the fall of Troy: they want to settle here. Aeneas calls on Jupiter, who responds with a storm that quenches the fires, which destroy only four of the ships. Anchises now appears to Aeneas in a dream. He must carry on to Italy with those who are brave and willing, leaving the cowards and the women behind. In Italy they will be tested by war, but before that Aeneas must visit the underworld, guided by the Sybil at Cumae, to meet the dead, including Anchises himself. After days of preparation and feasting, they leave. Venus persuades Neptune to give them favorable winds. On the way, though, the helmsman Palinurus falls overboard, asleep, and is lost (an echo of Elpenor in *The Odyssey*); but the fleet sails on safely past the Sirens' cliff.

Book Six tells of Aeneas's visit to the underworld. Aeneas and his men reach Hesperia at last. Landing at Cumae, they find the priestess of Apollo, the Sybil. Groaning and possessed, she prophesies their future. They will reach their promised land, but she sees wars, with the Tiber foaming with blood, and a new Achilles; Juno will continue to harry them; there will be a second foreign bride and, when they least expect it, help from a Grecian town. She tells Aeneas the way to the underworld, through the ever-open gates of hell and on through dark forests, over the black waters of the river Cocytus and then across the Styx, to get into Tartarus itself, where the dead live. To gain entry he must take a golden bough, sacred to Juno, to present to Proserpine (Persephone), the queen of the underworld. (It is worth remarking in this context that *The Golden Bough* is the title of Sir James Frazer's monumental and highly influential study of magic and religion, which sees the fundamental form of ritual as being the descent of the initiate into the underworld, to gain rebirth with the god rising again in the spring.)

En route to the entry to the underworld, Aeneas and his companions find the body of Misenus, a comrade of theirs, washed up from Troy itself. They burn it and give it proper burial. Reaching Lake Avernus, from which hell is entered, Aeneas finds the golden bough; and, led by the Sybil, he alone enters the cave. They pass Cares, Diseases, Age, Want, Fear, Famine, Toils, Strife, Death, and Sleep, all personified, as well as the Furies and all kinds of monsters, which Aeneas tries to attack, only to find they are empty phantoms. When they reach the boatman Charon they find a crowd of dead spirits, some buried, some unburied. Only the buried can be taken across Cocytus and the Styx into the underworld proper. Among the unburied they see Palinurus, who tells Aeneas that he was not in fact drowned, but murdered by Lucanians when he was washed up on their coast after three days in the water. He begs Aeneas to give him proper burial on his return, but the Sybil assures him that local people will appease his bones and build a tomb for him. Charon then challenges them. He may not take living bodies across, but the Sybil calms him with the golden bough. Landed on the other side, they have to get past the three-headed dog Cerberus, whom the Sybil sends to sleep with a drugged meal.

They then meet the dead: infants, the falsely accused, suicides; and then, in the Mournful Fields, famous women pining with desire—among them Procris, Phaedra, and Dido. To Dido Aeneas speaks, claiming that what he did, he did unwillingly and commanded by the gods, but

> In vain he thus attempts her mind to move
> With tears and pray'rs and late repenting love.
> Disdainfully she look'd; then turning round,
> But fix'd her eyes unmov'd upon the ground,
> And what he says and swears, regards no more
> Than the deaf rocks, when the loud billows roar;
> But whirl'd away, to shun his hateful sight,
> Hid in the forest and the shades of night;
> Then sought Sychaeus thro' the shady grove,
> Who answer'd all her cares, and equall'd all her love.
> Some pious tears the pitying hero paid,
> And follow'd with his eyes the flitting shade.

Aeneas then sees Trojans from the war, including Deiphobus, Helen's last Trojan lover, brutally mutilated by Ulysses (Odysseus) and the Greeks, and cursing the Greeks and Helen. They then come to a grim tower, surrounded by the river Phlegethon, in which the wicked are incarcerated and punished with insufferable torture. These include Tityus, who tried to rape Latona, the mother of Apollo and Diana (Artemis), who has his body stretched out and his insides plucked at by a vulture; Ixion, who attempted to rape Juno, and Pirithous, who tried to carry off Proserpine, who are attacked by Furies if they attempt to eat; and many others, endlessly pushing boulders or hung with burning wire on wheels of revolving spikes, and much else besides.

Aeneas and the Sybil then reach the Fields of the Blessed. There they meet Orpheus, the founders of the Trojan house and many others, all feasting and singing and sporting in verdant fields. There they also find the shade of Anchises, whom Aeneas embraces in vain. Anchises shows him the river Lethe, in which the souls due to be born again forget all that has happened before. He then explains that from the active mind which animates the universe come the souls of men, to be imprisoned in bodies. When their bodies die, the souls undergo what punishments they have earned. In a scene recalling Plato's *Phaedo,* those who are completely cleansed go back into the pure elemental air, while many others, after a thousand years in Elysium, are called to Lethe to forget their past, reentering new bodies.

Anchises then shows Aeneas the procession of his own progeny and of the future of Rome, starting with Silvius, Aeneas's own son by his future wife Lavinia. Many of the great names of Roman myth pass by, including Numitor, Silvius Aeneas, and Romulus, and then they see Julius Caesar and all his line, including echoes of the Fourth *Eclogue:*

> Augustus promis'd oft and long foretold,
> Sent to the realm that Saturn rul'd of old
> Born to restore a better age of gold

. . . extending Roman power and peace throughout. Then they see Numa, the great law-giver of Roman myth, and the Tarquin kings and the Brutus who extinguished their tyranny and set up the Republic, a consul first and a father second who ordered the death of his own sons for conspiring to bring back the kings. Then, among many others, Camillus, who rescued Rome from the Gauls, the two Scipios, who were the scourge of Carthage, and Fabius Maximus, who saved Rome from Hannibal by waiting rather than engaging the enemy. At this point Anchises gives voice to the mission of Rome, which is to exercise the imperial arts—to rule mankind by strength, to crown peace with law, to spare the conquered and to tame the proud.

They see Marcellus, another great general in the wars against Carthage and the Gauls, who killed the king of the Gauls in single combat. Next to him is a "godlike youth in glittering armour," but with gloomy face and downcast eyes. "Seek not to know who this youth is," says Anchises:

> This youth (the blissful vision of a day)
> Shall just be shown on earth and snatch'd away.
> The gods too high had rais'd the Roman state . . .
> No youth shall equal hopes of glory give,
> No youth afford so great a cause to grieve;
> The Trojan honour, and the Roman boast,
> Admir'd when living, and ador'd when lost!
> Mirror of ancient faith in early youth!
> Undaunted worth, inviolable truth!

This is the new Marcellus, nephew and intended heir of Augustus, and son of Octavia, his sister, the great hope of his time, but who died in 23 B.C. It is said that Octavia fainted when Virgil read her this passage about her son.

Anchises then takes Aeneas and the Sybil back up to the gate of the underworld, and Aeneas goes back to his ships.

Book Seven is the start of Virgil's *Iliad*; according to Virgil himself, early in the book, this is "the greater work"—not perhaps because *The Iliad* is a greater work than *The Odyssey,* but because the second half of Virgil's own poem actually gets us closer to Rome.

Cumae, on the bay of Naples, was some way down the west coast of Italy. Book Seven opens with the Trojans sailing further north. First they stop at the place called Caieta to bury Aeneas's old nurse of that name. They sail on, past Circe's isle, and, following a lovely description of dawn over the Tiber, they land on its banks. They are in the land of Latium, where King Latinus rules, living with his wife Amata and his daughter Lavinia, who is betrothed to Turnus, the prince of the neighboring Rutulians. But there is an omen: Lavinia will bring war to her people. Further, Latinus is told by an oracle that she will not marry Turnus, but a foreign prince. The Trojans, meanwhile, eat beneath a shady tree, using as plates cakes of bread, which they then eat. When this is pointed out by Ascanius, Aeneas realizes that it is the fulfilment of a prophecy of Anchises. The Trojans thank the gods that they have at last arrived.

Next morning Trojan emissaries go to Laurentum, the Latin city. Latinus realizes that Aeneas is the man intended to be his son-in-law and, welcoming them, tells them to bring Aeneas to him. Juno is, of course, enraged. She dispatches the Fury Alecto, "smear'd with black Gorgonian blood," to arouse resistance. Alecto first visits Amata, who is already angry at Turnus's displacement. Amata tries to dissuade Latinus, reminding him of the Trojan Paris, but she fails to move him. Amata spreads her venom around the city, behaving like a Bacchant. Alecto, meanwhile, disguised as an old woman, gets to work on Turnus, maddening him too. He prepares to fight the Trojans. The peace between the Trojans and the Latins is broken when Alecto leads Ascanius in a hunt to kill a stag sacred to the Latins. A battle ensues, with Turnus joining in. Latinus, besieged by calls for war, withdraws, refusing to open the gates of war (a Latin custom still observed in Virgil's time); but Juno does it for him. The other Latin tribes, led by Turnus, line up against the Trojans, including the Tuscans (led by the hated Mezentius and Lausus, his son), the Sabines, Greeks who had settled in Italy, led by Virbius, the son of Hippolytus, and the Volsci, led by the warrior maiden Camilla.

Book Eight finds Turnus raising the standard of war over Laurentum, and Aeneas oppressed with grief. The god of the river Tiber appears to tell him that he will find the sow prophesied earlier by Helenus. This will mark the place where in thirty years Ascanius will found the town of Alba. He himself should seek help from Evander, a neighboring king of Greek descent and a friend of Priam and Anchises. As they leave, they find and sacrifice the sow. Arriving in Evander's kingdom, Aeneas finds Evander and his people celebrating a rite in honor of Hercules. They are welcomed and Evander explains that this was the place where Hercules fought the monster Cacus, half-man, half-beast. Evander then shows Aeneas the area and its landmarks, which turn out to be the historic and sacred sites of the future Rome, easily recognizable as such by the Roman reader of Virgil's day.

In heaven Venus persuades Vulcan (Hephaestus), her husband, to produce armor for Aeneas, which he does by setting the Cyclopes to work in the forge of Mount Etna. In his city of Pallanteum, Evander promises Aeneas help against Mezentius, with a force to include Pallas, his own son. The pact and its outcome are sealed by thunder and lightning from Venus; Evander, too old to fight himself, takes sorrowful leave of Pallas. The force leaves, and on the way, in a secluded place, Venus, undisguised, brings Aeneas his armor. On the shield is embossed the history of Rome: the wolf with Romulus and Remus; the rape of the Sabine women (which produced what became the Roman nation); the defeat of Porsenna and Tarquin in their effort to restore the kings; Horatius Cocles holding the bridge against them; Manlius and the Gauls and the geese; scenes of leaping priests and chaste women; the traitor Catiline in Hades and the law-giver Cato; and more contemporary scenes: Augustus and Agrippa going into battle, Antony and Cleopatra and the battle of Actium in 31 B.C. overlooked by Apollo, Julius Caesar in triumph, and processions of conquered races and the rivers of the empire:

> These figures, on the shield divinely wrought,
> By Vulcan labor'd and by Venus brought,
> With joy and wonder fill the hero's thought.
> Unknown the names, he yet admires the grace,
> And bears aloft the fame and fortune of his race.

In Book Nine, with Aeneas absent, things begin to go badly for the Trojans. Turnus begins the assault on the Trojan camp from the Laurentine citadel. The Rutulians and their allies make to set the Trojan fleet on fire. Jupiter, though, causes the fleet to break away, sink in the sea and re-emerge as sea-nymphs. Turnus, though, rallies his troops, linking his situation to that of Menelaus:

> These monsters for the Trojans' fate are meant,
> And are by Jove for black presages sent.
> He takes the cowards' last relief away:
> For fly they cannot, and constrain'd to stay,
> Must yield unfought, a base inglorious prey . . .

'Twas giv'n to Venus they should cross the seas,
And land secure upon the Latian plains:
Their promis'd hour is past, and mine remains.
'Tis the fate of Turnus to destroy,
With sword and fire, the faithless race of Troy.
Shall such affronts as these alone inflame
The Grecian brothers and the Grecian name?
My cause and theirs in one; a fatal strife,
And final ruin, for a ravish'd wife.
Was't not enough, that, punish'd for the crime,
They fell; but will they fall a second time?
One would have thought they paid enough before,
To curse the costly sex, and durst offend no more.

Virgil now elaborates in Homeric fashion on the fury, heroism, and pity of war. As night falls, the Trojans, pinned behind their ramparts by the Rutulians, seek to build up their defenses. In the night, Nisus and the young Euryalus, like Odysseus and Diomedes before them, plead to be allowed to foray out from the camp in order to recall Aeneas from Pallanteum. In his father's absence, Ascanius lets them go, promising them rich rewards if they succeed. They kill enemies, many of whom are in drunken sleep still, but when dawn comes they are both themselves cut down by a force led by Volcens. First Euryalus falls:

. . . the sword, which fury guides,
Driven with full force, had pierc'd his tender sides.
Down fell the beauteous youth: the yawning wound
Gush'd out a purple stream, and stained the ground.
His snowy neck reclines upon his breast,
Like a fair flower by the keen share oppress'd:
Like a white poppy sinking on the plain,
Whose heavy head is overcharg'd with rain.
Despair, and rage, and vengeance justly vow'd
Drove Nisus headlong on the hostile crowd.

But he is hopelessly outnumbered. Though he kills Volcens, he falls himself. Turnus sticks the heads of the two Trojans on spears "smear'd over with filth obscene and dropping gore" to taunt the Trojans and encourage their enemies. Euryalus' mother is frenzied with grief, her shrieks and clamours demoralizing the Trojans themselves.

The Trojan ramparts are attacked, and their defenses torched. Ascanius brings down the vaunting Remulus, the brother-in-law of Turnus, his first success in arms, but he is then withdrawn from the battle by Apollo himself. The fighting is intense around the Trojan gate. Turnus finds himself inside the ramparts, but killing all around him wildly, he misses his chance to open the gate for the rest of the Latins. Had he opened the gate then, all would have been up for the Trojans, but Mnesthus and Serestus rally the defenders and Turnus has to back off towards the river. Eventually, to escape, he has to dive into the Tiber, where he is supported by the river god himself and returned to his troops.

Book Ten opens with a council of the gods in the hall of Olympus. Venus and Juno clash again, and as in *The Iliad,* Jupiter commands the gods to stay out of the war: "The Fates will find their way." The next morning on earth sees the Trojans, without Aeneas, under pressure again. Aeneas himself, following his success with Evander, manages to get support from an Etruscan city which has rebelled against the hated Mezentius, and his combined new force begins to sail back. On the way the nymphs who had been the Trojan ships meet Aeneas's new fleet and speed it on. Aeneas and his force join the beleaguered Trojans in the battle, which grows fiercer and bloodier. Prominent in the slaughter is Pallas, son of Evander, and so is Lausus, the young Latin prince, the son of Mezentius. Turnus, inspired by the nymph Juturna, his sister, decides to take Pallas on himself, and kills him. Boasting of his success, he strips the body of its sword-belt and wears it himself. Aeneas, as Achilles at the burial of Patroclus, sacrifices eight captive soldiers on Pallas' funeral pyre. He then enters the battle himself, and the balance shifts again:

> As storms the skies, and torrents tear the ground,
> Thus rag'd the prince and scatter'd deaths around.
> At length Ascanius and the Trojan train
> Broke from the camp, so long besieg'd in vain.

With the siege lifted, Jupiter allows Juno to intervene to save Turnus from the battle, which she does by impersonating Aeneas and leading Turnus onto a ship which takes him against his will back to his father's city. On the field of battle, the slaughter continues, with Mezentius and Lausus prominent for the Latins. Aeneas wounds Mezentius and Lausus rushes in to save his father. Aeneas kills the brave young man, and grieves:

> Poor hapless youth! What praises can be paid
> To love so great, to such transcendent store
> Of early worth, and sure presage of more?
> Accept whate'er Aeneas can afford;
> Untouch'd thy arms, untaken be the sword;

And all that pleas'd thee living, still remain
Inviolate, and sacred to the slain.
Thy body on thy parents I bestow,
To rest thy soul, at least, if shadows know,
Or have a sense of human things below
There to thy fellow ghosts with glory tell:
'Twas by the great Aeneas's hand I fell.

The wounded Mezentius is resting by the river when Lausus' body is brought to him. In despair he drags himself onto his horse to find Aeneas, but he too is killed, pleading at the last, despite the hatred of his own people, to be buried with his son.

Book Eleven opens the following day. Aeneas laments over Pallas, and sends the body, wrapped in cloaks of purple and gold, in a great procession back to Evander. Emissaries from the Latins arrive, to ask to collect their dead. Aeneas speaks warmly to them: he only ever sought peace and friendship with them. A twelve-day truce is agreed, during which the two sides mix freely. In Pallanteum, Pallas is received by the Priam-like figure of Evander, while all over the battlefield both sides cremate their dead on countless pyres. After three days of funerals, in Laurentum there is a move to seek peace and let Turnus fight alone. Further bad news for the Latins arrives when they hear that Diomedes—now building a city in Italy—will not fight for them; they, the Greeks, suffered too much already in the aftermath of Troy. Diomedes, having violated Venus at Troy, was prevented from returning to his wife and country; he has fought the pious Aeneas before, and will not fight him again. Latinus argues against further war. He is supported by Drances, an enemy of Turnus: we should make peace with Aeneas, and let him have Lavinia as bride. Why should we forfeit more lives "that Turnus may possess a royal wife"? He should fight Aeneas on his own. At this Turnus flares up. They have not lost the war; if Diomedes will not come, the Volscian Amazons will. But if a single fight between him and Aeneas is called for, he is ready.

The Trojans, meanwhile, march on Laurentum. Hearing of that, Turnus and his men storm out of the council, and Latinus withdraws once more, distressed that Lavinia is the cause of the fighting. On the field of battle Turnus is like "a wanton courser" freed from his reins, prancing over the plains. He is joined by Camilla and her Amazons. Turnus will ambush Aeneas and most of his force as they come down from the hills, while the Amazons and the Latins will take on the Trojans already in the field. In heaven, Diana (Artemis), Camilla's patron, laments her impending fate, reminiscing about her wild upbringing—pastoral, virginal, and fierce. The battle ebbs and flows around Laurentum, but

Resistless thro' the war Camilla rode,
In danger unappall'd and pleased with blood.
One side was bare for her exerted breast;
One shoulder with her painted quiver press'd.
Now from afar her fatal jav'lins play;
Now with her ax's edge she hews her way:
Diana's arms upon her shoulder sound.

She cuts great swathes through the Trojans, to their shame. But, as so often in Virgil, she over-reaches herself. During her rampage she is stalked by Arruns and killed by his spear which she never sees; but he in his turn is killed by one of Diana's nymphs. With Camilla fallen, the Latin forces are driven back into their city, suffering heavy casualties. Turnus, hearing of this, leaves his place of ambush, just in time for Aeneas and his forces to come through unharmed, as night falls.

The Twelfth and last book opens with Turnus in Laurentum in the night, raging at Latinus. Amata backs him, warning him against single combat, as Lavinia, blushing, looks on. But Turnus himself proposes to fight Aeneas alone, to end the war. Aeneas agrees.

The next day, the armies form up on the field for the fight between Turnus and Aeneas. But before it can begin, Juno plots with Juturna, Turnus' sister. The two warriors come out to fight. Aeneas offers sacrifice, agreeing that, if he loses, the Trojans will withdraw, never to return. If he wins, both nations will be equal in a union of the two, and the Trojans will build a town to be called Lavinia. Latinus confirms the pact. While this is going on, there is unrest in the Rutulian side, as they see Turnus as the weaker of the two. Juturna, in disguise, walks among the Rutulians. At Juturna's instigation, an eagle flies by, a huge swan in its talons. But the swan breaks free and falls unharmed into the river. The Rutulians see themselves as the swan, and their priest throws a spear into the Trojan side, bringing one of them down.

General fighting breaks out again. Aeneas tries to stop it, but is himself hit by an arrow. Turnus then plunges in, like the god of war himself, bringing wrath, terror, treason, tumult and despair. As the Trojans yield, Venus herself cures Aeneas. He returns to the field to seek out Turnus. Juturna, alarmed, takes over from Turnus' charioteer to remove her brother from Aeneas's grasp. The battle rages on until Aeneas resolves to raze Laurentum. As the Trojans march on, with Turnus nowhere to be seen, Amata hangs herself. Despair fills the city, and Turnus hears the lamentation. Recognizing Juturna, he turns on her. Doomed as he is, like Hector, he will fight on. Breaking through the Trojan line, he rushes into the city and finds Aeneas. The armies stop fighting, clearing a space for the final combat. Turnus' sword shatters on

Aeneas's armour, and Aeneas chases him round and round. As Aeneas strives to wrest a spear to throw at Turnus from an olive tree in which it has been stuck, Juturna gives Turnus another sword.

At this point, with both men armed, Jupiter and Juno settle their own differences. Juno admits she has been using Juturna, but agrees to desist in her pursuit of the Trojans—if they will no longer be known as Trojans. . . .

> When the nuptial bed shall bind the peace,
> (Which I, since you ordain, consent to bless),
> The laws of either nation be the same:
> But let the Latins still retain their name,
> Speak the same language which they spoke before,
> Wear the same habits which their grandsires wore.
> Call them not Trojans: perish the renown
> And name of Troy, with that detested town.
> Latium be Latium still: let Alba reign
> And Rome's immortal majesty remain.

The gods then send a Fury, disguised as a bird, to warn Juturna off, which warning despairingly Juturna accepts. Turnus is now alone. He tries to hurl a huge boulder at Aeneas, but it fails to reach him. Aeneas fells him with a spear throw to his thigh. Turnus concedes defeat, and asks only that his father should be respected, and that he, Turnus, should be returned to his home, alive or dead. Aeneas at first feels compassion, but then he sees Pallas' belt. Enraged, he drives his sword into Turnus's chest "and the disdainful soul came rushing thro' the wound."

The Ambiguity of *The Aeneid*

The Aeneid is, on the surface, straightforward enough. A pious hero fulfils the will of Fate and the gods, overcoming all obstacles on the way, and founds a great people with a great destiny. This destiny is also celebrated in the poem, as is Virgil's own ruler and patron. At the same time, the drift of Homer in both the Homeric epics is shadowed, but in crucial respects reversed.

If that were all that there is to *The Aeneid,* there might be some justification for Simone Weil's assessment that it is "cold, pompous and in bad taste." Against Weil we could set Berlioz's judgment—Berlioz having set his own version of Books Two and Four in *Les Troyens,* his own towering masterpiece. He wrote at the time: "Working at my opera intoxicates me. I swim with strong strokes in this lake of antique poetry. What gratitude we owe these great spirits, these mighty hearts, who give us such noble emotions as they speak to us over the centuries."⁹ Noble emotions and mighty hearts—of whom, of the main characters in *The Aeneid*, is this true? Aeneas? Dido? Turnus? Camilla? Latinus? Maybe both Weil and Berlioz are oversimplistic.

When we think about it, only comparatively minor and youthful characters, such as Pallas and Lausus, are unproblematically heroic, and this may be partly because they lack experience. To take our five principals in reverse order, Latinus is clearly weak and vacillating, his own feebleness a major cause of the war which tears his own people apart, as he himself recognizes. Camilla is certainly a powerful and memorable character, but is destroyed by her lack of judgment, by her fury when she is in battle. Turnus has some claim to be noble in the same way as Hector and even Achilles. But although his fate has some parallels with Hector's, his cause is far more questionable, and his eagerness to fight and to involve whole peoples in what is essentially a private quest for a princess shows a crucial lack of true greatness of heart.

Dido is tragic and doomed, to be sure. But her love is mad, a madness indeed inspired by the goddess Venus, if no less deep for that; she is maddened by it, and it ultimately destroys nobility in her. She forgets her husband Sychaeus and her vows to his memory, which had been sacred to her. She becomes unbalanced, and there is something pathetic in her "marriage," which is no marriage, and also in her desperate attempt to convince Aeneas that it is a marriage.

And Aeneas himself, pious we are constantly told by Virgil. But what we are told—and this is part of Virgil's genius—is not always what we are shown. Lingering in Carthage, in Eastern luxury with the Cleopatra-like figure of Dido, is not in Roman terms pious; even less so is the shameful manner of the escape from Carthage, more like a moonlight flit than the action of a mighty heart, although—and this is the predicament that Aeneas has got himself into by his initial impiety in neglecting his divine mission and lingering in Carthage in the first place—in leaving Carthage he is, technically, pious; for he does so at the command of a god, to fulfil his divine mission.

But actually Aeneas is very far from being a straightforward character at any point. Even at the start of his quest, we see him going back into Troy to fight, against the ghost of Hector's express command. At many crucial moments both in the wanderings and in the battle, Aeneas needs support, physical or mental—from Venus, his mother, or from other supernatural beings. And the end of *The Aeneid* is the most enigmatic passage of all.

If *The Aeneid* were a straightforward celebration of the noble and pious spirit of its hero and of Rome itself, why does Virgil show Aeneas at the end, in the slaughter of the defenseless Turnus, renouncing both humanity and clemency in a fit of ungovernable and indefensible rage? Aeneas, like Achilles, is enraged by the death of a beloved young hero. In both cases, the dead hero's armor is taken by his killer, which simply compounds the anger of the avenger, and in the case of Aeneas it is what provokes Turnus' slaughter. And here Aeneas, like Achilles, is—in Simone Weil's terminology—a killing machine and Turnus, the victim, a mere thing. And there *The Aeneid* ends. It is very, very different from the completely opposite end to *The Iliad* in which Achilles' ungovernable rage is transformed into clemency and humanity, in which the greatest killing machine of all becomes a compassionate fellow-sufferer. The very abruptness of Virgil's ending emphasizes the brutality of the deed, and leaves it unredeemed. And yet this is the start of the history of Rome, which Virgil is ostensibly celebrating in his work. There would be much to be gained by reading and re-reading *The Aeneid* with this ending in mind.

We might then conclude that, far from giving us an "official" Augustan version of the myth of the Roman imperium, what Virgil is doing is to create ambiguity and uncertainty around it, and at its heart. He is certainly not a critic of the enterprise overall. He probably does mean the words that he puts into Anchises' mouth in the underworld about the mission of Rome being to bring peace and to crown peace with law. And there are many noble and uplifting episodes in the Roman histories that Virgil regales us with in his poem, and with no sign of any authorial reservations about them.

Moreover, as T. S. Eliot says in "What is a Classic?," contrasting Homer and Virgil: "In Homer, the conflict between the Greeks and the Trojans is hardly larger in scope than a feud between one Greek city-state and a coalition of other city-states; behind the story of Aeneas is the consciousness of a more radical distinction, a distinction, which is at the same time a statement of the relatedness, between two great cultures, and finally, of their reconciliation under an all-embracing destiny."[10] Eliot, be it noted, says nothing about Carthage here (although elsewhere he does comment on the way that Dido's snub to Aeneas in the underworld is made to appear as the manifestation of Aeneas's own conscience). The two cultures are those of Troy/Rome and Greece, and Eliot is undoubtedly right to point to Virgil's profound sense in the poem of Rome, and of Rome's destiny as being something more than a merely provincial destiny. He also points out the way that Virgil—in contrast to Homer, for example—consciously draws on the literature of another people, and does so in order to establish the universality of Roman destiny.

But beneath this celebration of Roman destiny, Virgil is acutely aware of the ambivalence of the mission, or at least of the fallibility of those entrusted with its delivery, and the cost of the peace.

The whole of *The Aeneid* can certainly be seen in outline and on the surface as a struggle between civilization and barbarism, and between piety (*pietas*) and fury or madness (*furor*), with, as it were, Aeneas, a divine man (*theios aner*) at the start and another (Augustus) as the culmination of its future. We do see in *The Aeneid* the eternal Roman struggle of piety and humanity against savage and barbaric violence, and that struggle as divinely sanctioned. But at a deeper level, what Virgil also shows is that the struggle is as much within each of us as between barbaric people and civilized people. Yes, Camilla and her Amazons typically *represent* barbarism in classical mythology, but Virgil's Camilla is not a barbarian; nor, from what we see of him, is Turnus completely barbaric; and even if the Greeks at Troy are represented as behaving very barbarically, we can hardly imagine that Virgil thought of the Greeks as a whole as barbaric *sans phrase*. (After all, they had produced and continued to revere Homer, his own model in so many ways.)

Turnus and the Greeks, no doubt, behave barbarically in *The Aeneid*. But so does Virgil's divine man, his *theios aner,* the one entrusted with the divine mission to found Rome. What is striking about Aeneas is the way he fails over and over again to act piously. He disobeys the gods, his behaviour with Dido is unforgivable from more than one point of view, at times he seems unable to grasp or to execute his divine mission despite constant divine visitations, and of course in the death of Turnus he is as irrational and full of *furor* and mindless, ungovernable violence and vengeance as anyone in *The Iliad*. Yet he is the instrument of the divine mission, and the mission is fulfilled, and not by any means (always) despite Aeneas. His defects notwithstanding, he is, on balance, noble, and a good and successful leader.

So Aeneas is not an unambiguous hero (though he is a hero). Nor is the Trojan/Roman cause unequivocally just in Virgil's treatment of the myth. They had to plant themselves on the land of the Latins and beat them up when there was opposition. The gods said so. But it is hard to see that the cause was just in any straightforward way, and in this context it is worth remembering that Virgil himself was a countryman, not a Roman, and surely would have had some sympathy with the Latins. Yes, a great and divine future was made possible by this act of invasion, and yes, there is a sense that with the marriage of Aeneas and Lavinia the two peoples were united (as there was also with the rape and subsequent marriage of the Sabine women by the descendants of Aeneas's followers some generations later). But there is no disguising, and Virgil doesn't attempt to disguise, that there is a certain arbitrariness about all this, and a degree of violence in the conquest of the Latins, which is not entirely redeemed by the bravery of the Trojans in the battles. Like the founding myth of Greece, Virgil's founding myth of Rome has a crime at its very inception; or rather a series of crimes, for it was the Greek ravaging of Troy which set in chain the series of bloody events which led to the foundation of Rome and the empire, starting of course with the battle between Aeneas and the Latins, and followed by the rape of the Sabine women, the rape of Lucretia, the subsequent destruction of Carthage and so on, to say nothing of the suppression of the Roman Republic and the associated wars in Virgil's own time. Virgil is celebrating Augustus and the founding of the Roman Empire and the blessings it might bring; but in celebrating it in *The Aeneid* itself there is no hiding the dark side, for those with eyes to see.

All this points to a definite sense in which Virgil is a sentimental artist (in Schiller's sense). His is too humane and reflective a sensibility to be content with the simple telling of a story, however brilliant and however noble. In his characters and in his telling of the story there is more than a sense of the nobility and greatness of the mission and of Aeneas, its conduit. But at the same time, however unruffled the surface on a first reading, something of the complexity and ambiguity of the human condition emerges beneath, and is surely intended to emerge. It is for this reason that Virgil's characters foster interpretation and questioning, and have a psychological depth beyond what we find in Homer. And all this is leaving aside the magnificent description and dramatic poetry of *The Aeneid,* of which we have been able to give only the barest hint.

Ovid's *Metamorphoses*

In one sense the Metamorphoses *(dating from around A.D. 8) is a stylish and highly visual compendium of ancient myths and stories, over 150 in all. By turns savage, dramatic, witty, sensuous, and even occasionally pious, Ovid's* Metamorphoses *have proved to be an inexhaustible source for later writers and artists. But beneath the glittering surface and virtuoso effects of this poetic tour de force lies a vein of Pythagorean philosophy, as espoused and expounded by Ovid. Change is the only true reality. The permanence of forms is something of an illusion in a world itself subject to continual change and filled with beings undergoing endless cycles of birth and rebirth. Change may be brutal, fatal even, as it is in many of Ovid's tales, but ultimately everything that is survives, albeit transformed (hence "metamorphosis").*

Publius Ovidius Naso was born in 43 B.C. of a wealthy Roman family. He became one of the leading Roman poets of his time, famous particularly for his poetry on the subject of love, including *Ars Amatoria,* a witty handbook on the art of loving. It was partly because of the supposed immorality of this that he was exiled from Rome by Augustus in A.D. 8. He went to the Black Sea and never returned, dying there in A.D. 17 or 18.

Ovid's *Metamorphoses* was more or less complete when he was exiled. It is a virtual catalogue of Graeco-Roman myth and a well-spring for European art and literature. It is encyclopaedic in scope and virtuosic in construction, embedding story in story, and sweeping us on from the Creation and the Four Ages of early human existence and the Flood, right up to Augustus's supremacy in Ovidian Rome. Ironically, in view of the book's theme of change, there is a claim at the end of *Metamorphoses* that Ovid's own work and fame will be everlasting, and a hint that the Roman Empire will be as well: doubly ironic, perhaps, in view of Ovid's own fate at the hands of the Roman Emperor.

Among other things, the *Metamorphoses* melds Homer (*Iliad* and *Odyssey*) with Virgil (*Aeneid*) and the history of Rome. In the last section of the book (Book Fifteen) there is a magnificent 400-line exposition of the Pythagorean philosophy, which might also be seen as expressing the ideology of the *Metamorphoses* themselves. We are not, says Pythagoras, who is the narrator at this point, to eat animals. This is partly because the eating of flesh and blood is unnecessary and savage, savage in itself and making the flesh-eaters themselves savage. But more fundamentally, Pythagoras believes in the transmigration of souls:

> O men amazed with dread of death, why fear ye Limbo, Styx
> And other names of vanity, which are but poets' tricks,
> And perils of another world, all false surmised gear?
> For whether fire or length of time consume the bodies here,
> Ye may well think that further harms they cannot suffer more.
> For souls are free from death. Howbee't they, leaving evermore
> Their former dwellings are received and live again in new.
> (All translations from *Metamorphoses* are those of Arthur Golding
> (1565–67), modernized by the author.)

All this, of course, produces an attitude to death not wholly unlike that of Socrates and Plato, with the souls surviving the body and finding new existences in other bodies. But it also means that the animals we eat may have the souls of our parents or brothers or the spirits of others allied to us.

The message of Pythagoras—and Ovid—is that

> . . . the heaven and all that under heaven is found
> Doth alter shape. So doth the ground and all that is in ground.
> And we that of the world are part (considering how we be
> Not only flesh but also souls, which may with passage free
> Remove them into every kind of beast both tame and wild . . .

As we shall see, this removal of the souls of humans into beasts, plants and the elements of the earth is the constant theme of the *Metamorphoses,* and, horrific as it sometimes is, it can also be consoling, particularly if we follow Ovid's exposition of Pythagoras. This exposition goes into some detail about the changes which take place in the earth, of seas, volcanoes, and land; of the way animals and insects themselves are generated, change, and develop in strange and unsuspected ways; in the seasons and in our own lives from infancy to old age; and of the rise and fall of historical powers, such as Troy and Rome:

In all the world there is not that standeth at a stay.
Things ebb and flow, and every shape is made to pass away.
The time itself continually is fleeting like a brook,
For neither brook nor lightsome time can tarry still. But look
As every wave drives other forth, and that that comes behind
Both thrusteth and is thrust itself; even so the times by kind
Do fly and follow both at once and evermore renew.
For that that was before is left, and straight there doth ensew
Another that was never before. Each twinkling of an eye
Doth change.

Change, flux, then is the subject of the *Metamorphoses,* a word which itself means transformation; everything changes all the time, and everything is taking on new and different forms, including ourselves, and stability is just an illusory, superficial, semi-permanence over the endless activity beneath—which is why there is some tension between the work as a whole and any notion that the Roman Empire might usher in some "end of history."

The book itself is a compendium of interwoven stories, more than 150 in all. Most involve the transformation of some human character into something else, as the title suggests. Many are witty and urbane, others sensuous, some pointless, a number quite horrific, and, the prevailing tone of amorality notwithstanding, a few rather moral in tone and outcome. In many of the stories, Ovid shows considerable psychological acuity. In the actual writing he takes on all kinds of styles—pastoral, poetic, epic, heroic, even trying to out-Homer Homer in his description of the battle between the human Lapiths and the drunken Centaurs at the marriage feast of Pirithous and Hippodamia (Book Twelve). There is, then, a great variety of mood and treatment in the *Metamorphoses,* with wit and parody often predominant, but a serious purpose does emerge from the whole thing, particularly if we look back on the collection in the light of the Pythagorean philosophy, which Ovid himself clearly intended we should. It is a purpose which mocks pretension and pomposity, of course, but one which more fundamentally challenges common-sense notions of identity and stability. It sees us and our lives as part of an ever-revolving cosmic round. We are part of a living, developing whole in which life is not lost but only transformed. It is in this sense that, for all its surface amorality, the *Metamorphoses* can be consoling.

It would be impossible in a work like this to summarize or cover all of Ovid's tales. Nor do his fifteen Books fall into any clear-cut thematic groups. So what we will do is to pick on some themes which emerge from the collection as a whole.

The opening lines lay out in forthright terms Ovid's canvas and ambition:

> Of shapes transformed to bodies strange I purpose to entreat.
> Ye gods, vouchsafe (for you are they that wrought this wondrous feat)
> To further this mine enterprise. And from the world begun
> Grant that my verse may to my time his course directly run.

So this continuous work runs to the time of Augustus, as we have already noted, and it begins with a creation myth, and the ages of man before the present. Creation was out of chaos and the strife and disorder of chaos. First the god who is nature separated the earth from the sky, then the sea from the land. The land was distributed and zones of climate arranged, and then the heavens and the stars. Fishes, beasts, and birds emerged, and then a creature

> Far more divine, of nobler mind, which should the residue pass
> In depth of knowledge, reason, wit and high capacity . . .
> . . . made in the likeness of the gods, namely, Man.

Before the present time there were four ages, each one worse than the earlier (a striking contrast, by no means unfamiliar to the classical world, with our present-day myths of progress and advancement). In the Golden Age, that of Saturn, existence was edenic. There were no cities and no violence, and the earth itself produced plenty for sustenance. When Saturn was overthrown by Jupiter, there was first the Silver Age, a time when harsher climates necessitated the building of shelters and agricultural cultivation. The Bronze Age which followed was crueller but not as cruel as the Iron Age, in which viciousness entered the hearts of men. The earth itself was mined, weapons were made of iron, and gold was used; there were violence and war, and all manner of vice and treachery. Justice left the earth. During this period the Giants attacked the gods, but were crushed by them. Human wickedness and depravity were symbolised by Lycaon, the King of Arcadia, who had blasphemed against the gods and served human flesh to Jupiter himself. Jupiter then decided to flood the present lot of humans, as a prelude to the creation of a better race.

One man and one woman survive the flood: Deucalion and Pyrrha. Consulting an oracle in their desolate loneliness, they are told to cast the bones of their mighty mother behind their backs. They realize that their mother is the earth, and her bones are stones, so they scatter some stones as they were ordered. And in the first of the metamorphoses, these stones take on human form: a new, stony race of men is born, showing its origins in its destiny of toil.

Other creatures also emerge, including the terrifying Python, whom the god Apollo slays with his arrow, setting up the Pythian games as a commemoration of the event. But at that stage the victors were not crowned with laurel—and this, in a characteristic transition, leads Ovid into his first metamorphosis proper: the story of Apollo and Daphne. Apollo has just shot the Python when he encounters Cupid, who uses his arrows for a quite different purpose. He aims at Apollo himself and at Daphne, the daughter of the river Peneus. Apollo falls hopelessly in love with Daphne, but she, who has rejected many suitors and was hit only with one of Cupid's blunt arrows, is desperate to remain a virgin. Phoebus Apollo, inflamed with his love, chases Daphne on and on, pleading with her all the while, until Daphne is exhausted. She falls in the river Peneus, and calls on her father:

> This piteous prayer scarce said, her sinews waxed stark,
> And therewithal about her breast did grow a tender bark.
> Her hair was turned into leaves, her arms in boughs did grow;
> Her feet that were ere while so swift now rooted were as slow.
> Her crown became the top; and thus of that she erst had been
> Remained nothing in the world but beauty fresh and green.
> Which when that Phoebus did behold, affection did so move,
> The tree to which his love was turned he could no less but love.
> And as he softly laid his hand upon the tender plant,
> Within the bark new overgrown he felt her heart yet pant.
> And in his arms embracing fast her boughs and branches lithe,
> He proffered kisses to the tree; the tree did from him writhe.

Daphne has become a laurel tree, and Apollo determines that henceforth the laurel shall be sacred to him. His head and those of Roman generals and other victors will be wreathed in laurel leaves, and two laurel trees will stand on either side of the Emperor's palace—

> The laurel to his just request did seem to condescend
> By bowing of her new-made boughs and tender branches down
> And wagging of her seemley top as if it were her crown.

A charming tale—witty, sensuous and delicately poignant all at once—and one highly characteristic of Ovid. But many of the other tales are far more gruesome.

Take, for example, another tale involving Apollo, in Ovid's Second Book. Apollo once loved Coronis, a mortal woman. But she deceived him with a mortal man, and a white bird told on them. Incensed, Apollo shoots her in the belly with his arrow. Repenting too late, he fails to save Coronis, but as the mother is consigned to her funeral pyre he extracts from her womb their child. The child who is rescued from the ashes is brought up by a centaur and goes on to become Aesculapius (Asclepius), the god of healing, whose sanctuary and theater at Epidauros is still one of the most stunning monuments from ancient Greece. Apollo, though, is so angry with the sneaky bird that instead of thanking him, he turns his white feathers black—and so we have the raven. All this is a typical Ovidian conceit, playfully mixing high mythology with a natural fact—the raven's blackness—shown to be the result of a metamorphosis. This story, incidentally, is retold (without the myth of Aesculapius) by Chaucer in *The Canterbury Tales* as the Manciple's Tale.

More gruesome still than the fate of Coronis is another story involving Apollo, this time as god of music. In Book Six the satyr Marsyas, who plays the flute, challenges the god to a competition in music. Do not challenge the gods (as Arachne, also in Book Six, discovers when she takes on Athene at weaving, and in her tapestry dares to show Jupiter in disgraceful consort with mortals; she is given poison and turns into a spider—hence arachnophobia). Marsyas loses, of course, and is flayed alive by the cruel god, until his whole body is just one wound: his sinews discovered to the eye, his quivering veins without a skin beating nakedly, his intestines and the small strings in his breast all visible. But read on—the scene of horror turns into something beautiful and purifying and terribly sad but calm as well:

> The country fauns, the gods of woods, the satyrs of his kin . . .
> And all the Nymphs and all that in those mountains kept their sheep
> Or grazed cattle thereabouts, did for this satyr weep.
> The fruitful earth waxed moist therewith, and moisted, did receive
> Their tears, and in her bowels deep did of the same conceive.
> And when that she had turned them to water, by and by
> She sent them forth again aloft to see the open sky.
> The river that doth rise thereof, beginning there his race,
> In the very deep and shoring banks to seaward runs apace
> Through Phrygie; and according as the satyr, so the stream
> Is called Marsyas, of the brooks the clearest in that realm.

The horror is transformed, and the tears of the nymphs ennoble it. *The Flaying of Marsyas* is the subject of one of Titian's greatest and most remarkable paintings; even though it shows only the flaying, and not the tears and the river, there is something of a sacramental, ritualistic stillness about it which powerfully evokes Ovid, or maybe shows us something in Ovid which was not evident until Titian.

Titian also painted two other of Ovid's terrible stories, both involving Apollo's sister, Diana, the virginal goddess of the hunt. In Book Two Callisto, Diana's favourite nymph, is raped by Jupiter, who first disguises himself as Diana herself. Eight months later Diana, with her nymphs, is bathing in a pool. Callisto's pregnancy is revealed. She is cast out by Diana (the subject of the painting). When the baby is born, Juno, Jupiter's wife, also takes revenge, turning Callisto into a bear. In this form she is chased continually by huntsmen, until fifteen years later she is about to be killed by her own son, now himself a huntsman. But Jupiter intervenes, turning mother and son into the constellations of the Great Bear and the Little Bear, much to Juno's disgust.

There is a light touch to the story of Callisto, but not to that of Actaeon, the Theban prince in Book Three. One day, when out hunting in the woods, he comes across Diana and her nymphs bathing in a pool. He sees the nakedness of the goddess. Not having her bow and arrows to hand, Diana throws water at him, telling him to go and boast to his fellows that he has seen Diana bare—if he can. And

> . . . by and by doth spread
> A pair of lively old hart's horns upon his sprinkled head.
> She sharps his ears; she makes his neck both slender, long and lank;
> She turns his fingers into feet, his arms to spindle-shank;
> She wraps him in a hairy hide beset with speckled spots
> And planteth in him fearfulness. And so away he trots,

. . . a stag. He sees his reflection in a pool, and tries to cry out, but can only bay. His own dogs catch up with him and, hearing only braying when he tries to tell them that it is he, Actaeon, their master, they tear him to pieces, encouraged by the other huntsmen. Only then is Diana satisfied.

More horrific even than any of the stories we have so far considered is that of Tereus, Procne, and Philomela in Book Six, with its echoes of the story of Thyestes in Aeschylus's *Agamemnon* and a foreshadowing of Shakespeare's *Titus Andronicus*. It is a story of utter depravity and also of terrible revenge. Tereus, the King of Thrace, marries Procne, daughter of Pandion, the King of Athens. Despite the presence of a sinister screech owl above the bedroom on the first night of their marriage, Tereus and Procne produce a son, Itys, and enjoy five years of happiness. Then Procne pleads with Tereus to bring her sister Philomela to see her. So he sails to Athens to fetch her. But when he sees her, she is so pure and beautiful, he burns with fleshly lust. Unaware of any of this, in a prolonged leave-taking Pandion entrusts his second daughter to the care of Tereus. On the voyage back

> His eye went never off of her, as when the scareful erne [eagle]
> With hooked talons trussing up a hare among the fern,

Hath laid her in his nest from whence the prisoner cannot scape;
The ravening fowl with greedy eyes upon his pray doth gape.

When they land, Tereus shuts Philomela in a hut in a forest. He rapes her violently. When Philomela threatens to broadcast the crime to all and sundry, Tereus takes out his sword. But he does not kill Philomela. Instead he cuts out her tongue:

The tip fell down and, quivering on the ground,
As though that it had murmured it made a certain sound.
And as an adder's tail cut off doth skip a while, even so
The tip of Philomela's tongue did wriggle to and fro
And nearer to her mistresseward in dying still did go.

After this Tereus abuses Philomela at will. Eventually he returns to Procne, telling her that Philomela has died. A year passes, with Philomela dumb and imprisoned. But she manages to make some cloth on which she weaves her story, and to get the cloth taken to Procne. Procne hides her anger, but one night she joins in a Bacchic ritual, after which she bursts in on Philomela in her hut. She chides Philomela for weeping; this is the time for revenge—but how should she take it?

Returning to the palace with Philomela she sees Itys, and knows what she will do. After a short maternal hesitation, together with Philomela she kills him, as he is his father's son. She cooks the body, and serves it up to Tereus. After feasting on Procne's banquet, Tereus calls for his Itys. Procne tells him that the thing he is looking for he has within. Philomela leaps forward in triumph, tossing Itys' bloody head in his father's face. Tereus calls on the Furies for his own revenge and chases the sisters with his sword, but as he does so, they are transformed into a nightingale and a swallow, and he himself into a hoopoe, a bird of monstrous beak and crest.

The story, like many in Ovid, is an old one. It is referred to by Cassandra in Aeschylus's *Agamemnon,* who contrasts the solace that the shrill-voiced nightingale received from heaven, clothed with soft brown plumes and living apart from sorrow, with her own death by the sword. But Ovid tells it with terrific pace, sensuality and psychological insight.

The gods are not always cruel, nor does Ovid always conjure aesthetic delight out of horror. There is a poignancy about the short tale of Bacchus and Ariadne in Book Eight. Ariadne had helped Theseus to escape from the Minotaur in the Cretan labyrinth. Theseus carries her off as a lover, but on the way back to Athens he abandons her on Naxos:

Unkind
And cruel creature that he was, he left her post alone
Upon the shore. Thus desolate and making doleful moan,
God Bacchus did both comfort her and take her to his bed.
And with an everlasting star, the more her fame to spread,
He took the chaplet [crown] from her head and up to Heaven it
threw.
The chaplet thirled through the air; and, as it gliding flew,
The precious stones were turn'd to stars which blazed clear and bright
And took their place (continuing like a chaplet still to sight)
Amid between the kneeler-down and him that grips the snake.
Ariadne's crown becomes the constellation known as Corona (Borealis) or The Crown, between those of Hercules and Boötes.

In the story of Medea (Book Seven), it is the human being, the witch Medea, who works the transformations. She is one of the strongest characters in the *Metamorphoses,* to whom Ovid was clearly drawn. Strangely, perhaps, her revenge on Jason for deserting her for a new wife (killing the wife and the children she had with Jason), which is the subject of Euripides' *Medea,* is touched on by Ovid only in the most summary fashion. What fascinates Ovid is her initial love for Jason and then her own powers of sorcery. In loving Jason and in helping him to acquire the Golden Fleece, Medea is betraying her own father who owns the Fleece. Medea, like many of Ovid's characters, wrestles internally against "the uncouth heat that burneth in her tender breast." At first she seems prepared to renounce her love, but then she sees Jason again:

The flame that seemed quenched quite
Did kindle out of hand again. Her cheeks began to glow,
And flushing over all her face the scarlet blood did flow.
And even as, when a little spark that was in ashes hid,
Uncovered with the whisking winds, is from the ashes rid,
Eftsoones it taketh nourishment and kindleth in such wise
That to its former strength again and flaming it doth rise . . .

They go through a form of marriage, and Medea gives Jason magic herbs to enable him to go through various trials set by her father. He yokes fire-eating bulls, faces an army of soldiers springing from dragon's teeth, and finally drugs the dragon guarding the Golden Fleece itself. Jason and Medea then return with the Fleece, and Jason asks Medea to make his own father young again. In a great set-piece, Medea prepares herself for the magic. In the dead of night, under a full moon, her hair streaming, Medea turns around three

times, sprinkles her hair with water three times and wails aloud three times.
Then she kneels and prays:

> O trusty time of night
> Most faithful unto privities. O golden stars, whose light
> Doth jointly with the moon succeed the beams that blaze by day,
> And thou, three-headed Hecate, who knowest best the way
> To compass this our great attempt and art our chiefest stay,
> Ye charms and witchcrafts and thou earth, which both with herb and
> weed
> With mighty working furnishest the wizards at their need,
> Ye airs and winds, ye elves of hills, of brooks, of woods alone,
> Of standing lakes and of the night, approach ye everych one.
> Through help of whom (the crooked banks much wondering at the
> thing)
> I have compelled streams to run clean backward to their spring.
> By charms I make the calm seas rough, and make the rough seas plain,
> And cover all the sky with clouds and chase them thence again.
> By charms I raise and lay the winds, and burst the viper's jaw
> And from the bowels of earth both stones and trees do draw.
> Whole woods and forests I remove: I make the mountains shake
> And even the earth itself to groan and fearfully to quake;
> I call up dead men from their graves; and thee, O lightsome moon,
> I darken oft, though beaten brass abate thy peril soon.
> Our sorcery dims the morning fair and darks the sun at noon.
> The flaming breath of fiery bulls ye quenched for my sake
> And caused their unwieldy necks the bended yoke to take.
> Among the earth-bred brothers you a mortal war did set
> And brought asleep the dragon fell, whose eyes were never shut.
> By means whereof deceiving him that has the golden fleece
> In charge to keep, you sent it thence by Jason into Greece.
> Now have I need of herbs that can by virtue of their juice
> To flow'ring prime of lusty youth old withered age reduce.

Medea does indeed find the juices, flying for nine days in her dragon-pulled chariot and mixing her brew with a thousand other objects too. She then cuts the old man's throat and drains the blood out of his body, replacing it with her concoction, and Aeson emerges forty years younger, a striking counter to our normal expectations about human identity. She then contrives the murder of Jason's wicked uncle by his own daughters, after which she has to soar away on many journeys, eventually wreaking revenge on the now unfaithful Jason, and re-marrying in Athens.

The *Metamorphoses* are about change and identity, as already remarked, and there is in them a strong erotic vein too. So it is not surprising to find several tales which subvert notions of sexual identity and normality. In Book Nine, Byblis falls hopelessly in love with Caunus, her twin brother. As with Medea, there is a long internal monologue. Byblis questions the conventional bar on incest (the gods do it). She then confesses her desire in a letter to Caunus, but is angrily rebuffed. Byblis tries again and again in person, eventually forcing Caunus to leave for a foreign land. Byblis goes completely mad, wandering through various lands like a Bacchant. Eventually she collapses on the ground, watering it with her tears, caressed by the local nymphs. They produce an underground source for those tears, which could never dry up. Byblis herself fades away in her tears, "turn'd to a fountain, which in those same valleys bears / The title of the founder still and gushest freshly out."

The transformation of Byblis is followed immediately by that of Iphis. Iphis was born a girl, but because of her father's desire for a boy, was disguised as a boy by Telethusa, her mother, and brought up as such. At the age of thirteen, he/she is betrothed to Ianthe, a beautiful young girl, and they both fall in love. But Iphis is also appalled; she will never be able to enjoy the girl, and her love is unnatural: a cow never loves a cow, nor a mare a mare. "The ram delights the ewe, / The stag the hind, the cock the hen . . . never man could show / That female yet was ta'en in love with the female kind." She feels she would be better off dead. Ianthe, deeply in love too, is desperate for the wedding; but Telethusa, knowing what she does, keeps postponing it. In desperation, she takes Iphis to the temple of Isis, and the goddess seems to respond. When they leave, Iphis walks

> . . . with larger pace than ay
> She was accustomed. And her face continued not so white.
> Her strength increased, and her look more sharper was to sight.
> Her hair grew shorter, and she had a much more lively sprite
> Than when she was a wench . . .
> The vows that Iphis vowed [as] a wench he hath performed [as] a lad.
> *He* 'did take Ianthe to his wife and so her love enjoy.'

A more shocking story is that of Myrrha, who loves her father Cinyras (Book Ten). Ruminating on her hopeless passion, she notes that bulls sometimes mount heifers they have fathered, horses their own fillies, goats their kids, and so on, but morality rules our lives. Myrrha rejects all the suitors that Cinyras brings to her. She attempts to hang herself, but is discovered in time by her old nurse, who wheedles her secret out of her. The nurse tells Cinyras, when he is drunk, that a beautiful girl of Myrrha's age loves him. In the dark of the night, she brings Myrrha to his bed. Unaware of the identity of his bed-mate, Cinyras takes her virginity and impregnates her. Night after night Myrrha returns, until one night Cinyras brings in a torch to see who it is he is holding in his arms. He reaches for his sword, but Myrrha escapes. Full of disgust, Myrrha prays that the gods might alter her, thus denying her either life or death. There and then she is transformed into a myrrh tree, still weeping, her tears the drops of myrrh we find on the myrrh tree's trunk. (Her child is the beautiful Adonis, who is later loved by Venus. He is killed by a wild boar when, against Venus's advice, he goes hunting, and is turned into the delicate and ephemeral anemone.)

Finally in this set of tales of sexual polymorphism is the one about Salmacis and Hermaphroditus from Book Four. Hermaphroditus is a beautiful boy, the son of Mercury (Hermes) and Venus (Aphrodite). One day he comes to the pool of the nymph Salmacis, who spends her time luxuriously reclining there and grooming herself. Seeing Hermaphroditus, she wants to have him, there and then. If he is already married, "let me by stealth obtain that which shall pleasure both of us"; if he is not, "let me be then thy spouse and let us in the bridely bed ourselves together rouse." He does not know what love is, and blushes, increasing his beauty even more. Salmacis kisses him, but Hermaphroditus threatens to leave. Salmacis pretends to leave herself, offering Hermaphroditus her pool. As she hides in the bushes, he in childlike fashion begins to test the water, first a toe at a time. Eventually he strips off completely.

> When Salmacis beheld
> His naked beauty, such strong pangs so ardently her held
> That utterly she was astraught. And even as Phoebus' beams
> Against a mirror pure and clear rebound with broken gleams,
> Even so her eyes did sparkle fire.
>
> She can scarcely hold herself back, as the beautiful youth swims in the clear water. Having lightly thrown her garments off, she
> . . . flew to the Pool and cast her thereinto
> And caught him fast between her arms for aught that he could do.
> Yea, maugre [in spite of] all his wrestling and his struggling to and fro,
> She held him still and kissed him a hundred times and mo
> And, will'd he, nill'd he, with her hands she touched his naked breast.
> And now on this side, now on that, for all he did resist
> And strive to wrest him from her gripes, she clung unto him fast
> And wound about him like a snake which, snatched up in haste
> And being by the prince of birds borne lightly up aloft,
> Doth writhe her self about his neck and gripping talons oft

And cast her tail about his wings displayed in the wind;
Or like as ivy runs on trees about the utter rind;
Or as the crabfish, having caught his enemy in the seas,
Doth clasp him in on every side with all his crooked claws.
But Atlas' nephew still persists and utterly denies
The nymph to have her hoped sport; she urges him likewise
And, pressing him with all her weight, fast cleaving to him still,
"Strive, struggle, wrest and writhe," she said "thou forward boy, thy fill;
Do what thou canst, thou shalt not scape. Ye gods of heaven agree
That this same wilful boy and I may never parted be."

The gods do so agree. The two bodies are mingled and fastened together, no longer two, but one of double shape, neither boy nor wench, but both and neither. Hermaphroditus, seeing he is but half a man, calls on his parents to accord the same effeminate fate to any man who swims in this pool in the future.

From the most erotic of Ovid's tales we will end with the most moral, that of Philemon and Baucis in Book Eight. Jupiter and Mercury were once walking on the earth, disguised as mortals. Seeking shelter and rest, they were repelled in a thousand homes. They arrive at the humble dwelling of the aged couple Philemon and Baucis, who make them welcome. In a scene reminiscent of Odysseus's reception by the swineherd Eumaeus, Baucis cooks them a meal of cabbage picked from the garden by Philemon, and bacon that they had been saving. The gods recline at the wobbly table Baucis sets before them, with a plain country meal of olives and salad before the main course and figs and fruit afterwards, accompanied by a rough young wine. The old couple notice that the various dishes and the wine replenish themselves of their own accord, and begin to worry. Should they kill their only goose for their guests? The gods reveal themselves. They are not to kill the goose, but to remove to higher ground while their inhospitable neighbours are punished. As they climb the hill they see the whole valley below them being flooded, and their own hut transformed into a temple of marble and columns and sculpture. The gods ask Philemon and Baucis how they want to be rewarded. They will be the guardians of the temple and would like to die together, at the same time. When the time comes, the two old people each see their partner changing into a tree, Philemon into an oak and Baucis into a linden tree. And so we end our sampling of the *Metamorphoses* with a story of fidelity, marriage, piety, and humble hospitality, recalling moments from *The Odyssey,* and to which we will return in our last chapter.

We have referred to just over one tenth of the stories that Ovid tells in the *Metamorphoses,* but even this should be enough to indicate their kaleidoscopic variety and encyclopaedic scope. In Ovid, there is wit and eroticism and subversion, and also horror, magic and vice. There are also, at times, heroism and virtue. And Ovid's own range and virtuosity have to be admired.

But, beneath the fun, the vitality, the surface plenitude and variety, it is possible to see a serious purpose. The work is framed by the creation myth and the Pythagorean philosophy, and this is surely significant. Everything changes, nothing stays the same. Permanence is an illusion or, if not an illusion, highly relative. But what changes goes on, and even if change can be full of pain and suffering, nothing is lost; there is only transformation, but transformation in which what has been continues in one form or another.

We have already mentioned that the *Metamorphoses* have provided an apparently inexhaustible source for subsequent European art and literature, and we have mentioned three of Titian's paintings in this context. But Titian is only the tip of a huge iceberg here, among his contemporaries and successors, including Veronese, Velásquez, Rubens and Poussin, among many others. Writers who drew extensively on Ovid include Chaucer, Shakespeare, Milton, Ezra Pound and T. S. Eliot; we might note here particularly Shakespeare's borrowing from Ovid's Medea in *The Tempest* and Chaucer's use of Apollo and Coronis in the Manciple's Tale (both of which we will turn to later) and Eliot's use of the Philomela story in *The Waste Land*.

We might also refer to Ted Hughes's *Tales from Ovid* from 1997, truly a case in which a translation is a work of high poetry in itself. In his introduction Hughes tries to explain why Ovid has had such a hold on the European imagination: "Above all, Ovid was interested in passion. Or rather, in what a passion feels like to the one consumed by it. Not just ordinary passion either, but human passion *in extremis*—passion where it combusts, or levitates, or mutates into an experience of the supernatural."[11] And he goes on to point out that this transformation of passion through excess does not always require divine intervention, but—as in the case of Tereus and Philomela— sometimes comes about by virtue of the sheer excess of human passion.

What Hughes points to is certainly a part of Ovid, as we hope to have shown. It is also a part which would have particularly appealed to that poet, and perhaps to our time. But, as we also hope to have shown, though it is a part of Ovid, it is only a part. Different ages and different sensibilities will doubtless find other things in Ovid too: wit, philosophy, an intense sense of the natural world, and always the sheer joy in story-telling in all kinds of modes and moods.

Saint Augustine's *Confessions*

Saint Augustine, the Bishop of Hippo in North Africa, lived from A.D. 354 until 430. He is universally regarded as one of the central figures in the development of Christian doctrine, but it was only after a long and problem-filled spiritual journey that he was finally received into the Christian Church in the year 387, at the age of thirty-three. The Confessions *is his own account of that journey. Doctrinally it is notable for its fusion of Platonic philosophy and Christian thought, but the work is more famous (or notorious even) for its account of Augustine's struggle in his own person between his sensuality and the demands of the Christian life. This personal struggle reinforced Augustine's central contention that fallen humanity could rise only with the help of divine grace, a theme to dominate much subsequent Christian thinking. From the literary point of view, no one before Augustine had ever composed so detailed and exhaustive an account of the inner life. In this sense the* Confessions, *for all its doctrinal framework, is a profoundly modern work.*

Saint Augustine was born in A.D. 354 of a pagan father and a Christian mother in Thagaste in North Africa. He went to Carthage at the age of sixteen to read for law, but he became interested in philosophy and became a convert to Manichaeism.

Manichaeism was a religion founded by its prophet Mani in the 3rd century A.D. In Augustine's time it was so much a rival to Christianity that it was actually considered a Christian heresy. Manichees held that there were two creative powers, God (or Light) and Matter (or Darkness). Against the original intention behind the universe, which was to keep Light and Darkness apart to stop the contamination of the good by evil, in this world in general and in mankind in particular Darkness has exceeded its powers, mixing itself up with Light. Good and evil are thus intertwined, with, among other things, the originally all good Adam being seduced by Eve, which sets in motion the thralls of sexuality and the chain of human reproduction—and yet further admixture of good and evil. Various messengers, including Jesus, the Buddha, Zoroaster and Mani himself, are sent by God to assist mankind in returning to the light, releasing the soul from the body and matter at death to return to its true home. What, from the Christian perspective, is heretical about all of this—but also dangerously fascinating in its explanation of the presence and persistence of evil—is the notion that there are two fundamental creative powers, Light and Darkness, as opposed to the one supreme God postulated by Christianity, master and creator of all.

As a Manichee, Augustine founded his own school of rhetoric in Rome in 383. He moved to Milan, where he had been offered a professorship, and came under the influence of Platonists and the preaching of Saint Ambrose, Bishop of Milan. He was converted to Christianity and baptised in 387. He returned to Africa, founding his own community and becoming a priest in 391 in Hippo (during the Vandal invasion). He became Bishop of Hippo, the coastal town now known as Annabu in Algeria, remaining there with his community until his death in 430 during another Vandal invasion.

Augustine had immense influence as a preacher and teacher during his life, and even more afterwards as a Church Father and Doctor of the Church. He has been a major influence on all subsequent Christian thinking, particularly on such topics as God's grace, the nature of evil and human free will. In some ways he can be seen as producing a synthesis of Platonic or neo-Platonic thinking with Christianity, just as Saint Thomas Aquinas was later to do with Christianity and Aristotelianism. Specific Platonic themes in Augustine include dualism of soul and body, suspicion of the flesh, and a common approach to evil, to which we will come. Not coincidentally, these are topics also central to Manichaeism.

The *Confessions* is Augustine's own account of his life up to and including his conversion to Christianity. In the book, conversion is represented as a homecoming, an arrival at the place always sought and which one had always known in one's heart. It is thus a spiritual Odyssey, in the literal sense. In literary terms, the *Confessions* is the first of a huge number of similar works in the same spirit, not least the *Confessions* of Rousseau and Tolstoy. It is hard to think of anyone before Augustine who felt the need to produce such a volume of introspection and of critical self-examination. Comparing the tone and intention of Augustine's writing about himself with the cheerfulness, the blandness even, of Socrates' *Apology,* say, prompts the thought that there must be something distinctively Christian in Augustine's obsessiveness in self-interrogation, amounting at times almost to desperation. Plato and

Socrates did see philosophy as the care of the soul, but for Augustine the soul is so enmeshed in sin that its care can come only thanks to the infusion of God's grace, and only when the sinner realizes that in God's free gift lies his only hope of salvation.

Doctrinally, the notion that we need grace for salvation, and cannot be saved by our own efforts, comes from Saint Paul, particularly in his Epistle to the Romans. For Paul, it is not just those who have heard of Christ who feel the need for salvation; this is true also of pagans, to whom God has in their hearts revealed his wrath at ungodliness and unrighteousness, but whom, having by and large refused to admit this, God has given up to uncleanness through the lust of their hearts. Augustine would have concurred heartily. As he says right at the start of the *Confessions,* not only are our hearts restless until they rest in God—and the hearts of all of us, not just of those exposed to God's explicit word—but our unsaved condition is predominantly one of uncleanness.

For Augustine in the *Confessions* all this is not a matter of doctrine merely. It is a matter of long and tortuous experience, with the grace actually to convert coming only at the end of years of mental and physical exhaustion. The *Confessions* can be seen as an existential verification of the Pauline point. And Augustine does not just follow Paul in theory. In *Romans 7,* Paul elaborates, apparently autobiographically, on his inability to do what he knows he should:

> For that which I do I allow not: for what I would, that I do not; but what I hate, that I do . . . I delight in the law of God after the inward man: But I see another law in my members, warring against the law of my mind, and bringing me into captivity to the law which is in my members. O wretched man that I am! Who shall deliver me from the body of this death?

The answer, of course, is Christ through his death and resurrection, and the grace he pours into me individually, in Paul's case initially at his own conversion on the road to Damascus. Augustine's *Confessions,* the story of his own conversion and the struggle which led up to it, can be seen as an extended commentary on *Romans 7* and its amplification in one actual personal case.

The *Confessions* is divided into thirteen books, written in the form of an extended address to the Lord. The first deals with Augustine's infancy and childhood, and it opens characteristically with a lengthy prayer. Man cannot be content unless he praises God, because our hearts are restless until they rest in Him. We call upon the Lord, when we bear the mark of death, which is sin; yet we could not call on Him unless we already knew Him. We would be nothing unless we existed in the Lord, and from the Lord comes everything. Yet I have sinned. In ruins, I ask the Lord to remake the house which is my soul. The notion that we already know the Lord, albeit darkly—and that this is why deep down we know what we are seeking—is highly Platonic, as are Augustine's reflections on infancy. Far from being innocent, the baby is full of sin and self-centeredness, screaming and demanding and jealous, faults which we strive to eradicate as the baby grows up. Then as a boy, he moved from inarticulate sounds and gestures; he learned language by noticing that sounds were attached to objects. At school, he was beaten for failing to learn subjects which actually enable people in adult life to do less worthy things. He had to learn the Latin and Greek languages (he particularly hated Greek), and myths, such as that of Dido and Aeneas and of the doings of the pagan gods, in which there was no virtue and over which he foolishly felt sad. At the same time he neglected his own moral and spiritual development. He lied, he stole, he cheated. Was all this the "innocence" of childhood?

In Book Two, the time of adolescence, things got worse. During his sixteenth year he was gripped by sexual frenzy and lawlessness, but his family's only concern was for him to learn how to make public speeches and persuade others by means of the art of rhetoric. In fact they spent more money than they could afford on Augustine's education. His father, seeing him naked in the public baths, celebrated his newly developed manhood, and the grandchildren he would have. But his mother, the saintly Monica, began to be apprehensive, and warned him against the sins of the flesh (though it has to be added that she did not want him to get married young—and so possibly moderate his lust—because it might hold back his career). He got in with a depraved crowd, and, in an exercise of wrong-doing for its own sake one night, he robbed an orchard of pears which he and his companions did not even want. This incident is accompanied by a meditation on the nature of sin, and how whereas most sins promise tangible though illusory rewards, in this case what he wanted was nothing more than the pretence that he was making himself free by breaking God's law. He desired the sin itself, as making himself free of God's law. He sinks into an abyss of sin and frailty. Looking back on this time, he also realizes that no one can be chaste or free from sin, without help from the Lord. It may be worth questioning whether in Augustine's scheme of things it is actually intelligible to do evil for its own sake. Normally, as he suggests here, wrong-doing is seen as a misplaced desire for something which is in itself good, such as love, peace or sweetness (though ultimately these goods are to be found only in the Lord). Lust or sloth or extravagance are wrong not because of what they aim at, but because the means they use to get the goal are misdirected or out of proportion. Evil, in itself, is nothing, just the absence of the good; so how—from Augustine's perspective—can one positively desire it? The appearance of contradiction here is slightly softened by his adding that what the orchard robbers wanted was a bit of sport and mutual admiration, together with the thrill of having partners in the escapade.

In Book Three, "to Carthage then I came," a cauldron of lust where love, friendship and everything pure was sullied by depravity. He became a rabid theatergoer, but, like Tolstoy centuries later, he now wonders how he could ever have felt for merely imaginary characters. Officially he was studying for the law, learning to be unscrupulous, and he was at the top of the school of rhetoric, the art of persuasion. In all this sensuality and corruption, though, there was one redeeming feature, the philosophy of Cicero, which gave to Augustine the desire for a purer wisdom. He started to read the scriptures, but found them too simple. Unfortunately at the same time he fell in with a group of Manichaeans, who gave him only counterfeit truth, but it was what satisfied him at the time. It took him further than ever from the truth. He thought of God as in some sense material, rather than a spirit. He believed that evil was something positive, needing to be created, rather than merely the absence of good. He even believed nonsense, such as that particles of the divinity were imprisoned in fruit and could be freed if one of the elect were to eat it. He derided true Christians. Meanwhile, in the background his mother started to agonize over the blasphemy of his false beliefs. But a Christian bishop told her to leave her son to God. In time he would discover his own mistakes and the depths of his fall.

Book Four speaks of the nine years, from the age of 18 to 27, when Augustine was led astray and led others astray. First he taught rhetoric in Thagaste, teaching others how to win in debates. He also lived with "a woman" who is not named and whom he did not marry, but he was faithful to her; in this relationship, though, he learned the difference between the restraint and dignity of marriage—undertaken for the purpose of having children—and "a bargain struck for lust" in which children are begrudged. He hobnobbed with astrologers and soothsayers. But then he lost a dear friend to death, one who had recently been converted to Christianity. His own country became painful to him, being reminded everywhere of the one he had lost. Burdened with grief, he went back to Carthage. He meditates on the nature of friendship, on how in friendship two souls merge into one; but, as always with Augustine, it is God whom we really seek, and whom we can never lose, unless we forsake Him. Earthly beauty, too, is but a precursor of the higher, invisible beauty of God. In Carthage, when he is about twenty-six or twenty-seven, he writes a book on beauty as perfect proportion, all the time struggling but failing to catch the sound of God's secret harmony. He studies Aristotle, but finds the philosophy dry and useless.

In Book Five a famous Manichaean bishop named Faustus comes to Carthage. Augustine hopes that he will resolve various contradictions which he finds between the Manichaean teachings and books of science which he has been reading and with which he has been impressed. But Faustus proves a disappointment and Augustine realizes—though he does not actually leave the sect—that he will not be able to advance further in it. He leaves Carthage for Rome, where he falls ill and nearly dies. In Rome he teaches literature and rhetoric, and puzzles over the Manichaean beliefs in God as an infinite bodily substance and evil as an opposing stuff, also infinite, permeating the world. The belief that God and evil are two separate and opposing forces, Augustine calls the first fatal mistake, but one he is not yet able to shake off. In this state he accepts an invitation to Milan to teach. He falls under the spell of Ambrose, the Christian Bishop of Milan. Filled now with philosophical doubt about their doctrines, he decides to leave the Manichees to become a catechumen in the Christian Church. For Ambrose has shown him that the Old Testament may be interpreted in a figurative way, thus making previously unpalatable parts of it acceptable. Augustine is now able to accept that God is the Creator of all, and that created reality is basically or originally good. But he is still unable to take the final step of conceiving of God as a spiritual substance.

Book Six opens with his mother Monica arriving in Milan and placing herself under the direction of Ambrose. Ambrose appears to Augustine as the most fortunate of men—but for his celibacy. Augustine himself begins to move towards Christianity, but is thoroughly miserable, tortured with doubt, lust and worldly ambitions. One day he sees a beggar laughing and joking in the street, and contrasts his happiness with his own state of mind and his life enmeshed in lies, anxiety, and insincerity. With two friends, Alypius and Nebridius, Augustine attempts to find true wisdom, but all three cling on to their worldly hopes, because they can see nothing to put in their place. In contrast to Alypius who had earlier found sex degrading and is already leading a life of chastity, Augustine, now aged thirty, is bound down with sex and the toils and fetters of sexuality. He believes (falsely) that he can become master of himself and his desires without help from God, but he cannot escape from the lust which cannot be sated. In order to assuage this lust, Monica and Augustine between them seek to arrange a marriage for him. A young girl is found and accepts Augustine's proposal, but she is two years too young for marriage. Augustine dismisses "the woman" with whom he had been sleeping and whom he says he loved dearly. She goes back to Africa with their son, vowing never to have another man. But Augustine cannot wait for two years without sex and, distraught at the departure of his first mistress, he takes another. In his turmoil he toys with the pleasure-dominated philosophy of Epicurus, rejecting it only because he could not accept its denial of life after death. But why, however great his indulgence in pleasure, cannot he find happiness?

Book Seven interweaves philosophical reflection with Augustine's existential journey, the crux being that intellectual conviction is not enough for conversion. Augustine begins by arguing that if (as he believes is obvious) God is incorruptible and changeless, then the evil force postulated by the Manichees can do nothing against Him, and there would be no meaning to the cosmic battle they proposed. But, if God is all good, what, then, is evil, and how is it caused? Who put a bad will into me? These questions continued to torment Augustine, his difficulties compounded by his continuing to think of God as a quasi-material substance. Divine illumination begins to come to him when he starts reading the books of the Platonists (what we would call the neo-Platonists) and complementing what they said with the scriptures. God is true light, quite different from anything we know on earth. He is incorporeal, true love, and eternal truth. Everything created is, according to its level in creation, good. Evil, then, cannot be a created substance, because if it were, it would be good; so in itself it is nothing, literally. Platonism was crucial to Augustine at this point, because it led him to appreciate, against the Manichees, that there were genuinely immaterial realities, higher than the material. But though he could reason about these things now, and was drawn to God's invisible immaterial beauty, the flesh and the weight he carried in the habit of the flesh still held him back. He needed a mediator between his own fleshly state and the Platonic immaterial, but he himself did not yet believe that Christ is more than a man. To get beyond Platonism he still needed the revelation of Christ as man *and* God; and beyond the cold philosophy and the self-conceit it bred in him, he also needed charity. He began to read the Epistles of Paul and the Gospels: the grace of God in Christ, who is the image of the invisible God and co-eternal with God, sets man free through his death and resurrection. These thoughts of the active, redeeming love of God make his heart quiver, but . . .

At the start of Book Eight, Augustine is still held fast in the bonds of woman's love. He finds the thought of marriage irksome, but nor can he see how to make himself—in Paul's terms—a eunuch for the sake of the kingdom of heaven. His will is held by the enemy and he has become perverse and lustful. He is ruled by sin, sure intellectually of what he should do, but still a slave to passion. He wanted continence, but not yet: soon, presently, a little longer . . . He prays: "O Lord, make me chaste, but not yet," and even as he prays is scared that the prayer might be answered too soon. His self was a house divided against itself, all this division and weakness of will being the punishment we have all inherited as a result of Adam's sin. There are in him two wills contending, neither being his full will. He realizes that the division of the wills inside us is what causes us to do evil, rather than evil itself having any power over us (as the Manichees held).

Suffused with guilt, the higher part of his nature yearns for eternal happiness, while the lower is held back by earthly pleasures. His old attachments, too shameful to mention, pluck at the garment of his flesh, wheedlingly asking him if he intends to dismiss them; meanwhile the chaste beauty of continence beckons modestly to him. In the midst of this agonizing turmoil, he flings himself down in tears beside a fig tree, miserable, captive, unable to act or resolve the crisis. Then, from a nearby house, he hears a child singing out: "Take it and read, take it and read." He takes this as a divine command to open the Bible. He does, and reads Paul's words in *Romans:* "Not in rioting and drunkenness, not in chambering and wantonness, not in strife and envying. But put ye on the Lord Jesus Christ, and make not provision for the flesh, to fulfill the lusts thereof." His heart is flooded with light and peace. All his doubts are dissipated. With Alypius he goes in to his mother. He is converted, no longer wanting a wife or the fulfilment of any worldly hope. Monica is overjoyed that her prayers have been answered and her dearest wish has been fulfilled, dearer to her than would have been any children born of Augustine's flesh.

The aftermath of the conversion experience is covered in Book Nine. He is now free from temptation and filth, though puzzled about the inefficacy of his free will during the previous decade. Physically exhausted, he resigns as professor of rhetoric and retires to the country in the company of his son and friends (with whom he represents himself in some of his early writings as engaging in philosophical dialogue). He is baptized in Milan the following Easter, along with Adeodatus, his natural son, who returned from Africa. After the joint baptism, he is filled with wonder and joy, brimming with tears of joy and feelings of devotion and gratitude to the Lord for his salvation. He proposes to return to Africa in the company of Adeodatus and some like-minded companions, but on the way, at Ostia, his mother falls ill and dies at the age of fifty-six, having lived a life of quiet piety, chastity, and charity, even converting her husband on his death-bed. On her death, Adeodatus bursts out wailing, but Augustine himself is silent in his grief, crying only after she is buried. Her last wish was that she should be remembered and prayed for at the altar of the Lord, and this Augustine does, reflecting that her final request will be honored also in the prayers of those who read his confessions in the future.

Book Ten is thought to be a later insertion into the *Confessions,* telling us something of Augustine's spiritual journey after his conversion. In part it is a meditation on man's place in the cosmos, an interweaving of neo-Platonic and Christian themes, and as such it fills out some of the theological reflections of earlier books. It could be argued that in this meditation, as in much of his thought, Augustine wants to keep the core of the Platonic system, though without the notion that our birth in this world is a falling from an earlier actual existence. Nevertheless, Augustine retains enough of the Platonic framework to insist that crucial insights into true happiness, true value, the divinity itself, and even mathematics are not derived from the senses or from earthly experience. We "remember" these things not in the way that he remembers the sights and sounds of Carthage, but because they have been implanted in our souls by God. Man himself is part of a cosmic system, a universal hierarchy in which all things strive for and, according to their natures, "know" their true end and their true happiness. It is because deep down we "know" God as our true happiness that we seek him in our lives, however blunderingly, and are able to recognize him when, as Augustine did himself, we actually find him. Any truly significant teaching and learning—that which is concerned with the Platonic care of the soul and which may involve conversion of the soul—always requires movement in and by the learner, and based on what, deep down, the learner already "knows" in himself, which seems to leave the teacher as little more than the external occasion of the exercise (a paradox that Augustine explores in his dialogue *De Magistro*).

But in our case, things are complicated by our having free will and also by being marked by original sin, the guilt and disorder we all inherit as a result of the wrong exercise of free will on the part of our first parents. Evil is, as already remarked, nothing in itself. In an echo of the Socratic view that no one does evil knowingly, but only out of ignorance of the true order of things, for Augustine evil is a desire for things which are good in themselves but a distortion of the right relation of these parts in the system as a whole; only God is to be loved for himself, and so we must not see worldly things, which are good in their proper place, as ultimate ends. We can catch sight of God's invisible nature through his creatures, but things go wrong when we mistake means or lesser goods for ultimate ends. Then we become their slaves, a condition compounded by concupiscence—the lusting after these things—and by original sin, which makes us unable to resist the attraction of these lesser goods.

And so, as in Augustine's own case, we have to reflect:

> I have learned to love you late, Beauty at once so ancient and so new! I have learned to love you late! You were within me, and I was in the world outside myself. I searched for you outside myself and, disfigured as I was, I fell upon the lovely things of your creation. You were with

me, but I was not with you. The beautiful things of this world kept me
far from you and yet, if they had not been in you, they would have had
no being at all. You called me; you cried aloud to me; you broke the
barrier of my deafness. You shone upon me; your radiance enveloped
me; you put my blindness to flight. You shed your fragrance about me;
I drew breath and now I gasp for your sweet odour. I tasted you, and
now I hunger and thirst for you. You touched me, and I am inflamed
with the love of your peace.
(Translation by R. S. Pine-Coffin (Penguin, 1961).)

Nevertheless, the snare of concupiscence is ever-present in this life, even
for those disposed to obey God's commands. Conversion is never a purely
intellectual love of God. We have a continual struggle with evil, and we all
need grace always. When God's commands are obeyed, it is from God that
we receive the power to obey them. We must never forget that, nor that
temptation is never-ending. In Augustine's own case, even though he has
repudiated fornication, he is still tempted by gluttony. He is also tempted by
a kind of futile curiosity that he calls the "gratification of the eye." Just as
crowds flock to see mangled corpses (and as we in our time are fascinated by
road accidents), he likes watching lizards killing flies and spiders entangling
them in their webs. He likes to hear his own praises and he is liable to be too
pleased with himself. In these and all other temptations and sins, we need
a mediator who bridges the otherwise unbridgeable gap between God and
man. Jesus Christ, who has something in common with God and also something in common with man, is the mediator between God and men. We can
cast all our troubles on Him who died for us, and remembering the price of
our redemption, and even in our frailty we will be saved.

The last three Books (Eleven to Thirteen) of the *Confessions* are ostensibly a commentary on the first chapter of the Book of Genesis (that which
deals with the creation). Books Twelve and Thirteen are mainly of interest
to the modern reader because of Augustine's insistence that the scriptures
may legitimately be interpreted in different ways, so long, of course, as they
are seen to be teaching the love of God and of one's neighbour. While the
religious person will not go wrong if he does favor a literal or, in Augustine's
words, "child-like" interpretation, such fundamentalism (as it might now be
called) is not incumbent on us; indeed, as far as we can, we should seek out
the spiritual meanings behind the literal words of scripture. And the spiritual
meaning of the Genesis story is that God created not because He had need
of anything else, but simply out of the abundance of His goodness. There is
no change in God; in the changes which we undergo, by the gift of God's
grace and despite our desertion of God, collective and individual, we journey
towards the changeless Sabbath of God's eternal life.

If the last two books of the *Confessions* are difficult for those not concerned with scriptural exegesis, this is not true of Book Eleven, which is still studied today, even by those without the slightest interest in Augustine or his story. For it consists of what is still one of the profoundest philosophical examinations of the nature of time, and the dilemma it poses has still not been answered to general satisfaction. The context is the creation story. Creation itself is out of nothing (*ex nihilo*), and the creator, God, is conceived as timeless and unchangeable—as we have already seen, this doctrine is part of Augustine's Platonic inheritance. (The reason is that if God were changing, then He would be imperfect, for change implies that at any given moment one is incomplete or could get better (or worse).) So before the creation there is no time, only the unchanging God (whose own will and decision to create is itself seen as eternal, outside of our time). In creating the world, God created a system which, unlike himself, has temporal succession. But what exactly is time?

We think of time as consisting of past, present and future. But the past does not exist, and nor does the future. We think that whatever exists is present, and that the present exists, but the present is ever-vanishing and durationless.

We might say that we measure time as it passes (from past to present to future). But this is to say that it is coming out of what does not yet exist, passing through what has no duration, and going into what no longer exists. Further, how can we measure these things which do not exist? Some people say that time is the movement of bodies, but the movements of bodies are variable. They move at different speeds, and the same body is sometimes moving and sometimes at rest. It is rather that we measure the time *in* which bodies move. But how do we do this, given the nature of past, present and future, and given that there is nothing actually to measure—other, that is, than the ever-vanishing, ever-changing present point? Augustine is drawn to the conclusion that the passage of time is not objective, not something in reality itself. When we talk of the passage of time, all we are referring to are the changes in our own minds: that we expect what is not yet, that we attend to what is present, and that we remember what is past. Things change position from our limited temporal perspective, and only from that perspective, and that is what we call time.

But from the point of view of God, there is no change, even in creation. Everything in creation is always present to God. From our point of view things change, but they do not for God; nor is there change in God's knowledge, for God's knowledge, like God Himself, is changeless. To God, all is ever-present.

Although Augustine himself does not put it quite like this, we are led to the conclusion that time is related to human perception. If we had God's perfect perception, there would be no time. In that sense, time is a subjective artefact. It is a defect of our human perception. Our notions of time passing, of a non-existent past and future and a durationless present, are all illusions. It is perhaps surprising to find that many philosophers of science today will agree with this conclusion. They do not believe in Augustine's account of the creation, but they do hold that time is essentially subjective, and that in the universe there is no passage of time as we conceive it in ordinary life.

Of course, both Augustine and the philosophers have a problem with free will and the future. For how, if (in some sense) the future is already present (to God, or in some scientific reality), can we be free or the future open? Augustine indeed speaks in Book Thirteen of the history of the world, including the history of our salvation, individual and collective, being "predestined in eternity," which seems only to add to the problem. For if all, including my salvation, is predestined, how can I be free or responsible for what I do? But if I do change things, which do not happen or are not foreseeable until I do them, how can God know them in eternity? And if God has to wait until I do them, then neither He nor His knowledge is unchanging—and, from the scientific point of view, no science can ever be complete, for there will always be things it cannot predict. It is hard, if not impossible, to reconcile a belief in God's eternity and the changelessness and completeness of his knowledge with free will (though it has to be admitted that a similar problem arises for any belief in the future being already determined now, including scientific determinism).

Augustine says early on in his examination of time that "I know well enough what time is, provided that nobody asks me; but if I am asked and try to explain, I am baffled." Contemporary readers of Augustine may be baffled not just by the discussion of time, but more profoundly by the whole tenor of the *Confessions*. We are so far from condemning lust, or from believing more generally in human depravity or original sin and in the need for God's grace to overcome temptation, that it might seem almost impossible to understand Augustine's account, let alone sympathise with it. Even his admirers might find it hard to come to terms with his treatment of "the woman," unnamed though once loved by Augustine for a decade or more, and the mother of his beloved Adeodatus. And we hear nothing of the fate of his second, discarded mistress, or of the young girl he was engaged to. They all simply drop out of the picture once he has been converted. We might also wonder why his conversion to Christianity entailed a life of complete chastity from that point on. Then again, some have criticized Augustine for his obsessive dwelling on stealing the pears in comparison to his apparent absence of guilt over the women. Fair as this criticism is on the precise point at issue, we should, though, recognize that Augustine by no means underplays his guilt over sexuality in general, and this guilt may be taken to encompass the effects that his sexual confusion had on the women.

Nevertheless, even if we question Augustine's attitude toward sexuality, we should recognize his peculiar strengths and originality. He is a profoundly intellectual man, yet his religion is equally profoundly personal and first-personal. In a sense, compared to the objective stance of a theological treatise, in the *Confessions* he is an existentialist about religion. To most religious readers the *Confessions* is far more compelling than even the greatest work of theology—even, say, Aquinas's *Summa*. In contrast to the abstract tone and argument of the latter, the *Confessions* tells us what religious conversion and experience is like, and how it masters us. It involves decisions and commitments that Augustine makes—or, more accurately, decisions and commitments which are made for him, by the action of God's grace, and which he cannot but recognize. Augustine's genius is to weave the religious experience and the intellectual journey into a single seamless whole.

Even those who have little time for religion should be able to recognize Augustine's starting points: the morass and ambiguity of infancy and of the would-be tyranny of the infant; the difficulties of schooling; the insincerity of rhetoric and the law; the dryness of much of what passes for academic study; the fascination with stepping over boundaries; the pull of lust, and also its depravity and its insatiability and the way we can be sickened by it all. Some might protest at what they see as the exaggeratedly negative picture of life that Augustine paints prior to grace and conversion. But that was how it appeared to Augustine, certainly how it appeared to him after his conversion, and even if we accept the force of the objection, which would apply equally to Luther and Pascal, Augustine still provides a brilliant account of the complexity of human nature and its dividedness, which both Plato and Freud would have recognized. Moreover, even allowing for the prevailing negativity of his account in the first eight Books, we also see him inspired by the purity of Cicero, and even more by the dream of Platonism. It is undeniable that many of us, even in the midst of our materiality and self-centeredness, like Augustine, have aspirations to something higher, and that we find the hedonism of Epicureanism ultimately self-defeating.

Yet Augustine finds the Platonic vision on its own too abstract, too far from human experience. And here he touches on one of the profoundest aspects of Christianity, its insistence—against Judaism and later against Islam—on incarnation, the thought that in Christ, God is inextricably involved in the material world and in human suffering and destiny. God reaches out to us through Christ, who suffers like us and who calls to us. As he puts it in his early dialogue, *Contra Academicos:*

Even the most subtle chain of reasoning would never call back to this
intelligible world (of immaterial reality) souls that have been blinded
by the manifold shadows of error and rendered forgetful by the deepest
filth from the body, had not God the Highest, moved by a certain compassion for the Multitude, humbled and submitted the authority of the
Divine Intellect even to the human body itself. Our souls, awakened
not only by the divine precepts but also by his deeds, could return to
themselves and regain their homeland without the strife of disputation.
(Translation by Peter King (Hackett Publishing, 1995).)

It might be said that in this passage, Augustine's message is not entirely
favourable to the human body; even though God has "submitted" himself
to it, it is only so that we might escape its filth. Are there still remnants of
Manichaeism lurking beneath the Christian Augustine's views on the cor-
poreal and sexual aspects of human nature? But this negative view is to be
counterbalanced by what is said in the *Confessions* (Book Thirteen, line 22),
that in creating man, God has made us in his own "image and likeness"; and
(in *De Genesi ad Litteram*) that humanity is the element of creation closest to
God himself, closer even than the angels, precisely because in man spirit and
matter are integrated. As time went on, Augustine increasingly emphasized
the perfecting of both body and soul at the final Resurrection after the Last
Judgment.

That anyway is Augustine's vision, which he supplements with his own
original interpretation of evil (as nothing positive) and of original sin. We
may jib at original sin in the literal sense, but Augustine is surely right in his
unromantic notion of human nature and in his acute consciousness of the
forces in us drawing us to the bad. We may, though, puzzle rather more over
the privation doctrine, just as philosophers have always puzzled over the Socratic doctrine of evil as ignorance—for, if doing evil is a kind of blindness,
why do we succumb to the blindness? Original sin is Augustine's answer,
those bad dispositions we have inherited in our corrupted human nature:
"Behold I was shapen in wickedness, and in sin hath my mother conceived
me," as the Psalmist has it (*Psalms* 51:5), and Augustine would certainly
have concurred. But appealing to the effects of original sin simply pushes the
question further back. Why did our first parents or Lucifer succumb in the
first place, and so burden their descendants with the stain of their corruption? Why were they induced to choose the lesser good? And why did they,
in their state of full knowledge, opt for a mere privation or absence, rather
than the plenitude of good?

These doubts notwithstanding, Augustine's vision is coherent. And
even without sharing much or any of the vision, we can only wonder at the

strength of the account and the masterly and totally original way in which it is handled. There is no doubt that the type of penetratingly obsessive introspection that Augustine so brilliantly undertakes—for the first time in Western thought—has been immensely influential in subsequent ages. One need think only of Luther, Pascal and Kierkegaard, to say nothing of Augustine's countless secular followers, who may not even appreciate the original source of their internal Odysseys.

Dante
The Divine Comedy

The Divine Comedy (Divina Commedia) *was written by Dante (1265–1321) in the early years of the fourteenth century, after the poet had been exiled permanently from his native Florence. In its three parts, the work tells of the poet's journey through Hell, Purgatory and Paradise. In this journey he is guided first by Virgil, and then through the upper reaches of Purgatory and through Paradise by Beatrice, his beloved, who died in 1290 and who is revealed in the poem as a personification of divine wisdom. The work comprises, among much else, politics, history (including ancient history), philosophy, theology, and mystical experience, all bound together in sublime poetry. As rich in character and imaginative detail as anything in Western literature, it is nevertheless essential, hard as this can be for nonbelievers, to see all three parts and all the detail of the* Divine Comedy *as parts of Dante's single and over-arching vision. This is a vision of the universe as a whole—and all that is in it—as moved by and drawn to the love of God. To those who are able to enter into its spirit, whether believers or not, there is no more compelling account than Dante's of just what it might be like to experience the universe through a faith, at once sophisticated, intelligent, complex, and above all ardent.*

Inferno

Dante Alighieri was born in Florence in 1265. He was descended from Cacciaguida, a Florentine leader and crusader of the twelfth century, whom we will meet in Paradise. Dante himself was a gentleman citizen in the independent city republic. He may have fought for Florence against Arezzo in

1289–90, and by 1295, when he entered political life in Florence, he was already famous as a poet and as an exponent of the *dolce stil nuovo* (the sweet new style), a type of courtly love poetry. By 1295 he had composed *La Vita Nuova,* an interweaving of thirty-one poems with a prose narrative, which tells of his love for a lady called Beatrice. The real Beatrice, who becomes a major figure in the *Divine Comedy,* was born into the Portinari family. She died in 1290 at the age of twenty-four. We know little about her actual life, although we know that Dante had been in love with her since he was nine, and that this love took him over more and more completely during the years that followed (and even more so after her death, when she becomes for Dante an embodiment of divine goodness). All this was even though Beatrice had been married to someone else. Dante himself had married Gemma Donati, probably around 1283.

Dante's marriage was not a notable success, but even less successful was his foray into politics. In order to understand the *Divine Comedy,* we need to give a little of the political background. Italy in the thirteenth century consisted of a number of separate kingdoms and states in the north, the Papacy, which was a large secular state in its own right, mainly in the center, and the Holy Roman Empire, which controlled much of the rest of Italy, particularly the south (as well as large parts of what is now Germany). For much of the Middle Ages the Popes and the Emperors, who were of German origin, were at daggers drawn, and real power went back and forth. During Dante's time, Florence and much of the rest of Italy was split into two factions: the Guelphs, who were pro-Papacy, and the Ghibellines, who were pro-Emperor. The Guelphs were in the ascendancy in Florence, and it was as a Guelph that in 1300 Dante himself became a Prior of Florence, one of the six leaders of the city.

However, around this time the Guelphs themselves split into what later became known as the White Guelphs and the Black Guelphs, and it was as a White Guelph that Dante himself went to Rome in 1301. While he was in Rome the Black Guelphs, who were pro-French and pro-Boniface VIII, the Pope of the time, took over in Florence with the help of a French army. In 1302 Dante was condemned to death in his absence, for corruption and for conspiring against the French and the Pope. He spent the rest of his life in exile in various Italian cities, including Siena, Verona and finally Ravenna, where he died in 1321. Shortly after Dante's exile, however, the Papacy and the French fell out, which led to the so-called Avignon Papacy, a period in which the Popes lived in France, effectively prisoners of the French. There were also hopes that a new young Emperor, Henry of Luxemburgh (Henry VII), would take over in Italy and resolve the various disputes which were tearing Italy and the Church apart, but these hopes came to nothing when

Henry died in 1313. Both of these themes are reflected in the *Divine Comedy*.

During his exile Dante became increasingly anti-Papal and pro-Ghibelline. This stance is reflected in the *Divine Comedy,* which was written entirely in exile, though its action is represented as taking place over the days of Easter in 1300. The work as a whole is divided into three sections, *Inferno, Purgatorio* and *Paradiso,* each of 33 or 34 Cantos (100 in all) of around 130 to 140 lines each. The work recounts Dante's own journey down into Hell and through the earth into Purgatory on the other side, escorted by Virgil, and then up into Paradise, where his guide is Beatrice.

The choice of Virgil as his mentor and guide is significant. Dante is a sincere and committed Christian, but he sees aspects of pagan antiquity as foreshadowing the world as it is after Christ. Some pagans are praised by Dante for their virtue, and others blamed for impiety towards their gods. Dante's fusion of Christian and pagan images seems at times to foreshadow the Renaissance. But orthodox Christian as he is, no more than Augustine does he allow us to lose sight of the fact that the benefits arising from the Redemption wrought by Christ were closed off to the pagans, however worthy they may have been.

Hell is conceived as a vast pit, like an inverted cone or devil's punchbowl, beneath the northern hemisphere of the earth. There are eight circles around the inside walls of the cone, and finally a ninth region, a sheet of ice, which takes us to the mid-point of the earth. Lucifer is incarcerated in this ninth circle, but there is a subterranean stream leading through the very center and up into the southern hemisphere where Purgatory is situated. Dante and Virgil travel through Hell and up into Purgatory on the other side.

In each of the circles of Hell, the souls of different types of the damned are held. In the First Circle are the virtuous heathens, who cannot get to Paradise because they are unbaptized. Then follow four circles in which the weak are held, those without ill-will, but who have nevertheless fallen: the lascivious, the gluttonous, the avaricious and the prodigal, and then the wrathful. The boundary of the Fifth and Sixth Circles is the garrison city of Dis. It guards the descent into Hell proper, in which there are circles containing the violent and the fraudulent: heretics, the violent themselves, the fraudulent (divided into many subcategories), and finally the treacherous, including Satan.

Virgil is Dante's guide through Hell, and there are many echoes in Dante of Aeneas's descent into the underworld. In Canto I, Dante finds himself lost:

> In the mid-way of this our mortal life,
> I found me in a gloomy wood, astray

Gone from the path direct . . .
(All translations from the *Divine Comedy* are those of Francis Cary
(1861))

He had wandered in there during the night and was full of fear, but as dawn breaks (on Good Friday morning) he sees a hill leading out of the valley. But his way is impeded by three savage beasts, a leopard (representing lust), a lion (signifying pride) and a wolf (meaning covetousness). He despairs, but then he is met by the shade of Virgil, who reveals himself as the author of *The Aeneid*. Dante greets him as his master, and Virgil tells him that he must take another road if he is to escape from this place, for the wolf will let no one pass. Dante must follow Virgil not up, but down, first into Hell, down into the very center of the earth, and then up on the other side, into Purgatory, and then on into Paradise, where another will be his guide.

In Canto II, Dante first professes his unworthiness for the journey. He is neither Aeneas nor Paul. Virgil accuses him of cowardice, and tells him of his own visitation by Beatrice, who has travelled from Heaven to Hell to see him. Beatrice herself had been sent by the Virgin Mary, who pitied Dante and had sent Saint Lucy to commission Beatrice to help him find his way back to righteousness from his wanderings through life and away from the right path. Virgil again upbraids Dante for his cowardice. (Dante is in effect being filled here with the grace that the Christian needs for salvation.) Together they enter on "the deep and woody way."

Canto III opens at the gate of Hell:

> Through me you pass into the city of woe:
> Through me you pass into eternal pain:
> Through me among the people lost for aye.
> Justice the founder of my fabric moved:
> To rear me was the task of power divine,
> Supremest wisdom, and primeval love.
> Before me things create were none, save things
> Eternal, and eternal I endure.
> All hope abandon, ye who enter here.

After reading this inscription above the gate, they hear sounds of lamentation and sighing. These are the souls who are tepid, who have been neither good nor bad. They have no hope of death, because they were never alive. A great train of them goes by, so many that "I should not have believed that death had undone so many." Among them is one of Dante's villains, Pope Celestine V. He was in fact later canonized, but he had earlier let Boniface VIII, Dante's archenemy, into the Papacy by resigning the office himself, making what Dante calls "il gran rifuto" (the great refusal). These unhappy souls are stung by wasps and hornets, which make their faces stream with blood; mixed with tears, this is gathered at their feet by disgusting worms. Virgil and Dante then reach the shore of the river Acheron. Charon, the boatman, refuses to take Dante, a living soul, across. (Frequently in the *Commedia,* Dante's solid material form is commented on, in contrast to the weightless spectral forms of the dead, who will get their material bodies back only at the Last Judgment.) Charon gathers in his boat many damned souls, who, pursued by divine justice, are clamouring to get across the river, while Dante himself is transported by a mystical red blaze.

At the end of Canto III, it is worth remarking that we have had only 400 lines or so, and already so much incident and character and mood. Dante's speed and inventiveness is quite extraordinary.

In Canto IV, Dante and Virgil enter the First Circle, the medieval Limbo, a kind of ante-chamber to the lower reaches of Hell. This is the abode of those without sin, but who had not been baptized. Merit alone, which they have, is not enough to save them. Virgil reports that he was in Limbo when a mighty one (Christ) came down and took out the figures from the Old Testament, but not the good pagans. (It is worth mentioning here that at several points in Dante's journey through Hell, reference is made, often by Virgil, to Christ's "harrowing of Hell"—when, after his death and before his resurrection, he descended there and passed all the way through, shaking the place up physically and removing those who were to be saved.) Dante sees first poets in a blaze of light enclosed by darkness, led by Homer, Horace, Ovid and Lucan; then in a meadow of grass he sees heroes and heroines, such as Hector, Aeneas, Caesar, Camilla, Latinus and Lavinia, the ancient Brutus who drove the Tarquins out of Rome, Lucretia who was raped by Tarquin, and, surprisingly perhaps, Saladin, the Muslim ruler of Egypt and Syria in the 12th century and worthy scourge of the crusaders. He also sees philosophers, scientists and orators, such as Socrates and Plato, Cicero and Seneca, Euclid, Ptolemy and Galen, and the Islamic philosophers Avicenna and Averroes, all led by Aristotle himself. These figures are not in pain, for they have no guilt. They are, nevertheless, like Virgil himself, lost. They live without hope, but in desire: "sanza speme vivemo in disio."

Canto V takes Virgil and Dante into a much more turbulent and painful place, the Second Circle in which the lustful are punished. First the travelers have to pass the dreadful Minos, the judge of the underworld, who sends each soul to its proper place and who tries to stop Dante because he is not yet dead. Once past him, they hear sounds of pain and wailing and see a hellish, blackish storm which drives and whirls the spirits relentlessly on and on. These are the lustful: Semiramis, Dido, Cleopatra, Helen, Achilles,

Paris, Tristan, among thousands of others. As Dante pities them, two who are joined together in endless embrace come up, and one of the two speaks. She is Francesca da Polenta, and she was married to the crippled Giovanni Malatesta, son of the Lord of Rimini. She fell in love with his brother Paolo (whom Dante may actually have known). She and Paolo were both killed by Giovanni, who had taken them by surprise. She tells her story to Dante. Love seized both the lovers, and has not left her yet. Love has brought them to one death; the deepest Circle of Hell, meanwhile, awaits their murderer. (The souls of the dead often have the power to see into the future, as did Anchises in *The Aeneid*, though they often do not know about the present and often ask Dante for information about current events.)

Francesca then tells Dante of the start of the affair. One day she and Paolo were alone and reading together the story of Lancelot and Guinevere:

> Oft times by that reading
> Our eyes were drawn together, and the hue
> Fled from our alter'd cheek. But at one point
> Alone we fell. When of that smile we read,
> The wished smile so rapturously kiss'd
> By one so deep in love, then he, who ne'er
> From me shall separate, at once my lips
> All trembling kiss'd. The book and writer both
> Were love's purveyors. In its leaves that day
> We read no more.

Dante adds:

> While thus one spirit spake,
> The other wail'd so sorely, that heart-struck
> I, through compassion fainting, seem'd not far
> From death, and like a corpse fell to the ground.

The story of Paolo and Francesca is one of the most famous in the *Commedia,* the kiss and also the lovers in the grip of the whirlwind being made universally familiar in sculptural form by Rodin. On the sin and its punishment, the philosopher George Santayana asks whether an eternity in each other's arms would really be a punishment for lovers; he sees Dante as saying that to abandon oneself to a love which is nothing but love is to be in Hell already. As we will see, many of the punishments in Dante's Hell are essentially poetically heightened representations of the states that the sinners' souls were already in when they were alive on earth.

Canto VI sees the pilgrims in the Third Circle, a place of eternal rain, hail and snow, and foul stinking ground. Cerberus, the three-headed dog, presides over it, thundering at Virgil and Dante, and also the souls who have to wallow there, beaten down by the elements. They are the gluttons, among them Ciacco, another acquaintance of Dante, whose very name means hog. He tells Dante that the Black Guelphs will eventually be defeated in Florence, and also of the future damnation of some prominent Florentines. Ciacco then drops down asleep in the ground, to be awoken only at the Last Judgment. Virgil tells Dante that the Judgment will increase the capacity for both suffering and happiness.

At the start of Canto VII, Dante and Virgil have to pass Plutus, the classical god of wealth. His bullying, though, is quelled by a word from Virgil, and the giant falls to the ground like sails when the mast snaps. Virgil and Dante descend into the Fourth Circle, where a great crowd of sinners crash into each other howling, and with great weights on their chests. They are the avaricious and the spendthrift, both sets betrayed by wealth. They include many popes and cardinals. Virgil comments:

Not all the gold that is beneath the moon
Or ever hath been, of these toil-worn souls
Might purchase rest for one.

They carry on, further down, reaching the Styx. They are now in the Fifth Circle, where the angry are held in the marshy bog. They are full of rage, hitting each other and tearing each other with their teeth, and mire fills their mouths. In the next Canto, Virgil and Dante force their way on to the boat of Phlegyas (who, full of anger, had burned one of Apollo's temples) in order to cross the Styx. While they are on the boat, the shade of Filippo Argenti, a Florentine contemporary of Dante, tries to climb aboard out of the mire. To Dante's great satisfaction, Virgil thrusts him back, to be set upon by other angry spirits, finally tearing himself with his teeth. Phlegyas rows them on to the city of Dis, with its mosques and fires, the garrison guarding the lower Circles of Hell. The rebel angels refuse Dante entry; as Virgil considers what to do, they slam the gates. Dante is terrified. While Virgil ponders his course of action, three Furies appear on the tower, calling upon the Gorgon Medusa to turn Dante to stone. At this point there is a mighty wind, clearing away the fetid air and a thousand damned souls; an angel from Paradise orders the devils to allow Dante and Virgil in. All is now quiet. As they enter the city they see tombs with their lids open and fire issuing forth, and they hear the groans of those inside. These, Dante is told, are the heretics, and this is the Sixth Circle.

Canto X treats of the Sixth Circle. In one part they find Epicurus and his followers, who denied the immortality of the soul. Then from nearby sarcophagi rise Farinata, a Ghibelline, strong and erect, and, rather less heroically, Cavalcante, a Guelph. Farinata had been posthumously convicted of heresy and had been an enemy to Dante's family and cause. But he is portrayed by Dante as a genuine lover of Florence, and a figure of some nobility, a precursor of Dante's own hope that the factionalism of Florence will come to an end. He does, though, tell Dante that his and Dante's hopes will be dashed in the short term, warning him of his exile. Cavalcante, reputedly a religious sceptic, wants to know the fate of his son and Dante initially prevaricates, causing Cavalcante to fall back into his tomb. Only later, and to Farinata, does he give the news that Cavalcante's son is still alive (though in fact he was already sick and dying in 1300). As Dante and Virgil leave, Farinata tells them that among others in the Sixth Circle are the Emperor Frederick II and a Florentine Cardinal, Ubaldini.

In Canto XI, still in the Sixth Circle, they find Pope Anastasius, from the fifth century, who denied the divine birth of Christ. Before they descend further, Virgil explains the nature of Hell. In the lowest three circles are contained the worst sinners, those guilty of violence (which is defined very broadly to include blasphemy, sodomy and usury), fraud, and treachery. These manifest bad will, unlike the sins of incontinence, which just show weakness. Usury (lending money at interest), becoming increasingly common in Florence, is condemned because it is unnatural; it produces a fruit neither of nature itself nor of human industry.

Canto XII takes us into the Seventh Circle, that of the violent. Descending a slope of Alpine steepness, Virgil and Dante first encounter the Minotaur, the outcome of the unnatural desire of his mother, Pasiphae, for a bull. Then at the bottom of the scree they find centaurs, including Nessus, the slayer of Hercules, and Chiron, who brought up Achilles. They threaten them with arrows, but when Virgil explains his divine mission, Nessus himself becomes their guide for the start of the Seventh Circle, which is subdivided into three sections, that containing those violent against others, that containing the violent against themselves (suicides), and finally those violent against God (blasphemers), Nature (sodomites) and Art (usurers).

In the first section, they then see many tyrants shrieking in torment in a boiling red flood, including Alexander the Great, Dionysus of Sicily, Guy de Montfort, and Attila the Hun. Then, in Canto XIII, they enter a dense wood of poisonous thorn trees, in which Harpies are nesting and feeding from the trees. Dante breaks off some twigs from one of the trees. Blood flows and laments issue forth: the spirit imprisoned there explains that the trees are those who have committed suicide. This is the spirit of Piero delle Vigne, the adviser to the Emperor and a famous poet shortly before Dante's time, who had committed suicide while falsely imprisoned. As they listen to Piero, the shades of two notorious spendthrifts (regarded perhaps as a form of self-destruction) are chased through the wood by black bitches who proceed to tear them apart.

Then, in Canto XIV, they leave the wood and reach a sterile desert on which naked souls are writhing, rained on by flakes of fire. They are in the third section of the Seventh Circle, among the blasphemers. The first they encounter is a pagan, Capaneus, one of the seven kings who attacked Thebes, who blasphemed against Zeus; continuing to blaspheme, he is admonished by Virgil for his still unquenched pride. They then see a red stream flowing from the wood. In reply to Dante's questions, Virgil tells the story of the Old Man of Crete. Crete, now a waste land, was once a place of innocence and plenty, where the infant Jupiter had been hidden by his mother, who formed a mountain for the purpose. Within the mountain stands a huge man made of metals—of gold, silver, brass, and iron—apart from a foot of clay on which he mostly stands. Echoing Virgil's "sunt lachrymae rerum," tears run from a fissure in each part of this symbol of decay and decadence, except the gold. Flowing through the earth, they emerge as four rivers of the classical underworld: Acheron, Styx, Phlegethon and Cocytus. They have already crossed Acheron, the river of death, and Styx, the marsh of anger. The stream they see is a tributary of Phlegethon, running with the blood of murder, and Cocytus (running into the frozen lake of treachery) they will see later. Dante asks about Lethe, the classical river of forgetfulness. This too they will see, not in this abyss, but in the place where those who have repented bathe.

To avoid the fiery desert they walk along the side of the stream, and there, in Canto XV, they meet a troop of spirits coming alongside. One of them greets Dante, and under his burned visage Dante recognizes his old teacher, the Florentine scholar, lawyer, and administrator Brunetto Latini: "Are you here, Ser Brunetto?" In one of the most puzzling episodes of *Inferno*, they then engage in an elevated conversation about Dante's own poetic mission and future fame, his exile from Florence (which Brunetto foresees), the state of Florence itself, and Brunetto's estimation of various noted scholars. Nevertheless, though Dante does not refer to his sin directly, Brunetto eventually leaves him, racing to rejoin his troop of damned sodomites in their punishment by fire. In the next Canto, Virgil and Dante see three further Florentine sodomites bound up together in a sort of wheel, hitting and thrusting at each other. Dante professes grief rather than contempt for them, recalling their honored deeds and names, and further words are exchanged about the corrupt state of contemporary Florence.

When they have departed, Virgil and Dante hear the sound of water, which turns out to be a vast waterfall plunging into an abyss. In the abyss they see a huge and terrifying creature flying up towards them. This, we learn in Canto XVII, is the monster Geryon. He has a human face, the face of a just man, and is spectacularly decorated on his breast, back and flanks, but alongside all this he has a serpent's trunk, two great hairy paws and a huge tail with a sting at the end, a vivid representation of fraud. He is the one, Virgil says, who pollutes the whole world, but they have to make their way to the monster, for he is going to take them down into the abyss. On their way to Geryon they pass the last inhabitants of the Seventh Circle, the usurers being tormented with fire, usury being a particularly heinous sin for the medievals, as it creates a bogus form of wealth, based on no production of anything real or truly valuable. Among the usurers Dante recognizes various Florentines and Paduans, whose business was the lending of money. Virgil and Dante make their way to Geryon and mount his back. He flies slowly down, with Dante terrified, as if he were Phaeton or Icarus, mythical fliers who both toyed with the sun with disastrous results. Geryon lands them at the bottom of the abyss. They are in the Eighth Circle.

We learn in Canto XVIII that the Eighth Circle, itself surrounded by a wall of rock, is divided into ten enclosures, known as Malebolge, surrounded by ditches. Each Bolgia contains its own category of the fraudulent. In the first they find two processions of naked sinners being scourged by devils. These are panders (pimps), like Vendico Caccianemico, a Bolognese who gave his sister to a Marquis, and seducers, like Jason, who seduced—and abandoned—both Hipsypile and Medea. In the second Bolgia they find flatterers plunged in a filthy moat filled with human excrement.

Canto XIX takes us to the Third Bolgia, the place for simonists, those who have bought or sold sacred things for money. Dante's own anger is undisguised:

> Woe to thee, Simon Magus! Woe to you
> His wretched followers! Who the things of God,
> Which should be wedded unto goodness, them,
> Rapacious as ye are, do prostitute
> For gold and silver in adultery.

Simon (from the Acts of the Apostles) and his followers are upside down in holes in the earth, with their feet outside wreathed in flames. Dante addresses one: "Already standest there, O Boniface?" But Pope Boniface VIII, Dante's arch-villain (because he has corrupted the Church with worldly ambition, after procuring the Papacy by fraud), is still alive in 1300. Dante is actually speaking to an earlier Pope, Nicholas II, who tells Dante that Boniface will come there, to be followed by an even worse one to come, Clement V, who removed the Papacy to Avignon. Dante responds by asking Nicholas how much treasure the Lord required of Peter in giving him the keys to the kingdom of heaven, and he also refers to the whore of Babylon sitting in fornication with the kings of the earth (an image from the Book of Revelation, taken by Dante in this passage to refer to the Church in collusion with the secular powers), and also the Emperor Constantine. For Dante, Constantine is also a villain because of the so-called Donation of Constantine, a forged document allegedly giving the Church the Imperial Power. To Dante, this mixing of secular and sacred is the ultimate corruption of both, for each should plough its own furrow separately in purity of action and intention (which explains his later shift towards the Ghibellines, seen as a way of getting the Pope out of politics and the Church exclusively back to the things of God).

The Fourth Bolgia is the subject of Canto XX, the diviners or soothsayers. Their punishment is to have their heads back to front, so that their tears wetted the clefts of their buttocks. Dante is unusual among his contemporaries in standing out against astrology and magic, and he also parts from the author of *The Aeneid* here (who was widely regarded in the Middle Ages as a soothsayer himself). Dante's Virgil speaks out against the soothsayers, who include Tiresias and Manto, the prophetess daughter of Tiresias. Manto is supposed to have given her name to Virgil's own town of Mantua, but according to Dante's Virgil she left there nothing but dead bones and a tenantless body, in a place which already had considerable natural advantages. Eurypylus, too, is here, from *The Aeneid* (who was consulted by the Greeks about leaving Troy), and many women who wrought spells with images and herbs. The moon now is setting. We are in the Saturday after Good Friday.

We next enter the Fifth Bolgia (Cantos XXI and XXII). This is where the swindlers in public office or barrators are, incarcerated in boiling tar, as in the Venetian Arsenal. They are continually prodded into the tar by the Malebranche (Evil Hands), ten devils with rakes and hooks, who take a furious delight in what they are doing, farting, quarrelling and egging each other on. The devils try to stop Virgil, and then tell him that the ridge into the Sixth Bolgia has collapsed since the time of the great earthquake which occurred at the Crucifixion. They maliciously impart false advice about a different, unbroken ridge, and resume their sport with the swindlers, among whom there are many Tuscans and Lombards. Dante himself was accused of barratry, and during this episode he is threatened by the Malebranche, the only occasion in *Inferno* when he is personally threatened, but Virgil protects him. Eventually, while the devils are busy with one of the swindlers and fighting among themselves, Virgil and Dante make their way along the ridge of the Fifth towards the Sixth Bolgia.

They are, however, pursued by the Malebranche. Virgil, affirming his belief in Dante's innocence, gathers him up, and they slide down together into the Sixth Bolgia. There (Canto XXIII) they find the hypocrites. They are condemned to walk slowly round and round, with cowls like the monks of Cluny, gilded on the outside but weighted with lead on the inside. They find first two so-called Jovial Friars from Bologna, well known in Dante's day, one of whom points out a figure crucified on the ground that the others all walk over. This is Caiphas, the High Priest who condemned Jesus by saying that one man must suffer for the people; his father-in-law Annas and the rest of the Sanhedrin are being similarly punished for the greatest crime committed in the name of religion.

In Canto XXIV, Dante and Virgil struggle despondently over the rubble and up across the ridge between the Sixth Bolgia and the Seventh, the place of thieves. This is a ditch full of serpents intertwining themselves with the shades of the thieves and growing in and out of their bodies. One of the sinners is burned to ashes, only to be reconstituted in yet more pain. This is Vanni Fucci, the Beast of Pistoia, the violent leader of the Black Guelphs there. He had robbed the sacristy of the Cathedral, for which another was falsely hanged. In the rage of his misery, and so as to grieve him and to stop him rejoicing over his own suffering, he tells Dante that the White-Black contagion will spread to Florence and the Whites will be struck down. He then (Canto XXV) blasphemes against God, at which he is bound at the neck and arms by two serpents and flees, pursued by the centaur Caccus who is also wreathed with snakes. The rest of the Canto describes Ovidian metamorphoses, of a snake-thief first twining itself around and then growing into the human forms of one of the thieves, and then two further mutants interchanging their own forms and attacking each other; but in Dante's descriptions there is an imaginative and psychological horror more medieval than classical, no doubt intended to represent the deceit and perversion of personality inherent in theft.

Canto XXVI opens with ironic praise of Florence from Dante, for, apart from Vanni Fucci, the thieves of the previous Canto were all Florentines. In the Eighth Bolgia they find tongues of fire enclosing the evil counselors. First among them, in a single flame, are Diomedes and Ulysses (Odysseus), responsible for the fall of Troy, the presence of Achilles at Troy (and hence his death), and the theft of the Palladium—and indirectly for the founding of Rome. Ulysses tells them that on returning to Ithaca he was still consumed with the passion for new experiences, which neither fondness for his son nor love for Penelope could quench. So he sailed off again through the Pillars of Hercules (marking the end of the Mediterranean) and out, beyond Spain, into the ocean and on in pursuit of the unknown. Ulysses inspires his companions with the words:

Oh brothers! . . . who to the west
Through perils without number now have reach'd;
To this the short remaining watch, that yet
Our senses have to wake, refuse not proof
Of the unpeopled world, following the track
Of the sun. Call to mind from when ye sprang:
Ye were not form'd to live the life of brutes,
But virtue to pursue and knowledge high.

They sailed on in their mad flight, into the southern hemisphere, where eventually he and his companions were wrecked and drowned under a huge mountain which loomed up before them, and which we will later realize is Purgatory. Dante doubtless intends us to conclude that Ulysses, an evil counselor to be sure, but who is nevertheless majestic and noble in his questing, falls in the end, wrecked on Purgatory, because he cannot find in himself the repentance and humility that Purgatory demands. Aside from that, though, we can but marvel at the way in which Dante has taken Ulysses/Odysseus further than Homer, and understood more about his personality than we are given in Homer, where we are supposed to imagine Ulysses largely content to live out an old age in Ithaca. It is Dante's Ulysses, rather than Homer's, who is the subject of Tennyson's moving poem on the subject.

Canto XXVII continues in the Eighth Bolgia. They now find Guido da Montefeltro, a nobleman turned Franciscan friar, who died in 1298. His crime was to have been tricked by Boniface VIII ("the Prince of the new Pharisees") into endorsing Boniface's plan to destroy the town of Palestrina (which had already surrendered to the papal forces), and at a time when Christians should have been united against the Saracens who were at that time taking Acre, the last Christian outpost in the Holy Land of Palestine. For this not even Saint Francis could prevent the black cherubim from handing him over to the judgment of Minos.

The Ninth Bolgia is the subject of Canto XXVIII. Here there are makers of discord. Dante and Virgil see souls mutilated and cut in various ways, being slashed by devils and re-formed for the process to be repeated endlessly. The first they see is Mahomet, who was believed at the time to have been first a Christian and then Christianity's chief divider, and then Ali his son-in-law, who split Islam itself. Mahomet is depicted as a gross character, parading his wounds, which amount to disembowelment, and who thinks that Dante himself is about to be thrown into the Bolgia. After Virgil has defended Dante (who prided himself on supporting the unity of mankind), Mahomet tells them to warn Fra Dolcino, a noted schismatic, and still alive in 1300, to prepare himself to stop what is going to happen to him in 1307 (in effect a taunt, because Dante's readers would have known that the warning would have proved useless). Among other sowers of discord, they see one who swings his own severed head by the hair, as if it were a lantern. This is Betran de Born, a nobleman and troubadour of the twelfth century, and noble compared to Dante's Mahomet, but still a creator of division. He had incited the son of Henry II of England to rebellion against his father.

Dante is fascinated by what he is seeing, including a kinsman of his own who had been killed in one of the blood-feuds so common at the time in Italy, but Virgil hastens him away. It is already after noon on Holy Saturday, and they have more to do and time is short. The Tenth Bolgia (Cantos XXIX and XXX) is filled with spirits lying and crawling around, their limbs festering, their bodies covered with sores and scabs, the stench and sights of plague and leprosy all about. These are the alchemists and forgers, those who trade on greed and ignorance. The first to be seen are two alchemists from Siena, then a by-word for vanity. Dante invokes Juno's fury at Semele and Hecuba's distress at the death of Polyxena—but, he says, nothing in Thebes or Troy was as cruel as what he now saw, two souls running and biting the others. One is Gianni Schicchi, who falsified a will, and the other Myrrha (from Ovid, *Metamorphoses,* Book Ten), who deceitfully lay with her father. They then see a legless, dropsical one, tortured with thirst, who is Master Adam, a notorious counterfeiter. Adam points out to the pilgrims Potiphar's wife (who denounced Joseph in the Bible when he would not sleep with her) and Sinon, the duplicitous Greek from Troy. The three start fighting and insulting each other and Dante stares at them in fascination, which provokes Virgil to ironic anger.

Reconciled in Canto XXXI, Virgil and Dante now hear some great blasts on a horn and see what Dante takes to be great towers. Virgil points out that they are actually giants. They include Briareus, who fought the against the gods of Olympus, and Nimrod, who built the tower of Babel. Wicked though they are, savage and bullying, and rebellious against God and the gods, one of them, Antaeus, takes Virgil and Dante up and places them in the Ninth Circle, way below where they were.

The Ninth Circle (Cantos XXXII–XXXIV) consists of Cocytus, the fourth river of Hell, which is now a glacial, frozen lake consisting of four concentric zones of ice, with just the heads of the souls above the ice. These are the treacherous, thousands of them, among whose heads Dante and Virgil walk. Dante stumbles into one and forces him to speak by grabbing his hair above the ice. Some are close enough to butt and gnaw each other. There is an eternal chill down there and an icy wind, and an extreme of hate and bitterness among the damned who are there. The first ones encountered are those who have betrayed their kin and country, among whom are Mordred who was killed by King Arthur, Antenor who betrayed Troy to the Greeks, and, as would be expected, numerous Italians of the thirteenth century. Of these, the most famous—largely because of Dante's own account—is Ugolino, who is gnawing at the neck of his nemesis, the Archbishop Ruggieri. Ugolino was a Ghibelline from Pisa who was blamed for betraying his city's strong-holds to the Guelphs of Florence, though Ugolino's own crime is mentioned by Dante only en passant. Later on, Ruggieri imprisoned him, nailed up in a tower, with his four sons. After some months in the tower, food is no longer brought to them. They all begin to starve. One of the sons, seeing Ugolino biting his own hand, proposes that Ugolino, who has given them their flesh, should use it to save himself. Another cries out in desperation as he dies after four days of hunger. Over the next two days, the remaining three also die. Ugolino, now blind, crawls over them in his grief. But after two more days, "fasting got the mastery of grief." (We will meet Ugolino again in the Monk's Tale in Chaucer.) After Ugolino, who continues gnawing at Ruggieri's skull, in the third zone of Cocytus, Dante and Virgil find some of those who have betrayed and killed their guests, including Fra Alberigo, a friar who had murdered his brother and nephew at his own table, and who has been sent to Hell for this crime even before the death of his body on earth.

In Canto XXXIV we come to the central zone of Cocytus and the very center of Hell itself. Here, like a great windmill gradually appearing through a thick fog, half in and half out of the ice, stands the giant Satan himself. He has three faces and six great wings, which are the cause of the icy blast which keeps Cocytus frozen and which the pilgrims have already felt. In each of his mouths he crushes a sinner. These are the traitors by rebellion: Judas Iscariot, who betrayed Christ, and Brutus and Cassius, the assassins of Julius Caesar.

Virgil now commands Dante to climb down Satan himself. When they reach his legs they turn themselves around and start climbing up—not, as Dante originally thinks, back into Hell, but out of it on the other side, into the southern hemisphere. When Satan fell to earth, all the land of the south had gone to the north, except the island mountain, up to which they are climbing through a cave. Where it was evening on earth, here it is morning. After their descent into the depths of the centre of the earth, through an opening in the cave "thence issuing we again beheld the stars."

Purgatorio

Dante's Purgatory is an island mountain, the only land in the southern hemisphere, exactly opposite to Jerusalem. The Earthly Paradise (the Garden of Eden) is on its summit, from where purified souls ascend to Paradise.

Ascending the lower reaches of the mountain, there are four irregular slopes, occupied by souls whose purgation has been delayed, and who are waiting to get into Purgatory proper. From the lowest slope, these are the excommunicated, the lethargic, the unabsolved, and rulers who have been negligent. Purgatory proper, where purgation and purification is actually taking place, consists of seven terraces going around the mountain. These are occupied (from the lowest) by the proud, the envious, the wrathful, the slothful, the avaricious, the gluttonous, and the lustful. Above the terraces is the Earthly Paradise itself.

In contrast to the stasis, the darkness, and claustrophobia, the resentful anger and despair of Hell, Purgatory is filled with movement, at times with light and sacred song, and with hope, albeit for something distant. The suffering in Purgatory is not light, but nor is it fruitless, which makes all the difference. Many know only Dante's *Inferno;* this is doubly unfortunate because, thus restricted, they will misunderstand his intention and will also miss the extraordinary and beautiful change of mood between Hell and the early Cantos of *Purgatorio*.

On the other hand, for the non-religious reader, *Purgatorio* may present a problem, at least initially. The souls that Dante and Virgil meet there are singing religious songs and hymns, and doing so in groups. This signifies not only their repentance and expiation. That they are moving and singing in groups is a symbol of their movement towards entry into the greater group of the Church triumphant, the great group in Paradise where all the saved are part of one celestial rose, as we will see. This is what the souls in Purgatory are working towards in anticipation and expectation, and in doing so they are losing their grosser human personalities and individuality. There is here a significant and intended contrast with *Inferno,* in which characters like Francesca, Ulysses, and Ugolino are sharply delineated in their full humanity. The souls in *Purgatorio* are losing their earthly features, as well as their earthly passions and desires, and will eventually be cleansed of all their gross humanity in the River Lethe, forgetting all that is unworthy. But by contrast with the souls in *Inferno,* they are already less human, more evanescent and spirit-like, which is part of Dante's intention, but which from a certain point of view makes them less interesting as personalities than those in *Inferno.* Dante would say that personality in that sense is a little thing, a dangerous thing, and not something to be developed or striven for, but rather to be refined and burnt away in the fires of Purgatorio (a complete contrast with contemporary notions of self-esteem and finding your inner self, of course).

Canto I opens on Easter Sunday morning, with the planet Venus visible, and four stars never seen by mankind since the expulsion of Adam and Eve from the Earthly Paradise. Dante and Virgil meet a venerable old man, who challenges them forcefully as to how they came out of the valley of Hell, and Dante explains his commission from the three heavenly ladies. Virgil knows that this is Cato, a hero of the Roman Republic who killed himself when he realized that Caesar was going to prevail. Virgil tells Cato of his wife, Marcia, who is with him in Limbo. Cato ushers them on and they make their way over a lonely plain, "as one who returns to the road that has been lost"—a powerful reference to the opening of *Inferno*. As the dawn breaks, Virgil washes Dante's face with dew.

The sun rises (Canto II). A light speeds towards them over the sea. It is an angel steering a heavenly ship full of souls, who sing of the deliverance of Israel from Egypt, "in exitu Israel de Aegypto." (It is a feature of *Purgatorio* that many of the transitions are marked by hymns and psalms.) Virgil tries to embrace one of the souls, but finds only emptiness. The soul turns out to be Casella, a musician friend of Dante, who stays to talk and to sing one of Dante's own poems:

> Amor che ne la mente mi ragiona
> (Love that discourses to me in my mind)
> He began to sing so sweetly
> That the sweetness sounds within me still.

The souls stand rapt and attentive, but Cato upbraids them all for loitering and neglecting their task of purification. Like a wild flock of pigeons scattering, they all hurry off.

In Canto III, Virgil and Dante begin the ascent of the mountain. Dante wonders at Virgil's failure to cast a shadow before the now risen sun. How can insubstantial souls suffer? Virgil speaks of the limits of human reason before the eternal mysteries; Dante should be content to know what is the case, without having to know the reasons. As they ponder the best way up, they meet a crowd of souls who show them the way. One of them, beautiful in appearance, but scarred by wounds on his forehead and chest, reveals himself to be Manfred, a dashing Ghibelline hero from the thirteenth century, the illegitimate son of the Emperor Frederick II, who had been excommunicated by the Pope and then killed in battle by the forces of France and the Papacy in 1266. He tells Dante of his last-minute repentance and asks him to tell his daughter of his forgiveness by infinite goodness; but as an excommunicate, he has to stay for 30 years outside Purgatory proper unless he is prayed for by those below.

Virgil and Dante embark on a steep and difficult ascent, which eases off at the top (Canto IV). There behind a boulder they find a group of souls sitting, hugging their knees and resting. These are the lethargic, who, because they put off "the 'good sighs' of repentance" until their end, must wait for their whole lifetime before proceeding further, again unless prayer on their behalf rises from the heart of someone who is living in grace. Dante and Virgil, though, press on (Canto V). They meet a group singing the *Miserere*. These are those who were sinners up to their last hour and were then killed by violence, repenting only at the very last. Three ask Dante for help with prayers for them when he returns to earth. There is Casero of Fano, who died in a marsh trying to escape from the assassins of the Marquis of Ferrara. There is Buonconte of Montefeltro, son of the Guido we met in *Inferno* (XXVII). He was wounded in battle, and calling on Mary as he was dying, was rescued by an angel as his body was swept down in a flood into the River Arno. And there is also la Pia, of Siena, murdered by her own husband:

> . . . remember me.
> I once was Pia. Siena gave me life;
> Maremma took it from me. That he knows,
> Who me with jewelled ring had first espoused.
> (. . . ricorditi di me, che son la Pia;
> Siena mi fè, disfecemi me Maremma:
> salsi colui che 'nnanellata pria
> disposando m'avea con la sua gemma.)

In Canto VI, there are many others with similar requests. Dante questions Virgil, for had not he (in his account of the death of Palinurus) warned of the futility of praying for the dead? Virgil says that he was writing at an earlier time, when prayer had no access to God, and tells him to consult Beatrice in due course. As they go on, they find a soul seated alone and apart from the others. This is Sordello, a poet from Mantua. Virgil declares himself a fellow Mantuan; Sordello leaps up and the two embrace each other warmly. This touching scene leads Dante to lament the current state of Italy—a ship without a pilot, a brothel. Justinian's law is useless with no one to enforce it. The clergy meddle in the things of Caesar. The German Emperor Albert has abandoned them, neither he nor Rudolf, his father, ever coming to Italy. The great families feud (including the Montagues and the Capulets), Italy is full of tyrants, any villain can become a Marcellus (a popular leader in ancient Rome). And "my" Florence, Dante praises with bitter irony for its many changes of laws, money, offices, customs and leaders.

After this passionate digression, in Canto VII Sordello asks Virgil who exactly he is. He replies that he is Virgil, "for no sin deprived of heaven, except for lack of faith." Sordello greets him as if he were his lord, and Virgil explains his mission and his own fate in Limbo. Sordello offers to guide them over the next stretch, before night falls. In a flowery valley below them, they see the souls of the negligent rulers, including Rudolf, the Emperor who might have saved Italy, Ottocar and Wenceslaus of Bohemia, Philip III of France, the father of Philip IV (that "bane" of "foul and vicious life") who took the Papacy to Avignon, Charles of Anjou, who killed Manfred, Henry III of England, and numerous others. Apart from Henry, all had been involved in the struggles of Dante's time, and all had brought grief on their peoples.

As dusk falls (Canto VIII) two angels with flaming swords fly down to watch over the valley. As the three travellers go down, Dante is overjoyed to meet Nino Visconti, grandson of Ugolino and an old friend of his. As the stars of the evening appear, Sordello points out that a snake, the devil, such as gave Eve the apple, is crawling through the valley. The angels chase it out. Meanwhile, another shade, Conrad Malaspina, prophesies that Dante himself will be banished, and will become a guest of the Malaspini.

In Canto IX it is night in the Valley of the Princes, but only Dante sleeps. He dreams that he is taken up by a golden eagle into the sphere of fire between the earth and the moon, where both are burned. When he wakes, he finds himself in an unknown place, higher up. Virgil explains that as he slept, he was taken by Saint Lucy to the entrance of Purgatory proper. They find a gate, guarded by an angel, who lets them pass on to the steps of Purgatory, tracing seven Ps on Dante's brow. One will be removed on each interior terrace. The gate is then unlocked and they enter to the sound of voices singing the *Te Deum*.

They climb up a narrow path, and on to the First Terrace, where sins of pride are purged (Cantos X–XII). On the inside of the terrace there is a wall of white marble, adorned with magnificently carved images of humility. They see the Annunciation, with Mary and the Angel Gabriel, David dancing before the Ark of the Covenant and Michal deriding him, and the Emperor Trajan speaking compassionately to a poor widow in the midst of a triumphal procession. The proud then shuffle by, bowed down by great rocks on their backs. One of these souls, a Tuscan aristocrat overproud of his birth and killed for his scorn of others, shows Virgil and Dante the way to the next terrace. Another is Oderisi, once a leading illustrator of his day and proud of it, but whose fame has now been eclipsed, just as in painting Giotto has dimmed the fame of Cimabue: "the noise of worldly fame is but a blast of wind." Oderisi then addresses Provezan Salvani, a proud Sienese leader: "Your renown is as the herb, whose hue doth come and go." He was, though, saved because he did once abase himself in the marketplace of Siena to secure the release from prison of a friend, and Dante himself says that Oderisi's words allay a great swelling in his own breast. As they walk on, they see on the road beneath their feet thirteen images of pride. These include Lucifer himself, Briareus and Nimrod, two of the giants in Hell (*Inferno* XXXI),

Niobe, who boasted she was a better mother than Latona, mother of Apollo and Artemis (Diana), and had all her fourteen children killed, Arachne, who dared to challenge Athene (Minerva) and was turned into a spider, and Holofernes, the Assyrian leader beheaded by Judith. There is also Troy in ruins and ashes. Dante marvels at the skill of the depictions, at what he had referred to as "visible speech" earlier on the terrace. Reflecting the increasing realism in the art of his time, he now speaks of the dead seeming dead and the living living in the images before him, produced by some master of brush or chisel and of shape and outline. But these reflections are cut short. An angel hastens them up a sacred stairway towards the next terrace. Dante feels lighter than he did; one of the seven Ps has been removed from his brow.

The pattern we have observed on the First Terrace (of images of the virtue corresponding to the sin being purged preceding the sinners themselves, who are then followed by famous examples of the sin and then by an angel taking Virgil and Dante up to the next terrace and removing one of the Ps from Dante) is repeated on each of the remaining terraces.

The Second Terrace (Cantos XIII–XIV) is plainer than the First, consisting of bare rock, without carving or shade, and a path of reddish stone. It is devoted to purging the sin of envy. First Virgil and Dante hear the voices of kindness: Mary asking Jesus at the marriage feast of Cana that "they have no wine," then Pylades pretending to be his friend Orestes, so as to suffer his execution, and finally "love those from whom you have suffered wrong," a verse from the Sermon on the Mount. The sinners are in sack-cloth, their eyelids sewn up with iron wire, moving and huddling together like blind beggars. One of them is a Sienese lady called Sapia, who rejoiced at the misfortunes of others, and particularly at the defeat of Provezan Salvani, whom we have just met on the First Terrace. But she sought peace with God at the end of her life, and was, in addition, prayed for by a hermit. Two further souls discover from Dante that he is from the Arno valley. This provokes one to speak of the hogs, curs, dogs and wolves who live there now, and of the grandson of the other who will slaughter the Florentine wolves. The speaker is Guido del Duca and his companion Rinier da Calboli; though they had been envious in their lifetime, both are now downcast at Italy's current decadence. When Virgil and Dante pass on, they hear the voices of Cain, the first murderer, and of Aglauros, an Athenian girl turned to stone for envying her sister.

An angel of dazzling brightness comes down to take Virgil and Dante up to the Third Terrace. As they go, Virgil explains to Dante that, in contrast to earthly goods which are lessened by sharing, which is the root of envy, the gifts of God increase by being handed round; and also that the second P has now left him. We have reached the Third Terrace, that of the angry (Cantos XV–XVII). Dante now has visions of three instances of mercy: Mary's sweetness on finding Jesus in the Temple; Pisistratus, an Athenian lord, who, against the wishes of his wife, had showed mercy to a man who had kissed his daughter, saying: "How shall we those requite, who wish us evil, if we thus condemn a man who loves us?"; and Stephen, the first martyr, begging forgiveness for those stoning him to death. When evening begins to fall, a black smoke approaches, the fog of anger. Voices are heard singing the *Agnus Dei,* praying for mercy.

They see a crowd of spirits, and one of them—Marco from Lombardy—speaks, saying who he is. Dante asks him why the world is so wicked. Marco explains that it is a result of human free choice, which would be destroyed if everything were done by heavenly necessity. So, though heaven initiates our impulses, the cause of evil is in us. The soul "like a babe" first goes after whatever delights it, so human beings need laws to curb and guide them, but, let down by both king and shepherd, we do not observe them. We are badly guided, particularly in the blurring of the proper division between the Church and the secular power, the "two suns of Rome," "whose several beams cast light on either way, the world's and God's." But now that the sword is grafted on the crook, each quenches the other. The secular power no longer upholds courtesy and valour, but rather the opposite, while the Church falls into the mire of secular politics, defiling both itself and its burden. As the smoke begins to thin out with the beams of the setting sun visible through it, Marco leaves them.

Dante sees visions of those destroyed by anger: Procne, from Ovid's *Metamorphoses,* Haman, crucified by Esther in the Bible, and Amata from *The Aeneid,* who killed herself over the loss of Lavinia (and in Dante's vision has Lavinia weeping for her). Anger now purged, the next angel then takes them up to the Fourth Terrace, that of sloth or accidie. Virgil now gives Dante a lecture on love, which owes something to Augustine and to Aquinas: love itself is by nature without error, but it can be evil if it swerves, misdirected by the mind, desiring evil for others, as in pride (where one hopes to excel by putting others down), envy (where one fears to lose honor and so is aggrieved by another), and anger (where one wants to compensate for an insult by harming the other). These are the sins purged on the first three Terraces, but there are also goods which fail to produce happiness if pursued in the wrong proportion, sloth on this Terrace, and avarice, gluttony, and lust higher up. So not all loves are good, for some are misdirected by human perception. We have the power to control our love, the faculty of free will, that which counsels, which gives us power to guard the threshold of assent.

It is almost midnight and Dante is feeling sleepy when he sees a great crowd of people running and calling for haste. Those in front mention Mary hastening to Elizabeth after the Annunciation and Caesar rushing to Spain in the civil war against Pompey. The slothful sinner whom Dante focuses on is a twelfth-century Abbot of San Zeno at Verona; it is not clear why exactly, though his introduction does allow Dante to castigate the present Abbot, who has secured the succession for his illegitimate son. There is also mention of the Israelites who failed to reach Jordan and the Trojans from Aeneas's expedition who remained in Sicily.

Dante now (Canto XIX) dreams of the Siren who, in medieval legend, seduced Ulysses; in the dream, Virgil tears off her clothes, revealing a loathsome smell coming from her belly. This causes Dante to awake to the new day. The angel who leads them to the Fifth Terrace, that of avarice, tells Dante that he has now seen how man may be freed from the old enchantress (the Siren). On the terrace they see souls prostrate on the ground and weeping, still fixed on earthly things. Among them is Pope Adrian V, who converted late from avarice, realizing that his heart was not at rest, and whose hopes on earth rest with the prayers of his niece.

In Canto XX, Dante meets examples of generosity or of indifference to wealth: Mary, again, this time at the manger, Fabricius, the Roman consul who refused a bribe to betray the Republic, and Saint Nicholas, who provided dowries for three poor girls who might otherwise have gone into prostitution. Dante and Virgil are then addressed by Hugh Capet. He was the son of a butcher in Paris and the founder of the Capetian dynasty in the tenth century, and as he says himself, "the root of that evil plant whose shade such poison sheds o'er all the Christian land"—France, the Flemish lands and even Sicily and the south of Italy. Among his descendants are Charles of Anjou, who was suspected of poisoning Thomas Aquinas in 1274 (and who, strangely perhaps, we already met in Canto VII in the Valley of the Princes), and Philip IV (of France) who mocks Christ a second time by seizing Boniface VIII and suppressing the Knights Templar. (It is noteworthy that even though Dante cannot abide Boniface, Philip's crime is against the Papacy itself, and as such an attack on Christ.) Pygmalion, who killed Dido's husband Sychaeus for gold, King Midas and Ananias from the Acts of the Apostles, who kept back part of his tithe to the Church, are then recalled by Capet, along with others undone by greed. When Dante and Virgil leave Capet, there is a great earthquake, and sounds of the *Gloria,* as the shades resume their weeping on the ground.

In Canto XXI, Virgil and Dante meet a new soul, one who appears cleansed. The soul himself explains that no change in Purgatory happens without reason. The earthquake happened because after more than 500 years, he has been redeemed, and the *Gloria* is praise from the spirits on the mountain. This soul says that he is Statius, a Roman poet of the 1st century, author of the *Thebaid* and the unfinished *Achilleid* (and whom we will meet again in connection with the Knight's Tale in Chaucer). Statius adds that he would have consented to a greater punishment had he been able to have lived at the same time as Virgil. Virgil himself first enjoins silence, but Dante smiles. Virgil relents and Dante reveals the identity of his guide.

Dante, Virgil, and Statius all ascend to the Sixth Terrace, Dante having another P removed by the escorting angel. (From now on Statius will accompany Dante, right up into Paradise itself, and after Virgil has returned to Limbo.) Under questioning from Virgil, Statius admits to having been a spendthrift. He then tells Virgil that he was enlightened by the latter's Fourth *Eclogue,* in Dante's version:

> Lo!
> A renovated world, Justice return'd,
> Times of primeval innocence restored,
> And a new race descended from above.

He became a Christian under the Emperor Domitian, but because of the persecutions remained hidden and lukewarm; so he was consigned to the Fourth Terrace for more than four centuries. Statius then asks Virgil about other Roman poets, including Terence and Plautus. Virgil then tells him about Limbo, where they are, along with poets such as Homer and Euripides, as well as Antigone, Ismene, Thetis, and many others. Virgil and Statius walk on in converse, up on to the Sixth Terrace, that of gluttony. Dante walks behind, listening to them. They come across a beautiful tree, but a voice commands them not to eat its fruit. It then reminds them of examples of abstinence, of Mary at the marriage feast of Cana, of Roman women preferring water to drink, of Daniel preferring wisdom to the meat and wine of the king. The voice tells too of how in the Golden Age acorns were savoury and every brook seemed like nectar, and of the honey and locusts which were the food of the Baptist in the desert.

On the Sixth Terrace (Cantos XXIII–XXIV) they find emaciated shades, pallid and wasted. One of them is Forese Donati, a relative of Dante's wife and a close friend of Dante, who had died recently. Forese explains that the odour and spray from the tree they had just passed inflames the desire to eat and drink, but without satisfying it. He has got through Purgatory thanks to the goodness of his wife, but he castigates the shamelessness of the Florentine women of the day. In reply to questioning from Dante, he adds that Piccarda, his sister, is already in Paradise. But among the gluttons of Purgatory are still many other nobles and churchmen, including the father of Ruggieri (*Inferno,* XXXIII) and Pope Martin IV, famous in his day for cooking eels in wine. One of these gluttons is Buongiunta, a poet, who mentions the name of Gentucca, a lady thought by some to be loved by Dante in his exile. Alluding to Dante's exile, Buongiunta asks whether he sees before him the author of one of Dante's poems; having this confirmed, he laments that as a poet he did not achieve Dante's: "new and sweeter style" (the *dolce stil nuovo*). Forese and Dante then speak of the troubles of Florence, and Forese foretells the fall (in 1308) of Corso Donati, the leader of the Blacks who, with the French, had taken Florence in 1301 and had exiled Dante, and of Corso's own death falling from a horse when he himself was trying to escape. When Forese leaves, Dante, with Virgil and Statius now, sees another great tree with people fruitlessly begging beneath it. A voice tells them to pass on; this is an offshoot of the tree of Eve, which is higher up. The voice tells them of some ancient sins of gluttony, and then the next angel, whose wings shed ambrosial fragrance, points them towards the Seventh Terrace.

Canto XXV consists mainly of a lecture on the soul from Statius in response to a question of Dante as to how mere souls (the gluttonous they have just seen) can feel hunger. When a human child is conceived, the male's blood, which is active, mingles with the female's, which is passive, and enlivens it. First an embryonic vegetative form emerges, which then develops into an animal form, with all its limbs and organs. When the brain of the animal is perfected, God himself infuses the human soul. The soul becomes the active, unifying principle of the whole new human being, just as the sun's heat becomes wine when it is mixed with the juice of grapes. At death the soul leaves the body, along with all our faculties, and goes to whichever place it is destined. There (in a point original to Dante) it is given a shadowy body, with organs for feeling and sight.

As they reach the Seventh Terrace, that of lust, they see spirits in flames, who are singing of the virginity of Mary and of Diana (and her punishment of Callisto, from Ovid, *Metamorphoses,* Book Two), and also of chaste wives and husbands, as their own sins are burned away. Up on the Terrace (Canto XXVI), two troops of souls rush past on the burning path, nuzzling each other with kisses. One group consists of homosexuals, who refer to Sodom and Gomorrha, and also to Caesar. The other group is made up of those whose heterosexual lust makes them refer to Pasiphae, the Queen of Crete, entered by a bull (which produced the Minotaur). One of the latter group reveals himself as Guido Guinizelli, a poet whom Dante reveres as an artistic father, the founder of the sweet new style, but who himself points out one "who surpassed them all," Arnault, the Provençal love poet from the early-thirteenth century, who speaks to Dante in Provençal before hiding himself again in the refining fire.

In Canto XXVII, to the strains of *Beati mundo corde* (blessed are the pure in heart), an angel sends the three travelers through the purifying fire which leads to Beatrice and to the earthly Paradise. The burning is intense,

1. Leda and the Swan. Leda is the Queen of Sparta and the Swan is Zeus. One direct result of this encounter is the birth of Helen, and so an indirect one is the Trojan War. We will meet Leda, the Swan, and Helen again in *Faust, Part Two*, as the setting of Goethe's poem moves to classical Greece. (Correggio (Antonio Allegri) (1489–1534), *Leda and the Swan*, c. 1532; © Gemäldegalerie, Berlin/Bridgeman Art Library)

2. A gold death mask from Mycenae, actually somewhat earlier than the possible time of the Trojan War. Nevertheless, it gives a sense of the magnificence and riches associated with the Homeric kings. On excavating it in 1876, the great archaeologist Heinrich Schliemann is said to have declared: "Today I have gazed on the face of Agamemnon." (Funerary mask from Mycenae, formerly thought to be that of Agamemnon, Mycenaean, sixteenth century BC; © National Archaeological Museum, Athens/Giraudon/Bridgeman Art Library)

3. (*above*) Paris chooses Aphrodite as the most beautiful of the three goddesses. In his quest for the eternal feminine, he gains Helen as his reward, but incurs the hatred of the other goddesses, Athene and Hera. The chain of events he thus sets in train brings about the destruction of Troy. (Peter Paul Rubens (1577–1640), *The Judgment of Paris*, c. 1632–35; © National Gallery, London, UK/Bridgeman Art Gallery)

4. (*left*) Diomedes, the youngest and one of the most exciting of the Greek heroes in *The Iliad*, as envisaged by the contemporary sculptor Anthony Caro. In his sequence of works devoted to the Trojan war, Caro pares his subjects down to their essence. (Anthony Caro (b. 1924), *Diomedes (The Trojan War)*, 1993–94, photo by David Buckland; © Barford Sculptures Ltd.)

5. The classical ideal of beauty, here depicting Athene, the patron of Odysseus and, as we learn from Aeschylus, the presiding deity of the laws and civilization of the city of Athens. But the "calm simplicity and noble grandeur" of works like this, which so appealed to classicists of the eighteenth and nineteenth centuries, was bought at the price explored in the tragedies. (The Head of Athene, from the metope of the Stymphalian Birds, Museum of Olympia, 1956 (b/w photo) by Nikolaos Tombazis (1894–1986); © Benaki Museum, Athens/ Bridgeman Art Library)

6. In Turner's great painting, Polyphemus is effectively part of the landscape which looms over the tiny Odysseus (Ulysses) and his fragile ship. (J. M. W. Turner (1775–1851), *Ulysses Deriding Polyphemus*, 1829; © National Gallery, London/Bridgeman Art Library)

7. (*left*) Agamemnon would have left his city by this gate en route for Troy, and would have returned through it to meet Clytemnestra and his fate. The classical Greeks were overwhelmed by the sheer scale of the walls of a city built centuries earlier, attributing their construction to Cyclopean giants. (Lion Gate over the entrance to the Palace of Mycenae, Greece, fifteenth century BC; © Private collection/Bridgeman Art Library)

8. (*below*) Antigone leads her beloved father Oedipus away from Thebes and into exile. He is now blinded and Thebes polluted by his crimes. She will return only after his death, to meet her own tragic destiny. (oil on canvas) (Ernest Hillemacher (1818–87), *Oedipus and Antigone being exiled from Thebes*, 1843; © Musée des Beaux-Arts, Orléans France/ Giraudon/Bridgeman Art Library)

9. (*left*) As the hemlock takes hold and his followers become increasingly distraught, Socrates remains calm, speaking of his release into a better world. (Gaetano Gandolfi (1734–1802), *The Death of Socrates*, 1782 (private collection/photo); © Bonhams, London/Bridgeman Art Library)

10. (*below*) Turner captures the luxury and opulence of Dido's Carthage, and also a sense of decadent lethargy even as it is being built (as did Berlioz in *The Trojans*). And no more than Virgil and Turner can we, the spectators, forget the ultimate fate both of Dido and of her city. (J. M. W. Turner (1775–1851), *Dido building Carthage*, or *The Rise of the Cartheginian Empire*, 1815; © National Gallery, London/Bridgeman Art Library)

11. Virgil is reading from Book Six of *The Aeneid* to his friend and patron the Emperor Augustus, and also to Livia, Augustus's wife, and Octavia, his sister. Virgil relates how Aeneas visits the

underworld to hear predictions from his dead father Anchises regarding the course of Roman history, and has reached the death of Marcellus, son of Octavia and nephew and intended heir of Augustus. As she hears this, Octavia faints. (Jean-Auguste-Dominique Ingres (1780–1867), *Virgil Reading* The Aeneid *to Livia, Octavia, and Augustus*, c. 1812 (oil on canvas); © Musée des Augustins, Toulouse, France/Bridgeman Art Library)

12. The god Apollo is about to catch the reluctant nymph Daphne, to have his way with her, but she is saved by being changed into a laurel tree. Bernini's sculpture is a superbly sympathetic and dramatic portrayal of Ovid's tale. The transformation happens before our eyes, with Daphne, now as much tree as woman, eluding his grasp just as his hand enfolds her. (Giovanni Bernini (1598–1680), *Apollo and Daphne*, 1622–25 (marble); © Galleria Borghese, Rome/Lauros/Giraudon/Bridgeman Art Library)

13. As Ovid relates, the satyr Marsyas dared to challenge the god Apollo in a contest of musicianship, and pays the price. In Titian's painting, King Midas, sitting on the right, is taken to be a self-portrait of the artist. Titian had introduced him from another of Ovid's tales, in which the King found in favor of Pan and against Apollo, and was rewarded for his pains with the ears of an ass. No matter, Titian's painting is a remarkable meditation on suffering, beauty, poignancy, and transformation, wholly in the spirit of Ovid. (Titian (Tiziano Vecellio) (1488–1576), *The Flaying of Marsyas*, c. 1570–75; Kromeriz, Erzbischöfliches Schloss; photo: akg-images/Erich Lessing/Art Resource, NY)

14. (*opposite top*) Rubens' painting shows us the humble Baucis and Philemon (from Book Eight of Ovid's *Metamorphoses*) being led by the gods whom they have entertained to higher ground, to escape the flood that is about to punish their inhospitable neighbors. But it could equally well represent Ovid's earlier story in which the pious Deucalion and Pyrrha alone are saved from the flood which engulfs the whole of mankind. Either way, in true Ovidian spirit, Rubens' painting conveys a strong sense of nature's turbulence and transformative power. (Peter Paul Rubens (1577–1640), *Landscape with Philemon and Baucis*, (oil on panel) c. 1625; © Kunsthistorisches Museum, Vienna/Bridgeman Art Library)

15. (*opposite bottom*) A late painting of Titian, of one of Ovid's metamorphoses. Its subject is Diana's cruel revenge on Actaeon, who has unwittingly observed the virgin goddess naked; he is savaged by his own hounds when they hear his cries as the braying of the stag he is being turned into. There is, nevertheless, a sense of resolution in the handling, a sense that nothing in nature is wholly destroyed but it only changed. (Titian (Tiziano Vecellio) (1488–1576), *The Death of Actaeon*, c. 1565; © National Gallery, London/Bridgeman Art Library)

16. (*above*) Still a Manichaean, Augustine teaches wordly rhetoric and philosophy in Rome. (Benozzo di Lese di Sandro Gozzoli (1420–1497), *St. Augustine Reading Rhetoric and Philosophy at the School of Rome*, 1464–65; © S. Agostino, San Gimignamo, Italy/Giraudon/Bridgeman Art Library)

17. The Father of the Church at his desk, no less passionate than in his earlier days, but now with a passion of the spirit. (Sandro Botticelli (1444/5–1510), *St. Augustine in his Cell* (fresco), c. 1480; © Ognissanti, Florence/Bridgeman Art Library)

18. (*below*) Dante, with the book of his poem. On his left is the city of Florence and on his right the universe of the *Divine Comedy*: the pit of Hell, the terraces of Purgatory, and the spheres of Paradise. (Domenico di Michelino (1417–91), *Dante and his poem the "Divine Comedy"* (tempera on panel), 1465; © Duomo, Florence/Bridgeman Art Library)

19. Ugolino is placed by Dante in the Ninth Circle of Hell, that of the traitors. As well as treachery, he is guilty of eating his own children. In common with many later readers, however, in this poignant image Blake sees him more as a victim than as a sinner. (William Blake (1757–1827, *Count Ugolino and his Sons in Prison*, illustration for Dante's *Inferno* Canto 33, c. 1827 (tempera on panel); © Fitzwilliam Museum, University of Cambridge/Bridgeman Art Library)

20. (*right*) Beatrice and Dante are drawn up into Mercury, the second sphere of Paradise, received by hundreds of redeemed spirits, radiant in streams of light. (Gustave Doré (1832–83), *The Angels in the Planet Mercury: Beatrice Ascends with Dante to the Planet Mercury*, illustration for Dante's *Paradiso*, c. 1860–68 (engraving); © Private Collection/Bridgeman Art Library)

21. The source of all his troubles—a more Romantic view of the deluded resident of La Mancha than that of Cervantes. (Honoré Daumier (1808–79), *Don Quixote Reading*, 1865–67 (oil on canvas); © National Museum and Gallery of Wales, Cardiff/Bridgeman Art Library)

22. (*below*) Don Quixote takes on the world, followed by Sancho Panza. (Honoré Daumier (1808–79), *Don Quixote and Sancho Panza*, 1865–70 (oil); © Private collection/ © Agnew's, London/ Bridgeman Art Library)

23. A sense here of the drear extent of Pandemonium, and of its "darkness visible." (John Martin (1789–1854), *Satan on his Throne*, illustration for Milton's *Paradise Lost* (1608–74), 1858 (litho); © British Library, London/ © British Library Board/All rights reserved/Bridgeman Art Library)

24. Blake suggests the ambivalance involved in the knowlege of good and evil, just as Milton did himself. (William Blake (1757–1827), *The Temptation and Fall of Eve*, illustration for Milton's *Paradise Lost*, 1808; © 2007 Museum of Fine Arts, Boston/Museum Purchase with funds donated by contribution/All rights reserved/ Bridgeman Art Library)

25. Rubens' painting dates from half a century before Racine's *Phèdre*. But in this horrific image of one of the scenes described by Racine, it conveys the play's stifling atmosphere and its sense of the ineluctability of destiny. (Peter Paul Rubens, *The Death of Hippolytus*, c. 1611–13 (oil on canvas); © Fitzwilliam Museum, University of Cambridge/Bridgeman Art Library)

26. The disillusioned scholar in his dusty study, visited by the diabolical tempter. (Eugène Delacroix (1798–1863), *Faust and Mephistopheles*, 1827–28 (oil on canvas); © Wallace Collection, London/Bridgeman Art Library)

27. They race from the witches' Sabbath in a vain attempt to rescue the stricken Margareta. Of Delacroix's illustrations to *Faust, Part One*, Goethe wrote that the artist had "seized all the original gloom" of the work, accompanying "an unruly, restless hero with an equal unruliness in his drawing," even surpassing his own conceptions in these scenes. (Eugène Delacroix (1798–1863), *Mephistopheles and Faust riding in the Night*, illustration for Goethe's *Faust*, 1828; © Bibliothèque des Beaux-Arts, Paris/Lauros/Giraudon/Bridgeman Art Library)

28. The medieval city close to ancient Sparta, where Goethe has Faust—now a knight from the north of Europe—receiving the classical Helen on her return from Troy. Mistra was founded by the Frankish crusaders who took over the South of Greece, but under the Byzantines, who quickly captured it, it became famous as a center of neo-Platonic study; and so a fit setting for Goethe's synthesis of the classical and the medieval. (Nicholas Egon (b. 1921), *The Emperor's Palace*, Mistra, 1998 (w/c and pastel on handmade paper); © Private collection/Bridgeman Art Library)

29. We end our illustrations where we began, with the eternal feminine. Raphael's incomparable Galatea was seen by Goethe on his visit to Rome in 1786. In *Faust, Part Two*, it is such a vision of Galatea riding on the sea in a shell-chariot which leads the weirdly cerebral Homunculus to shatter the vat in which he is encased. He disappears into the sea to begin his long evolution to fully organic human existence, drawn on by the power of love. Raphael (Raffaello Sanzio of Urbino) (1483–1520), *The Triumph of Galatea*, 1512–14 (fresco); © Villa Farnesina, Rome/Giraudon/Bridgeman Art Library)

but Virgil heartens Dante by talk of Beatrice, now the embodiment of divine love and wisdom. Having gone through the fire, the way up is steep, and night is falling. Dante sleeps, and dreams of Leah and Rachel, representing the active and the contemplative life respectively. At dawn, Virgil tells Dante that he can guide him no more. Things now are beyond his understanding. The way is now less steep, the sun is up and the scene is of forest glades of grass, flowers and trees. For the time being, says Virgil, Dante must find his own way, taking his own pleasure for guide, and he invests him with crown and mitre.

Dante is now in the earthly Paradise, the garden of Eden (Canto XX-VIII). A stream bars his way. On the other bank, a beautiful lady, alone and walking like a dancer, is singing and gathering flowers. Smiling at Dante, she tells him that here the air itself scatters seeds around, and that from a divine fountain flow the two rivers of Paradise: Lethe, to erase from men's minds the memory of sin, and Eunoe, to motivate good deeds. This place, she says, is what the poets in ancient times dreamt of as the age of gold; hearing this, Virgil and Statius, two poetic dreamers, smile.

Dante and the lady continue to walk on opposite sides of the river (Canto XXIX). A sudden brightness, becoming a blazing fire, and a sweet melody fill the air (which leads Dante to curse Eve for losing all this to us). Various figures, mainly from the Book of Revelation, then appear in procession: seven gold candlesticks in the sky (= the seven gifts of the spirit: wisdom, understanding, counsel, might, knowledge, piety and fear of the Lord); twenty-four elders, clothed in white (= the twenty-four books of the Old Testament); four living creatures, each with six wings and crowned with green leaves (= the four evangelists); between them a triumphal chariot, drawn by a griffin (= the Church, and the griffin, a combination of eagle and lion, representing the two natures of Christ); three ladies dancing to the right of the chariot (= faith, hope and charity) and four on the right (= the cardinal virtues: wisdom, courage, justice, and prudence); and finally seven old men (= the later books of the New Testament and the Book of Revelation). There is then a clap of thunder, and the procession stops.

From the divine chariot, voices of a hundred elders and angels sing; in the new dawn, clouds of flowers drift down from the hands of angels. Suddenly, in the chariot, is a lady clothed in a white veil, a green cloak and a red dress. Dante turns to Virgil, but Virgil has gone. A voice tells Dante not to weep over this; he has yet to feel the edge of another sword, and to weep for that. It is the veiled lady speaking, who tells Dante to look at her; it is Beatrice. Dante is full of shame. When the angels sing to him to hope in the Lord, his anguish only increases. Beatrice recounts the story of Dante's life; his early promise, and how at the start she sustained him; how he gave himself to another, and after her death took a way which was not right; she visited him in dreams, but he fell lower and lower, until he could be saved only by seeing Hell, which was why she herself went down there. But Lethe can be crossed only if Dante repents and weeps.

At the start of Canto XXXI, Beatrice, from the other side of Lethe, demands an answer from Dante. Dante pours forth tears and confesses that he had gone after false pleasure. Beatrice admonishes him still further, but then tells him to look up. Across the stream, Beatrice appears even more beautiful. Remorse, which has caused Dante to fall to the ground, gives way at last to confidence. Next to him is the first lady he saw by the stream. She plunges him into Lethe and washes him. She then leads him into the dance of the four virtues, and then to the three of faith, hope and charity. They lead Dante to the griffin, and at their pleading, Beatrice unveils herself to him.

In Canto XXXII, Dante, entranced, continues to gaze on Beatrice and her smile, after a gap of ten years; but as he does, the procession wheels around, with Beatrice in the chariot and Statius, Dante, and Matelda (the lady by the stream) following. They reach the Tree of Knowledge, now stripped of leaves and foliage (because of Adam's fall). The griffin then ties the chariot to the Tree, and as a sign of the New Covenant which Christ produced between God and man, the tree reblossoms. Dante falls asleep, but when he wakes, all is transformed. Beatrice is on the ground, with the seven virtues, by the chariot. Beatrice tells Dante to watch, to write about it when he returns. He sees an eagle (= the Roman Empire) swooping on the Tree, tearing its bark and destroying its leaves and fruit (= the persecutions of the Christians in the early Empire). A fox (= heresy) jumps in the chariot (= the Church), but is driven off by Beatrice. The eagle's feathers fall over the chariot (= the Donation of Constantine, giving the Church the western Empire and mixing it up in secular power). At this, a voice from heaven calls out: "O poor bark of mine, how badly art thou freighted." A dragon (= Mahomet) drags part of the chariot away. What is left springs plumage, and seven monstrous heads sprout from the chariot (= greed in the Church for power and wealth). On this monster sits a harlot (= the Queen of Babylon = the Papacy of Dante's time), with a giant (= Philip IV of France) standing beside her, and they are kissing each other. The giant drags the monster/chariot through the wood and out of sight (= removal of the Papacy to Avignon in 1305).

In the final Canto (XXXIII) the seven virtues weep. Beatrice, sighing and sad, commands Dante and Statius to follow them and her. Beatrice prophesies a new power in the land who will slay the harlot and the king, and those who attack the Tree, which has now been robbed twice, will be punished. Dante must tell all this to those "who live that life, which is a race to death." As the effect of his earlier immersion in the river Lethe, however, Dante cannot now remember his estrangement from Beatrice. The little group now stops at the river Eunoe, in which Matelda immerses Dante and Statius in order to revive the good part of his weakened memory:

> I return'd
> From the most holy wave, regenerate,
> E'en as plants renew'd with foliage new
> Pure and made apt for mounting to the stars.

Paradiso

In *Paradiso* Dante is guided by Beatrice, not just as Dante's idealized inamorata, but also as the personification of divine wisdom and love. Through her smile, Dante ascends to the beatific vision of the blessed in Paradise, taken up into God's love. This journey consists of a movement through the nine heavenly spheres of medieval cosmology. These are conceived of as concentric spheres that move around the earth, which is still and at the center. The spheres are those of the moon, the five planets, the sun, the fixed stars, and finally the ninth, the Crystalline (which moves the rest). Outside of and beyond the Crystalline Sphere is the Empyrean, which is beyond matter altogether and outside space and time. While the Empyrean is the true home of God's presence and also of the angels and the blessed, each of the preceding spheres, as well as the Empyrean, is part of Paradise. Each has its own angelic order, and its own redeemed inhabitants, reflecting their earthly careers. How this all works out is explained by Dante as he takes us through Paradise.

Compared to *Inferno* and *Purgatorio, Paradiso* may seem static. There is not the struggle involved in the other parts, and Dante and Beatrice rise effortlessly from one sphere to the next, as if carried along by the force of divine love. Certainly there is in it more philosophy and more dogma than in the other books of the *Commedia,* and less dramatic tension. To some Christians there may also be a question as to the dominance of Beatrice and the comparative absence in *Paradiso* of the figure of Christ, either crucified or glorified. Nevertheless, largely due to the presence of Beatrice and to Dante's own characterization of her, and to what is symbolized by that, *Paradiso* has its own special contemplative, visionary and mystical quality.

In Canto I, after Dante has called on Apollo to help him render what he has seen in Paradise, we find him on the summit of the earthly Paradise. Drawn on by Beatrice, he looks at the sun, and sees things that humans cannot see. Beatrice herself is fixed on the eternal spheres. Dante can only look at her, but is changed within. He passes beyond the human, up into a harmony and a lake of flame and light that he has never before experienced. Beatrice explains that the divine order attracts us upwards, as fire rises to the moon. Having free will, we can turn our original impulse downwards, towards the earth, but his current ascent is no more unnatural than a torrent falling down a mountain.

In Canto II, due to their innate impulse for God, they have risen beyond the mortal world into the First Sphere, that of the moon. Dante asks why there are dark patches on the moon's surface. Emphasizing the continuous activity of the divine from the Empyrean itself and through the spheres, Beatrice explains that this is not because of differences on the moon's surface, but because of the different way in which the divine intelligence is diffused through the universe, according to the nature of each part, just as our own soul is diffused differently through different parts of the body.

In the Sphere of the Moon, the lowest of the heavenly spheres (Canto III), there are redeemed souls who had been inconstant in their vows. They appear to Dante as insubstantial as reflections in water, but Beatrice assures him they are real. One of them speaks to Dante. She is Piccarda, the sister of Forese and Corso Donati (one in Purgatory and the other destined for Hell, *Purgatorio* XXIII and XXIV). She had been a nun, but was forced to marry by Corso. For this blemish she is in the lowest heavenly sphere. Nevertheless she is content. The divine does what is necessary and she, and the desires of all the heavenly souls, are conformed to their place in Paradise:

> In his will is our tranquillity.
> (E'n la sua volontade è nostra pace.)

. . . a line singled out by Matthew Arnold for its beauty and resonance, and perhaps recalling the Augustinian saying "In bona voluntate, pax nobis est" (In good will is our peace). Piccarda also points out Constance, the mother of Frederick II (*Inferno* X) and grandmother of Manfred (*Purgatorio* III), who had suffered a similar fate, but who, like Piccarda, had never inwardly renounced her vow.

Beatrice now (Canto IV) explains to Dante that the souls he sees in the lower spheres are in reality all wholly in the Empyrean (and not, as Plato thought, returned to their original star after their death). They appear to Dante to be in a lower place to symbolize to his human weakness the less exalted state of their blessedness. Moreover, free will would have allowed anyone to resist whatever force was offered to them, as it kept the martyr Lawrence on his gridiron as he was roasted and the hand of the Roman hero Mucius in the flames when he was put to the test. As she speaks, she looks at Dante

with eyes that shot forth sparks
Of love celestial, in such copious stream,
That, virtue sinking in me overpower'd,
I turn'd; and downward bent, confused, my sight.

It is as if Dante needs the experience of Beatrice's love, and its physical embodiment in her eyes and smile, as well as her vision and her teaching.

In Canto V, Beatrice's teaching continues. Vows are sacred, compacts between men and God, and should not be undertaken lightly or perversely (as Agamemnon did over Iphigenia). They should not be lightly renounced or dispensed either, and this leads Beatrice to condemn the wicked greed of professional pardoners. Beatrice falls silent; she turns towards the brightest part of the universe, and in the radiance of more than a thousand splendours, they are drawn up into the Second Sphere, that of Mercury and of service marred by ambition (Cantos VI and VII). The redeemed souls, here and in the subsequent spheres up to but not including the Empyrean, appear as "splendors" or flames, or enclosed in flames.

Justinian, the Roman Emperor from A.D. 527 to 565 and codifier and reformer of Roman law (as he says), is the first to speak. Admitting that initially he had held heretical views about Christ, he later took his way alongside the Church, to fulfil his "great task." He then tells of the growth of Roman might and of the Pax Romana, the peace secured by Rome, from Aeneas right up beyond his own time to Charlemagne, before inveighing against the factionalism of the Guelphs and the Ghibellines and the French disruptions in Italy. In his account, Justinian highlights the peace wrought by Augustus before the birth of Christ, the crucifixion of Christ under the third Caesar (Tiberius)—by which vengeance was executed for the wrath of Divine Justice—and how Titus, in destroying the Temple at Jerusalem, executed vengeance on that vengeance. Thus Christian salvation history is seen as inextricably bound up with Roman history. At the same time, in Justinian's whole orientation a model is developed of the correct relationship between Church and state, equal but different, and co-operating in their different spheres. And, doubtless with his own fate in mind, Dante has Justinian ending his discourse by pointing out one Romeo, a wise Provençal courtier, who, inspired as Justinian was by heavenly justice and its sweet harmony, nevertheless died poor and old, "begging his life by morsels."

Canto VII has Beatrice giving her own account of the double vengeance alluded to by Justinian, and which deeply puzzles Dante. By abusing his freedom, the first man fell; mankind lay sick for many ages, banned from Paradise until, in an act of love, God united himself with human nature and suffered on the cross the penalty for human sin, which pleased both God and the Jews. In punishing Christ's human nature, God's retribution was just, but in punishing the divine nature, the Jews themselves deserved retribution. God himself needed to do this, because after man had sinned, man

> ever lack'd the means
> Of satisfaction, for he could not stoop
> Obeying, in humility so low,
> As high, he, disobeying, thought to soar.

Though man could not pay his own satisfaction, God could simply have forgiven the fault; but for the Son of God to take on mortal flesh in this way, and to be punished himself for the fault, shows an even greater love. Only this way could dignity and strength be restored to human nature, and man become able to raise himself again. And in closing her discourse, Beatrice refers to the human soul, which like the angels and the heavenly spheres is immortal, ever thirsting after God, in contrast to the mortality and corruptibility of the earth and the other animals.

Cantos VIII and IX take us into the Third Sphere, that of Venus and of love marred by wantonness. Beatrice becomes ever more beautiful as they rise among the new dance of divine lights. One steps near, and reveals that he is an old friend of Dante, Charles Martel, who had been the son of the King of Hungary and the heir to the kingdoms of Naples and Provence, but who died before succeeding and was thus unable to prevent the evil his brother went on to cause. Charles explains to Dante that different functions on earth require different natural gifts, ending with a dig at his brothers, one of whom who was fitted for the crown and became a priest, while the other, originally a priest, became the evil ruler he has already complained of. It is unclear why Charles Martel is in the Sphere of Venus, but this is not the case with Cunizza, the next spirit. She had been the sister of Ezzelino, a cruel tyrant in Hell (*Inferno* XII). Overwhelmed by Venus, she had been the lover of Sordello (*Purgatorio* VI), among many others, but had also performed many acts of kindness for which she was redeemed. Next to her is Folco, a troubadour lover, who became a bishop. After pointing out Rahab, the harlot in Joshua who saved the Hebrew spies, Folco inveighs against Florence (where florins were invented) and the Roman Papacy, who together neglect the Gospels and the Doctors of the Church, and are concerned only with money-making.

After the Third, the spheres contain people who have not been marred by specific faults. The Fourth Sphere (Cantos X–XIV) is that of the sun, the abode of thinkers and theologians. They ascend there without Dante being aware of it, any more than one is aware of the start of a thought before it comes. The sun itself is brighter than can be imagined. Dante is so entranced and given up to the love of God that Beatrice is eclipsed; but she only smiles joyfully. Around them are flashing lights, which dance and sing around the travellers in a crown. One of them is Saint Thomas Aquinas, the greatest of the medieval theologians, who leads twelve others, including Boethius and Siger of Brabant, in life an opponent of Aquinas and charged with heresy, but here singing with him and the others in harmony.

Aquinas next explains that Providence had ordained two princes to guide us on earth, one seraphic in fervency, the other in wisdom a cherubic light. These are Saint Francis and Saint Dominic, the founders of the Franciscans and the Dominicans respectively. Aquinas praises Francis as one wedded to poverty and blessed with the stigmata, but laments the fact that his own order, the Dominicans, had since the time of Dominic himself fallen into greed.

At this point, Saint Bonaventure, an early Franciscan, steps forward to repay the compliment. He praises Dominic as the institutor of Christian learning and the scourge of error, but, in symmetrical fashion, goes on to lament the current divisions among the Franciscans. He does, though, point out various Franciscan saints, who are shining around him, among them Abbot Giovacchino (Joachim) of Fiore, praised for being endowed with "soul prophetic." This is significant because Joachim, an immensely influential figure among followers of esoteric teaching, had been condemned by the Church in the person of Pope Boniface VIII, Dante's great enemy, with a place reserved for him in Hell. The Church objected to Joachim's doctrine of the three ages, and in particular for what he said about the Third Age: the ages were that of the Law (the Old Testament and God the Father); that of Faith (the New Testament and Christ); and the age of Enlightenment, in which there would be no further need for the Church or other institutions of religion (the "Eternal Gospel," referred to in the Book of Revelation, and the Holy Spirit). If Dante did not share the precise hopes and expectations of Joachim and his followers, he certainly longed for a new and better age.

The stars dance round and Aquinas now resumes his own speech. Everything, mortal and immortal, is part of the plan which God, in loving, creates, right down to things which are no more than "brief contingencies." In this way, the diversity and multiplicity of things are created, and all, even the most humble, are part of the divine system. At times in this process, nature works like an imperfect artist with a faltering hand; in the case of human nature, the full light of "primal virtue" shone only twice, in the cases of Adam and Christ. Aquinas now praises Solomon as an exemplar of vision and of kingly judgment, in contrast to poor philosophers, heretics, and those who pass hasty judgements on others. Solomon himself then speaks of the resurrection of the body, after which the blessed will be seen in their true forms, but even brighter than they are now. The light already there is augmented by yet more lights and, possibly in a reference to Joachim's Third Age, by what Dante calls the "sparkling of the Holy Ghost." Dante and Beatrice now ascend into the Fifth Sphere, that of Mars and of Christian soldiers and martyrs. Dante sees an incommunicable vision of Christ on the cross, white against the red of Mars, itself surrounded by the lights of the soldiers and martyrs and their singing.

In Canto XV, one of the spirits reaches out to Dante with the same affection with which Anchises greeted Aeneas in the underworld. It is Cacciaguida, Dante's own great-great-grandfather, who died in the Second Crusade (1147–49). As with the early Rome, recalled by the reference to Aeneas and by Cacciaguida himself, in Cacciaguida's time, Florence was peaceful, sober and chaste. The people were poor and pious and the ladies unpainted. But things started to decline when people from outside started moving into the city, and Cacciaguida tells of how some of the ancient families started to become corrupt, until the murder of Buondelmonte, for jilting a girl in 1215, which initiated the continuing strife between the Guelphs and the Ghibellines. Dante asks his ancestor about his own fate. He will soon be exiled from Florence at the prompting of Pope Boniface, in Rome, where throughout the day "gainful merchandise is made of Christ":

> Thou shalt prove
> How salt the savour is of other's bread;
> How hard the passage, to descend and climb
> By other's stairs.

He will be dishonored by those with whom he falls, so much so that isolation will be an honor. He will stay first with the Lord of Verona, and will befriend his younger brother Can Grande, who, before Henry VII is betrayed by the Avignon Pope, will show heroism and generosity. But Dante himself should not envy his enemies, for his life will long outlive their treacheries; and Cacciaguida tells him that what he has to do is to make plain the vision of the journey he is on, for the "vital nourishment" of those who will hear:

> The cry thou raisest
> Shall, as the wind doth, smite the proudest summits;
> Which is of honour no light argument.

And for that telling, in the deep, on the mountain and in the realm of Paradise, the spirits he has been shown are those who are famous.

In Canto XVIII, Dante tastes his bitterness. Beatrice smiles and tells him to attend to the spirits that Cacciaguida is going to present, all fighters for faith, including Joshua, Judas Maccabaeus and Charlemagne. As they and

Cacciaguida withdraw, Dante and Beatrice are raised to the Sixth Sphere, that of Jupiter, of justice and good rulers. The spirit lights there gradually spell out the words DILIGITE JUSTITIAM QUI IUDICATIS TERRAM—"love justice, ye that judge the earth." The spirits then form themselves into an eagle. Dante prays for divine action against the contemporary Church, which buys and sells in the temple whose walls were built with miracles and martyrdom, and which refuses the sacraments to those who need them.

In Canto XIX the souls, still formed into the eagle (representing earthly justice and the good empire), sing, as one voice, just as they are formed into one figure, that being just and merciful, "I [that is, the souls formed into the eagle speaking as one voice] am exalted to this height of glory." Dante, speaking of the unfathomability of divine justice, now asks about the fate of the good, unbaptised pagan, on the banks of the Indus, say, who wants to do good. "Where is the justice that condemns him?" The eagle reasserts the unfathomability of the eternal judgment, and also that no one who does not believe in Christ either before or after his crucifixion will be allowed into Paradise (before allows in the good Jews, who awaited and anticipated Jesus). However, many Christian rulers have been and are far less just than the good pagans. The eagle now proceeds to individuate its eye and eyebrow into those who make it up. Shining in the pupil of the eye is David, while the eyebrow is composed of Trajan (the good emperor from *Purgatorio* X, who was supposed to have been restored to life after his death, so as to receive baptism), Hezekiah, the Emperor Constantine (his "donation" notwithstanding), William the Good of Naples, and the Trojan Ripheus from *The Aeneid* (Book Two, line 246), where he is described as "the most righteous" and "the greatest lover of justice." He was so righteous that he firmly believed in the coming Christian redemption, and the three ladies of *Purgatorio* XXIX (faith, hope, and charity) waited more than a thousand years after his death to baptize him. But, the eagle tells Dante, mortals should refrain from making judgments about divine predestination, because we have scant knowledge of the workings of the First Cause and do not know the numbers of those chosen. Trajan and Ripheus, the pagans who had been saved, dance to these words, as a pair of twinkling eyes.

In Canto XXI, as they ascend to the Seventh Sphere, Beatrice does not smile. She tells Dante that, were she to smile now, he would be burned like Semele, for her beauty increases as they ascend. They move into the Sphere of Saturn, that of the contemplatives, and named after the god who presided over the classical age of gold. Dante sees a ladder going up, far out of sight, with the lights of a multitude of spirits moving up and down and around it. (We learn later that this is Jacob's ladder, populated with angels, in the Book of Genesis.) For once Dante hears no music of the spheres; a spirit explains that this is for the same reason that he does not see Beatrice's smile. Dante asks him why he has been chosen to speak to him, but he warns Dante not to question the ways of divine Providence. The spirit then explains that he is Saint Peter Damian, a famous Benedictine ascetic and contemplative from the eleventh century, who, late in life, was forced to become a cardinal of the Church. He then inveighs against the greed and gluttony of the "modern shepherds." At this there is a tremendous shout from all the flames wheeling about. Dante is terrified, and Beatrice calms him. Saint Benedict, who founded the monastery of Monte Cassino, now speaks of his early foundation, of Jacob's ladder leading up to the last sphere where all will be fulfilled, but which no one from earth now attempts to climb, and of the current corruption of his and the other religious orders, all of which have sunk far below the ideals of their founders. Beatrice and Dante then ascend the ladder themselves, to the Fixed Stars. Looking back through the seven spheres they had passed through, Dante sees the earth, so pitiful in comparison, then all the other spheres, before turning back to Beatrice's eyes.

Cantos XXIII–XXVII take us into the Eighth Sphere, that of the Fixed Stars and the Church Triumphant, the part of the Church consisting of those saved in Paradise. Beatrice points out to Dante the hosts of those who are triumphant. As he looks at the thousands of lights, he sees the sun (Christ) which gives them all light. He is dazzled. Beatrice explains that he is being overcome by the wisdom and power which has opened the way for him between heaven and earth, but he must not resist. His soul breaks out, as lightning from a cloud, in a manner he cannot remember. Beatrice commands him to open his eyes, so as to see her and her smile as they really are, but he cannot describe what he saw. Beatrice then tells him to look on the rose in which the divine Word was made flesh, Mary herself. He sees many splendid lights, without any longer seeing the source of their light. Mary descends as a sapphire, "the beautiful sapphire, with which the sky is so brightly ensapphired." She is encircled by angelic love (the Angel Gabriel), which, with all the other lights, sings her praises. As Mary rises higher again, to the strains of *Regina Coeli* (Queen of Heaven), sung by the remaining lights, among whom is Saint Peter, Dante loses sight of her.

Saint Peter now questions Dante on the nature of faith, as in an examination in the medieval schools (universities). Faith, says Dante, is the substance of things hoped for and the evidence of things not seen, though backed up by miracles. After further scholastic probing from his examiner, Dante moves from the realm of sober intellectual conviction to a passionate expression of his faith in the one God, alone and eternal, who, unmoved himself, makes the whole of heaven move with love and desire. Saint Peter leaves him, but not before showing his approval by circling his brow three times.

Dante now laments over his exile, and looks forward to being honored once more in the place where he was baptized (which never happened, of course). Another light, Saint James, approaches Dante, telling him to take hope. Beatrice replies that Dante is filled with hope, which Dante then defines as a certain expectation of future glory, springing from divine grace and earlier merit. Dante's hope is above all for resurrection of soul and body ("double raiment") in the life to come. All around him the lights sing and dance, when a third splendour shines out in his direction. Beatrice tells Dante it is Saint John, the beloved disciple. Dante looks for his body, but is only dazzled by the brightness. Saint John tells him that his body is still in the earth; so far only two lights, Christ and Mary, have ascended in bodily form. Dante turns to look at Beatrice, but can see nothing. He is blind.

Still blind, Dante is now questioned by Saint John on love. The good, says Dante, once known, fires love, according to the amount of good in it. So, to those who understand, the preeminent good, from whom every other good is but a beam from its light, must move us with love the most. Saint John asks Dante to name the teeth by which this love bites him, and Dante replies that they are the world's existence and his own, and Christ's death, which have drawn him away from the sea of sick love to the shore of a just love. At this his sight is restored, and along with the apostles, he sees a fourth light approaching. Beatrice tells him to see Adam within. Questioned by Dante, Adam speaks of the Fall, caused not by eating the apple, but by the pride which underlay the act; of his expulsion from the earthly Paradise, and of the long wait for redemption in the First Circle; and also of the transitory nature of all earthly things, including even his own language, extinct before Nimrod's people built the Tower of Babel.

The color around Dante now changes to a fiery red. Peter denounces his current successor, Boniface VIII, for turning his tomb (Rome) into a sewer of blood and filth. Beatrice blushes for shame. Peter goes on: he and the other martyrs did not shed their blood in order for their successors to create schisms, or to wage war on Christians, or to enrich themselves. But as with Scipio, who saved Rome for the glory of the world, Providence will bring succor soon, as will Dante himself by his words. The spirits in flames ascend, and Beatrice and Dante look down on the earth, seeing how far they have travelled from it.

Dante looks even more rapturously on Beatrice, seeing the divine light which shone on him from her smiling face. Together they ascend into the Ninth Sphere, the Crystalline, the Primum Mobile (or the first thing moved) and abode of angels, which, as Beatrice explains, moves all else in the universe and is itself moved only by the Divine Mind. By contrast, she says, humans as they grow up lose their innocence to covetousness, greed, infidelity and corruption. We should not wonder at this, given that there is no one to rule; but there will be a time of renewal before long.

In Canto XXVIII, at first Dante gazes into Beatrice's eyes. When he turns away he sees a tiny but intense fixed point of light. Around it spin nine circles of fire, the circles of the angelic orders. The innermost is the one which is most inspired by the truth of the divine spark, and it moves fastest because it is closest to the burning love which moves it. (Notice how, for Dante, the vision of the divine and its truth go along with the love it inspires and which we have for it.) Dante asks how it is that in the sensory world the outermost spheres are the most divine, whereas here the reverse is true. Beatrice explains that the spheres increase in size according to their degree of blessedness. This sphere, which moves all the others, is physically the greatest, and from the physical point of view the most powerful angelic circle is at the outermost circle of the sphere. But—and here physical space is giving way to spiritual reality—the most loving angels, and the greatest in power and intelligence (the Seraphim), are the innermost within the Crystalline Sphere itself and closest to the fixed point at the center, and so on through the nine categories of angel.

In Canto XXIX, Beatrice gazes on the fixed point at the centre, and begins to explain the process of creation. God is Eternal Love, subsisting purely in Himself, but reveals Himself in new love. He created the angels, which were pure mind and pure act, and purely passive formless matter, which was given form and activity through the angelic spirits to become the world we know—a combination of forming activity and receptive passivity. Soon after the creation, out of pride, a section of the angels rebelled, fell, and convulsed the earth, while the rest continued in loving submission to God, and, through their intelligence, continued to move the other spheres. The good angels never turn away from God's face, but we humans below are carried away in our philosophising by love of appearances. Forgetting the blood that the divine scripture cost, and the humble spirit in which it should be approached, our preachers and theologians silence the Gospel with idle tales and preach with jests and jibes, all the while growing fat themselves. The angels, though, in their countless numbers, receive the radiance of the primal light according to their various conditions, and reflecting and diffusing it without destroying its unity.

The four final Cantos (XXX–XXXIII) present the Tenth and final sphere, the Empyrean, the heaven that is pure light, "intellectual light, full of love." In ascending, Dante looks on Beatrice, but even the memory of it dispossesses his mind. Her beauty now defeats his artistry, as they prepare to see Paradise and all its forces as one, and its inhabitants in their bodily form as they will be at the Last Judgment. As happens to all those who enter

Paradise, Dante is bathed in a dazzling light, rendering everything else invisible. He then sees a river of light, flowing between banks with all the colours of spring. Living sparks jump in and out of the river. To see the truth of all this, Dante himself has to bathe his eyes in the river. The river now becomes an endless circle of light, reflected from the summit of the Primum Mobile, which draws from it its life and power. Above the light, Dante sees those of us who have been saved forming into a huge eternal rose. Within the rose is the assembly of the saved, its seats almost full. Beatrice tells Dante that by the time he gets there, Henry VII will already be there. By contrast, the Pope of Henry's time (Clement V) will go to the Eighth Circle of Hell, with Boniface VIII even deeper.

Round the white rose of the blessed, the angels, with faces of living flame and wings of gold, fly like a swarm of bees, dipping in and out of the great flower, but without disturbing its splendor or its unity. Dante is struck dumb, as a barbarian in imperial Rome. After he has grasped the general form of Paradise, he turns to Beatrice for enlightenment; but she is gone, her place taken by the figure of an old man, Saint Bernard of Clairvaux (a monk famous for his mystical devotion to the Virgin). Beatrice has sent him to replace her, and she may be seen enthroned high above. Dante sees her, and thanks her; Beatrice smiles in reply, and turns her face back to the eternal fountain. Saint Bernard tells Dante to look up yet higher. In a scene of indescribable and unimaginable beauty, he sees Mary, the Queen of Heaven, surrounded by more than a thousand angels.

Saint Bernard now explains to Dante the layout of the rose, picking out some of the saints enthroned within. On one side, Eve is at Mary's feet, and below her Rachel with Beatrice. Lower still are Sarah, Rebecca, Judith and other Old Testament figures who had faith in the coming of Christ. John the Baptist is on a throne opposite that of Mary, and on his side of Paradise are those who "look'd to Christ already come," such as Francis, Benedict, and Augustine. Lower are children who died too young to have any real choice, but who are saved nonetheless. Grace is bestowed variously, at God's pleasure, but not without cause, Bernard says, before telling Dante to look once more on the face of Mary. Dante sees joy raining down on her, brought by angels, including Gabriel, who announced Christ's incarnation to her. Close to Mary are Adam and Peter, John the Evangelist (who, as author of the Book of Revelation, foresaw the travails of the Church) and Moses, Saint Anne (the mother of Mary) and Saint Lucy, who sent Beatrice to Dante. But Dante must now ascend to the Primal Love itself.

Bernard first prays to Mary, through whom all grace comes, to assist Dante to rise yet higher to his final salvation. Mary looks at Bernard and the Eternal Light, and grants the prayer. Bernard tells Dante to look up, but he is doing so already. Praying for the grace to recount a little of what he had seen then, Dante tells us that in looking into the Eternal Light he saw everything that there is, and which is scattered through the universe, enclosed within and fused together by love as one simple light. Looking at that light, which contains all that is good, it is impossible to turn one's gaze elsewhere. As he looks, the single radiance he sees is transformed into three circles of three colors, two reflecting each other, as in a double rainbow, and the third as fire breathed forth from both (Father, Son and Holy Ghost). This is the Eternal Light, which lives in itself, and which knows itself, and which, so knowing, loves and smiles on itself. As he muses on this circling, he sees within, painted in its own color, our image: a human likeness (just as, much earlier, Saint Augustine had seen the human form as that element of creation closest to the Godhead). Dante wishes to see how the human image fits in the circle (Christ in God, God in Christ, humanity and the Godhead inextricably mingled). His own power of thought is insufficient, but his wish is nevertheless granted in a flash of insight.

> Here vigour fail'd the towering fantasy;
> But yet the will roll'd onward, like a wheel
> In even motion, by the love impell'd,
> That moves the sun in heaven and all the stars.
> (All'alta fantasia qui mancò possa;
> ma gia volgeva il mio disio e 'l velle,
> si come rota ch'igualmente è mossa
> l'amor che move il sole e l'altre stelle.)

Dante: Summing Up

To someone who has just finished reading the *Divine Comedy,* it may seem extraordinary to realize that the 100 Cantos consist of little more than 13,000 or 14,000 lines. For the *Comedy* as a whole is as monumental and as fertile and teeming with characters as anything in European literature. If one were to claim that Dante and Shakespeare were the two most imaginative and creative writers our civilization has produced, one would be saying something almost too obvious to need repeating. Yet the speed and concision and brevity of the Italian is equally amazing, as Carlyle forcefully recognized:

> Tacitus is not briefer, more condensed . . . It is strange with what a
> sharp decisive grace he snatches the true likeness of a matter: cuts into
> the matter as with a pen of fire, Plutus, the blustering giant, collapses at
> Virgil's rebuke; it is "as the sails sink, the mast being suddenly broken."
> Or that poor Brunetto Latini, with his cotto aspetto, "face baked,"

parched brown and lean; and the "fiery snow" that falls on them there, a "fiery snow without wind," slow, deliberate, never ending! Or the lids of those Tombs; square sarcophaguses in that silent, dim-burning Hell, each with its Soul in torment; the lids laid open there; they are to be shut at the day of Judgement, through Eternity. And how Farinata rises; and how Cavalcante falls at hearing of his Son, and the past tense "fue"![12]

And as well as Dante's speed and incisiveness is the beauty and mellifluousness of his poetry, something one is bound to lose in translation. Dante's style is indeed a sweet style, which does not mean that it is not strong and forceful as well. Even for those with little or no Italian, it is well worth getting hold of a dual language edition of the *Comedy,* just to get something of a feel for its language.

The *Divine Comedy* is many things. Apart from the hundreds of characters delineated in it, it is a political treatise. It is a compendium of medieval Christian thought, philosophical and theological. It is a work of much and great passion, and in many ways deeply personal. It is perhaps the closest thing we have to the full elaboration of an all but ineffable mystical vision. It is all this, and much more. But the detail and the themes never detract from the architecture of the whole. Like the great gothic cathedrals which were contemporary with Dante, all the richness and diversity is held and unified within a tremendous soaring and sweeping structure, to which every detail contributes, but without compromising its line or its visionary purpose.

We should also be aware that, like the great cathedrals it resembles, the *Divine Comedy* is built up on numerical patterns and relationships. Each of the domains that Dante visits is divided into nine sections: circles, terraces and spheres respectively. The nine spheres of Paradise, of course, correspond to the nine choirs of angels. Each of the books of the *Comedy* consists of thirty-three Cantos (excluding the very first introductory one), and thirty-three is the number of years Christ lived on earth. The rhyme form that Dante used is based on the number three, which for the medievals is the sign of the Trinity. And nine, the number underlying the Dantean geography—and hence the geography of the cosmos—is not just the square of the Trinitarian three. It is also, Dante tells us in his *Vita Nuova,* the number preeminently associated with Beatrice: "this lady was accompanied by the number nine, to give to understand that she was nine; that is a miracle whose root is the wondrous Trinity alone." So even in construction and form, the *Divine Comedy* mirrors the reality of the Christian world.

Further, Beatrice is, as we have already noted, not just a beatified person, but also a symbol for Dante of divine wisdom and love. Nearly two centuries later, Botticelli (whose illustrations to Dante are in themselves a masterpiece) made his Venus and his Primavera signs of divine love and life. This symbolism is often taken as a manifestation of the neo-Platonism which was dominating the Florence of the Medici, according to which earthly beauty was a veil of a deeper spiritual reality, but way before that the great Florentine poet was thinking and operating in the same way.

Dante is, of course, highly original, and in the invention particularly of Virgil and even more of Beatrice, his theological and philosophical vision is deeply personal. Beatrice and (to a lesser extent) Mary are as much or even more the embodiments of God's love as the crucified Christ for Dante, but the crucified Christ is always there, and always presupposed if not always in Dante's foreground. Unlike Blake, say, Dante is never cranky or idiosyncratic. He is held within a strong and vibrant tradition of thought and practice and orthodoxy, which prevents the *Comedy* from ever being quirky or hermetic. That said, orthodoxy does not prevent Dante from showing considerable sympathy for the ecclesiastically suspect Joachim of Fiore. But then Dante was never an uncritical supporter of the institutions of the Roman Church. He was indeed among their severest critics, all the more forceful for coming from within a genuine and deep orthodoxy and understanding of the Christian tradition, from which he never significantly deviates.

As far as Dante's own development of that tradition is concerned, particularly notable is the sense that Dante gives to the need for incarnation. Divine wisdom is Beatrice and her smile, and no abstract or bloodless philosophical category. The blessed spirits are visualized as both eagle and rose, in both cases still individuals, but, in contrast to the spirits in Hell, with their individuality purified and refined, and part of a greater coherence held together by divine love. And there can be few more striking and haunting expressions of the divine itself as intensely personal than the image in the final Canto of a face—of Christ, of man, of a human person—somehow within and behind the triple arc of the divine light. The world for Dante is suffused not just with the divine in an abstract sense. It is suffused with the personality of the divine. The divine for Dante is personal, albeit eternal and unchanging; a mystery no doubt, verging on contradiction, but one that Dante's thought and image helps to elucidate and to embody.

We can certainly and legitimately see Dante as a medieval figure, but perhaps we should also see him as a Renaissance figure too. Like his near-contemporary Thomas Aquinas, who brought Aristotelian philosophy into Christian and synthesized the two, Dante synthesizes classical learning with the biblical and Christian tradition. This is not just in his choice of Virgil as his initial guide and mentor, and also his frequent shadowing of *The Aeneid* within the *Comedy*, inspired and moving as these things are; but also in the numerous other characters he introduces and refers to from classical poetry and myth, mainly from Latin sources, but not exclusively so. We feel in reading the *Comedy* that its author was familiar with the classics, and in many ways lived and breathed their spirit, and was inspired by them.

Reference to the pagan influence on Dante brings us to the most ticklish question for the modern reader of Dante: Hell itself and the exclusion from Paradise of pagans, with only two exceptions who do not even include Virgil. Personally I find the First Circle, where the good pagans live in desire but without hope, harder to take than Hell itself. For those condemned to Hell actually embody the state of their souls in life, when governed by their specific sins: thieves like snakes, makers of discord themselves slashed about, the gluttonous wallowing in a bog, those obsessed with money bowed down with heavy weights, the violent simmering in a river of boiling blood, hypocrites also weighed down beneath their garments, traitors as ice-cold as their hearts, gnawing and being gnawed, the lustful caught on an endless and obsessive tornado of their desires, and so on. Even for those who have no truck with the notion of eternal damnation, Dante certainly gives us vivid images of the sins and of their corrupting effects.

Even so, by no means all the sinners in Hell seem, from what Dante tells us, to merit their punishment, either in this life or the next. It would be, as Carlyle observed, "a paltry notion" that *Inferno* is "a poor splenetic impotent terrestrial libel, putting those into Hell whom he [Dante] could not be avenged-upon on earth." Some of the damned Dante clearly likes or admires, such as Francesca (who might, as a child, have sat on the poet's knee) and Brunetto Latini (his revered teacher). They are in Hell, but being there are, in Carlyle's view, pitied by Dante; but with the pity that only one who knows rigor can bestow. And two of Dante's most memorable characters from the whole *Comedy* are Ulysses and Ugolino, who seem strangely out of place where they are, the one a genuinely heroic figure, and the other, as pictured by Dante anyway, more a victim than the worst of sinners, in the Ninth Circle. Why, we may ask, are these four characters in Hell at all, given that others just as bad or worse are in Purgatory or Paradise?

We will get no direct answer from Dante, either to this question or to the more general question about the virtuous pagans. And perhaps, from Dante's own perspective, we should not expect an answer. We know that love rules the universe, but we are not to expect to follow its workings in detail. Hell is not the whole story. And we should remember the inscription over the gate of Hell: hard as it may be for moderns to accept on an intellectual level, for Dante what made the gate were the divine power, wisdom and love. The entry to Hell must be seen in the light of Paradise and the final Cantos of the *Comedy,* and this is signaled by Dante at the very gate of Hell. His genius may get us even as unbelievers to see and feel what it might be like to take all together, from the lowest to the highest, from the smallest to the greatest, from the least significant to the most, all as expressions of the love which rules the universe.

And while in Hell the damned are strongly individuated and strongly expressive of their sins, almost as the incarnations of their sins with their very punishments part of their essence, in Purgatory there is a subtle difference. The punishing fire is not part of the sinner, but something apart from him or her, purifying and burning away the sin and the bad self, so much so that in Canto XXVI, Arnault the Provençal poet actually willingly dives back into the purifying fire, "Poi s'ascose nel foco che gli affina," a line quoted to great effect by T. S. Eliot both at the end of *The Waste Land* and in his great essay on Dante which he wrote in 1929.[13] In *Purgatorio,* too, in the final Cantos we see Dante himself undergoing his own refinement, his leaving of Virgil and the secular world and his initially painful encounter with Beatrice, in many ways the most personal part of the whole poem, in which the husk of Dante's personality is hollowed out prior to entry into Paradise. And in Paradise itself, the mystical vision draws us and Dante continually upwards, in a succession of ever more brilliant visions of the state of the blessed. That, Dante is showing us, should be enough for us, individually and collectively. For the rest, "e'n la sua volontade è nostra pace."

In considering the divine economy of hell and heaven, we should also re-member that for the medievals the awfulness of hell was always outweighed by the consolation offered by the mercy of God, and was always seen in that context. An instructive parallel here might be the numerous medieval representations of the Apocalypse, such as the great tapestry at Angers. The terrible punishments meted out to the wicked are always there, graphically enough, but in contrast to more modern representations of apocalyptic vi-sions and the horrors of hell, the symbols which dominate in the end are those of the New Jerusalem and of the crystal river of life. The whole is always presided over by the figure of Christ as the Lamb, meek, kind, vul-nerable, but always triumphant and the leader of the elect. There is indeed a closer parallel here, for in the Apocalypse the figure of John the Evangelist makes a visionary journey and is instructed to regale the seven churches with what he sees, good news in the sense of the ultimate vindication of good over evil and the redressing of wrongs by the divine mercy. Dante goes on his own revelatory journey, also with instructions to report back on what he has seen, and the whole *Comedy* is also presided over by the saving mercy of God, as personified here by the figure of Beatrice. We misconstrue both the Apocalypse and Dante if we do not see everything in the context of the wis-dom, love, and mercy of God, and if we do not see the messages they convey as consolatory through and through, precisely as encompassing sin, struggle, suffering, purgation, and the ever-present reality of damnation, all things we moderns will tend to deny or water down. In doing so, from the point of view of Dante and the medievals, we will also water down the meaning both of salvation and of the divine mercy.

We should also remember that Dante's final vision is of the love which moves the sun and the other stars, and by which his own desire and will are now moved, as by a wheel which spins with even motion. It is a vision of harmony above all, a vision with deep roots in both Greek and Christian thought (as Simone Weil has pointed out), and which surely underlies the *Comedy* as a whole. Harmony is the reconciliation of opposites, and Christianity, particularly of the type espoused by Dante, is a doctrine of multiple harmony. Creation itself, on this view, is an initial act of disharmony on the part of the Creator, in which the unity of the Godhead is disturbed, and in which there is now matter (and all that that implies) as well as divinity. Creation involves a renunciation by God of his unity and plenitude. As Simone Weil dramatically puts it: "the act of Creation is not an act of power. It is an abdication. Through this act a kingdom is established other than the kingdom of God. The reality of this world is constituted by the mechanism of matter and the autonomy of rational creatures. It is a kingdom from which God has withdrawn, God having renounced being its king can enter it only as a beggar."[14] This may be over-stark for some Christians—who will recall that in Mark's Gospel (1:15), creation is invited back into God's kingdom—and maybe for Dante too; and maybe it is more accurate as a description of the world after the Fall, when humans and the rest of creation outside the Garden of Eden (or Earthly Paradise) become subject to all the pains and ills of mortality without remission. For the orthodox, after Christ's redemptive sacrifice, creation is drawn back into God's kingdom. Nonetheless, even if Weil's description is not wholly accurate regarding the creation in its pure essence, all would agree that there is a partial withdrawal of God in creation. There has to be. God has to allow space for other things to be, including living and freely willing things, and in allowing this space God has to withdraw, to be invisible. And, with God withdrawn and invisible, the world will on the surface look to creatures as if God is not there. Faith, grace or some moral or aesthetic insight is needed to see behind the mechanisms of nature.

In the creation of the world, there are now things and, in the case of mankind, separate wills in the universe. There is in the world disharmony, suffering and evil. And in *Inferno* there is nothing but the mechanisms of nature, conceived of as the inevitable working out of sinful karma, and the autonomous wills of the damned. But, in the Incarnation and the Passion,

God as Christ takes on the nature of a suffering, abandoned person, a beggar. God becomes man so that man might become God; God's face is human (as Dante shows us), and the harmony which was initially fractured by the Creation itself is restored, partially now, and only completely to be restored at the Last Judgment. Even the vision granted to Dante, and conveyed to us in *Paradiso,* is of the cosmos before the Last Judgment, when the blessed are still not in their final resurrected form. Only at the Last Judgment will that which had been broken by the sin of Adam, and partially restored by Christ's sacrifice and resurrection, be fully restored. Only then, at the end of time—after all the labours and sufferings to which we humans and the world itself are still subject, even after Christ's redemptive work—will the cosmos be fully and lovingly and triumphantly vindicated.

In Dante's vision, human beings are centers of activity and will, and many of these never harmonize their will with that of the divine love. Here, I think we can see the true nature of the sin of Paolo and Francesca; they did decenter their own wills, but only to center them on another, limited, self, and hence their eternal punishment forever bound up in each other. On the other hand, those souls in Purgatory and Paradise have their own will and intelligence harmonized with that of the divine love, as we see in the images of the eagle and the celestial rose, to which all conform, but without losing their own individuality. And, as Dante says, in the beatific vision, everything formerly scattered through the universe is bound together by love, and that which is elsewhere imperfect is here perfected. From Dante's perspective, love ruling all, we have to take this to imply that all is somehow taken up here and transformed and harmonized, including evil things; or, if that way of looking at things is inconsistent with the existence of the Inferno that Dante has travelled through, we have to see *Inferno* and those in it as part of that which goes to make up the divine order, here revealed with both divine and human countenance, moving and infusing all with love.

Dante's genius as a poet and as a thinker is not just that he develops and expounds that position in a theoretical way. It is that he gives even to those of us who do not agree with the position, and who are still troubled by the damned and the unbaptized, some sense of what it might be to live with Dante's faith, and to experience the spiritual life which follows from it. Above all, in his final Canto, God is presented not as a remote philosophical First Cause but rather as present in the whole of creation and infusing all, from the smallest things to the greatest, with the power and attraction of his love, encompassing and embracing them all, and where we will let him, burning away the defects of personality and individuality until, in our humanity, we are at one with the divine, just as the divine is itself revealed as ultimately having a human form and face.

Chaucer
The Canterbury Tales

*Geoffrey Chaucer, a Londoner, lived from around 1343 until 1400,
writing* The Canterbury Tales *towards the end of his life. At the end
of the fourteenth century, twenty-nine pilgrims set off from Southwark in London to Canterbury Cathedral, the shrine of the saint and
martyr Thomas Becket. It is a highly diverse group, full of strongly individual characters. On their journey, to pass the time, the pilgrims recount tales, twenty-four in all, of many types and styles, from tragedy,
high romance and delightful fancy through the pious and the moral
to the most earthy and bawdy. But over and above the tales they tell,
Chaucer also gives us incisive portraits of the tellers themselves, and
of their own reactions to each other. In the tales and in the portraits
of their tellers, over and above illustrating the more enduring traits
of vice and virtue, Chaucer gives us a fascinating picture of medieval
society, particularly of the state and influence of the Church and of the
position of women at the time. Although the pilgrims are on a religious
pilgrimage and ultimately—like Dante—en route (as Chaucer tells
us through his Parson) for the heavenly Jerusalem, Chaucer's interest,
and ours—in contrast to Dante's—is fixed firmly on the engagingly
earthly characters encountered on the earthly journey.*

G eoffrey Chaucer was born around 1343, in London. He was the son
of a wine merchant, and became a page to the Countess of Ulster. He
fought in France, as a squire, was captured in 1359, and was ransomed by the
King in 1360. In between visits to Ireland and Spain, he married a lady in
the court of the Queen. It is not known how happy this marriage was. There
was also an incident in which Chaucer was accused of rape. He campaigned
in France again in 1369 and then visited Italy, making further visits to both

countries in the 1370s on royal missions. He became a justice of the peace and a knight of the shire, and was patronized particularly by John of Gaunt (the brother of Edward III, uncle of Richard II, and also Chaucer's brother-in-law). He received further preferment under both Richard and the man who displaced him, Henry IV. On his death in 1400, Chaucer was buried, laden with honors, in Westminster Abbey. As well as being a man of action and of affairs, he was extremely well read in Latin, Italian, and French. All this experience and reading is reflected in his writing, including *The Canterbury Tales.*

The Canterbury Tales was mostly written between 1387 and Chaucer's death. Although, as has been said, it is full of learning, it is a work which carries its learning lightly. It does not strive for the epic or the tragic or for the elevated philosophical and religious seriousness of Dante, say, though in it there are tales and moments of tragedy, epic, and seriousness. But its overriding tone is one of rumbustiousness and of a sense of the fertility and disorder of life. Chaucer does make judgments about what he sees, but without the fervor and vituperativeness of Dante or (as we will see) of Milton. There is a generous humanity about Chaucer which allows him to prick our pretensions and laugh at our foibles, as well as occasionally condemning them. He is the first and perhaps the greatest comic writer in English, not a tragedian; although, as we will see, he is highly sensitive to the charms of nature and is capable of writing poetry of great beauty and pathos.

It has been said that in *The Canterbury Tales* Chaucer presents a cross-section of contemporary English society, warts and all. Although there may be no actual serfs and no actual royalty in the *Tales,* the pilgrims do range from the very poor to the very grand. As far as warts go, it is striking that the majority of the pilgrims are, to say the least, hypocritical or in other ways vicious; two of the poorest, the Parson (a man of "holy thought and work") and his brother the Ploughman (who lives "in peace and perfect charity"), are two of the best. These genuine exemplars are exceptional both within Chaucer's writing and, one suspects, within the society in which he lived. The England of Chaucer's time was one in which there was a rising merchant class and also a clergy of immense extent and influence, in both cases of often rather dubious morals. The trading class and the clergy are well represented by Chaucer at all levels, as well as the aristocracy and nobility, and also—very important for Chaucer—women; for a constant theme in his writings and in a good proportion of the *Tales* is the relationship between the sexes. Two of the most memorable characters in the *Tales* are the Prioress and, above all, the Wife of Bath, who threatens at one point to take the whole thing over, as she tells not just her tale but, in graphic detail, the story of her life.

Like Ovid's *Metamorphoses*, Chaucer's *Canterbury Tales* consists of a string of interlinked tales and of tales within tales, and, again like Ovid, the vast majority of Chaucer's tales and the framework of the work itself are in verse. Chaucer hit on the clever device of having the tellers of his tales, including himself, as characters within the overall tale in which the separate tales are embedded. So at any point there may actually be two tales going on: the over-arching tale of the pilgrims on their way to Canterbury and of the relationships between them, and, within that frame, the smaller tale being told at the time by one of the pilgrims, which itself usually reflects back on the character of the teller. Within the work as a whole, we have the illusion that the pilgrims are real people, compared to the characters in the tales they tell. In Chaucer's handling of his characters, few escape authorial judgment. Many of the clergy in particular are shown to be acting in flagrant contradiction to their calling. But the judgments Chaucer makes are usually indirect, emerging from what he tells us in describing his characters, rather than by any explicit censure or condemnation. Chaucer is a wry and witty observer of human character, not a preacher or moralizer.

The setting is a pilgrimage from the Tabard Inn in Southwark to the cathedral of Canterbury. Before the pilgrims depart, the Host or Landlord of the Tabard, Herry Bailey, a real figure who is also on the pilgrimage, proposes that, to while away the time on the journey, each member of the group will tell four stories, two on the way out and two on the way back, with a free dinner at the end for the teller of the best tale. In fact, apart from Chaucer himself who embarks on two tales (but completes only one of them after being stopped in full flow by the Host, who demands something more interesting and actually gets something much more boring), no character tells more than one tale. Of the twenty-nine pilgrims who start from Southwark, twenty-two tell tales and there is a further tale from the Canon's Yeoman, a figure who joins the group on the road; so, with Chaucer himself telling two, there are twenty-four tales in all. The work as we have it, possibly incomplete and certainly potentially expandable, begins with a Prologue in which there are portraits of twenty-two of the pilgrims and of Herry Bailey himself. It ends with a tale from the Parson, in effect a lengthy sermon on the virtues and their corresponding vices, and a "Retraction" from Chaucer himself in which he asks for prayers from his readers for divine forgiveness for the vanity of some of his writing and for the grace to make a good end to his life.

Like T. S. Eliot's *The Waste Land*, Chaucer's *Canterbury Tales* opens with an invocation of April. But Chaucer's April is not the cruellest month. It is the sweetest, and is also the harbinger of the life and fertility which is to come, an apt metaphor for what is going to unfold in Chaucer's own work:

When that Aprill with his shoures soote [sweet]
The droghte of March hath perced to the roote,
And bathed every veyne in swich [such] licour
Of which vertu engendered is the flour;
And Zephirus eek [also] with his sweete breeth
Inspired hath in every holt and heeth
The tendre croppes, and the young sonne
Hath in the Ram his halve cours yronne [run],
And smale foweles maken melodye,
That sleepen all the night with open ye [eye]
(So pricken hem [them] nature in hir corages [their courage]);
Thanne longen folk to goon on pilgrimages . . .

It is English. Try reading it out loud, and the sense will emerge, as well as a lovely feel for the season of spring: sweet showers, the sap rising in the plants, the gentle winds in every grove and heath, the tender crops, the new sun, the small birds singing and sleeping through the night with eyes open—nature then pricking them all and encouraging them; and also folk longing to go on pilgrimage, in England, and, as it emerges a few lines later,

. . . to Canterbury they wende
The holy blissful martir for to seke . . .

. . . in his already (in 1387) magnificent cathedral. And, as all of Chaucer's contemporaries would have been conscious, the pilgrimage to a shrine like Canterbury was a metaphor for the journey that each soul makes through life to the heavenly Jerusalem; with the great cathedrals like Canterbury, with their soaring arches and liquid, coloured light—itself a sign of the light of the Holy Spirit—the best and most vivid intimation we have on this earth of the heavenly Jerusalem. This link is made explicit by Chaucer's Parson in the prologue to his tale, as the pilgrims come within sight of Canterbury (and imagine what an impression that would have made in the Middle Ages, the cathedral rising up out of the landscape on the horizon ahead, unimpeded by the architectural detritus of the modern age):

And Jhesu, for his grace, wit me sende
To shewe yow the wey, in this viage [journey],
Of thilke parfit [the same perfect] glorious pilgrimage
That highte [was called] Jerusalem celestial.

But pilgrimage and its existential meaning are only the context for Chaucer's tales, important though that context is. The tales themselves are not just concerned with what happens here below; taken as a whole, they delight in what goes on here below, from the most elevated to the most earthy.

The pilgrims themselves fall into a number of groups. From the upper ranks of society there is first the Knight, a natural gentleman and the veteran of many campaigns, including forays against the Moors in Spain and North Africa and against the Turk in the eastern Mediterranean. His son the Squire has already seen service in France and Flanders, and they are accompanied by just one servant, the Yeoman, clad in green, a proper forester. By contrast, the Prioress—Madame Eglantyne, a daughter of the nobility—is all daintiness and affectation, while very sure of her position. She keeps little dogs and wept for a mouse caught in a trap, though not (as we will see) for Jews. She has a retinue of another nun and three chaplains. Finally from the upper classes there is a Monk, a Prior, though more conversant with the practice of hunting than with the rule of Saint Benedict.

The pilgrims from the middle reaches of society include Hubert, a Friar, "a wantone and a merrie," making a living from selling absolution to sinners and spending the proceeds in taverns and on barmaids, this noble "post" of his order marrying off the girls he seduced. Then there is the Merchant, with his Flemish beaver hat, such a pompous man that none knew he was in debt. There is a Clerk of Oxenford, unworldly and expert on Aristotle, a Sergeant of the Law (a barrister), and an epicurean Franklin (a landowner). From various guilds there are a Haberdasher, a Dyer, a Carpenter, a Weaver, and a Carpet-Maker, whose characters are not developed, though the Cook who is with them, a vulgar character, is. There is a Shipman, a captain, knowledgeable, brave, and skilful at sea, but ruthless in drowning the prisoners he captures and quite happy to steal wine from his clients. He is, in other words, both a trader and a pirate, a combination familiar in Chaucer's time and subsequently. A learned Doctor of Physik (a physician) knows that "gold in physik is a cordial / Therefore he loved gold in especial." And finally from this group there is Alisoun, the Wife of Bath, bold-faced, red-haired, and wide-hipped, a devotee of both Mars and Venus, who has had five husbands, apart from other company she had had in her youth, well traveled, and well versed in love, knowing "of that art the olde daunce." She is, however, somewhat deaf from having been struck about the ear by her fifth husband, as we learn later, who had been angered by her tearing three pages from a misogynist tract he was reading to her.

Of the characters from the lower sections of society, apart from the Cook, there are first the "poor" Parson "of a town" and his brother the Plowman (who does not actually get to tell a tale), two honest, hardworking, and wholesome characters, and also a Manciple (or steward) from the law courts, who is a shrewd, frugal, and dishonest administrator. The rest are real lowlife: the gross, oafish Miller, a dishonest, red-bearded giant with a great hairy wart on his nose; the Reeve, "a slendre choleric man," a one-time carpenter and now the agent for a lord on an estate, feared by those below him while he enriches himself; and finally the Summoner and the Pardoner, the most corrupt of all, and, significantly, both in the employ of the Church. The first of these, "as hoot [hot] he was and lecherous as a sparwe [sparrow]," with the fire-red face of a cherubim, though pitted with spots and pimples, tyrannizes the people with the threat of the ecclesiastical court, enriching and pleasuring himself in the process. The Pardoner is physically repulsive, with lank yellow hair hanging down to his shoulders, eyes glaring like those of a hare, a voice like that of a goat, beardless and judged by Chaucer to be a gelding or a mare. He is festooned on his person with relics and indulgences with which he enriches himself, getting more silver from one day's preaching than an honest parson would get in a couple of months.

This somewhat ill-assorted company, introduced in Chaucer's *General Prologue,* is then corralled and choreographed by the Host of the Tabard, a large and genial man (and a real character from Chaucer's day). On the first evening Herry Bailey sets up the tale-telling competition, and as the pilgrimage progresses, he comments on the stories which have been told, he calls upon the next speaker, and he also intervenes in the disputes which sometimes crop up. Most of the tales have their own prologue, uttered by the story-teller, in which the character of the teller is further developed—in the case of the Wife of Bath, to almost Falstaffian proportions. Few of the tales are original to Chaucer, though the telling of all is; some are thought to be traditional, while others are borrowed from literary sources such as Ovid, Dante, Petrarch, Boccaccio, and medieval romances. It is neither necessary nor desirable here to go into any great detail on the tales, which are on the whole clear and straightforward enough, but we will pick out some salient features of each, so as to emphasize their variety and scope.

The first pilgrim to give us his tale is, as befits his status, the Knight. Appropriately enough, the Knight gives us a chivalric romance, derived partly from Boccaccio and more remotely from Statius (whom we encountered with Dante), both of whom wrote epics about ancient Thebes, where Chaucer's tale is partly set. It is about two Theban knights and cousins, Palamon and Arcite, who are taken prisoner by Theseus in his battle with Thebes, and imprisoned in a tower in Athens, where both fall in love with Emelye, the sister of Theseus's wife, whom they see walking in the garden beneath their tower. The cousins become rivals, and after various vicissitudes and adventures are set by Theseus to decide their suit by competing against each other in a tournament. In the arena where the tournament is to take place, there are temples dedicated to Venus, Mars, and Diana, and these are described as bedecked with appropriate images, anticipating in their drama and vigour the art of the next century and a half: Venus, naked, rising from the sea (Botticelli); in Mars's temple, "the smylere with the knyf under the cloak" (Titian's Bravo); and in Diana's, the story we encountered in Ovid of Actaeon (Titian again). Palamon is the devotee of Venus, Arcite of Mars, and Emelye, who does not want to marry at all, of the chaste Diana. Arcite wins, but is immediately thrown from his horse, and dies in Emelye's arms commending Palamon to her. After some years of general mourning following Arcite's funeral, Theseus speaks to his subjects. When the First Mover made the earth, he bound the whole of creation in "the faire cheyne of love." We should "maken vertu of necessitee": Emelye and Palamon should now marry, which they do to their own and to general satisfaction.

After this high-minded and somewhat philosophic romance, the Host is minded to call on the Monk, but the drunken Miller insists on telling a story of his own. It is, of course, utterly scurrilous, and involves the young wife of an old carpenter enjoying herself with a young student. As the sin comes about through a grotesque parody of Noah's ark—with the carpenter sleeping marooned in a boat suspended from the roof, which the student has got him to build in case of another Flood—the story is somewhat blasphemous too; and the attendant bawdy also includes the wife in the middle of the night of love-making baring her lower parts at a window to be kissed there by another would-be lover, and, in revenge for this, her actual lover having a red-hot poker stuffed up his arse by his rival.

The Reeve is greatly offended by this insult to a carpenter, and now tells his own story, almost as ridiculous as the Miller's, about two more students robbing and cuckolding a dishonest miller and deflowering his daughter. The Cook now threatens to out-do both the Reeve and the Miller in bawdy, with a story about an apprentice who has been sacked by his master, and who goes to lodge with a friend, whose wife is a prostitute, but for some reason the tale ends at that point, just as it is about to start. The Host, wanting no more tales of the sort we have just been hearing, next calls on the Man of Law to raise the tone, which he duly does with a pious romance taken from the Anglo-Norman Chronicle of 1335. It concerns Constance, the daughter of a Christian emperor of Rome, who is married first to a Moorish (!) Sultan in Syria and then to a pagan king in Northumberland, both of whom she converts to Christianity. But both times she is dogged by a murderous mother-in-law and set adrift in a boat on the open sea. This indeed is the central and abiding image of the tale, a complete passivity of the soul before the will of God, as, in her purity and her trust in God, Constance never does anything to defend or explain herself. Needless to say in Constance's case, the will of God reunites her both with her father and her Northumbrian husband, before, on the latter's death, she returns to Rome for the last time, piously to await her own.

Next we have the Shipman's tale. It is about a merchant who is so concerned to plough his business that he forgets to plough his wife. In desperation she turns to a monk, a friend of the family who is staying in their house, begging him for the loan of 100 francs so she can repay money that she owes on clothes. The monk borrows the 100 francs that the wife needs from the merchant, who is about to travel on business, claiming that it is needed by his monastery. In the husband's absence, he and the wife enjoy each other. When the merchant returns, the monk tells him that he has repaid the 100 francs he owes him to the wife. The husband then pays the wife the attention she had missed hitherto, and all are happy; an immoral tale no doubt, but far less shocking to readers of the twenty-first century than the Prioress's tale, the next to be told, and to us a horrible confection of sentimental piety and anti-Semitism.

A pious widow has a son who is seven years old, who makes his way to school each day through the ghetto where the Jews then lived, supported by the Crown and practicing their hated trade of money-lending ("foule usure and the lucre of villeynye"). At school he learns a Marian hymn, which so appeals to him (though he does not understand its Latin words) that he sings it en route to and from school. This irritates the Jews so much that one of them slits his throat and throws his body into a pit of excrement. The distraught mother seeks her son and prays to the Virgin, who causes the son, even though dead, to sing the hymn from the bottom of the pit. The Jews are rounded up and the guilty ones are publicly drawn and hanged. The dead boy continues to sing until he is given proper burial, his little martyr's soul continuing to sing the new song of the Book of Revelation, alongside the virgins before the Lamb of God.

There were many versions of this story, including the one in which the boy is Saint Hugh of Lincoln. The Jews were in fact expelled from England in 1290, so Chaucer is here drawing on a dark ancestral prejudice, unenlivened by living exemplars for a century or so. It should not need saying, but, in contrast to Dante, say, writing about Mohammed, we cannot assume that Chaucer agrees with the sentiments of the Prioress. Indeed, his acerbic portrait of the Prioress in the *Prologue* might lead us to think that Chaucer is deliberating contrasting her overdainty manners and love for little dogs with the cruelty of her unthinking prejudice. On the other hand, in her own prologue to her tale, the Prioress does speak a beautiful hymn to the Virgin ("O mooder [mother] Mayde! O mayde Mooder free!"), comparing her to Moses' burning bush and emphasizing that it was on account of her humility that the Spirit "ravished" her. It is uncomfortable: genuine religious feeling coexisting with atavistic prejudice and unconscious hypocrisy (and whatever virtues Madame Eglantyne possesses, humility is not one of them).

Perhaps the Prioress's tale is a bit much for the Host, too, for he now calls upon Chaucer himself to tell a tale of mirth. Chaucer begins his first tale, that of Sir Thopas. On the face of it, this is a knightly romance about a chaste knight who hears birdsong in the woods, falls in love with an Elf-queen, encounters a three-headed giant, and, planning to slay him, sleeps under the stars, drinking water from a well like Perceval. In fact, two centuries before Cervantes, Chaucer is poking fun at the romances. Thopas actually runs away from the giant, and threatens to return to kill him by the distinctly unchivalric method of piercing his belly with a lance. Thopas' appearance too is comic, with a face as white as bread but with livid patches, and his hair and beard the color of saffron, both going down to his girdle. No matter: it is too much for the Host, who cuts Chaucer off as he launches into the second part of Sir Thopas's adventure. Chaucer tries again with the pious and didactic Tale of Melibee, which is an English translation in prose of a French version of a Latin original. Melibee is a man whose house is broken into and whose daughter is attacked, but who is persuaded by Dame Prudence, his wife, not to take revenge on his enemies but to forgive them, and so earn a reputation for mercy. The debate runs for a thousand lines or so, and is filled out with references to many authorities, including Job, Ovid, Seneca, Cicero, Saint Paul, Saint Augustine, and Saint Jerome. The pilgrims apparently listen to all this, and at the end the Host comments merely that his own wife is not at all like Dame Prudence. She urges him continually to beat and avenge those who insult and cheat the Bailey family.

The hunting Monk is now called upon, with some choice comments from the Host about his potential to be an Abbot and, rather more pointedly, about the loss to the nation that the Monk will not exercise his lust in engendering offspring. The Monk may not engender offspring, but this does not mean that he is faithful to his vocation. We have already learned from the *Prologue* that he keeps many a dainty horse in his stables, in violation of his monastic vow of poverty. His corpulent figure and his greed are both in violation of the rule of Saint Benedict, which forbids gluttony and the eating of meat. Although this particular rule had been relaxed by Chaucer's day, our Monk's behavior is hardly in accordance with its spirit. But genial and worldly as he may be, in his tale the Monk responds surprisingly, not to say hypocritically. He follows a model set by Boccaccio (in *De Casibus Virorum Illustrum*) with a succession of accounts of the downfalls of the great, including Lucifer, Adam, Hercules, Nero, Alexander the Great, Julius Caesar, Croesus, and, among more modern examples, Dante's Ugolino. After seventeen of these, the company has had enough. The Knight asks for something less gloomy, and is seconded by the Host. The baton passes to one of the Prioress's chaplains.

The Nun's Priest's tale takes the form of an Aesopian fable about Chauntecleer, a strutting cock. His beauty and his prowess over his seven wives are lovingly dwelt on, especially over Pertelote, his favourite. Chauntecleer has a bad dream one night, and Pertelote tries to reason him out of it, citing Cato as an authority. Chauntecleer responds with counter-examples in which dreams had been taken seriously and come true, both from recent times and from ancient history, including those of Daniel, Joseph, and Andromache. At the end of the debate, Chauntecleer cheers up. Parodying Saint John's Gospel, "In Principio" [in the beginning]; he says, "Mulier est hominis confusio" [woman is man's confusion]; which he mistranslates (for the benefit of his wife) as: "Womman is mannes joye and al his blis." He "feathers" and "treads" Pertelote twenty times before daybreak. Puffed up by this, Chauntecleer parades around the yard, until he sees a fox. Instead of making his escape, he is flattered by the fox (a new Iscariot, a new Sinon), and he agrees to sing for him. As he does, with his eyes shut, the fox seizes him and runs off with him in his mouth. A lamentation rivalling that of the fall of Troy ensues, we are told, together with a hue and cry like that of the massacre of the Flemish during the Peasants' Revolt (of 1381), but the terrified Chauntecleer keeps his wits about him. He tells the fox to exult in his triumph and shout insults at his pursuers. As he does, Chauntecleer flies from the fox's mouth, out of reach. (The moral, of course, is that flatterers should not be listened to.)

The Nun's Priest's tale is rightly regarded as one of Chaucer's masterpieces, on all sorts of levels, not least in the delightful absurdity of the cock as an epic hero and learned to boot. Take the fruit of it and let the chaff be still, says the Nun's Priest at the end; but Chaucer's genius is surely in the "chaff."

The Physician's tale is adapted from Livy (*History of Rome,* Book Three, lines 43–49), as Chaucer says. It tells of Apius, a corrupt judge, who wants for his own pleasure Virginia, the daughter of Virginius. Apius contrives a situation in which a slave named Claudius will come to his court claiming that Virginia is really his daughter, stolen from him when she was very young (to hand her over to Apius, once the court has decided in Claudius'ss favor, which it duly does). Virginius tells his daughter that to preserve her virtue, he must kill her, which he also does. Virginius is taken to Apius's court for this crime, but there is a popular uprising. Apius and the slave are arrested, Apius killing himself in prison and Claudius being sent into exile. Tales of this sort were popular in the Middle Ages and in Elizabethan and Jacobean times. It must be said, though, that Livy's original account is better than

Chaucer's. First there is more detail of characterisation, including both an uncle and a fiancé for Virginia, but further, Livy compares the incident to the equally sordid story of the rape of Lucretia. Just as Lucretia's death led to the end of the Tarquin dynasty in Rome and the instigation of the Republic, so the uprising following the crime of Apius brought about the demise of the tyrannous decemvirs (of whom Apius was one) and their replacement by the tribunes. In Livy, both stories thus had a political and historical point quite absent in the case of Chaucer's Physician's retelling of the story of Virginia.

The Physician is followed by the Pardoner, who takes for his theme the tag *Radix malorum est cupiditas* (avarice is the root of evil). After having graphically explained in his prologue how he makes his own living out of avarice, he tells a rather effective tale in which three men meet their death through their own greed. Interestingly, in the long introduction that he gives to his tale proper, this rather repulsive figure inveighs against gluttony particularly. In line with much medieval preaching, in which gluttony is sometimes represented as a form of idolatry (in which men take for their God their bellies), the Pardoner tells his audience that Adam was driven from Paradise for this sin. He goes on to speak of the dung and foul corruption that gluttony produces, and the way that our throats become sinks for the excesses of drink—and all this despite the fact that, as he himself tells us, he will not actually preach without food and wine even from the poorest widow and a wench in every town, and quaffs a quantity of ale before he starts his tale. When his moralizing tale is finished, and his earlier self-revelations notwithstanding, the Pardoner then tries to sell some relics and indulgences to the pilgrims. Furious at this effrontery, the Host says he would rather have the Pardoner's (non-existent?) balls in his hand than one of his relics. Order is restored by the Knight, and the Wife of Bath takes the stage.

The Wife of Bath's prologue is longer than many of the tales. In it she defends marriage or, more precisely, the opposite of virginity. Virginity may be a perfection, but why were we given organs both for the "purgation of urine" and for generation, if not to use them for both? She goes on to recount her experiences with her five husbands. The first three were rich and old, and sexually deficient—according to Alisoun, husbands have to pleasure their wives, and she exploited them for their wealth. The fourth was a drunkard and a fornicator, who kept a mistress and who died when she was on a pilgrimage to the Holy Land. Before his death, though, Alisoun had walked out and flirted with Jankyn, the parish clerk. He, at the age of twenty, became Alisoun's fifth husband; she was then aged forty. Fantastic as he was sexually—she could not withdraw from him her "chamber of Venus" (one of many euphemisms in the account)—he also beat her and regaled her with learned stories of troublesome wives, including Pasiphae, Clytemnestra and Delilah.

It was during such a reading that the fight occurred which led to Jankyn reeling backwards into the fire, and to the retaliation which caused her deafness, after which they lived in a kind of truce, with Alisoun regaining the upper hand (which, according to her, is the secret of a successful marriage).

Alisoun's tale, a variant of the Arthurian legend of the Loathly Damsel, continues her debate with Jankyn. A knight rapes a country girl. He is handed over to Arthur's Queen, who agrees to spare his life if after a year he can answer the question as to what it is that women most desire. On the last day of the year, he meets the Loathly Damsel, an ugly old hag, who, on condition that he does what she requires of him, will tell him the secret. In despair, the knight agrees. The answer to the question is that women desire the same sovereignty over their husbands as over their lovers. The Queen is satisfied and the knight is free, but the old crone demands his hand in marriage. In bed together, the Damsel, quoting Dante, Boethius, and Seneca, preaches gentleness to the knight. She asks him whether he would prefer her as she is, old and foul, but faithful and humble, or young, pretty and possibly flirtatious. Worn out, the knight simply cedes mastery to his wife, whereupon she is revealed as young and fair. "For joye he hente [caught] her in his armes two / His herte bathed in a bath of blisse." And the bliss continues as she continues to delight him, while the teller of the tale prays to Christ to send women "Housbondes meeke, young and fresh abedde, / And grace t'overbyde hem [to outlive them] that we wedde," and to cut very short the lives of those who won't submit to their wives.

The Friar and the Summoner are enemies, and they trade insults in the prologues to their tales, which follow Alisoun's, and in the tales themselves. In the Friar's tale, a summoner en route to extort money from a poor widow encounters a yeoman, who seems to have a similar metier, but who turns out to be a devil. They carry on together in companionable conversation. When the summoner threatens the innocent widow with court or excommunication if she does not pay him a bribe, the widow prays that he should be carried off to hell, and the summoner's companion duly obliges. The Summoner responds to this by telling in his prologue of a visit to hell by a friar, in which he sees at first no brothers of his—because all 20,000 of them are lurking in Satan's arse. His tale continues in this scatological vein. It has an avaricious friar being insulted by a sick man who lets off a tremendous fart at him, as the payment that the friar is demanding for himself and for the other members of his convent. The offence is compounded when the squire of the local lord, to whom the friar complains, works out a way of sharing a fart between the friar and his twelve companions (by allowing the air made by the fart to travel through the spokes of a wheel at which the friars are sitting).

After this, which is received without comment, something more edifying. The philosophic Clerk, called on to produce something lively, actually gives a rather serious version of a story by Petrarch. It concerns Walter, a marquis, who gives up a life of pleasure to marry a beautiful and virtuous village girl, Griselda, the daughter of Janicula, the poorest of the peasants. Though the marriage is, on the surface, happy, and Griselda both humble and gracious, Walter decides to test her virtue and her patience. He has her young daughter taken away from her, and later her son—both, unbeknown to Griselda, deposited with his sister. Then, when the daughter is twelve, he forges a papal divorce and sends for his "lost" daughter to be his new wife. He sends Griselda back to Janicula, in rags at her insistence, and as if that were not enough, then summons her back to be the servant of his new bride. Griselda has lost her maidenhead, her children and her station, but the nearest she comes to complaining is to beseech Walter that he "prikke with no tormentynge / This tendre mayden, as ye han doon mo," that is, as you have done to another (not even to "me"!). At this, Walter reveals all, and all is resolved and all restored. To this paean to the virtue of wifely patience, however, and with a nod to the Wife of Bath, Chaucer adds a rider, urging present-day wives not to emulate Griselda but to stand up for themselves with, if necessary, the strength of a great camel or the eagerness of a tiger in India.

Even less is the Merchant able to stay silent at this point. He has been married only two months and already his wife is revealed as a shrew, worse than a fiend. He has to tell his tale. January, a rather disgusting old knight, to satisfy his own lust, marries a young wife, May. Much is made of January's preparation for the wedding night and of his efforts then, though May is less impressed. Seeing the old man in the morning, "in his night-cappe, and with his necke lene / She preyseth [reckoned] nat his pleying worth a bene." Damian, the knight's squire, has meanwhile fallen in love with May, and she with him. After another bout of vigorous love-making (in which he insists that May remove all her clothes), January goes blind, but clings to May like a leech. With references to the Song of Songs, traditionally taken to be the song of mystical love of the soul for God, though for a quite different purpose, May persuades January to let her lead him into the orchard (presided over by the gods Pluto and Proserpine), where Damian is hiding. Urged on by May, Damian climbs a pear tree, and May gets January to help her climb up the tree too, ostensibly to get a pear: "And suddenly anon this Damyan / Gan pullen up the smock, and in he thong [thrust]." Outraged by this indecency, Pluto restores January's sight. May indignantly insists that he did not see what he did see, that she was actually fighting in the tree, that her smock was not pulled up over her breast, etc. She jumps down from the tree into January's arms, who kisses her and strokes her womb "full soft," from which one supposes one can deceive oneself as much as one likes when possession, deception, and lasciviousness are at issue. The Host, however, expatiates on the fickleness of wives generally, and on the shrewishness of his own, on which he will not expand for fear of its being reported back to her by one or other of the pilgrims. He then summons the Squire to tell his tale.

The Squire's tale is, predictably enough, a romantic concoction featuring a Tartar king, a strange knight coming to a feast bearing magical gifts from the King of Araby and India, including a brass horse that will fly its rider anywhere, which suddenly vanishes, and (in a second section) the King's daughter who, the morning after the feast, finds a distressed falcon in the garden, who tells her a tale of the infidelity of her fiancé, who is eventually prevailed upon to repent. Thankfully, perhaps, the Squire is interrupted by the Franklin just as he is about to launch into a third section, the Franklin praising the virtues of the Squire in comparison to the indolence and wastefulness of his own son. The Franklin, a generous and hospitable man, though mocked by the Host for his pretensions to gentility, then tells his tale.

It is, the Franklin tells us, a Breton lay of olden days, and deriving from Boccaccio. Arveragus, a knight in Brittany, has a virtuous wife, Dorigen, and they live in marital ease and mutual confidence. Arveragus, though, goes to Britain for two years, to seek honor and adventure. Dorigen walks the castle ramparts in sadness at his absence; she sits and muses on the fearful sea and rocks:

> [She] caste her eyen dounward fro the brynke.
> And when she saugh the grisly rokkes blake,
> For very feere so wolde hir herte quake
> That on hire feet she mighte hire noght sustene.

She is fainting with fear at the fate of ships and sailors on that dreadful coast. To cheer her up, her friends organize a picnic for her in a beautiful garden. At this picnic a squire, Aurelius, who loves her, declares his love. Dorigen refuses his suit, but adds playfully that she would entertain it if Aurelius could clear the coast of Brittany of all its rocks, so that no more ships should go down on them. Arveragus returns, and for two years Aurelius languishes in despair, until he hears of a magician in Orleans who can work wonders. He travels there, and the magician conjures up marvelous scenes of hunting, and also of his beloved Dorigen dancing as knights jousted. For a thousand pounds, the magician agrees to do what Aurelius needs, and they travel back to Brittany. It is winter, the cold, frosty season of December, beautifully described (as are the jagged rocks of the Breton coast). Phoebus (the sun) had grown old, his face pale and dull:

The bitter frosts, with the sleet and reyn,
Destroyed hath the grene in every yerd.
Janus sit by the fyr, with double berd [beard],
And drynketh of the bugle horn the wyn:
Biforn hym stant brawen [stood the meat] of the tusked swyn,
And 'Nowel' crieth every lusty man . . .

. . . a description anticipating Brueghel's painting of winter.

Eventually, after much calculating and observing, the magician (or nature) works the trick. The rocks are indeed covered by the sea, and Aurelius goes to claim his prize from the horrified Dorigen. She is distraught, and tortures herself with images of the faithful women of antiquity—Lucretia, Alcestis, Penelope and many others who preferred death to dishonor. Arveragus, who had been away, finds her in this distressed state, and she tells him the reason. With great confidence, he tells her to honor her bargain in secret. The story then quickly unravels. Dorigen meets Aurelius and tells him that Arveragus has sent her to fulfil her promise.

Unto the garden, as myn housbonde bad [bade],
My trouthe [promise] for to hold, allas! allas!

Aurelius, astounded at the honesty and poignancy of this, and understanding Dorigen's feeling, cancels the arrangement. Arveragus and Dorigen last out their days in happiness, while the magician, on hearing what had happened, releases Aurelius from his debt.

For all its air of wizardry and romance, the Franklin's tale is a high point in Chaucer, in its descriptions of nature and of the Breton coast, and in the directness of its emotional appeal. By contrast, the Second Nun's tale is one of the weakest, a comparatively colorless and conventional account of Saint Cecilia, a somewhat stock Christian martyr of Roman times. Cecilia, a Christian, wishes to remain a virgin after her marriage to the pagan Valerian. She overcomes his doubts, and he is converted, and then his brother too. Both the brothers are martyred, and their torturers themselves are converted. Cecilia is then condemned to death, but mocks the judge Almachius for worshipping a stone idol as a god. She survives a bath of red flame, and continues to preach for three days after a botched attempt to cut off her head, before finally rendering up her soul to God. This recitation, Chaucer tells us, covered five miles of the journey.

The party have now reached Boghtoun under Blee (about ten miles from Canterbury), when they are joined by two somewhat travel-stained riders, who gallop up. These turn out to be a Canon, who rather unsuccessfully practices alchemy, and his Yeoman servant, who is not entirely enamored with his master's efforts, and whose face has become discolored as a result of the Canon's experiments. The Canon accuses the Yeoman of slander, and rides off, worried that his secrets are to be revealed. The Yeoman now tells a story attacking alchemy and the seven years he has wasted in the Canon's service. The first half is simply a description of the physical dangers (including explosions and handling all manner of noxious chemicals), the monetary losses, the failures, the recriminations and the heartbreak involved in alchemical experiments. In the second part of his tale, the Yeoman tells how another canon alchemist—a Judas, he calls him—deceives a gullible priest into parting with forty pounds for a completely useless powder which is supposed to turn copper into silver. In a long postscript, the Yeoman condemns not just the deceit of alchemists: the very intention of alchemy is to uncover secrets which should not be revealed, and this is contrary to God's will, a powerful and heartfelt message.

As the pilgrims ride on, nearing their goal, the Host points to the Cook, drunk and half-asleep on his horse. The Manciple, dwelling further on the Cook's drunkenness, volunteers a story instead. The Cook lunges at him, and falls off his horse. The Host berates the Manciple for his censoriousness, and also for the way he fiddles the amounts and accounts, with which, as we learned in the *Prologue,* this lewd fellow outpaced the wisdom of a heap of learned men. His tale is a version of the story of Apollo and Coronis in Book Two of Ovid's *Metamorphoses.* A caged white bird tells Phoebus (Apollo), who was at that time living in Thebes, that his wife was deceiving him with another man. Apollo responds by summarily killing his wife with an arrow. He then tears out the white feathers of the bird and replaces them with black, and he also changes his beautiful voice into a croak. The tell-tale has become a crow, which (rather than the wife's deception and murder) is the moral of the Manciple's tale, which is rather thin and unpoetic in comparison to Ovid's much fuller original.

We are now almost at Canterbury. It is 4 p.m. on April 20, and time for one last tale before the pilgrims' arrival. The Host calls on the Parson, who, in line with his own manifest integrity and seriousness, declines to give them fable or romance or even rhyme, but will give them something appropriate for their ultimate journey to the heavenly Jerusalem. It is his long sermon about the virtues and vices, during which he calls on them all to repent of all the sins they have committed in "delight of their thoughts," for, as he puts it, "delit is ful perilous." And this, of course, is the cue for Chaucer's somewhat paradoxical *Retraction,* which follows directly on the Parson's "tale."

An obvious point about *The Canterbury Tales* is the diversity of styles, themes and intentions to be found within them, which is part of what contributes to the sense in Chaucer of a great richness and fertility. In different tales we find romance, chivalry, poetry, and virtues such as constancy, prudence, chastity, and courage. We also find a vein in quite a number of the tales of religious feeling, not necessarily adapted to modern taste, but a sense of the unquestioned truth of religion and of a providential background. This religious vein, incidentally, seems even stronger and less questionable in the long prose disquisitions of the Parson and of Chaucer himself in the tale of Melibee, than it does in the somewhat problematic tales of the Prioress and the Second Nun, while it is hard to know just how a modern audience should approach the rather improbable characters of Constance and Griselda in the Man of Law's tale and the Clerk's tale. In common with much medieval literature, the characters in these tales are indeed so thinly drawn from a modern point of view that they are hardly more than symbols for the virtues being extolled in the stories concerned—though we do not get the feeling in reading them that, thin as these characters and their stories might be, we are meant to question the underlying message. There the Christian framework survives intact, and the tales appear as allegories of the virtues, a form familiar to Chaucer's contemporaries. (It is a matter of debate as to the extent to which many of Chaucer's *Tales* are to be taken as allegories; a reasonable response might be to say that in few of the *Tales* are the characters drawn with the psychological depth of a nineteenth-century novel; nevertheless, the characters of Dorigen, say, in the Franklin's tale, or January in the Merchant's, while doubtless exemplifying specific virtues and vices, are rather fuller drawn and thereby more plausible and more human than the frankly improbable Constance and Griselda.)

But alongside the serious, the religious and the high-minded, there is a marvelous vein of wit in many of the tales, from the delightful intellectual dancing in the Nun's Priest's tale, through the parody in Sir Thopas and the broad humor in the description of the Wife of Bath, to the outright bawdy of tales such as those of the Miller, the Reeve, the Shipman, and the Merchant, the Merchant's tale itself having many other things as well, including psychological acuity and a rich sense of the magic of nature. Descriptions of the natural world are indeed one of Chaucer's great strengths, in a whole range of tales, especially perhaps the Knight's (itself almost a catalogue of chivalric virtue and description) and the Franklin's. In contrast, we also have the scatological and the spiteful from the likes of the Friar and the Summoner, to say nothing of the intriguing and detailed account of the practice and danger of alchemy from the Canon's Yeoman.

Amid all the diversity of approach and mood, and a sense of the immense fruitfulness both of nature and of human invention and ingenuity, two themes are especially prominent: religion and love (or sex). Apart from the overall religious context—both of the pilgrimage as a whole and of many of the stories—we learn a great deal in the *Tales* of the extent to which people's lives were dominated by the Church and its functionaries and hangers-on. The picture is not a flattering one to the Church, which looks like a great umbrella under which many of mankind's more worldly and sensual vices can shelter and flourish. One could say that this is all but inevitable in any human organization which becomes as large and powerful and all-encompassing as the medieval Church. While this is no doubt true, it is, of course, the Church's mission to stand for unworldliness. Perhaps more than Dante, precisely because he gives us so much detail and characterization of clerical and paraclerical figures, we can see in Chaucer the soil in which reform movements such as those of Wycliffe and the Lollards (contemporary with Chaucer) and, in central Europe, Jan Hus, and eventually the Protestant Reformation itself, could grow and develop. While on the topic of the social conditions of Chaucer's time, it is perhaps surprising that in the *Tales* there is no explicit reference to the great plague which had hit and decimated the populations of Europe in the mid-fourteenth century, although there is a lot in the margins about the poverty and hardships of many people, which was one of its results.

On love and sex—perennial themes, and perhaps why modern story-tellers and filmmakers are continually drawn to Chaucer—we have the whole gamut from the constancy of Constance and the knightly yearnings of Palamon and Arcite, through the desperate and ultimately honorable yearning of Aurelius for his lady, the wedded bliss of that lady and Arveragus and the almost neurotic testing of Griselda by Walter, down to the lust of January for May, May's romping in the tree with Damian, and the even lower scenes depicted by the Miller, the Reeve, and the Shipman. Towering above all is the Wife of Bath, with her prologue and tale, and her questions about dominance in sex and marriage. It is one of the delights of Chaucer that all these different attitudes are there, without, on this theme, authorial attitude or position; it is as if Chaucer himself is too aware of the complexity and diversity of the relations between man and woman, and the strength of the desires involved, to be prepared to schematise or regulate. If such was his attitude, then a series of tales and characters exploring all these differences was the perfect vehicle for its development and expression.

Chaucer is not Dante, as we have already observed. He has neither Dante's desire to systematize nor his ambition to poetry of a high mystical seriousness or even really of tragedy or epic in any consistent or extended sense. Even though there are many different characters in both authors, and both are, in a sense, on a pilgrimage, where Dante sees everything in terms of the ultimate love and purpose of the Godhead, Chaucer, notwithstanding his *Retraction* and the moral earnestness of the tale he puts last, is content (more than content) to keep his eyes firmly on the earth and on what goes on there. Even here his vision is somewhat constrained. He may write about tragedy (in the Knight's tale, perhaps) and about high romance (in the Squire's tale), but his center of gravity is elsewhere, in a much more realistic world.

And this leads us to a final observation. For all the fascination, detail, learning, wit, poetry, vulgarity, and much else besides which are displayed in the tales, how many of them are believable, except as tales told to pass the time on a journey? Don't the tales, in a sense—however vivid some may be in the telling—pale in comparison to their setting and their tellers? By contrast to the tales themselves, the pilgrimage and the pilgrims grow in reality as the journey develops. The frame for the tales is the first reality in Chaucer, and the tales remain tales within a tale. And while, like all of us, the pilgrims are on a pilgrimage—ultimately not to Canterbury but to the heavenly Jerusalem—what fascinates and delights Chaucer is the journey and those on it, rather than the destination. His *Retraction* may not be wholly sincere, but it does have a point; he and his readers are opting for delight on the way as much as for the religious consolations of the goal, be it Canterbury or the heavenly Jerusalem.

Shakespeare

Shakespeare lived from 1564 until 1616, and, according to traditional reckoning, wrote thirty-seven plays, equally traditionally divided into comedies, tragedies and histories. Of these, twenty-five or more would count in any list of the world's greatest literature. In European literature, only Dante even comes close to Shakespeare in fertility of imagination, in richness of detail, or in poetic genius. There is, though, a huge contrast between the two. Dante's poetry is tightly constrained, even in its linguistic form, and subordinated to an over-arching theological and philosophical vision. And if Dante achieves the impersonality some would see as the mark of great poetry, we always know what Dante's own position is on any matter of importance, its passionate idiosyncrasy and originality masked by the perfection and coherence of the whole edifice.

Shakespeare was, as everyone knows, a working dramatist. But this in itself cannot account for the untidiness and, in classical terms, disunity of his productions. It is rather as if Shakespeare is convinced of the disunity of life itself, its lack of tidy forms and the way in which people—and often the same people—run the whole gamut of emotions, feelings, and attitudes, from the highest to the lowest. This lack of unity—of tone, of mood, of character, of plot sometimes, and of language—was an outrage to those schooled in the classical tradition in France especially; Shakespeare was a barbarian compared to Racine or Corneille, spewing forth untamed wildernesses of plot and feeling, in comparison to their tightly constructed and impeccably manicured machines (one of which we will look at shortly). The appearance of Kemble's Shakespeare company in Paris in the 1820s provoked a veritable culture war, with the Young Turks of Romanticism (Delacroix, Stendhal, Alexandre Dumas, Victor Hugo, Berlioz, etc.) all lining up on one side and the academicians and classicists on the other. If you want to know the mind-blowing effect all this had at the time, listen to the music of Berlioz, especially the *Symphonie Fantastique,* which Berlioz dedicated to and had performed before Harriet Smithson, the flame-haired Irish Ophelia and Juliet in Kemble's productions, who had not at the time even deigned to speak to him, but who later (and tragically) became his wife.

It would be quite anachronistic to think of Shakespeare as a Romantic or even as a protoRomantic. Shakespeare is far too multifarious, far too all-encompassing for any such classification. On the other hand, English-speakers can become so used to Shakespeare's plays and language as to overlook the extent to which, for those unaccustomed to his sheer profligacy of invention, there is something profoundly shocking about Shakespeare: a full realization in his plays of what Vaclav Havel has called "the scandalous chaos of life and its mysterious fertility." Hence the untidy plots, the teeming and often apparently uncontrolled characters, escaping, it sometimes seems, from the mind of their inventor to take on existences of their own, and above all the language which makes visible and audible to us every human predicament, attitude, and emotion.

And where is Shakespeare himself in all this? Shakespeare was, as we have observed, a working dramatist. His works are dramas, to be put on and acted and appreciated for their dramatic power and invention. They are not philosophical treatises, to be worked over for their arguments (though there are arguments in them), and to be scrutinized for their mutual consistency. Scandalous as it may be to the mind of a dogmatist, there is no reason why a dramatist may not express different attitudes in different plays or even in the same play, without us, the audience, being able to impute any attitude to the writer himself outside of the play. It is, of course, the very protean nature of Shakespeare's personality, as manifested in his plays, which has led critics and writers to conscript him for various positions, from crypto-Catholic to conservative to agnostic humanist to subversive to nihilist. In a sense all are right and all are wrong. Perhaps Jorge Luis Borges comes closest to the truth when he writes of Shakespeare[15]—about whom we actually know surprisingly little—as being both nothing and everything, as being able to be everything because he himself is nothing (or at least gives nothing of himself away in his work).

In this chapter we will look briefly at three of Shakespeare's plays. More than anywhere else in the book, there is a degree of arbitrariness about the choice: one comedy (*The Tempest,* if *The Tempest* is a comedy), one tragedy (*Hamlet,* but why not *King Lear?*), and one history (*Henry V*—but in its unrepentant patriotism, chauvinism even, surely too politically incorrect in the twenty-first century?).

There is no defense to the charge of arbitrariness here, though I would insist that all three of the chosen plays have their own particular and incomparable genius. More broadly, they all in different ways deal with themes of civilization, order, and authority, and their antitheses: disorder, anarchy, and untamed nature. They also deal with love, sexuality and domesticity, both in themselves and as threatened by savagery, violence, infidelity, and the sheer unpredictability of instinct and chance. But then, one way or another, these themes are in a host of ways omnipresent in Shakespeare, as in all great literature. There is also, as we will see, in at least two of these plays, much related to the theatricality of the theater, and of life itself.

This playing with the notion of theater itself is not by any means confined to *Hamlet* and *The Tempest*. In *A Midsummer Night's Dream*, for example, we also have a play within a play, and characters in the play—whom we take for real, for a time—commenting on the play that we and they are watching. And the whole play oscillates between dream and reality, but a reality which we, the audience, know itself to be but a dramatic presentation, and for which (as at the end of *The Tempest*) we are asked to forgive the dramatist. As far as we can see, there is no such self-consciousness and questioning of the dramatic medium itself, playful or otherwise, in ancient tragedy (though there is much of the same in playful mode in Shakespeare's contemporary Cervantes). In this sense Shakespeare looks modern, or at least looks forward to modernity. But, as we will see in *Hamlet* particularly, the framework of belief in Shakespeare is not modern. With whatever questioning Shakespeare allows himself of the details of dogma, there seems to us to be little questioning of the existence and rightness of a sacred moral order itself. Though Claudius in *Hamlet* tries to shuffle off his guilt, and to secure forgiveness without renouncing his crown, there is in fact no shuffling (as Claudius himself says). There is no escape from the moral order or from its transcendent underpinning. What Caliban does in trying to rape Miranda is absolutely evil; and, as we will see in *Henry V*, for all the logic-chopping about the Salic Law, and for all Henry's leadership and heroism, Shakespeare leaves the legitimacy of the war against France very much an open question. There are absolute rights and wrongs in Shakespeare, of an order not of our choosing, however much characters may shuffle and prevaricate.

On the other hand, Shakespeare is certainly acutely aware of the tenuousness of civilization and of the difficulty of maintaining the order which makes civilized life possible. This is a theme which emerges in different ways in each of our chosen plays. Does this mean that he himself is a conservative or traditionalist, as some have argued? And they can also point to Ulysses' great paean to hierarchy and order in *Troilus and Cressida*:

Take but degree away, untune that string,
And, hark! What discord follows; each thing meets

In mere oppugnancy: the bounded waters
Should lift their bosoms higher than the shores,
And make a sop of all this solid globe:
Strength should be the lord of imbecility,
And the rude son should strike his father dead:
Force should be right; or rather, right and wrong,
Between whose endless jar justice resides,
Should lose their names, and so should justice too,
Then every thing includes itself in power,
Power into will, will into appetite;
And appetite, an universal wolf,
So doubly seconded with will and power,
Must make perforce an universal prey,
And last eat up himself . . . (Act One, Scene 3)

Hobbes, in his most pessimistic mood, could not have put it better, this need for strong government and for hierarchy to preserve us from what Hobbes called the war of all against all, and lives "nasty, brutish and short." But it is Ulysses speaking, and we know from Dante that Ulysses is a false counselor, an impression that Shakespeare does not exactly dispel.

And there are in Shakespeare all the "others" as well, those who would not subscribe without qualification to Ulysses' creed: subversive spirits like Falstaff, Caliban and even Ariel; Hamlet in his realism and criticism of the legal system and examples of realpolitik (and can we not easily imagine Ulysses pumping up Claudius with just the speech we have quoted?); then there are Gonzalo's utopian fantasies, contrasted (favorably?) with Prospero's rigidity; and finally there are Henry V's own doubts about monarchy, and the contrast he draws between his position and that of the "wretched slave." With these and other questions in mind, we will now turn to *Henry V.*

Henry V

Shakespeare portrays the English king Henry V in the play of that name (1599) as the most heroic of rulers as he takes on the French, first at Harfleur and then defeating them against the odds at Agincourt (in 1415). Shakespeare's dramatization of Henry's supreme leadership and martial valor (particularly in the battlefield speeches) can hardly fail to stir even the most churlish and disapproving, which is perhaps why the play is often treated in our less patriotic times with caution or even suspicion. And even on a straightforward reading of Shakespeare's version of events, we have to admit that perhaps due to his early death, Henry's triumphs quickly turned to ashes in the hands of his successors. But Shakespeare's Henry is actually a reflective and complex character as well as a dashing and inspiring leader. He is well aware of the dubious way in which his father gained the throne, and of the need to compensate for that, and also of the painful burdens borne by monarchs. And there is his earlier history in the background, as portrayed in the Henry IV *plays, to say nothing of the question of Falstaff, absent from the stage of* Henry V, *but still casting his larger-than-life shadow over events and over the young king.*

We know from internal evidence that the play was written in 1599, and in its theme and treatment of character it follows on directly from the two parts of *Henry IV* and from *Richard II.* In *Richard II*, Henry Bolingbroke, as he then was, had deposed his cousin Richard II (who was subsequently murdered), to become Henry IV. In the two *Henry IV* plays, much of the focus is on the tension between the King and his son Prince Hal (the future Henry V), who prefers low life in the taverns of Eastcheap in London to his dynastic duty. Characters from his Eastcheap days—such as Mistress Quickly, a tavern "hostess," Bardolph, Nim, Pistol, the Boy, and, above all, Sir John Falstaff—all have a role in *Henry V.* Indeed, *Henry V* can be seen as completing the transformation of Hal into King Henry, a hero unifying and inspiring a nation divided by internal strife, a transformation which was implied even at the beginning of *Henry IV Part One,* and maybe even in this unifying transformation going some way to legitimate the brutal seizure of power by his father. (Both Henrys always have the injustice of Bolingbroke's treatment of Richard lurking in the back of their consciousness.)

In Act One, Scene 2, the Prince speaks of his life in the stews and taverns and of the "unyok'd humour" and idleness of his companions:

> Yet herein will I imitate the sun
> Who doth permit the base contagious clouds
> To smother up his beauty from the world,
> That when he please again to be himself,
> Being wanted, he may the more be wonder'd at,
> By breaking through the foul and ugly mists
> Of vapours that did seem to strangle him.

He will throw off this "loose behavior" of himself and his companions, so that when he reforms, he will show himself off to better effect than if he had had no fault, though there is never any suggestion that he did not thoroughly enjoy himself in his pranks and escapades and in annoying his father. However, he does fight at the battle of Shrewsbury, where he actually kills the unblemished Hotspur, to whom his father has compared him unfavorably.

When Henry IV is dying at the end of *Henry IV Part Two* (Act Four, Scene 5), Henry and his father are in fact reconciled. Significantly for what is to occur later, in this scene Henry IV offers his son this advice:

> Therefore, my Harry
> Be it thy course to busy giddy minds
> With foreign quarrels; that action, hence borne out
> May waste the memory of the former days.

He then asks forgiveness for the way he himself acquired the crown, to which Prince Hal responds:

> My gracious liege,
> You won it, wore it, kept it, gave it me;
> Then plain and right must my possession be:
> With which I with more than a common pain
> 'Gainst all the world will rightfully maintain.

This he does, to a large extent by following the advice about foreign quarrels—in *Henry V;* but before the end of *Henry IV Part Two,* there is Falstaff to be seen off. Falstaff has been Hal's chief guide and companion in his youth, a second father to the Prince, rivalling Henry IV in his affections. Sir John Falstaff is an ageing, witty and pleasure-loving knight, of formidable girth and presence. He is cowardly in himself and unscrupulous in his dealings with others; in one incident he presses some comparatively wealthy yeomen into the King's army and then allows them to buy themselves out, pocketing the money himself, and replacing them in the army with a bunch of ragged scarecrows and ne'er-do-wells, who will march to almost certain death. This gargantuan and engaging reprobate is Prince Hal's guide, philosopher, and friend, but only until Hal succeeds. Falstaff, full of hope, runs to his royal friend with all the eagerness almost of a puppy greeting his returning master, but his hopes are cruelly, summarily and unexpectedly rebuffed:

> *Falstaff:* My king! my Jove! I speak to thee, my heart!
> *Henry V:* I know thee not, old man: fall to thy prayers;
> How ill white hairs become a fool and a jester!
> I have long dream'd of such a kind of man,
> So surfeit swell'd, so old and so profane;
> But being awak'd, I do despise my dream.
> Make less thy body hence, and more thy grace.

Leave gourmandising; know the grave doth gape
For thee thrice wider than for other men.
Reply not to me with a fool-born jest.
Presume not that I am the thing I was;
For God doth know, so shall the world perceive,
That I have turn'd away my former self,
So will I those that kept me company . . .

So does Henry deal with Falstaff and his past, though we are promised in the
Epilogue to *Henry IV Part Two* that we will see Falstaff again in *Henry V.*

Act One

In *Henry V,* each of the five Acts is preceded by a Chorus which sets the scene
with references to the language and imagery of Virgil and Homer, but which
also invites the audience to use their imagination in seeing in the "cock pit"
of the theater the "vasty fields of France" and the events of the battle of Agincourt and the rest.

In Act One, we are given the background to Henry's expedition to France.
Scene 1 has the Archbishop of Canterbury and the Bishop of Ely discussing
how to fend off a proposal of Henry IV to take half the possessions of the
Church. Canterbury praises Henry's personal reform, and the two churchmen plan to deflect the crown from the Church in England by encouraging
Henry in his claim to the crown of France. It is this claim which occupies
the whole of the long and somewhat complicated second scene. The scene,
though not easy to follow, is important in the context of the play, dramatically as a slow introduction to the events which are to follow, and thematically because what is at issue is the very legitimacy of the actions that we—as
audience—will identify with.

Anglo-French relations had been interwoven in the Middle Ages in part
because, going back to the marriage of the English Henry II with Eleanor of
Aquitaine (who was also the divorced wife of the King of France) in 1152,
the kings of England were also the dukes of Aquitaine (Gascony); but as such
they had to recognize the overlordship of the kings of France, and this led
to constant friction and a strong sense of injustice on both sides. But then,
over and above that, after four French kings in quick succession, in 1328
Edward III of England claimed the French throne for himself, through his
French mother, Isabella. This led to an English campaign in France, the so-
called Hundred Years War, which began in 1337 and lasted intermittently
until 1453. Edward's own campaign included a victory at Crécy (1346), the
victory of his son, the Black Prince, at Poitiers (1356), and in 1359, Edward

himself marching on Rheims, where the French kings were traditionally crowned. But, following the peace of Bretigny in 1360, the campaign petered out, with the English being ceded Gascony and Calais unimpeded and largely withdrawing from the rest of France, until Henry V himself renewed the claim to the French throne in 1413.

Leaving aside the military campaigns, the French had always strenuously rejected the English claim because of what was known as the Salic Law, an ancient Frankish custom, according to which the throne could be inherited only through the male line. Edward's claim was therefore invalid. In Scene 2 of *Henry V,* the ecclesiastics argue that the Salic Law applies only to the Franks in Germany, but not to the Franks in France; and in any case, there have been instances in French history where succession has been through the female line. So Henry's claim is good. Assuming that Scotland (a traditional ally of France) could be kept quiet, Henry should invade France.

At this point the Dauphin's ambassador enters, bringing a "tun" of treasure, which turns out to be filled with tennis balls. This insult dramatically deflects attention from the question of the legitimacy of the English cause. In a spirited reply, Henry says that the English will match "our rackets to these balls." The campaign is on, with, as the Prologue to Act Two has it, all the youth of England "on fire."

Act Two

Before we go to France, there is the first of two scenes set in Eastcheap (Act Two, Scene 1). Involved are Nim, Bardolph, Pistol, the Boy, and Mistress Quickly (the Hostess). Pistol has just married the Hostess, Bardolph's former betrothed. There is much bravado and three drawing of swords in the scene, but half-way through the Boy comes in with the news that Falstaff is ill. As Mistress Quickly says, "the King has killed his heart." On being told by her that "as ever you come of women, come in quickly to Sir John," they all leave, reflecting on Falstaff's fate and the King, even though Nim insists that the King is a good king. The King, meanwhile, is in Southampton, from where the fleet is about to sail (Scene 2). He traps three nobles who he knows are plotting against him into condemning another supposed traitor; and then, exposing their own plot, sentences them decisively and ruthlessly, after which he orders the invasion of France. Falstaff, meanwhile, has died, in Arthur's bosom, the Hostess insists, "if ever man went to Arthur's bosom" (Scene 3). As he was dying, he "cried out of sack" and of women, and "said they were the devil incarnate":

> *Hostess:* A could never abide carnation, 'twas a colour he never liked.
>
> *Boy:* A said once the devil would have him about women.

Hostess: A did in some sort, indeed handle, women—but then he was rheumatic, and talked of the Whore of Babylon.

Boy: Do you not remember, a saw a flea stick on Bardolph's nose, and a said it was a black soul burning in hell?

Bardolph: Well the fuel is gone that maintained that fire. That's all the riches I got in his service.

Nim: Shall we shog? The King will be gone from Southampton.

Pistol: Come, let's away . . .

For the three rogues and the Boy, now bereft and penniless with the death of Falstaff, are going to France as part of Henry's expedition.

From the slums of London and the urgency of Henry's court-martial in Southampton, the scene (Scene 4) turns to the opulence and luxury of the French court, where the Dauphin speaks slightingly of Henry, "a vain, giddy, shallow, humorous youth." The King (Charles VI) is more circumspect, reminding the court of the exploits of the Black Prince. The Duke of Exeter then arrives, as Henry's ambassador, demanding the crown of France. The Dauphin reminds him of the "Paris balls" he sent Henry, to match "his youth and vanity," to which Exeter replies that Henry will "make your Paris Louvre shake for it."

Act Three

In Act Three, Henry and his army are besieging Harfleur, a French port at the mouth of the Seine. The French had offered Henry Catherine, the King's daughter, and some "petty and unprofitable dukedoms" as a dowry, but this had been rejected. But there appears to be stalemate. The town's walls have survived a hammering. Leadership is required from Henry, who, like Alexander the Great, is going to be the first to scale the wall:

Once more unto the breach, dear friends, once more,
Or close up the wall with our English dead.
In peace there's nothing so becomes a man
As modest stillness and humility.
But when the blast of war blows in our ears,
Then imitate the action of the tiger.
Stiffen the sinews, conjure up the blood,
Disguise fair nature with hard-favoured rage.
Then lend the eye a terrible aspect.
Let it pry through the portage of the head
Like the brass canon, let the brow o'erwhelm it

As fearfully as doth a galled rock
O'erhang and jutty his confounded base,
Swilled with the wild and wasteful ocean.
Now set the teeth and stretch the nostril wide,
Hold hard the breath, and bend up every spirit
To his full height. On, on, you noblest English,
Whose blood is fet from fathers of war-proof,
Fathers that like so many Alexanders
Have in these parts from morn to even fought,
And sheathed their swords for lack of argument.
Dishonour not your mothers; now attest
That those whom you called fathers did beget you.
Be copy now to men of grosser blood,
And teach them how to war. And you, good yeomen,
Whose limbs were made in England, show us here
The mettle of your pasture; let us swear
That you are worth your breeding—which I doubt not,
For there is none of you so mean and base
That hath not noble lustre in your eyes.
I see you stand like greyhounds in the slips,
Straining upon the start. The game's afoot.
Follow your spirit, and upon this charge
Cry, 'God for Harry! England and Saint George!'

Henry's will, alone it seems, and his invocation of Englishness, here prevails. The wall is breached, but Henry's army is not in good shape. In Scene 2, we see Fluellen, a Captain, beating in the three somewhat reluctant Eastcheap "swashers," as the Boy calls them, before revealing that they have already been involved in stealing and looting. In the next scene, to underline the Britishness of the expedition, Shakespeare shows us four captains: a Scot (Jamy), an Englishman (Gower), an Irishman (Macmorris), and the Welsh Fluellen, discussing tactics and the discipline of war.

The town now wants to discuss terms for peace. Henry, though, is implacable. He threatens to unleash his "enraged soldiers" on an orgy of destruction, rape, and slaughter of old and young alike, if there is not total surrender. The Governor, realizing that the Dauphin is not going to lift the siege, yields, and the triumphant English enter Harfleur.

From the barbarism of war to the sweets of peace: in Scene 4, spoken in French, Princess Catherine of France is having an English lesson from her nurse, full of delightful Gallicisms and double entendres. This is followed by a discussion at the French court. There is some surprise at the English advance. They have now left Harfleur and have crossed the Somme. On the other hand, we learn that their numbers are few and that sickness is spreading through the army.

In Scene 6, we are back with the English army, with Exeter holding a bridge. Pistol enters and explains to Fluellen that Bardolph has stolen a pax from a church and has been condemned to death by Exeter. Pistol pleads for him, but Fluellen will have none of it. Henry enters, and Fluellen asks him to judge. Henry, without so much as recognizing Pistol or Bardolph, "would have all such offenders cut off." His transformation is complete.

Montjoy, the French Herald, enters, demanding surrender and a ransom from the English. Henry admits to enfeeblement, but he will march on to Calais:

> We would not seek a battle as we are
> Nor as we are we say we will not shun it.

In Scene 7, it is night in the French camp. The French nobles foppishly boast of their horses, joke about their mistresses, and look forward to hammering the English, who are camped only 1,500 paces away. By ten o'clock the next morning we'll each have a hundred Englishmen.

Act Four

Act Four, which deals with the battle of Agincourt, opens with the Chorus comparing the two armies by night: "the confident and overlusty French" and "the low-rated English . . . this ruined band." The first scene takes up this theme in a manner reminiscent of Book Ten of *The Iliad,* the night before the third day of the battle when Agamemnon is deeply worried and goes round the Achaean camp calling a council of the leaders. Here, Henry tells his nobles of the danger they are all in, and an old knight, Sir Thomas Erpingham, plays the role of Nestor. Henry takes Erpingham's cloak so he can wander round the camp incognito.

Henry is first challenged by Pistol, who does not recognize him, Henry claiming to be a Welshman. He then overhears Fluellen insisting on the need for military discipline. Other soldiers, including Bates and Williams, come up; and the three of them, with Henry still in disguise, discuss the nature of kingship. Henry says that he is serving under Erpingham, and that Erpingham is worried about the outcome of the battle. Bates asks if Erpingham should not communicate this to the King. Henry says no: "I think the King is but a man, as I am," and has fears the same as other men. The cause being just, it is their duty to follow the King. Williams asks: but what if the cause be not good; then the King will be responsible for all the deaths which occur. Henry argues that it is the duty of the men to follow the King, but if they die, the state of their soul is on their own head; so the King will not be guilty of their damnation. Bates agrees, but Williams impugns the King's integrity, saying that he will let the men fight to their deaths, and then seek a ransom for himself. Henry and he exchange gloves, agreeing to resolve the quarrel after the battle, when they will see whether the King betrays his men or not.

Alone, Henry reflects on the burdens of kingship:

Upon the King.
'Let us our lives, our souls, our debts, our care-full wives,
Our children, and our sins, lay on the King.'
We must bear all. O hard condition,
Twin-born with greatness; subject to the breath
Of every fool, whose sense no more can feel
Than his own wringing. What infinite heartease
Must kings neglect that private men enjoy?
And what have kings that privates have not too,
Save ceremony, save general ceremony?
What art thou, thou idol ceremony?
What kind of god art thou, that suffer'st more
Of mortal griefs than do thy worshippers?
What are thy rents? What are thy comings-in?
O ceremony, show me but thy worth.
What is thy soul of adoration?
Art thou aught else but place, degree and form,
Creating awe and fear in other men? . . .
I know
'Tis not the balm, the sceptre and the ball,
The sword, the mace, the crown imperial,
The intertissued robe of gold and pearl,
The farced title running fore the king,
The throne he sits on, not the tide of pomp
That beats upon the high shore of this world—
No, not all these, thrice gorgeous ceremony,
Not all these laid in bed majestical,
Can sleep so soundly as the wretched slave
Who with a body filled and vacant mind
Gets him to rest, crammed with distressful bread . . .
And but for ceremony such a wretch,
Winding up days with toil and nights with sleep,

Had the forehand and vantage of a king.
The slave, a member of the country's peace,
Enjoys it, but in gross brain little wots
What watch the King keeps to maintain the peace,
Whose hours the peasant best advantages.

A different slant, one might feel, on order and ceremony from that of Ulysses; but we should note that for all Henry's recognition of the emptiness and tawdriness of ceremony, and for all his envy of the condition of the "wretched slave," he still insists on the necessity of ceremony and on the King's watch, precisely so that the peasant can have his advantages.

Erpingham rouses Henry from his reverie. His nobles need him and Henry sends Erpingham off to gather them. Alone again, Henry prays to the God of battles to steel his soldiers' hearts. And he also reflects on the sin of his father in grabbing the throne. He has re-buried Richard himself, and has provided for many prayers and masses for his soul: "More will I do, / Though all that I can do is nothing worth / Since that my penitence comes after ill. . . ."

The French camp once more provides a contrast. "The sun doth gild our armour." They are impatient for battle and for victory, as well they might be, having 60,000 men to Henry's 12,000—as is pointed out by the Earl of Warwick in Scene 3. Warwick wishes they had more. In reply, to the whole army, Henry declaims his Saint Crispin's Day speech, unmatched in qualities of leadership and inspiration:

What's he that wishes so?
My cousin Warwick. No my fair cousin.
If we are marked to die, we are enough
To do our country loss; and if to live,
The fewer men, the greater share of honour.
God's will, I pray thee wish not one man more.
By Jove, I am not covetous for gold,
Nor care I who doth feed upon my cost;
It ernes me not if men my garments wear;
Such outward things dwell not in my desires.
But if it be a sin to covet honour
I am the most offending man alive.
No, faith, my coz, wish not a man from England.
God's peace, I would not lose so great an honour
As one man more methinks would share from me
For the best hope I have. O do not wish one more.
Rather proclaim it presently through my host

That he which hath no stomach to this fight,
Let him depart. His passport shall be made
And crowns for convoy put into his purse.
We would not die in that man's company
That fears his fellowship to die with us.
This day is called the feast of Crispian.
He that outlives this day and comes safe home
Will stand a-tiptoe when this day is named
And rouse him at the name of Crispian.
He that shall see this day and live t'old age
Will yearly on the vigil feast his neighbours
And say, "Tomorrow is Saint Crispian."
Then will he strip his sleeve and show his scars
And say, "These wounds I had on Crispian's day."
Old men forget; yet all shall be forgot,
But he'll remember, with advantages,
What feats he did that day. Then shall our names,
Familiar in his mouth as household words—
Harry the King, Bedford and Exeter,
Warwick and Talbot, Salisbury and Gloucester—
Be in their flowing cups freshly remembered.
This story shall the good man teach his son,
And Crispin Crispian shall ne'er go by
From this day to the ending of the world
But we in it shall be remembered,
We few, we happy few, we band of brothers.
For he to-day that sheds his blood with me
Shall be my brother; be he ne'er so vile,
This day shall gentle his condition.
And gentlemen in England now abed
Shall think themselves accursed they were not here,
And hold their manhoods cheap while any speaks
That fought with us upon Saint Crispin's day.

Notice the familiar, almost conversational opening and the slow build-up, meditative and introspective, but establishing the kind of man the leader is; then the apparently gracious concession to any who wish to go, but put in such a way that any who took it would be ashamed; then the establishment of the Crispin Day theme, repeated and repeated, as to what it will mean in terms of honor in the future, and the pride of those who were fortunate enough to be there, a select band in contrast to those who were not; then, in the rousing peroration, the association of all with the noble enterprise and with the nobles and the king in blood-brothership.

After this, Montjoy comes to offer terms for the ransom of the English, which are, naturally enough after the Crispin's Day speech, dismissed: "We are but warriors for the working day . . . Our hearts are in the trim." On the field of battle (Scene 4), we first see Pistol capturing a French soldier, and then releasing him for a ransom of 200 crowns. The Boy is disgusted with Pistol and compares him unfavorably to Bardolph and to Nim, who it appears has also been hanged for looting. The incident, though, is symptomatic of the way the battle has been going. The French have been pushed back, but prepare for another attack. Henry, learning of the deaths of York and Suffolk, and hearing of this new attack, orders his men to kill the French prisoners they have. It then emerges, in a conversation between Fluellen and Gower, that the French have committed the unforgivable crime of killing all the English boys who had been left guarding the supplies. Fluellen, the Welshman, points out that Henry was born in Monmouth (in Wales). As he is to be compared to Alexander the Great, Monmouth may be compared to Macedon; and although, unlike Alexander, Henry did not kill his best friend, he did turn away "the fat knight."

Henry enters with the English army and French captives. Full of anger now at the slaughter of the boys, he orders that all French prisoners they take be killed. Montjoy arrives to concede defeat and to ask to bury his dead. He gives the name of the place as Agincourt. Henry, in conversation with Fluellen, emphasises his Welshness. Williams appears, seeking the Englishman he tussled with the previous night. After some complicated by-play, Henry reveals himself as Williams' opponent. It emerges finally that 1,500 French nobles and 10,000 French in all died at Agincourt, compared to four English nobles and twenty-five men. Acknowledging that "God fought for us," Henry orders the singing of *Non nobis* ("Not to us, O Lord") and the *Te Deum* ("We praise Thee, O God"), before they journey on to Calais.

Act Five

Act Five is something of an epilogue to the rest of the play, and somewhat skeletal in itself. We are told by the Chorus that Henry returned in triumph to London, following Agincourt. Various events, including the death of the Dauphin and the English campaigns of 1416–19, are passed over, and we are with Henry and his troops on their expedition to France of 1420. In the first scene, we are with Fluellen, Gower and Pistol. Pistol, ribbing Fluellen about his Welshness and the leek in his cap, is beaten for his pains and told off by Gower. Now the last of Hal's Eastcheap companions, Pistol tells us that "his"

Doll (the Hostess?) is dead of venereal disease, and that he will now return to England, to steal.

The final scene takes place in the French court, and is a scene of high comic reconciliation and romance. Henry is welcomed by the King and Queen of France, and also by the Duke of Burgundy, who extols the "lovely visage" of France and emphasises the need for peace. Henry sends his dukes to negotiate the peace, while he himself woos Catherine. With Henry posing as a plain soldier, the lovemaking is charmingly conducted in a mixture of English, French, and Franglais. But there is a serious dynastic point as well. Together, Henry says, they will "between Saint Denis and Saint George, compound a boy, half-French half-English, that shall go to Constantinople and take the Turk by the beard." Catherine (now Kate to Henry) agrees, and, against her professions of modesty, Henry kisses her on the lips. The courts then return with an agreement, with Henry to be King of England and Heir to France, so that, as the French King puts it, "the contending kingdoms . . . may cease their hatred."

We learn, though, in the Epilogue what all of Shakespeare's audience would have known: that Henry VI succeeded as an infant, and that so many then "had the managing / That they lost France and made his England bleed."

Conclusion

Henry V is, on the surface, straightforward and straightforwardly patriotic, too much so apparently for some modern sensibilities, which are scared of the sheer power of the Saint Crispin Day's speech and also perhaps by the combination of Hal/Henry's easygoing popularity and his sheer steel. And steel there is, not just in the rejection of Falstaff and the summary execution of Bardolph. By today's standards, the Henry of Harfleur is a potential war criminal and the Henry of Agincourt, slaughtering the French prisoners even before the killing of the boys, very probably an actual one. All this is quite apart from the dubious pretext for the war (a "false prospectus" if ever there were one).

From the English point of view, Henry is a fine leader. He unites a divided country, apparently carrying all the factions and sub-nations with him. Again, his leadership is doubtless the secret. No doubt when in action he enjoys what he is doing, but as Shakespeare makes very clear in the reflections before the battle of Agincourt, Henry is acutely aware of the cost of kingship, and he also has his answer to the question we posed in connection with Homer: peaceful commonwealths are founded on original crimes, and need order and force to keep them peaceful. It would not be wrong to see the glorification of Henry by Shakespeare as some sort of retrospective justification of the Bolingbroke coup. There is still, of course, the problem of the legitimacy of the invasion of France, magnificent as it seemed at the time. Does Henry really believe the advice given to him in Act One about the Salic Law legitimating his claim to France? One doubts that so acute and self-conscious a character did, or that Shakespeare intended us to think he did, even if, as could be maintained, the underlying claim to some English suzerainty over France may have had merit within the twisted and interwoven history of the two countries. Does the romance of the ending, the union of the two countries, make up for the deficit at the start? More, even apart from the misfortune of Henry's early death (1422), did it ever seem likely that an Anglo-French union could have survived long in the 15th century? At the end of *Henry V,* history gives way to romance; we are in the world of the comedies rather than that of history. But before that, in the Saint Crispin's Day speech and in the hours leading up to it, Shakespeare has given us so moving and powerful a testament to patriotism and its strength that contemporary audiences, reared on a diet of internationalism and pacifism, are filled with discomfort at their warming to the heroic young king and his country.

Hamlet

Shakespeare's Hamlet *(1600) tells the story of the Danish prince called on by his father's ghost to avenge his murder. The assassin is Claudius, the old king's brother, who then assumed the throne and married Gertrude, Hamlet's mother. But Hamlet's mission is frustrated by what looks like his continual procrastination, which leads directly or indirectly to the death of eight characters. Among the eight are Hamlet himself and Ophelia, the young girl whom Hamlet initially loves and then abuses horribly when he suspects her of being used by his enemies. What takes Shakespeare's play beyond the revenge tragedies of the time is the character of Hamlet himself, a source of endless fascination and reinterpretation from Shakespeare's time on.*

Hamlet was probably written in 1600, so just after *Henry V.* Like *Henry V,* its hero is a young prince, but a prince of a very different character and in a very different situation. Although his father—the old Hamlet, King of Denmark—has died, Hamlet is not the ruler. This position has been seized by his uncle Claudius, who has also married Gertrude, the widow of old Hamlet and young Hamlet's mother. As Hamlet learns early in the play, it appears that Claudius has murdered his brother. But, in contrast to how Prince Hal would have acted in a similar situation, Hamlet appears indecisive, and the disastrous events which unfold in the play are largely a consequence of this. On the standard interpretation of the play, Hamlet is a dreamer rather than an actor, more at home in the world of the theater than in the scheming milieu of his uncle's court; but this is not because of a lack of courage or intelligence, for he is courageous and intelligent, but rather because of a surfeit of self-consciousness.

It is because of Hamlet's damaging propensity for introspection, together with self-paralysing reflectiveness and sensitivity, that he became an icon for the Romantics, almost a prototype of the modern Romantic hero or anti-hero. As we will see, however, this is not a complete picture of Hamlet, who at crucial points in the play is as much a creature of his own time (or rather Shakespeare's) as of the future. In many ways he is a Renaissance prince, in a Renaissance court, isolated and surrounded by enemies, but still quite capable of decisive, unscrupulous and courageous action. It is not clear that his indecisiveness is altogether the fault of some defect in his character, as the Romantic interpretation would have it. Nor does the play make full sense except within the context of Christian belief about judgment, and on the assumption that Hamlet and others in the play accept this belief unquestioningly.

Act One

The play opens at midnight on the battlements of the castle of Elsinore, Elsinore being the site of the Danish court. The soldiers of the watch have seen a ghost on previous nights, and they have brought Horatio, a scholar and friend of Hamlet, to watch with them. They see the ghost, whom Horatio recognizes as the old King Hamlet. He also explains that Hamlet defeated and killed King Fortinbras of Norway in a duel, gaining lands as a result. His son, young Fortinbras, is preparing for war to reclaim what Norway has lost, so there are preparations for war in Denmark too. The Ghost appears again, and Horatio and the soldiers resolve to speak to Hamlet about what they have seen.

The second scene is a complete contrast. Claudius, the King, recently crowned and recently married, is holding court. He dispatches envoys to Norway to curb young Fortinbras. He also gives Laertes, the son of Polonius, an old Privy Councillor, permission to return to France. Throughout all this, Hamlet, clad in black like some medieval representation of melancholy, himself broods to one side. He responds angrily to the attempts of Claudius and Gertrude to shake him out of his melancholy, and when the court has gone, he utters the first of the soliloquies for which the character is renowned:

O that this too too solid flesh would melt,
Thaw and resolve itself into a dew,
Or that the Everlasting had not fixed
His canon 'gainst self-slaughter. O God! O God!
How weary, flat, stale and unprofitable
Seem to me all the uses of this world!
Fie on't! O fie, fie! 'Tis an unweeded garden
That grows to seed; things rank and gross in nature
Possess it merely. That it should come to this!
But two months dead—nay, not so much, not two—
So excellent a king, that was to this
Hyperion to a satyr, so loving to my mother
That he might not beteem the winds of heaven
Visit her face too roughly. Heaven and earth,
Must I remember? Why she would hang on him
As if increase of appetite had grown
By what it fed on, and yet within a month—
Let me not think on't; frailty, thy name is woman—
A little month, or ere those shoes were old
With which she followed my poor father's body,
Like Niobe, all tears, why she, even she—
O God, a beast that wants discourse of reason
Would have mourned longer!—married with my uncle,
My father's brother, but no more like my father
Than I to Hercules; within a month,
Ere yet the salt of most unrighteous tears
Had left the flushing in her galled eyes,
She married. O most wicked speed, to post
With such dexterity to incestuous sheets!
It is not, nor it cannot come to good.
But break, my heart, for I must hold my tongue.

What is significant about this speech is that Hamlet's *Weltschmerz,* and his attitudes to Claudius, to his mother and to her over-speedy marriage, and to sex (above all to sex), are all established at this point, and *before* he learns anything about how his father died. This is the Hamlet who foreshadowed Goethe's Werther and who fascinated Coleridge, the author of "Dejection: An Ode," in which he wrote of "A grief without a pang, void, dark and drear, / A stifled, drowsy unimpassioned grief / Which finds no natural outlet, no relief." For this aspect of Hamlet, we do not need the Ghost and his revelations, and Hamlet does not need any objective proof of sin or guilt on the part of Claudius or Gertrude. It is all in his mind and his disposition already. He already has, like Coleridge, "viper thoughts that coil around his mind," and also, we may feel, a degree of exaggeration about his plight (for example, whatever Gertrude might or might not have done, despite Hamlet's complaint, beasts that want discourse of reason are not found wandering around in mourning after the deaths of their mates). To Hamlet, already, the world and the court are like an unweeded garden, possessed by things rank and gross in nature. Objective proof, though, of genuine disorder in the court is what Hamlet is about to get, because at this point Horatio and the soldiers tell him what they have seen, and he agrees to go with them onto the ramparts later that night.

In the third scene we see first Laertes, bound for France, and his sister Ophelia. Hamlet has been "trifling," as Laertes sees it, with Ophelia's affections, and he warns her off. Polonius, their father, then dispenses advice to Laertes, advice notable mainly for its combination of wordiness and practical uselessness. Laertes is in effect told to avoid every extreme in his conduct, holding just the right position in between; Ophelia, on the other hand, is told to distrust Hamlet and to avoid him.

On the ramparts (Scenes 4 and 5), Hamlet and the others encounter the Ghost. The Ghost takes Hamlet off alone, and tells him that he is currently suffering terribly in Purgatory because he died "in the blossoms" of his sins, with no chance to repent or be absolved. But he did not die, as was put out, of a serpent's sting. He was actually murdered by Claudius, who put poison in his ear while he was asleep one afternoon in his orchard. Hamlet is to avenge this crime, but must do so without "tainting his mind" against his mother. That the Ghost is telling Hamlet to commit just the crime that Claudius committed—and maybe to be liable to a far worse punishment that the Ghost—is glossed over by both characters, however. When the others reappear, Hamlet, reinforced by the Ghost, enjoins them to secrecy. He also tells them that he may act mad ("put an antic disposition on") in order to pursue his ends.

Act Two

In the first scene, Polonius, the eternal bureaucrat, sends a servant to spy on Laertes in Paris. Ophelia enters, saying that Hamlet is behaving very strangely towards her. Polonius concludes that this must mean that Hamlet really does love Ophelia, and decides to inform the King.

In the following scene, in the court, two student associates of Hamlet, Rosencrantz and Guildenstern, are brought before Claudius, who sets them to spy on Hamlet. The ambassadors from Norway return with the news that the new king there has persuaded young Fortinbras to divert his attentions from Denmark to Poland, and to seek permission to pass through Denmark en route. Polonius brings Claudius and Gertrude evidence of Hamlet's mad love for Ophelia, and they plot to observe Hamlet in conversation with her. Hamlet then enters. Pretending to be mad, he sends Polonius up unmercifully, though dropping bawdy hints about his interest in Polonius's daughter. Rosencrantz and Guildenstern enter, and Hamlet initially bandies words with them—about Fortune (a strumpet), Denmark (a prison), ambition (dreams and shadows). He then confronts them with having been sent to spy on him, which they admit.

Hamlet tells them that he has lost all mirth. Everything in the world appears sterile and foul to him, even man:

> What a piece of work is a man, how noble in reason, how infinite in faculty, in form and moving how express and admirable, in action how like an angel, in apprehension how like a god—the beauty of the world, the paragon of animals! And yet, to me, what is this quintessence of dust? Man delights me not—no, nor woman neither, though by your smiling you seem to say so.

He is then told that a troupe of travelling players are arriving in Elsinore, and Hamlet welcomes them with enthusiasm. He gets their leader to declaim a rhetorical speech in which Aeneas recounts to Dido the deaths of Priam and Hecuba, after which he asks him in private to put on a play before the court called *The Murder of Gonzago,* to which he, Hamlet, will add a few lines.

Hamlet is then left alone, and in his second soliloquy he reflects on the passionate way in which the Player acted over Hecuba:

> For Hecuba!
> What's Hecuba to him, or he to Hecuba,
> That he should weep for her?

He contrasts his own inactivity and lack of gall "to make oppression bitter" with the tears and words and gestures of the actor. He will, though, use the play—in which there will be something like his father's death—to test his uncle, to see if he reacts to it with guilt.

Of course, as Hamlet does himself, one could also say that it is not just the uncle who is going to be tested by the play, but also his father's ghost (or what seems to be his father's ghost). Equally, the remarks about the player and the death of Hecuba could also be applied to Shakespeare's *Hamlet.* By this stage, if the performance is any good, the audience will be far more gripped than anyone would ever have been by the Player's speech. But we are still an audience of a play, a make-belief, not of Hecuba and her sorrows, but of Hamlet and of Shakespeare's manipulation of our reactions to his creation.

Act Three

The first scene opens with Rosencrantz and Guildenstern telling Claudius and Gertrude about the play that Hamlet is organizing. Polonius and Claudius then set up Ophelia to be observed by them in conversation with Hamlet. As the two men hide, with Ophelia pretending to read a prayer book, Hamlet enters and speaks:

> To be, or not to be—that is the question:
> Whether 'tis nobler in the mind to suffer
> The slings and arrows of outrageous fortune,
> Or to take arms against a sea of troubles,
> And by opposing end them? To die, to sleep—
> No more; and by a sleep to say we end
> The heartache and the thousand natural shocks
> That flesh is heir to—'tis a consummation
> Devoutly to be wished: to die, to sleep.
> To sleep, perchance to dream. Ay, there's the rub;
> For in that sleep of death what dreams may come,
> When we have shuffled off this mortal coil,
> Must give us pause. There's the respect
> That makes calamity of so long life.
> For who would bear the whips and scorns of time,
> The oppressor's wrong, the proud man's contumely,
> The pangs of disprized love, the law's delay,
> The insolence of office, and the spurns
> That patient merit of the unworthy takes,
> When he himself might his quietus make
> With a bare bodkin? Who would these fardels bear,
> To grunt and sweat under a weary life,
> But that the dread of something after death,
> The undiscovered country from whose bourn
> No traveler returns, puzzles the will,
> And makes us rather bear those ills we have
> Than fly to others that we know not of?
> Thus conscience does make cowards of us all;
> And thus the native hue of resolution

Is sicklied o'er with the pale cast of thought,
And enterprises of great pith and moment
With this regard their current turn away
And lose the name of action.

Hamlet, who might commit suicide, will not because he does not really believe that death is the end; as we have already seen in the first soliloquy, he believes that God has forbidden suicide. Strangely, though, in this speech Hamlet makes no mention of the edicts of the Almighty, and is apparently doubtful about what might happen after death; as for the undiscovered country, to Hamlet's own knowledge has not at least one traveler returned (his father)? This speech is so familiar that we tend to forget its strangeness in the context of the play up to that point, and also in the light of what Hamlet (and Claudius) will in due course say about Christian judgment. "To be or not to be" reads and sounds more like the musings of a Roman stoic, of perhaps a Renaissance philosopher (which in a sense Hamlet is), than like the thoughts of the character we are shown in the rest of the play. But in the speech Hamlet also says that the pale cast of thought deprives us of the will or power to act. These are thoughts of high generality and appeal, particularly to tortured youth, quite apart from their place in the action of the play. But there is the play, and the action:

Soft you now,
The fair Ophelia,—Nymph, in thy orisons,
Be all my sins remembered.

The nymph, Ophelia, is a sweet girl whom Hamlet proceeds to treat brutally. Admittedly, as emerges, he knows that she is in on the plot, but she is hardly to blame for that. Ophelia begins by reminding Hamlet of the things he has said to her. He asks her if she is honest—and fair. She struggles. He did love her once, he admits, but she should not have believed him: "Get thee to a nunnery," so she will not breed sinners; and then he castigates her, and through her all women, for painting the faces God gave them. "You jig, you amble, and you lisp, and nickname God's creatures, and make your wantonness your ignorance . . . we will have no more marriages. . . ." As always, Hamlet is obsessed with the sexual aspect of love, and it shatters Ophelia's fragile confidence as to who Hamlet is:

O, what a noble mind is here o'erthrown!
The courtier's, soldier's, scholar's, eye, tongue, sword . . .
Th'observed of all observers—quite, quite down!
And I, of ladies most deject and wretched,

That sucked the honey of his music vows,
Now see that noble and most sovereign reason
Like sweet bells jangled out of tune and harsh . . .

Equally jangling and insensitive, Claudius and Polonius now enter, in effect dismissing Ophelia—Hamlet's "affections do not that way tend," says Claudius, and decides to send Hamlet away to England. Polonius proposes that after the play Gertrude tries to find out what is really troubling him.

Scene 2 opens with Hamlet addressing the Players, just before the play is to be presented: "Speak the speech, I pray you, as I pronounced it to you, trippingly on the tongue." They are not to over-act or distort what is written in an effort to "out-Herod Herod." Nor are the clowns to do more than is set down for them. Before the play actually begins, Hamlet eulogizes Horatio:

Give me that man
That is not passion's slave, and I will wear him
In my heart's core, ay, in my heart of heart,
As I do thee.

He then fills Horatio in on the plot, asking him to observe the demeanor of Claudius during the play.

As the play begins, before the whole court, Hamlet positions himself in Ophelia's lap, occasioning ribald comments from him about country matters and lying between maids' legs, as well as invective against his mother. The play itself is in effect run twice; first there is a mime of old Hamlet's death through having poison poured in his ear, and then the whole thing is repeated with speeches, principally from the Queen, in which she professes her undying love for the King and her hostility to second marriages. The King in the play falls asleep, and Hamlet asks his mother how she likes the play. She replies: "The lady protests too much." Claudius, becoming rattled, asks Hamlet the play's title. Hamlet says it is called *The Mousetrap*. The action proceeds with the King's nephew pouring poison in his uncle's ear, accompanied by a commentary from Hamlet. At this Claudius leaps up, calling for lights.

In the disarray which ensues, Hamlet and Horatio see what has happened in the play as confirmation of their suspicions, and then Rosencrantz and Guildenstern, followed by Polonius, summon Hamlet to Gertrude's room. Hamlet accuses Rosencrantz and Guildenstern of attempting to play on him, as on a pipe. Left alone, Hamlet ponders on how he will treat his mother:

'Tis now the very witching time of night,
When churchyards yawn and hell itself breathes out

Contagion to this world. Now could I drink hot blood,
And do such bitter business as the day
Would quake to look on. Soft, now, to my mother.
O heart, lose not thy nature. Let not ever
The soul of Nero enter this firm bosom.
Let me be cruel, not unnatural.
I will speak daggers to her, but use none . . .

Hamlet could drink hot blood—now; but he won't use daggers to his mother. As things turn out, neither is exactly the case. The scene which follows (Scene 3) is in some ways the nub of the action. It opens with Claudius instructing Rosencrantz and Guildenstern to escort Hamlet to England, and Polonius volunteering to hide himself in Gertrude's room to overhear the meeting between Hamlet and his mother. Left alone, Claudius tries to pray:

O, my offence is rank, it smells to heaven.
It hath the primal elder's curse upon't—
A brother's murder.
But he cannot pray, because he is unwilling to renounce the fruits of his crime. As he struggles internally, on his knees, Hamlet passes by:
Now might I do it pat, now he is praying,
And now I'll do't.
[*He draws his sword*]
And so he goes to heaven . . .

. . . while his own father is suffering in Purgatory. This is no revenge. He will wait until Claudius is "drunk asleep, or in his rage, / Or in th'incestuous pleasure of his bed." The irony is that Claudius rises, unable to pray.

With Polonius hiding behind a screen, Hamlet enters Gertrude's room. Each is angry with the other, Gertrude making to leave. Hamlet tries to stop her, and she cries out for help. Polonius too cries out, and Hamlet thrusts his sword through the screen. He then discovers that it is Polonius he has killed, not Claudius, as he had imagined. To Gertrude's reproach he replies that what he has done is not so bad as killing a king and marrying his brother. Gertrude's reaction convinces Hamlet that she was not party to the murder, but he declares that he will now wring Gertrude's heart. He shows her pictures of old Hamlet and of Claudius, and accuses her of being "stewed in corruption, honeying and making love / Over the nasty sty." As Hamlet goes on vilifying Claudius and Gertrude, the Ghost appears to Hamlet, though not to Gertrude, "to whet [Hamlet's] almost blunted purpose." Gertrude thinks Hamlet mad, the Ghost only the work of his imagination. But Hamlet now moderates his attack on his mother, who admits that he has split her heart in two parts. As she repents, Hamlet enjoins sexual abstinence on her; and, reminding her that he has to go to England, drags the body of Polonius away.

Act Four

The last two acts of Hamlet move fast to the denouement of what has gone before. In the first scene of Act Four, Gertrude tells Claudius about the killing of Polonius. Claudius sends Rosencrantz and Guildenstern after Hamlet (Scene 2), who bring Hamlet before Claudius (Scene 3). Hamlet tells Claudius that Polonius is at supper, a supper "not where he eats, but where he is eaten"—by the worms. Hamlet leaves for England, and we learn in a soliloquy from Claudius that Claudius is sending letters calling on the King of England to put Hamlet to death when he lands there. In Scene 4 we see Fortinbras and his army marching through Denmark, with the permission of Claudius.

The fifth scene is the centerpiece of the Act, and the most poignant one in the play, played out largely between Ophelia, Gertrude and Claudius, and latterly Laertes. Ophelia has become unhinged by grief over the death of her father. She comes before Gertrude and Claudius with her hair down, singing half-mad ditties about death, flowers, and maids losing their virginity. As she goes out, Claudius is deeply worried about the consequences of all that has happened, and also about the way he has had Polonius buried in haste and in secret, the more so when he hears that Laertes is back in Denmark and being hailed by the people as their chosen king. Laertes enters in a fury, seeking instant revenge and demanding to know the truth. At this point Ophelia returns, still singing pitifully of her father's death, and giving wild flowers to Laertes and the others. As she leaves, Laertes explodes with fury. Claudius asks Laertes to establish the facts to his satisfaction, and Laertes demands a proper burial for Polonius.

In Scene 6, Horatio receives a letter from Hamlet. He escaped from the ship taking him to England when, in a fight, he boarded a pirate ship which was attacking them and which has brought him back to Denmark. In the final scene of the Act, Laertes—who now accepts that Hamlet is to blame for Polonius's death—and Claudius learn of Hamlet's return. Because he is loved by his mother and by the people, they will have to act circumspectly. Laertes will challenge Hamlet to a fight with foils, ostensibly for a wager, but Laertes' sword will be tipped with poison, and, as a backup, there will also be a poisoned drink prepared for Hamlet. Gertrude now enters with terrible news. Ophelia, garlanded with flowers and singing, has drowned, having fallen into a brook as she tried to hang some of her flowers on the branches of a willow.

Act Five

The first scene (of two) takes place in a graveyard, and contains one of the few moments of light relief (of sorts) in the play. Two gravediggers or clowns are discussing in mock-serious tones the legitimacy of Ophelia being given Christian burial, as she may have willed her own death in the water. They discuss the durability of various professions, concluding that the gravedigger is the strongest of all, because his houses last till doomsday. Hamlet and Horatio appear, and one of the clowns throws up skulls as he digs. After some macabre joshing between Hamlet and the Clown, it emerges that one of the skulls is that of Yorick, the King's jester. Hamlet takes the skull and reflects:

> Alas, poor Yorick. I knew him, Horatio, a fellow of infinite jest, of most excellent fancy. He hath borne me on his back a thousand times. And now how abhorred in my imagination it is! My gorge rises at it. Here hung those lips that I have kissed I know not how oft. Where be your gibes now, your gambols, your songs, your flashes of merriment that were wont to set the table on a roar? Not one now to mock your own grinning? Quite chop-fallen? Now get you to my lady's chamber and tell her, let her paint an inch thick, to this favour she must come. Make her laugh at that.

Hamlet throws the skull down with disgust, and reflects that Alexander himself must look and smell like this in the grave; and also that his dust, and Caesar's, might by now be stopping a beer-barrel or plugging a hole in a wall. At this point Ophelia's funeral cortege appears. Owing to the doubt surrounding her death, she is to be allowed only a short service. Laertes, himself maddened with grief, jumps into her grave. Hamlet reveals himself and jumps in too, to fight Laertes, claiming that he too loved Ophelia, more than forty thousand brothers could. As they are separated, Claudius assures Laertes that they will soon enact their plan.

This they do in the final scene, which opens with Hamlet telling Horatio how he disposed of Rosencrantz and Guildenstern. Finding in their cabin the letter to the King of England asking for his death, he replaced it with one demanding theirs. He goes on to say that it is the King, rather than Laertes, who is his enemy, at which point Osric, a foppish courtier, enters with the challenge from Laertes. Hamlet accepts, and the court enters. Hamlet begs pardon of Laertes, which Laertes partially accepts. As they take their foils, drinks are brought in, one of which Claudius poisons. The duelists fight, Hamlet winning the first two bouts. Gertrude drinks to Hamlet's success— from the poisoned cup, to Claudius'ss horror. In the third bout, Hamlet is pricked with Laertes' poisoned foil; but in scuffling they exchange rapiers, and Hamlet poisons Laertes too. As Gertrude dies of the poison, Laertes confesses to the plot. Hamlet stabs Claudius and forces him to drink as well. Claudius dies, as does Laertes, reconciled at the last to Hamlet. Horatio tries to drink too, but Hamlet forbids him. As he dies, he instructs Horatio:

> If thou didst ever hold me in my heart,
> Absent thee from felicity awhile,
> And in this harsh world draw thy breath in pain,
> To tell my story.

Hamlet's own last words are to bequeath the reins of power to Fortinbras, who enters to eulogise Hamlet and to have the four bodies on the stage borne off.

Conclusion

An obvious point to begin a consideration of *Hamlet* would be to ask whether it is true, as Fortinbras says, that Hamlet "was likely, had he been put on / To have proved most royally." We have already mentioned a contrast between *Hamlet* and *Henry V,* but there are within the play itself two other obvious comparisons. Compared to Laertes and Fortinbras, Hamlet lacks the simplicity and directness that a leader requires. These both act decisively when this is demanded, and both act out of a necessity to right a perceived wrong (though Fortinbras is later weaned off his cause). It is not that Hamlet lacks physical bravery, for he demonstrates plenty of that in the final scene and in his dispatch of Rosencrantz and Guildenstern. But at least in one side of his character he is a dreamer, unsuited to action (as he tells us himself in "To be or not to be"), and he is also more at home—despite his protests about overacting—in the world of the Players than in the complication and mess of the court.

Hamlet's febrile mental state has led to speculation about the Ghost. Are we to take the Ghost and even the crime itself as simply fabrications of Hamlet's over-heated imagination? While such an interpretation might make it easier to see the play in modern terms, it would be hard to make such an interpretation stick. Hamlet is not the only person to see the Ghost, nor is he the first. And what Hamlet learns from his encounter with the Ghost is, of course, corroborated in the play scene, and indeed in Claudius's subsequent attempt to pray.

Mention of this scene raises another aspect in which *Hamlet* is profoundly unmodern. Without a belief in judgment and the after-life, and despite

Hamlet's own apparent vacillation on the point in "To be or not to be?," it is hard to make sense of much of the dynamic of the play. Hamlet's conscience and much else in the play is conditioned and given structure by this belief, and we cannot understand much of the action without taking it seriously. Furthermore, Hamlet, in criticizing Gertrude, becomes the upholder of the sacred order which Gertrude has breached in marrying her husband's murderer so quickly. (Even if she does not realize that Claudius is actually a murderer, the speed is certainly unseemly, as is her apparent enjoyment of Claudius's bed and her insistence to Hamlet that there is nothing questionable in what she has done.)

It might be, though, that the appearance of the Ghost in the scene between Hamlet and his mother is intended to be imaginary. It is the only time that the Ghost appears in which it is not seen by more than one person, and it happens precisely at the psychological heart of the play. For the mainspring of much of Hamlet's motivation is his tortured relationship to his mother, and in particular his almost physical loathing of her sexuality and her sexual congress with Claudius. Hamlet's psychology seems to be driven far more by sexual motivation and obsession, mainly negative, than by the classic rationality of a pure desire to know. Much of the strongest poetry in the play centers around Hamlet's relation to his own sexuality and to that of others close to him. His hatred of Claudius is more dominated by this than by any sense that he might have cheated him out of the crown. Indeed, from what we learn in the play about Fortinbras, there is no sense that the crown would automatically have passed to the son of the previous ruler.

We do not have to be too Freudian to think that what Hamlet wants most of all is the love of his mother, particularly perhaps after the death of a somewhat idealized and shadowy father; and this love has been cruelly denied him by his uncle's ambition and his mother's sex: so, "frailty, thy name is woman"—said, we might recall, before Hamlet has been addressed by the Ghost. And, in a psychological transference which does not show Hamlet in a good light, it is Ophelia who bears the full force of his animus against his mother, which could not be directed frontally against Gertrude without destroying the possibility of the love he actually wanted.

There is no doubt that Ophelia loved Hamlet, and that Hamlet did love her (as Hamlet himself says, and as is shown too in the graveyard scene). Ophelia also sees and knows Hamlet in his best light ("O, what a noble mind is here o'erthrown"). It is true that Ophelia is party to the manipulation of Hamlet by Claudius and Polonius, but she is in no position to decline; and Hamlet also manipulates her cruelly by pretending to be mad, and then throwing in her face his hyperbolic views on the nature of sex and breeding. With the death of Polonius too, it is not surprising that Ophelia goes mad.

Nor is it surprising that in her own madness she turns with instinctive insight to Gertrude, Hamlet's other woman, the indirect cause of her trouble and the one most likely to empathize with her predicament, as the prime recipient of her songs and her flowers.

If Hamlet sees sex and breeding in reductive terms as loathsome, so he becomes increasingly obsessed with death as the play goes on. He sees as strongly as any character in literature the skull beneath the skin. He sees the plays of actors as greasepaint and fantasy, but in the context of death he sees the work of human civilization in a very similar light. Hamlet has no compunction about killing others himself—as we see in the deaths of Polonius or Rosencrantz or Guildenstern—and this has been taken as a sign that he is a true aristocrat of the Renaissance; he is ruthless and able to do down his enemies and those inferior to him with hardly a moment's thought. For this Hamlet, "the readiness is all" (as Hamlet says just before unraveling the whole situation in the duel with Laertes). His indecisiveness is partly owing to the situation he is in.

For Claudius's court is a Renaissance court, tightly controlled and full of spies and intrigue. Claudius is an exponent of Machiavellian realpolitik. Even if her own situation becomes perilous with the death of the elder Hamlet (and possibly her son's too), Gertrude is a scheming woman quite able and content to use her sex to make her way in the world of assassination and power, even to the extent of appearing to forget her first husband in her rush to marry Claudius. When Hamlet upbraids her in her boudoir and asks her if she sees the Ghost, she protests to Hamlet that there is nothing there, "nothing but ourselves."

This may be read as a purely literal description of what she sees, or does not see, or it may be the ultimate expression of the modern, unShakespearean morality: there is nothing but we ourselves, no sacred order, nothing but the choices and values we ourselves accord. From this point of view, Hamlet is not just the "ambassador of death" (as he was called by the critic L. C. Knights)—he is also the spokesman for the order beyond human choosing, which Gertrude and Claudius have breached.

For Hamlet at this point there is indeed something more than ourselves: there is the sacred order in which widows mourn their husbands, sons honor their fathers appropriately, and tormented souls consigned to Purgatory revisit the living. But Hamlet is not entirely consistent on the sacred order. In his "To be or not to be" soliloquy he is not nearly as certain about the reality of God or the afterlife as he should be, given the Ghost's recent appearance to him and the orthodox Christian belief he expresses when Claudius is at prayer. He himself says to Rosencrantz and Guildenstern that "there is nothing either good or bad, but thinking makes it so"; and his messengership, if we may so put it, is partly compromised by his own uncertainty and indecision, his sense that the time is out of joint, quite apart from the objective wrongs he is supposed to right. And then compounding his own doubt about the sacred order, he is let down by his friends (apart from Horatio) and, crucially, by Ophelia, who is too weak to resist her manipulation by Claudius, Polonius, and, to an extent, Gertrude. Hamlet is a victim of the power game and constrained in what he can do by the nature of his position.

But objective victimhood, so to speak, is only part of the truth. For Hamlet, as we have just observed, the time itself is "out of joint," as he puts it after he has been given his mission by the Ghost. Life itself is out of joint; or rather, by the end of the play he cannot see life except in terms of death. It is this general uncertainty and indecision in Hamlet which led T. S. Eliot to speak of a lack of "objective correlative" in connection with the emotions he expresses. For all the appalling situation in which he finds himself, it hardly justifies his wholesale disillusion with the world and with life, as expressed in the "To be or not to be" soliloquy. In his relentless stripping away of what he would see as the veneer of life, Hamlet is the antithesis of Henry V or of the Ulysses of *Troilus and Cressida*.

Hamlet is not, however, a pure dreamer, even though he (rightly) criticizes himself for his tendency to indecision and introspection. He can be decisive and cunning. In the end he defeats his enemies in a difficult and dangerous environment, although at considerable cost, and, due to his oversensitive proneness to reflection, possibly at more cost than Henry V or Fortinbras, had either been in a similar position. But if Hamlet is noble, his nobility is of a more modern sort than that of those other leaders. It is that of an individualist, who, for whatever reason, is deeply suspicious of human bonds and human affection, and who can see little between himself and the biological realities of birth, copulation, and death, in which the surface of the human world is itself a dramaturgical act as fragile and febrile as the productions of a band of strolling players. Some of what Hamlet does presupposes the sacred order assumed by medieval and even Reformation Christianity, and the action of the play makes little sense outside that context, and to that extent the play is unmodern; but there are within Hamlet's personality and character feelings and thoughts which put the old theological order in question, and it is these aspects of *Hamlet* which have fascinated readers and commentators ever since, particularly since the Romantic era.

The Tempest

The Tempest, *thought to be Shakespeare's last play, may be seen as a comedy, in that in the end all ends well, or it may be a "romance," along with some of Shakespeare's other late plays, in which long-lost relations and enemies are found and reconciled. Prospero, the one-time Duke of Milan, has been deposed by Antonio, his scheming brother, and with his infant daughter Miranda lands on an island inhabited only by the spirit Ariel and Caliban, a sad creature, half-animal, half-human, the child of the Sycorax. Prospero, a magician, in what is often seen as a comment on the colonial adventure of Shakespeare's time, uses his powers to press both Ariel and Caliban into his service. Twelve years later, when Antonio and his ally Alonso, King of Naples, are returning from the marriage of Alonso's daughter in Tunis, Prospero conjures up a storm (the tempest of the title). All the travelers are wrecked on Prospero's island, including Ferdinand, Alonso's son. Guided by Prospero, with help from Ariel, Ferdinand and Miranda fall in love, the ancient enemies are punished and eventually reconciled, Ariel is freed, and the malignant Caliban left on his island, as Prospero and the now betrothed Miranda return to Italy. A marriage in Tunis (= Carthage), a shipwreck in the Mediterranean, a new dynasty in Italy? Is Virgil not called to mind? And if that is not enough, Shakespeare has Prospero using a paraphrase of the very same speech which Ovid's Medea declaims when she conjures up one of her most powerful spells. In addition there is a masque celebrating the marriage of Ferdinand and Miranda, replete with classical gods and reference. The Tempest is, in a sense, Shakespeare's homage to his classical antecedents, but it also drips with some of his most magical and most English poetry, as well as containing some of his most tantalizing speculations on the relation between reality and dramatic illusion, all bound together in a dramatic reconciliation of enemies and opposites.*

The Tempest has traditionally been thought of as Shakespeare's last play and also, because of Prospero's abjuration of his magic, as Shakespeare's own farewell to the stage, the abjuration of his own stage magic. Both of these ideas have been disputed, but *The Tempest* is certainly a very late play, written around 1610–11. It was performed in 1611 and also—and perhaps significantly—in 1613 as part of the court celebrations to mark the marriage of the daughter of James I to the Elector Palatine.

Although traditionally placed in Shakespeare's works as the first of the comedies, it is not now regarded straightforwardly as a comedy. Following Coleridge, it is now more often seen as a "romance," along with the other late plays (*The Winter's Tale, Pericles, Cymbeline*), in which we also find scenes of the reconciliation of age-old disputes, with the disputants fortuitously brought together and lost children found. It is also, in view of the masque at its center, a celebration of marriage; and, perhaps more questionably, in the character of Prospero, a meditation on wisdom, magic, and rulership.

It is not only the genre to which the play belongs which is complicated. Prospero, the play's central character, along with much else in the play, turns out to be far more ambiguous than might appear at first sight. Also, particularly for modern audiences, it becomes impossible to read the play without thinking of the Elizabethan and Jacobean voyages of exploration and colonization, which again makes Prospero problematic, for he is a character who has seized a land from its native inhabitants, however unprepossessing they might be. And, important in the context of this book, and as we will later show, there are in the play very explicit references to both Virgil and Ovid, showing Shakespeare to have been very conscious of his classical heritage.

Act One

Scene 1 shows the tempest of the title raging, from the point of view of those on a ship caught up in it. These include Alonso, the King of Naples, his brother Sebastian, and Antonio, the usurping Duke of Milan. They are returning from the marriage in Tunis of Alonso's daughter Claribel to the King of Tunis (though this is only revealed later). On the ship, the Boatswain and Gonzalo, an "honest old counsellor," discuss the storm and their prospects. They are joined on deck by Sebastian and Antonio as, with waves and timbers crashing about, the ship appears to be all but lost.

In Scene 2 we meet Prospero, the rightful Duke of Milan, and his daughter Miranda, who are on an island. We learn from Miranda right at the start that it is Prospero, who is a magician, who has caused the tempest. Miranda pleads for the safety of those on the ship, and Prospero assures her that no harm will be done, and that all is being arranged for her benefit. He then explains their situation. Twelve years earlier, he, Prospero, was Duke of Milan, and she his only child. But while he turned his attention to the "secret studies" of magic and the liberal arts, his brother Antonio ran the state. With Prospero "neglecting worldly ends," his library "dukedom large enough," Antonio opened Milan to the old enemy, the King of Naples, and put Prospero and the infant Miranda to sea on a rotting boat. They had food and water and also, by virtue of the charity of Gonzalo, various other necessities and, most important, Prospero's library. By good fortune they eventually landed on the island where they now are.

Prospero now sends Miranda to sleep and summons Ariel, his spirit, who tells him he has done his bidding with the tempest. The King's ship has been brought safely to the island, but the rest of the fleet, supposing it lost, has sailed on to Naples. Ferdinand, the King's son, jumped ashore and is now alone, while the other passengers are dispersed elsewhere on the island. Prospero praises Ariel for carrying out his orders exactly, but he has more for him to do:

> *Ariel:* Is there more toil? Since thou dost give me pains
> Let me remember thee what thou hast promised,
> Which is not yet performed me.
> *Prospero:* How now? Moody? What is't thou canst demand?
> *Ariel:* My liberty.

Prospero reminds Ariel—a free spirit, but Prospero's slave—that he owes him more. Before Prospero came to the island, the "foul witch" Sycorax had been banished from her native Algiers and dumped there by sailors. The delicate Ariel had then been her servant. When Ariel had refused to enact her commands, she imprisoned him in the trunk of a pine tree. He remained there for a dozen years, because Sycorax had died giving birth to her son, the monstrous creature Caliban, and there was no one to release Ariel until Prospero came to the island and freed him. On being threatened by Prospero with imprisonment in an oak, Ariel flies off to do Prospero's bidding.

Prospero awakens Miranda, and they go off to seek Caliban, "my slave." Caliban curses Prospero, claiming that the island is rightfully his through his mother Sycorax. When Prospero first arrived, he made much of Caliban, and with Miranda taught him to speak; in return, Caliban showed him around the island. Prospero points out that he had treated Caliban "with humane care" . . .

> . . . till thou didst seek to violate
> The honour of my child.
> *Caliban:* O ho, O ho! Would't had been done!
> Thou didst prevent me—I had peopled else
> This isle with Calibans . . .
> You taught me language, and my profit on't
> Is I know how to curse. The red plague rid you
> For learning me your language.

Threatened with cramps and aches by Prospero, Caliban goes off to fetch fuel, and Ferdinand enters, led on by a song from the now invisible Ariel. Miranda sees him, and is amazed: "a thing divine, for nothing natural / I ever saw so noble"—she has never seen a human being apart from her father. Ferdinand is equally amazed at Miranda, "the goddess / On whom these airs attend." Prospero, who is controlling all this, affects sternness towards Ferdinand: the young couple are falling in love, but the prize must not be too

230

light. Ferdinand will be Prospero's prisoner. Ferdinand threatens Prospero with his sword, but, still entranced by Miranda who pleads on his behalf, he is pacified by Prospero's magic.

Act Two

In the first scene we see the royal party, with the good-hearted Gonzalo being taunted and sent up by Antonio, Sebastian and Adrian, another lord. There is some discussion as to whether Claribel is the fairest queen in Tunis since Dido, and also whether Dido should be called a widow and Aeneas a widower. Alonso is devastated by the apparent loss of Ferdinand, but is blamed by Sebastian for having married his daughter to an African, which was the proximate cause of the disaster. Gonzalo asks for less harshness and gives expression to the ideal commonwealth that he would institute, had he control of the island:

> I'th' commonwealth I would by contraries
> Execute all things, for no kind of traffic
> Would I admit; no name of magistrate;
> Letters should not be known; riches, poverty,
> And use of service, none; contract, succession,
> Bourn, bound of land, tilth, vineyard, none;
> No use of metal, corn, or wine, or oil;
> No occupation, all men idle, all
> And women too, but innocent and pure;
> No sovereignty—
> *Sebastian:* Yet he would be king on't.
> *Antonio:* The latter end of commonwealth forgets the beginning.
> *Gonzalo:* All things in common nature should produce
> Without sweat or endeavour. Treason, felony,
> Sword, pike, knife, gun, or need of any engine
> Would I not have, but nature should bring forth
> Of it own kind all foison, all abundance
> To feed my innocent people.
> *Sebastian:* No marrying 'mong his subjects?
> *Antonio:* None, man, all idle—whores and knaves.
> *Gonzalo:* I would with such perfection govern, sir,
> T'excel the golden age.

We will return later to Gonzalo's "golden age" and its antecedents, but after his vision of innocence, Ariel sends the whole party to sleep, except

Antonio and Sebastian. Antonio, who has displaced his brother, begins to plot. With Ferdinand drowned, Claribel (Alonso's next heir) in Tunis, and Alonso asleep on the ground, Sebastian should silence his conscience and, like Antonio, seize his chance. Antonio will kill Alonso, thus simultaneously releasing himself from the need to pay Naples tribute and allowing Sebastian the crown, while Sebastian himself will get rid of the prating Gonzalo. But, as they draw their swords, Ariel sings in Gonzalo's ear, awakening him. The moment passes.

In the second scene, in another part of the island, Caliban is carrying wood and moaning about the tortures with which Prospero's spirits continually afflict him. Trinculo, a jester from the ship, wanders in and Caliban, taking him for another of Prospero's spirits, hides himself under his cloak. As a storm brews, Trinculo too goes under the cloak for shelter. Stephano, a drunken butler, now appears, and thinks he sees a four-legged monster. Caliban emerges, and Stephano gives him some of his drink, and then pulls Trinculo out from under the cloak. Caliban is quickly intoxicated, and offers to show the two clowns the island, hoping with their help to free himself from Prospero.

Act Three

In Scene 1, Ferdinand is working. Miranda appears and offers to help him. The two are watched by Prospero, as Miranda reveals her name. Ferdinand says that this "admired Miranda / Indeed the top of admiration" is the best of women; Miranda replies that she knows none of her sex, but could imagine no one to rival Ferdinand. Ferdinand professes his love for Miranda, and Miranda says she is either his wife, if he will marry her, or if not, she will die his maid. Prospero has, of course, choreographed it all:

> So glad of this as they I cannot be,
> Who are surprised withal, but my rejoicing
> At nothing can be more. I'll to my book,
> For yet ere suppertime must I perform
> Much business appertaining.

But before Prospero's business we see the progress of the two plots on the island.

First Caliban and the clowns (Scene 2). After a certain amount of slapstick and mutual beating, in which Ariel takes a playful hand, Caliban explains that the three of them will go to Prospero's cell when he is asleep in the afternoon, seize his books, and batter in his brains; they will then seize

Miranda; Stephano will have her and rule the island. They sing to the success of their plot ("Thought is free"), but Ariel is there, invisible, and plays another tune. Stephano and Trinculo are worried by the mysterious sounds, and, in a most poignant speech, Caliban reveals his soul:

> Be not afeard, the isle is full of noises,
> Sounds and sweet airs, that give delight and hurt not.
> Sometimes a thousand twangling instruments
> Will hum about mine ears; and sometimes voices,
> That if I then had waked after long sleep,
> Will make me sleep again, and then in dreaming
> The clouds methought would open and show riches
> Ready to drop upon me, that when I waked
> I cried to dream again.

He cried to dream again, and when Prospero is destroyed, they will have his music for nothing.

The court party is in Scene 3. Alonso is still disconsolate, and Antonio and Sebastian continue to plot. Prospero, above them, conjures up a show of spirits bringing in a marvelous banquet. But when the mortals try to eat, to thunder and lightning, Ariel, disguised as a Harpy, makes the banquet vanish:

> You are three men of sin, whom destiny,
> That hath to instrument this lower world
> And what is in't, the never-surfeited sea
> Hath caused to belch you up, and on this island,
> Where man doth not inhabit—you 'mongst men
> Being most unfit to live. I have made you mad;
> And even with such-like valour men hang and drown
> Their proper selves.

Alonso, Sebastian, and Antonio draw their swords on Ariel, but Ariel reminds them of their crime in supplanting Prospero and setting him and Miranda adrift. The loss of Ferdinand is punishment. Prospero, invisible, praises Ariel and exults at having his enemies in his power. Gonzalo, seeing the consternation of the guilty three, comments:

> All three of them are desperate: their great guilt,
> Like poison given to work a great time after,
> Now 'gins to bite their spirits.

Act Four

The fourth Act consists simply of one long scene, of which the focal point is a magical masque laid on by Prospero to celebrate the engagement of Miranda and Ferdinand. First Prospero explains to Ferdinand that his trials were simply to test his love for Miranda. He has passed, and he now offers Miranda as his future wife. He does, though, warn strongly against breaking her "virgin-knot" before the enactment of "all sanctimonious ceremony." He then summons up the masque, the main characters in which are Iris, the messenger of the gods, Ceres (played by Ariel), the goddess of corn, of harvest, and of fertility, and Juno, as goddess of marriage.

Iris first appears, calling on Ceres. As Ceres enters, Juno's chariot appears, suspended above. Ceres is told by Iris that she has been summoned to celebrate a contract of true love, and Ceres asks if Venus or her son (Cupid) are in the offing: Cupid is an enemy of Ceres since he lured her daughter down to Pluto in the underworld. Iris reassures Ceres that Mars's "hot minion" (Venus) has returned to Paphos and her son has broken his arrows: "no bed-right shall be paid / Till Hymen's torch be lighted" (that is, there will be no consummation until proper marriage).

Juno and Ceres then sing, blessing the marriage and its fruitfulness. As Prospero explains to Ferdinand that the spirits are called up by his art, Iris summons up choruses of nymphs and reapers, who start a graceful dance. But suddenly Prospero leaps up; he has forgotten Caliban and the conspiracy against his life. He brings the masque to an abrupt end, telling Ferdinand and Miranda:

> Our revels now are ended. These our actors,
> As I foretold you, were all spirits, and
> Are melted into air, into thin air,
> And like the baseless fabric of this vision,
> The cloud-capped towers, the gorgeous palaces,
> The solemn temples, the great globe itself,
> Yea, all which it inherit, shall dissolve,
> And like this insubstantial pageant faded,
> Leave not a rack behind. We are such stuff
> As dreams are made on, and our little life
> Is rounded with a sleep.

The young couple are sent to rest in Prospero's cell, while he summons Ariel. Ariel has led the conspirators through prickly undergrowth into the dirty pond outside. As they emerge, Ariel hangs Prospero's clothes on a nearby tree. The drunkards see the clothes. Against the urging of Caliban, who wants to get on with the murder of Prospero, Trinculo, and Stephano start putting on the clothes. Ariel and Prospero unleash spirits in the form of hunters and dogs, who chase the conspirators away.

Act Five

Again a single scene. Prospero, in his magic robes, discusses with Ariel the culmination of his work. The King and the court, currently imprisoned by magic, are to be released and brought to Prospero. Prospero himself draws a magic circle, and in a stunning paraphrase of Medea's speech in Ovid (*Metamorphoses*, Book Seven), addresses his supernatural forces:

> Ye elves of hills, brooks, standing lakes, and groves,
> And ye that on the sands with printless foot
> Do chase the ebbing Neptune, and do fly him
> When he comes back; you demi-puppets that
> By moonshine do the green sour ringlets make,
> Whereof the ewe not bites; and you whose pastime
> Is to make midnight mushrooms, that rejoice
> To hear the solemn curfew, by whose aid—
> Weak masters though ye be—I have bedimmed
> The noontide sun, called forth the mutinous winds,
> And 'twixt the green sea and the azure vault
> Set roaring war; to the dread rattling thunder
> Have I given fire, and rifted Jove's stout oak
> With his own bolt; the strong-based promontory
> Have I made shake, and by the spurs plucked up
> The pine and cedar. Graves at my command
> Have waked their sleepers, oped, and let 'em forth
> By my so potent art. But this rough magic
> I here abjure; and when I have required
> Some heavenly music—which even now I do—
> To work mine end upon their senses that
> This airy charm is for, I'll break my staff,
> Bury it certain fathoms in the earth,
> And deeper than did ever plummet sound
> I'll drown my book.

Prospero, unlike Medea, is about to abjure his rough magic, which is why audiences have seen this speech as Shakespeare's own valediction to the stage.

But first, to solemn music, Ariel leads the court figures into the magic circle. Prospero promises Ariel freedom, very soon, and Ariel sings:

> Where the bee sucks, there suck I,
> In a cowslip's bell I lie;
> There I couch when owls do cry;
> On a bat's back I do fly
> After summer merrily.
> Merrily, merrily shall I live now
> Under the blossom that hangs on the bough.

Prospero now reveals himself to the court party as who he really is. He embraces Alonso and Gonzalo. To Antonio and Sebastian, he warns that he could reveal their treachery, and he demands his dukedom back from Antonio. Alonso, while seeking pardon for his wrongs, wants more proof that it really is Prospero before him. Prospero toys with him, saying that as he has lost a son, so he, Prospero, has lost a daughter.

He then reveals Ferdinand and Miranda playing chess, with Miranda accusing Ferdinand of "playing me false." "No, my dearest love, / I would not for the world." "Yea, for a score of kingdoms you should wrangle, / And I would call it fair play." Ferdinand sees his father and kneels before him. Miranda expresses her wonderment at the people she sees:

> O wonder!
> How many goodly creatures there are here!
> How beauteous mankind is! O brave new world
> That has such people in't!

Prospero comments, perhaps a little acidly, "'Tis new to thee." The reconciliations, though, continue, with the possible exception of Antonio, who seems neither repentant nor joyful. In Gonzalo's analysis, Claribel has found a husband in Tunis, Ferdinand a wife, and the rediscovered Prospero a dukedom. The Boatswain and the crew then turn up, safe and sound, followed by the bedraggled trio of Stephano, Trinculo, and Caliban. Prospero forgives Caliban, invites the court to his cell, and charges Ariel to speed the fleet to Naples, after which he will be free. As for Prospero himself, after the marriage of Ferdinand and Miranda . . .

> [I'll] thence retire me to Milan, where
> Every third thought shall be my grave.

His "charms," as he says in the Epilogue, now "are all o'erthrown."

Conclusion

The Tempest is, as already remarked, something of a Shakespearean homage to Ovid and to Virgil. We have already seen how Prospero conjures up his magical forces in the same terms as Ovid's Medea. Sycorax, too, owes not a little to Medea, even her name reflecting Ovid's epithet for Medea, the "Scythian raven." It will be pointed out that while Medea and Sycorax show no signs of doing so, Prospero gives up his magic, and uses it to good ends. But from certain points of view—Caliban's, say—the parallels between Prospero and Sycorax are also marked. Both are banished to the island, and both use their magical powers on it. Both, indeed, use Ariel as a slave (Prospero's own term). And, whatever we think of Caliban—and Shakespeare leaves us in no doubt of the wickedness of Caliban's attempt on Miranda—there is certainly a sense in which Prospero deprives Caliban of both land and liberty.

As did Aeneas in Latium to some of the original Latins and their allies. The references in *The Tempest* to *The Aeneid* are also striking. We have already mentioned the debate about Dido in Act Two, Scene 1. But there is also Ariel as a Harpy at the magic banquet, reflecting the Harpies who destroy the Trojans' feast in the Strophades; the words in which Ferdinand first greets Miranda in Act One, Scene 2 ("most sure the goddess on whom these airs attend") are the same as those with which Aeneas greets Venus, his mother, after his shipwreck on the coast of Libya; and the greeting that Ceres offers to Iris in the masque ("Hail, many coloured messenger . . . who with thy saffron wings upon my flowers diffused honey drops, refreshing showers . . .") is so close to the words with which Virgil describes Iris in Book Four of *The Aeneid* ("Iris, bathed in dew, flew down on saffron wings, trailing all her colours across the sky") as to be surely intended.

Do these references and surface similarities portend any deeper or thematic similarity? Both works start with a shipwreck, caused by magic. But in one case, the wreck is of a ship travelling from Italy to Tunis, and in the other the reverse. In the one case there is a marriage in Tunis, in the other a nonmarriage in Tunis, though both have sanctified marriages in Italy (Aeneas–Lavinia and Ferdinand–Miranda), which unite previously separate peoples (Trojans and Latins, Neapolitans and Milanese). And in both cases the journeying and the story end in Italy, though in the one case with the seizure of power there and the setting up of an empire, in the other case with a restoration of power in Italy and (we are to suppose) its speedy renunciation.

Any comparison between Virgil and Shakespeare here will have to compare the respective heroes, Aeneas and Prospero. In a very general sense both are wise, though flawed, rulers, working in some sense for good, arguably under divine direction. And both have to use force and/or magic to achieve their ends, and in doing so ride roughshod over others. But, whereas Aeneas never gives any sense of thinking that ruling is not his ultimate good and goal, with Prospero things are far more equivocal. It is, indeed, because he takes his eye off the ball in Milan in the first place that he is ousted. And while this moves him to anger and to plan to recapture his dukedom, once he has got it back, he looks to renounce it again. We could also ask about Prospero's own integrity. He seems interested in (magical) power for the sake of having it, and he uses it to enslave Caliban and Ariel and to punish and terrorize his enemies. Of course, one of the ultimate ends may be good, but the means are questionable. Nor do we know why or to what effect he opened graves, let out the dead, and the rest. If there are elements of white magic and benevolence in Prospero, they are mixed with Faustian and necromantic traits.

What is the attitude in the play to rulership, Prospero's or Alonso's? Hard though it might be to make sense of its intent, it is equally hard to overlook Gonzalo's anarchist speech in Act Two, Scene 1. Commentators tell us that the immediate source of this speech is Montaigne's essay "Of the cannibals"; and that itself is interesting, for Caliban/cannibal was to some extent living in the sort of state that Gonzalo describes before the arrival of Prospero and Miranda. We could also see the storm which shipwrecks Prospero's enemies as nature overpowering the arts and crafts of civilization, and it makes those thrown on to the island, as was Prospero himself, subject to the forces of nature.

But we need to recognize that the tempest is no natural storm, but one summoned up by Prospero's art, and we also need to recognize that in the calibanic or cannibalic state of nature there may not have been innocence or purity either. No, the Eden that Gonzalo is describing is that of Ovid's Golden Age, the age of Saturn, an age of plenty, of fertility, of streams running milk and wine and honey, and above all of peace without law, punishment, or property.

It is the age depicted in Titian's *Venus of Pardo,* say, in the Louvre. But a dream of Eden is also in the masque in *The Tempest,* in the very nature of Ariel and his songs, and—most poignantly of all—perhaps also in Caliban's heartrending dream of music taking him somewhere better. It might be possible to see much of *The Tempest* itself, in its poetry, its fantasy, and its sense of fertility, as a hymn to such a dream.

But not all. For, just as Prospero calls us back to reality from the masque, we know that the play in which the masque is set is itself all a dream, a work of theater—and surely the reference in that speech to the "great globe itself" would be taken by the audience to indicate partly the theater of that name, but only partly. For the ultimate sense of the speech is, rightly or wrongly, that the world itself is no more than a dream, and so neither more nor less real than what we see on stage. Certainly, much of what we see on the world's stage—the strutting on it of politicians, lovers, celebrities, and so on—is hardly more real than what we see on a theatrical stage, which may well be part of what Prospero is getting at. But a yet deeper and more puzzling philosophy seems to be part of the play and its meaning, and one which erodes *any* ultimate difference between dream and reality, between theater and the real world.

If Prospero can be seen as a type of magus figure, it was only a few decades after the play that the philosopher Descartes raised a whole system of philosophy on attempting to refute the hypothesis that we could never know that we were not in a dream—and for most readers of Descartes, the skeptical belief seemed more convincing than Descartes' refutation of it. *The Tempest* is not a skeptical treatise, but at the end of the great dramatist's career it plays tantalizingly on a number of levels with contrasts between dream and reality, theater and the outer world, and leaves the audience in some doubt as to the solution of these puzzles. Nature is not real, because what seems to be natural (Caliban, the tempest itself) is in fact the work of magical forces. The pride of life and rulership are seen to crumble beneath Prospero's deconstruction of them. The lovers' vows and feelings may be sincere, but are they more real than the masque that Prospero so brutally brushes aside? And Prospero's own prospering back in Milan is but a momentary interlude before he returns to—his meditations? his magic?

So often in Shakespeare we are posed with contrasts and conflicts and overlappings between image and reality, theater and the world, illusion and truth. Within this continual questioning of our sense of reality, there are, to be sure, real moral conflicts and judgments; but, at the end of the day, just as Hamlet wondered how the Player could so weep for Hecuba, so we might ask ourselves whether we do not think we know Falstaff, say, better than many a real acquaintance. Our greatest dramatist lived at a time when, perhaps, because of the murderous disputes which were going on over the niceties of theological belief, skepticism among the educated and thoughtful was flourishing (as we will shortly see again in connection with Cervantes). Despite his firm grip in his plays on the notions of right and wrong upheld by the sacred order of his time, Shakespeare is clearly troubled at times by the substantiality of reality—or at least by the substantiality of our conceptions of reality—and never more so than in his putative last play, as we see in the meditations and activity of Prospero. It would be a nice irony if the great dramatist's reflections on the very substantiality of his plays and of the characters within them were to give another twist to the very modern thought that the hold that any of us has on reality is tenuous in the extreme—that we all, to a greater or lesser extent, live in worlds we imagine, individually and collectively.

Cervantes
Don Quixote

Cervantes (1547–1616), a veteran of the wars against the Turks, wrote the two parts of Don Quixote *in the last two decades of his life. The first part of Cervantes' book was so successful that a pirated sequel appeared, which so angered Cervantes that in his own second part he took the pseudo-Quixote to task. Don Quixote and his "squire," the peasant Sancho Panza, are two of the seminal figures in European literature, so much so that the characters have long outgrown their genesis, like Shakespeare's Falstaff taking on in the popular imagination an existence of their own. Don Quixote is a slightly deranged elderly gentleman who, long after they were actually taken seriously, takes the romances of knights and courtly love for literal truth. He enlists in his service the somewhat reluctant Sancho Panza, declares as his courtly mistress a peasant girl whom he christens Dulcinea del Toboso, and calls his old nag by the high-sounding name of Rocinante. The Don and Sancho travel around Spain, supposedly righting what the Don takes to be wrongs and rescuing what he supposes to be damsels and others in distress. Appearances to the contrary—as when the Don charges at windmills in the belief that they are hostile giants, or takes a lowlife inn as being a castle in which he can celebrate a chivalric vigil at arms—are all explained away as being the work of wicked enchanters. Proof against commonsensical rebuttal, the Don engages in hosts of comical misunderstood "adventures," and is often severely punished for his pains, to the delight of Cervantes' readership. The inherent cruelty of the situation is reinforced in the second part of the book when characters who have supposedly read the first part actually set him up, to general amusement. Somehow, however, through it all the Don retains not just pathos but also a degree of dignity. When, at the end, he admits that he has been deluded all along, and falls into a decline from which he dies, it is hard not to feel that something valuable has been lost.*

Miguel de Cervantes, the author of *Don Quixote,* was born in 1547. He served as a soldier in Italy, and fought bravely in the naval battle of Lepanto in 1571, a decisive encounter in the struggle for the heart of Europe between a combined Christian force and the Turkish empire, then the major and still advancing Islamic power. Cervantes, though, was captured by pirates when attempting to return to Spain in 1575 and taken to Algiers, where he was enslaved to a renegade Greek. He tried unsuccessfully to escape several times, and returned to Spain only on payment of a ransom in 1580. His career thereafter continued to be mixed. He worked as a tax inspector, attempted to become a writer, and was imprisoned twice. It was indeed while in prison (for fraud) in 1597–98 that he had the idea for *Don Quixote,* as he tells us himself in the Prologue to Part One of that work. This was published in 1605, and was an immediate and growing success, so much so that a second part, not by Cervantes but by some unknown person writing under the name of Alonso Fernandez de Avellaneda, appeared in 1614, while Cervantes was hard at work on his own sequel, and much to his annoyance. The genuine Part Two appeared in 1615, and Cervantes died in 1616.

Cervantes' own experience, a huge amount of reading on his part, and the whole tenor of his time, including the struggles between the Christians and the Islamic Moors (who had been expelled from Spain only in 1492), all infuse his novel, which is almost Shakespearean in its range of reference and character. It is Shakespearean in another sense too. Like Falstaff, like Bottom, like Malvolio, its two major characters, Don Quixote and Sancho Panza, seem to take on lives of their own, establishing their own reality beyond the imaginations of their authors, which seem to be forever running behind and attempting to catch up with what were originally their inventions. However, in a very significant way *Don Quixote* is not Shakespearean. It is not a play, but a novel, one of the very earliest, and indeed the only one we consider in this book. The fact that Cervantes is something of a pioneer here may partly account for his somewhat uneven deployment of multiple narrators, stories within stories and other novelistic devices, but his sense of the potential of the form does allow his imagination to roam in a way which would be well-nigh impossible in a more tightly constructed play or poem.

The comparison here with Falstaff and the clowns is not unintentional. For what is most prominent in Cervantes is a spirit of robust and deflationary earthiness, amounting at times to a degree of subversiveness. There may be an underlying humanity in *Don Quixote*—though that is something we will have to examine—but, in contrast to Shakespeare, there is little that is noble or truly tragic. How, indeed, could there be, when the whole point of the book is the deflation of heroic romance and its ideals through an almost plebeian mockery of such things? In the high noon of the Spanish empire, with its autocratic monarchy and its aristocracy of honor and swagger, the very tone of *Don Quixote,* quite apart from its theme, would look like a calculated gesture of defiance from below.

There is, to be sure, a very consistent theme running through *Don Quixote,* and a very consistent joke. The theme is the contrast between the high ideals (ridiculously high ideals, in Cervantes' view) of chivalry and medieval romance, and the reality of real life. High-flown and flowing romances and ballads about knights-errant, wicked enchanters, ladies admired from afar with courtly love, damsels in distress, dragons to be slain, Moors to be conquered and quests to be fulfilled had been the stuff of popular literature in Spain and elsewhere for some considerable time, at least up to a short while before Cervantes wrote, and they had even influenced figures as serious as Ignatius of Loyola, the founder of the Jesuits, and Teresa of Avila, the great mystic and reformer of convents. The joke—and the means that Cervantes uses to puncture the chivalric ideals—is the madness of Don Quixote, the self-styled Knight of the Sorrowful Countenance, who wanders through the Spanish countryside in the company of his "squire," the peasant Sancho Panza, in search of knightly adventures to dedicate to the honor of his courtly mistress, the incomparably beautiful and virtuous Dulcinea del Toboso (in reality Aldonza Lorenzo, the rough peasant maid whom Don Quixote had seen but four times in his whole life).

Don Quixote's adventures are all based on misinterpretations in his own brain of perfectly ordinary and humdrum events and situations. Maddened by his reading of romances, the otherwise sane and even sensible *hidalgo* (or landowner), Alonso Quixano from the village of La Mancha, sees himself as Don Quixote, the Knight of the Sorrowful Countenance, continually deceived by enchanters who make things look quite different from how they really are. So giants appear as windmills, hostile armies as flocks of sheep, knightly castles as inns, and so on. Most poignantly of all, in the second part, Dulcinea herself is seen as lurking beneath the form of an ugly and foul-mouthed peasant girl (who is not even the original Aldonza). Sancho maintains a running commentary on all these events, spiced with ever more outrageous proverbs and sayings, by and large commonsensical, but going along with his master just enough to keep alive his hope of ultimate reward, either the governorship that Don Quixote has promised him or, more realistically, some money.

But whatever Sancho does or says, or however forcefully, brusquely or cruelly reality attempts to break in, on the matter of his madness, Don Quixote is utterly insulated by his watertight explanations: the mismatch between what he and everyone sees, and what is actually the case, is due to the malign operation of enchanters changing the appearances to deceive everyone. However things seem and however the enchanters have arranged things, Don Quixote *knows* that the windmills are really giants, the sheep really soldiers, the inns really castles, and the young crone really Dulcinea. There is indeed precedent in the romances for such deceptions: in the Arthurian legends, for example, as we have seen in Chaucer's Wife of Bath's tale, there is a Loathly Damsel, hunchbacked, bearded, and rat-faced, whose true beauty will be revealed only when a pure knight embraces her as his bride, thus releasing her from the spell laid on her by a wicked enchanter. Don Quixote, being a walking encyclopedia of the romances, would undoubtedly have been aware of this and of many other such deceptions, as he points out from time to time. What we, as readers, have to grasp, though, is that Don Quixote never denies that the appearances are as they are; he is—or after some initial confusion, becomes—perfectly well aware that the "giants" look and behave like windmills, etc. Indeed, in this case, Quixote explains to Sancho, when Sancho tells him that he had only been tilting at windmills, that the sage Feston has made the giants look like windmills precisely to deprive him of the glory of his victory over them.

Though filled out with an immense amount of detail and incident, and also embracing many subsidiary stories and stylistic genres, including the epic, the picaresque, the didactic, and the romantic, as well as ballads and poetry, the general framework of the book is relatively simple. In view of the overall simplicity of structure and the sheer prodigality within, it is neither necessary nor possible here to do more than sketch an outline of the overall structure.

As already mentioned, Alonso Quixano is a landowner from the village of La Mancha. He is a voracious reader of knightly romances and becomes convinced that he must become a knight-errant himself. He puts on some old armor which had been rusting and gathering dust in his house for centuries. Lacking a proper helmet and visor, he concocts a contraption out of cardboard and steel, convincing himself that its obvious inadequacy is unimportant, and to add to the ramshackle appearance and equipment of the new knight, a barber's basin is later co-opted for use as his helmet. He names his old horse Rocinante. He declares that Aldonza Lorenzo will be his lady, for whom he will fight, now to be known as Dulcinea del Toboso, and he sets off for his adventures. He stays at an inn, which he takes to be a castle, and attempts to keep his vigil of arms there, so as to enter the order of chivalry.

The innkeeper, whom Quixote takes to be the castle governor, initially plays along with this delusion, but after Don Quixote starts fighting with some muleteers who he thinks have insulted him and his lady, with the help of his serving maids, he quickly dubs him knight and sends him packing. Quixote then attempts to free a servant boy who is being flogged by his master, whom Quixote takes for a knight, though as Quixote rides off, the boy is beaten all the more. He then challenges six traveling merchants to pay homage to Dulcinea's beauty and virtue, but charging at one of them, falls off his horse. Encumbered by his armor, he is himself beaten up and left immobile on the ground. He is rescued by a farmer who is a neighbor of his, and is taken back to his village, where his two friends, the priest and the barber, along with his niece and his housekeeper, discuss what is to be done, for they all realize that Quixote is obviously deranged.

Don Quixote's friends and relations do not, of course, succeed in curing him, which would have brought the book to an early conclusion. They do, though, destroy a sizeable part of his library of romances (which gives Cervantes the opportunity to list and critically analyze these crucial texts). Don Quixote then sets off again on his adventures, this time accompanied by his newly engaged "squire," the peasant Sancho Panza, on his donkey. The very first thing that the newly formed partnership encounters are the giants/windmills, which Don Quixote charges at, ending up on the ground with his lance shattered. Interestingly, as this is probably the most famous and memorable of all the adventures, the whole episode takes up only two pages out of a total of close to a thousand.

In a way, we now know all we need to know about the structure of the story, for the dozens of episodes which follow are all in some degree or other variants on the ones already described: mistaken identification by Don Quixote of some pretty normal occurrence in the Spanish countryside; high-flowing rhetoric by Don Quixote about what he perceives as having been transformed from its true (knightly) reality by malicious enchanters, frequently followed by a knightly challenge to bemused participants in the scene; growing amusement or irritation on the part of the participants, who often, for a time at least, play along with the madness; a violent encounter in which Don Quixote often inflicts considerable physical injury on his amazed antagonists and is himself actually quite brave; followed, nine times out of ten, by some equally or more severe physical punishment or beating of Don Quixote, and sometimes of Sancho Panza too; post mortem on the part of Don Quixote and Sancho, with Sancho expressing himself in ever more elaborate strings of proverbs and Don Quixote serving up his standard "enchanter" explanation.

As the pair make their way along, their relationship develops, Sancho being kept happy by the promise of a governorship (or at least some material reward) when Don Quixote achieves his knightly goal, but Don Quixote also coming to rely increasingly on psychological support from his often acerbic but ultimately loyal servant. There is also another conceit invoked by the author who is initially telling the story (Cervantes himself). Quite early on, he pretends that the account of Don Quixote's adventures which he has been using has broken off in mid-adventure (with Don Quixote charging at a Basque whom he has imagined to be part of a plot to kidnap a princess and who is reduced to using a cushion to shield himself against the Don's blows). Cervantes makes out that he is then stymied until he finds in Toledo an Arabic history of Don Quixote, written by a Moor named Cide Hamete Benengeli, which he has to get translated into Spanish, but which conveniently picks up where the previous one left off. The Benengeli manuscript and complications which arise from it, like the Quixote-Panza relationship, becomes a running theme or joke as Cervantes' work progresses. Much has been made of this by modern commentators worrying over the nature of authorship and of pretence by subsequent novelists to authorial omniscience; we may doubt that Cervantes himself was a proto-postmodernist, but the digressions about the various authorial hands involved certainly add charm and diversion to the work, and may indeed indicate a certain nervousness or at least self-consciousness about the nature of the novel at this early stage in its development. (Who is telling this story? How does he know what he is telling us? What is his relationship to his characters, who are his invention, but whom we readers are to suppose as real?)

In the first part of *Don Quixote* there are a number of subsidiary stories told by various participants interwoven into the main story. There are also stories about other characters whom Don Quixote meets wandering around forlornly in the remote countryside, including one who is almost as mad as Don Quixote and who also postures as a knight. These characters seek and sometimes find their true loves or their long-lost relations, in one case a brother who had, like Cervantes himself, disappeared after being captured by pirates after the battle of Lepanto and enslaved in Algiers. Unlike Cervantes, though, this lost brother is rescued by a ravishingly beautiful and fabulously wealthy Moorish girl who can hardly speak Spanish, but who falls in love with him nevertheless, deceives her father in Algiers and helps him to get back to Spain and to his family—which gives a flavor of the romance that Cervantes can and does himself weave from time to time. These stories have a certain charm, and amusingly from the point of view of Cervantes' own work, their manner (with lovelorn youths and the like acting out the life of the shepherds of fable, singing ballads among the rocks, and faithful or betrayed maidens following them into the wilderness), and the often improbable coincidences on which they rest, owe not a little to the very romances which Cervantes is in the main parodying. Incidentally, though, the revolutionary nature of *Don Quixote* as the book which single-handedly slew the courtly romance may have been somewhat exaggerated by later readers. By the time Cervantes was writing, the romance form was already outdated and hardly taken seriously by readers; it had indeed been satirized more than a century earlier by Chaucer in his own tale of Sir Thopas. Cervantes' readers evidently enjoyed the joke, though, as well as Cervantes' own mixture of parody, satire, slapstick, and well-told, engaging nonsense, rather as we do today.

Also notable in the first part are the serious and largely sensible disquisitions which Don Quixote from time to time pronounces, on such topics as arts and letters, the superiority of the military life as opposed to the life of letters, the nature of chivalry, and, perhaps most striking, on the Golden Age, which, like Gonzalo's vision in *The Tempest*, derives directly or indirectly from Ovid: all things held in common, in a land of plenty and ease, without need for ploughing, with people living in peace, modesty, and security. Don Quixote professes that it is to restore such an age, and in particular to protect maidens and widows and to succor orphans and the needy, that the order of chivalry was formed, and that this is the purpose of his own mission.

At the start of the second part of the book, Cervantes himself, through the mouth of Sanson Carrasco, a graduate, who is amused by Don Quixote's adventures but who also turns out to be an accomplice of the priest and the barber in trying to cure him of his madness, lists the most notable adventures from the rather rambling and discursive first part: the windmills; the episode of the noisy fulling mill which terrifies Don Quixote in the middle of the night and which seems to him to portend a gigantic adventure (and during the course of which Sancho vividly and noisily answers a call of nature); the two flocks of sheep which Don Quixote takes for two armies; the grisly procession taking a corpse for burial to Segovia, which Quixote takes for that of a knight on a bier, and whose attendants he beats up, thinking they have insulted him; Don Quixote's freeing of a chain gang of convicts; and the ridiculous misinterpretation of two Benedictine monks and a Basque, who are escorting a coach, as abductors of a noble princess. We could also add the hilarious scene in an inn/castle in which a whoreish servant girl attempts an assignation with another traveler who is attempting to sleep in the same room as Don Quixote and Sancho, with all its predictable ensuing bedlam, ending with an encounter with the local police and Sancho being tossed in a blanket in the courtyard of the inn for nonpayment of the bill, as Don Quixote, now for once genuinely undeceived, makes his way off protesting that knights-errant never pay money for their lodging.

During Part One, the priest and the barber attempt to follow the wanderings of their friend. They eventually catch up with him and get him back to La Mancha, lying on top of a hay cart, after they have rescued him from an incident in which he laid into a statue of the Virgin being carried by a band of penitents (for Don Quixote, an eminent lady being carried off against her will) and was himself struck down for his pains. It should be said that during his adventures in both parts of the book, Don Quixote both gives and receives a fair amount of physical punishment; and, mad though he is, he is not lacking in physical and even moral bravery, though this is somewhat easy to overlook, given his madness and the inevitably absurd situations which his madness contrives. But the situation having been contrived, the Don usually conducts himself if not with nobility, at least with strength and directness of purpose in which he is never a coward (in contrast, of course, to Sancho Panza who, being under no illusions, sees no call for bravery or indeed any justification for the beatings he also frequently receives from the Don's opponents).

Compared to Part One, Part Two is far more direct and far more focused. It is less meandering and there are far fewer long digressions or subplots. Cervantes himself seems more surefooted, though possibly less engaging, partly because he is clearly angry with the author of the false second part which appeared in 1614, one year before Cervantes' genuine work. The false Part Two is, of course, testament to the success of the 1605 publication, and to the way that, within a decade, Cervantes' Don Quixote had already entered public consciousness. Spitting with rage in the prologue to his Part Two, Cervantes says that what he is here offering is "cut by the same craftsman and from the same cloth as the first one," and further, in this genuine second part, "I give you Don Quixote prolonged and finally dead and buried"—thus obviously cutting the ground from under the feet of any more would-be plagiarists or breachers of copyright.

The fame of Don Quixote after Part One is the occasion for much of the action of Part Two. For now so many people have heard of him, characters in Part Two recognize him and want to encourage him in his lunacy—for good or ill. So an additional theme enters, the manipulation of Don Quixote by people who know of him and of his madness already, and who want to use him for their own ends and for their own amusement. The dates do not, of course, stack up; for Don Quixote is supposed to be dead before the author of Part One compiled the account to which the characters in Part Two are reacting. But never mind: the joke of a character in a narrative being treated as real by characters in an extension to the same narrative is a good one. What, though, is more worrying about Cervantes' new device is that as a result of his exploitation of it, a degree of cruelty towards Don Quixote enters on the part of those knowingly exploiting his lunacy for fun. It is, indeed, hard not to see in Cervantes himself a degree of vicarious cruelty himself in supposing that his audience would be amused by this.

Having said this, though, the first character to appear who knows about Don Quixote's exploits from having read about them is the graduate Sanson Carrasco, whom we have already mentioned. At the start of Part Two, he travels to La Mancha to meet the heroes of the earlier tales, and he tells them that their exploits have not only been translated from Arabic into Spanish (Cide Hamete Benengeli again), but also into many other languages. With encouragement from Sanson, who finds Sancho even funnier in the flesh than in the earlier novel, and much to the anger of the priest and the barber and Don Quixote's faithful niece and housekeeper, the two adventurers then set out on Don Quixote's third quest for adventure (to expressions of "Blessed be Allah" from Cide Hamete Benengeli, who is still in charge of the narrative).

During the course of this third quest, Sanson Carrasco turns up a number of times as a knight, in an attempt to get Don Quixote home again; fortunately or unfortunately (depending on one's point of view), Quixote initially defeats the "Knight of the Spangles," and so is only reinforced in his delusion. Before that, however, occurs the incident which is the occasion of much of Part Two, and in a way the saddest thing of all. Shortly after leaving La Mancha, and—as Don Quixote thinks—en route for Toboso where his Dulcinea lives, Sancho and Don Quixote encounter three peasant girls. For fun, Sancho addresses the most unpleasant and ill-favored of the three in courtly language, calling her the "princess and universal lady of El Toboso," which the girl contemptuously brushes aside. As the false "Dulcinea" attempts to ride off, she falls off her ass, Don Quixote attempting unnecessarily to rescue her. As the three girls ride off, Don Quixote, who is convinced by Sancho's lunacy, launches into yet another enchanter explanation (about Dulcinea having been transformed into the ugly creature before them). For Sancho, all this simply reinforces his joke, but, as we will see, he becomes hoist with his own petard. The joke is not so easily forgotten.

After various other adventures, including one in which he attempts bravely but foolhardily to fight with some lions from a circus, Don Quixote undergoes what looks like a sort of mystical experience. He enters a cave of mythic reputation and in it he imagines that he meets the knight-enchanter Montesinos, who takes him into various wonderful palaces, shows him various characters from the romances, and discusses various legends. Then, still in the cave, Don Quixote "sees" the three peasant girls, including "Dulcinea" (who runs away from him as fast as she can); but Don Quixote vows to find a way of disenchanting her. Sancho is amused, but also horrified. His joke is taking root to a degree he could not have imagined.

The mainspring of Part Two is the encounter of Don Quixote and Sancho Panza with a beautiful Duchess and her husband the Duke, who are not otherwise identified, but who are thrilled to meet the errant pair, having heard so much about them. And they are not disappointed in their expectations. Sancho proves even more amusing than they had expected, and Quixote falls only too readily into the various jokes and traps they lay for him. The crux comes when Sancho tells the Duchess about the cave of Montesinos and the appearance there of the "enchanted" Dulcinea. The Duke and Duchess arrange a moonlight spectacle after a boar hunt, filled with Moors, devils, and the enchanter Merlin himself, who announces that Dulcinea can be disenchanted, but only after Sancho Panza has freely lashed himself three thousand and three times on his buttocks. With bad grace and considerable reluctance Sancho agrees that he will do so, but before this happens, the two of them are tricked into thinking that they have ridden up into the heavens on a magic horse at the behest of the enchanter Malambruno. The story then splits into two strands.

In the first strand, Don Quixote himself is further toyed with by various servants of the Duke and Duchess, impersonating various magical and mystical figures, some of whom attempt to make love to him and all of whom produce humiliations and even beatings for him, including being attacked by a sackful of cats which was lowered into his window (which he naturally interprets as an enchantment). Meanwhile, Sancho is set up as Governor of the "island" of Barataria (in reality a town of the Duke's). Sancho, who spends about a week in this position, is called upon to make various judgements of a Solomonic complexity. As would be expected, his pronouncements are spiced with proverbs, but also with a high degree of wisdom and common sense, implying, of course, that a peasant can be as good a ruler as a king. A mock attack on his town, however, proves too much for Sancho's nerve, and he renounces his governorship to return to his old freedom (as he sees it) and the service of Don Quixote. On the way back, though, Sancho has his own Montesinos moment. After a friendly encounter with a Morisco neighbor of his, a converted Moor who despite seeing himself as Spanish has just been expelled from Spain, Sancho falls into a pit on the side of the road, together with his donkey. He cannot get out, and would have died there had Don Quixote, en route to right a wrong which one of the Duchess's servants had invented for him, not come along and heard him. The pair are naturally greatly pleased to be reunited.

After one more fake battle at the court of the Duke (which Don Quixote actually wins), Quixote and Sancho take to the road again. Amid ever more ridiculous adventures, the Don—who is making for the jousts at Saragossa—is told, to his chagrin, that this is what the false second part has him doing. So—to underline the authorship joke—Quixote changes his plan. He will go to Barcelona, where they also have excellent jousting in which he can show his prowess. Meanwhile, he continually nags Sancho about the lashings he has to undergo.

On the way to Barcelona, there is a macabre nocturnal encounter with the bodies of some hanged bandits, swinging from trees, and a more friendly meeting with some live bandits, led by a Robin Hood figure. But it is in Barcelona itself that Quixote receives his greatest humiliation. While Sancho helps to rescue a girl who is dressed as a boy and turns out to be the lost daughter of his Morisco friend from earlier on the road, Don Quixote is paraded around the city by a "friend" with a parchment stuck to his back declaring "this is Don Quixote de la Mancha," forced to dance until he literally drops, and then deceived about the cave of Montesinos by a talking statue (transmitting the voice of the friend's nephew). But it is all about to end.

Quixote is now challenged by the Knight of the White Moon, as always on the quality of Dulcinea del Toboso. But this knight insists that if Don Quixote loses, his penalty will be to cease his quest and retire to his village for a year. He does lose, and his vanquisher is revealed as Sanson Carrasco, concerned ultimately for Quixote's well being. After a brief and involuntary stop at the Duke's castle, Sancho and Don Quixote make their way back to La Mancha, but not before the final insult. The gloomy knight presses Sancho to lash himself, and this Sancho pretends to do, whipping a tree in the dark along with bloodcurdling cries which cause the grateful Don Quixote to implore him to desist. Lamenting the temporary end of his knight-errantry, however, the delusion continues: seeing pictures of the fall of Troy and of Dido and Aeneas, the Don avers that, had he been there at the time, he would have killed Paris, thus preventing all the ensuing calamities.

They arrive back in the village, Sancho at least rewarded with money from his master. Quixote explains to his friends the temporary cessation of his quest, but—to their consternation—begins to dream up a fantasy about them all playing the roles of classical shepherds and shepherdesses. It is not to be. Don Quixote takes to his bed in depression and fever for six days. At the end of the six days, he comes to his senses at last, no longer Don Quixote de la Mancha, but plain Alonso Quixano, a good man, and henceforth the sworn enemy of Amadis de Gaul and all the "profane" histories of knight-errantry which brought on his madness. His friends, including Sanson Carrasco and Sancho Panza, are amazed. But they realize he is dying. With the ending of his madness, his spirit has left him. He dies calmly and Christianly, though not without a final sally at the author of the false second part of the history, a point echoed in the final paragraph by "Cide Hamete": "For me alone was Don Quixote born, and I for him; it was for him to act, for me to write; we two are as one, in spite of that false writer from Tordesillas . . . My only desire has been to make men hate those false, absurd histories in books of chivalry, which thanks to the exploits of my real Don Quixote are even now tottering, and without any doubt will soon tumble to the ground. Farewell." (Translation by John Rutherford (Penguin, 2000).)

Absurd Histories in Books of Chivalry

We have already suggested that Cervantes' dragon of chivalry may already have been in decline by 1605, and so his ostensible purpose of slaying it was somewhat otiose. It has even been argued that in an age of censorship and inquisition, an author such as Cervantes with a work of subversive knockabout needed an alleged moral purpose (in his case the destruction of harmful stories likely to turn young heads from the straight and narrow) to deflect the attention of the authorities from his subversion. But even if this were not so, we still need to ask about the power of *Don Quixote*. For it would be hard to pretend that Cervantes' book is believable, either in detail or in the whole. To what extent do the exaggeration and caricature involved in Don Quixote and his exploits militate against the work?

Don Quixote may well appeal to contemporary taste precisely because of its ragbag nature, its skepticism about ideals, and also because of (rather than despite) its manifest implausibility. There is no authorial omniscience or omnipotence here, but rather an attempt to develop a theme of intellectual and moral deflation by whatever means come to hand, and at the same time telling many a joke and many an entertaining yarn. *Don Quixote* is not, of course, a work of "magic realism" in the modern sense, but in many of its devices and even more in its spirit and in its very exaggerations it is not too far from works by Márquez or Rushdie.

Obviously we are not going to find nobility, grandeur, or even beauty in *Don Quixote,* at least not in any straightforward sense. But here again the book may well appeal to an age in which we are suspicious of high ideals and of setting ourselves goals we know (or believe) we cannot attain. Sancho Panza is, for better or worse, not just a man for all time; he is a man particularly of our time, a man of democratic earthiness and realism, an early adept in satire and comic deflation of pretension and nonsense. Don Quixote himself is of course the prime target of the deflation, but so are many of the subsidiary figures, involved as they are in ludicrous situations and adventures.

There is, though, the tone of the book. Over and above its relentless lack of verisimilitude—for could anyone be mad and deluded in quite such a way and to quite such an extent as Don Quixote, but only episodically?—there is a relentless vein of cruelty in the writing, as both Don Quixote and often his opponents too are severely beaten about. This gets worse as the book goes into the second part, where characters in the novel manipulate the madman for their, and our, amusement. Thomas Mann once posed the question as to whether all this cruelty, to Sancho Panza as well as to Don Quixote, did not in the end look like self-flagellation, self-revilement, and self-castigation. More prosaically, we could simply ask whether it is really funny to laugh at a madman so much and for so long. Once one has seen the point, is there not a certain sinking of the heart when yet another situation is contrived simply to expose Don Quixote's delusion and to beat him up for it?

No doubt different answers will be given to this question, depending in part on the taste of the respondent and, crucially, on just how funny the various incidents are found—a somewhat subjective matter, one supposes. There is also a romantic view of Don Quixote as, beneath the pathos and the suffering, a noble figure, almost an innocent abroad in a harsh and unforgiving world, but one who through it all maintains a degree of purity and integrity. This is perhaps the feeling that Richard Strauss conjures up in his beautiful (over-beautiful?) tone poem on the subject. And there are also countless touching images of the ill-sorted pair wandering in their bumbling way through the Spanish countryside and conducting endless conversations on what they find there, almost like two philosophers reflecting on the whole of human life, or a somewhat more earthy Dante and Virgil making their way not through Hell, but through what, for all its enchanting aspects, is fundamentally a vale of tears.

It might indeed be possible to see *Don Quixote* in this somewhat more elevated way, and as a timeless metaphor for the journey each of us has to make through life, with its poignant interplay of idealism and realism. For those who know only images and extracts, it may be hard not to see it in this way. But can Cervantes' text actually support such a reading? Or is it in the end a shallow book, made shallow by the thinness of a greatly overextended joke and the delight that the author clearly takes in punishing his hero, whose only crime is to be sadly deluded? We mentioned that Cervantes, like his contemporary Shakespeare, can be seen as engaging with and in the skeptical discussions of their time; but it has to be said that the effect in Cervantes is not so powerful, as the illusions and ideals which form the material of the debate in his case are so obviously illusory and impracticable. In a way, a closer comparison would be with Chaucer, seeing the characters of Don Quixote and Sancho Panza as the string connecting a ragbag of tales of different sorts, their own characters and conversation in the end being more substantial than the events which befall them and the stories which are told. For it is for the two characters he has bequeathed to us that Cervantes will always be mainly remembered and rightly valued.

Milton
Paradise Lost

John Milton (1608–74) wrote Paradise Lost *mostly in the years following the failure of the Cromwellian Commonwealth in 1660, a cause with which Milton had been closely identified.* Paradise Lost *is an epic on the grandest scale, and while its author is highly conscious of his classical forebears, unlike Homer and Virgil it is in no sense a national epic. Its theme is no less than the justification of the ways of God to men. It attempts to do this by recounting in the grandest terms the Christian account of the Fall. The key events are the original rebellion of Satan and his followers against God, the creation of the human race to replace the fallen angels, the temptation of Eve by Satan, the sin of Adam and Eve, their (and our) expulsion from Paradise, and the promise of eventual redemption for the now fallen human race by means of the Incarnation and sacrifice of the Son of God. There is no doubting the grandeur of Milton's poetry or the magnificence of his achievement. What has divided readers from the very start is Milton's uncompromising adherence in his poem to the letter of his religious faith. Many distinguished critics have concluded that the true hero is not God but Satan, who dares to question the oppressive authority of the God that Milton describes; and that (in the words of William Blake) Milton is, without knowing it, really "of the devil's party." This view may be attractive on the surface, particularly to those who dislike Christianity, but is it consistent with the poem Milton actually wrote?*

John Milton was born in 1608 in London, and was classically educated at Saint Paul's School and Christ's College, Cambridge. After a visit to Italy in 1638–39, he became a protagonist on behalf of the Presbyterian (anti-episcopal) cause. During the English Civil War he supported the Parliamentarians against the King (who was executed in 1649, with Milton's approval). Milton defended the revolution and worked for the new Commonwealth, right up to the Restoration of the monarchy in 1660 (which, to the surprise of some, he survived). It was after this that he completed *Paradise Lost,* on which he had been working intermittently for most of his adult life (it was published in ten Books in 1667 and in twelve Books in 1674). Milton married three times, and during desertion by his first wife became notorious for defending divorce (in pamphlets published from 1643–44). His *Areopagitica* of 1644 is one of the most famous defenses of free speech in English. He died in 1674, having been blind for over twenty years, which goes to make the composition of *Paradise Lost* all the more remarkable.

Paradise Lost is Milton's self-conscious attempt to compose an epic to rival Homer and Virgil, and to recall Greek tragedy as well. As a poem whose subject is the Fall of Man, with its ostensible purpose to "justify the ways of God to men," it has proved as controversial in its reception over the centuries as its writer was in his lifetime. For many readers and critics, including Dr. Johnson, T. S. Eliot, and F. R. Leavis, its very self-consciousness—together with the grandeur and eloquence of the writing—have militated against its meaning and its spontaneity, and against the reader's ability to do more than succumb to the power of the diction. More acutely, the dynamic of the struggle recounted in the poem has puzzled its readers since the earliest days. For Blake, Milton, the anti-monarchist, is "of the devil's party," though "without knowing it." For Shelley, Milton's Satan is "a moral being," one "far superior to his God as one who perseveres in some purpose . . . in spite of adversity," with God complacent "in the cold security of undoubted triumph." And, according to the twentieth-century critic William Empson, "the Christian God the Father, the God of Tertullian, Augustine, and Aquinas, is the wickedest thing yet invented by the black heart of man,"[16] Milton's particular triumph being to display the truth of this view beyond all doubting.

Are these later readers anachronistically reading their own prejudices and preoccupations back into Milton? We might direct our own reading of the poem partly towards considering this question. Whatever we decide on the moral import of the work, Milton is dealing with the most intractable theological problems: reconciling (or attempting to reconcile) divine omnipotence with free will, divine omniscience with eternal punishment, divine creation with the creation and existence of evil. . . . And if Milton fails in his stated endeavor (if), that may be because the endeavor itself, if honestly undertaken, is impossible.

Book One

> Of man's first disobedience, and the fruit
> Of that forbidden tree, whose mortal taste
> Brought death into the world, and all our woe,
> With loss of Eden, till one greater man
> Restore us, and regain the blissful seat,
> Sing Heav'nly Muse, that on the secret top
> Of Oreb, or of Sinai didst inspire
> That shepherd, who first taught the chosen seed,
> In the beginning how the heav'ns and earth
> Rose out of Chaos: or if Sion hill
> Delight thee more, and Siloa's brook that flowed
> Fast by the oracle of God; I thence
> Invoke thy aid to my advent'rous song,
> That with no middle flight intends to soar
> Above th'Aonian mount, while it pursues
> Things unattempted yet in prose or rhyme.
> And chiefly thou O Spirit, that dost prefer
> Before all temples th'upright heart and pure,
> Instruct me, for thou know'st; thou from the first
> Wast present, and with mighty wings outspread
> Dove-like sat'st brooding on the vast abyss
> And mad'st it pregnant: what in me is dark
> Illumine, what is low raise and support:
> That to the heighth of this great argument
> I may assert Eternal Providence,
> And justify the ways of God to men.

Thus the first twenty-five lines of *Paradise Lost*. One cannot help being struck by the magnificence of the diction, which sweeps us along, the details of the sense notwithstanding. From the very start, Milton mixes references from Old and New Testaments with the classical, Aonia being Helicon, the mountain sacred to the classical Muses, but on a first reading it hardly matters whether we know this or not, or indeed the precise details of Oreb, Sinai, or Siloa; we are simply swept along, as we are past often imprecise and even contradictory descriptions. We may also note the similarity of the opening of *Paradise Lost* with that of *The Aeneid,* both stressing the one man who will restore an ancient glory.

But more than any of this, one cannot help but be struck by the sheer presumptuousness of Milton's claim to be pursuing "things unattempted yet in prose or rhyme," and specifically to "justify the ways of God to men."

We can actually narrow down the intended sense of "things unattempted": specifically they are unattempted in English. Milton is here following the position advocated by Sir Philip Sidney at the end of his *Defence of Poesie*,[17] that we should write in our own language. In his words, Milton is claiming that English is a legitimate language for serious poetry and serious themes, and here perhaps for the most serious theme of all: the justification of God to men. But, the reader may ask, why do God's ways have to be justified to men? And, more specifically, why is it John Milton, this new Moses (the shepherd on Oreb (Horeb)—or was it Sinai?), inspired not just by the same Heavenly Muse, but also by the creating Spirit itself, who is charged with the task over which for centuries, as Milton implies, theologians and philosophers have labored unavailingly? And why in epic rhyme as well? It is, of course, a testament to Milton's greatness that despite these questions and despite the presumptuousness, nearly five centuries on, *Paradise Lost* continues to delight, to intrigue, to baffle, and to inspire—even those noisy critics who reject its message with something bordering on hatred. At the very least, Milton is vindicated in his use of English poetry for the highest and most difficult of themes.

After the preamble, Satan, who dared to challenge God, is depicted just defeated by God. He and his angels have fallen for nine days, and they are in the torment of having lost everything and of being in eternal pain as well. He is in the "dungeon horrible" and the "darkness visible" (line 63) of Hell, a dark chaos, with a burning lake for the damned. (The darkness visible, we are told, from "one great furnace flamed; yet from those flames / No light"— just the first of many imprecise if not implausible passages of description, yet whose very imprecision seems to sweep us on into an ever-mightier realm.) But still, from his dungeon Satan rallies Beelzebub, his lieutenant:

> What though the field be lost?
> All is not lost; the unconquerable will,
> And study of revenge, immortal hate,
> And courage never to submit or yield:
> And what else is not to be overcome?
> That glory never shall his wrath or might
> Extort from me. (105–11)

"All is not lost" because the rebel angels still have their "unconquerable will." "Ever to do ill" will be their "sole delight" (160). They will seek to subvert all God's plans, although as Milton points out, this will be only at the consent of God, and how enraged Satan will be to see

> How all his malice served but to bring forth
> Infinite goodness, grace and mercy shown
> On man by him seduced . . . (217–19)

For it is, of course, the Fall of Man that Satan will engineer to defy God. But from Satan's point of view, in Hell they remain free, and he will continue to reign: "Better to reign in Hell, than serve in Heav'n." (263)

Satan now rouses his troops, who are lying prostrate in the lake of fire. Many of the rebel angels are described individually, in terms drawn from the Old Testament and classical myth. They move forward, with ten thousand banners and a forest of spears, in a great phalanx. Satan, his heart filled with pride, "under brows of dauntless courage" (603), gives the devils hope of regaining Heaven. He foretells the creation of Man, and how this will give the rebel angels a chance of revenge and the exercise of malice. They will have a council to prepare war. Pandemonium, the devils' palace, now rises up, at once heavenly and diabolical (714 ff.); its architect is Mulciber (i.e. Vulcan/Hephaestus). The devils gather for their Consult.

Book Two

Book Two opens with the Consult in Pandemonium. This is like a parliamentary debate among the Princes of Hell. In his opening speech Satan establishes his position as leader, invoking the notions of consent, merit, a just right to his position, and the fixed laws of Heaven to underpin his legitimacy as leader. They should not give up Heaven for lost, but use their "immortal vigour" to win it back. The other leaders then speak. Moloch recommends a frontal assault on God and Heaven—even if this leads to destruction, that would be better than existence in Hell, in this "abhorred deep" (87); Belial counsels keeping quiet in the hope that if they do so, God might "remit / His anger" (210–11) and slacken the flames of Hell; Mammon concurs—they should concentrate on Hell, where they are at least free; Mammon is applauded, and it is left to Beelzebub to act as Satan's mouthpiece. Rather than either appeasement or a frontal assault, they should lead God to "abolish" his own work by seducing Man "to our party" (368). This wins the day, but only Satan is willing to go up out of Hell to set the plot in motion. He is praised for his bravery, "that for the general safety he despised / His own" (481–82). The devils disperse, some to violence, others to philosophy, and Hell is described in terms reminiscent of Virgil's *Aeneid* (Book Six, lines 273–300) and of Dante's *Inferno*. At the gates of Hell, Satan is confronted with the hideous monsters, Death and Sin. Sin is Satan's daughter, born out of his head like Athene out of Zeus, but she has also been his lover, together producing the monster Death. Together, Sin and Death produce yelling monsters who are all around, and who continually devour their mother. Sin—whom Satan will introduce into the race about to be formed, along with Death, whose famine will now be filled—unlocks Hell. Satan moves into the realm of Chaos, where the "embryon atoms" (900) will remain in confusion

> unless the Almighty Maker them ordain
> His dark materials to create more worlds. (915–16)

Satan struggles in the abyss and reaches Chaos and Night. Chaos ushers him on along the route where, after the Fall of Man, Sin and Death paved a great bridge between Hell and Earth. Satan sees Heaven and, hanging from it, the universe, "this pendent world" (1052), to which he hurries "fraught with mischievous revenge" (1054).

Book Three

Milton invokes God as light, and refers to his own blindness, the "ever-during dark" (45) which surrounds him and cuts him off from the cheerful ways of men. God now addresses his Son about Satan and about the Fall of Man. But it will be Man's fault. Divine foreknowledge does not imply influence or causation:

> They themselves decreed
> Their own revolt, not I. If I foreknew,
> Foreknowledge had no influence on the fault . . .
> I formed them free, and free they must remain
> Till they enthral themselves: I else must change
> Their nature, and revoke the high decree
> Unchangeable, eternal, which ordained
> Their freedom; they themselves ordained their fall.
> The first sort by their own suggestion fell,
> Self-tempted, self-depraved; Man falls, deceived
> By the other first: Man, therefore, shall find grace;
> The other, none. In mercy and justice both
> Through Heaven and Earth, so shall my glory excel;
> But mercy, first and last, shall brightest shine. (106–33)

So Man will be saved by God's grace. But how? He cannot atone himself, and there is no one in Heaven who will. The Son of God then prays: "on me let thine anger fall; / Account me Man" (238). By taking God's anger on Himself, He will redeem the attempt of Man to make himself God. The

Father promises that when the Son rises, Man will rise with him, and the Son will be given all power. The praise in Heaven of the angels is described. Satan, meanwhile, comes to the outermost region of creation. He reaches the gate of Heaven, and the stairs from Heaven to Earth. Finding Uriel in the Sun, Satan disguises himself as a cherub, enquiring about God's "new happy race of Men" (679); Uriel directs him to Adam's abode in Paradise.

Book Four

The book opens with Satan's self-hatred and remorse: "which way I fly is Hell; myself am Hell" (74), ending with the affirmation: "Evil, be thou my good . . ." (110). The landscape, plenty and beauty of Paradise is described, with Satan prowling in it wolf-like, like the "lewd hirelings" which infect the Church (193). He sits on the Tree of Life observing the scene. Adam and Eve come in . . .

> In naked majesty, seemed lords of all,
> And worthy seemed; for in their looks divine
> The image of their glorious Maker shone,
> Truth, wisdom, sanctitude, severe and pure—
> Severe, but in true filial freedom placed,
> Whence true authority in men: though both
> Not equal, as their sex not equal seemed;
> For contemplation he and valour formed,
> For softness she and sweet attractive grace;
> He for God only she for God in him,
> His large fair front and eye sublime declared
> Absolute rule; and hyacinthine locks
> Round from his parted forelock manly hung
> Clustering, but not beneath his shoulders broad:
> She, as a veil down to the slender waist,
> Her unadorned golden tresses wore
> Dishevelled, but in wanton ringlets waved
> As the vine curls her tendrils—which implied
> Subjection, but required with gentle sway,
> And by her yielded, and by him best received,
> Yielded with coy submission, modest pride,
> And sweet, reluctant, amorous delay.
> Nor those mysterious parts were then concealed;
> Then was not guilty shame. (290–312)

Satan looks on as they feed and drink and play, among the tame beasts. He is envious and malicious: "Hell shall unfold, / To entertain you two, her widest gates . . ." (380). Adam warns Eve about the Tree of Knowledge, next to the Tree of Life. Death will be the result, but he does not know what death is, apart from being something dreadful. Avoiding this tree is to be the sign of their obedience to God. Adam and Eve embrace:

> half her swelling breast
> Naked met his, under the flowing gold
> Of her loose tresses hid: he in delight
> Both of her beauty and submissive charms
> Smiled with superior love, as Jupiter
> On Juno smiles, when he impregns the clouds
> That shed May flowers. (495–501)

Obvious shades there of Zeus/Jupiter and Hera/Juno in Book Fourteen of *The Iliad,* though Eve is not here ensnaring an unwitting partner. Adam and Eve are, like Juno and Jupiter, thus "imparadised in one another's arms" (505). Satan's envy at their innocent bliss reaches fever pitch. He begins to plan to use the Tree of Knowledge. Uriel meanwhile warns Gabriel that he has lost sight of Satan. Adam and Eve retire to their bower and their nuptial bed, to start the race which will fill the earth (733). They make love, un- troubled by hesitation or shame or lust or the falsenesses of harlots or court amours. Lulled by nightingales, embracing, they sleep. As they sleep, Satan is found by two of Gabriel's angels, "squat like a toad" by the ear of Eve, try- ing to tempt her in a dream. They bring him before Gabriel. They prepare to fight, but God intervenes. Warned by Gabriel, Satan flies off.

Book Five

The next morning, Eve is troubled by her dream, and of the voice telling her to eat from the Tree of Knowledge, fruit "to make gods of men" (70). Adam comforts her, telling her that merely to have involuntary thoughts of evil is not blameworthy. They pray and go to work. In Heaven, meanwhile, God briefs Raphael concerning Adam. He is to advise Adam of his happy state, free but mutable, and to warn him of the danger ahead, in order to render Man inexcusable, should he transgress. Raphael finds Adam and Eve, happy and innocent in their nakedness, greeting Eve as later Mary would be greeted (385). They eat, and Adam asks about obedience. Raphael speaks about free service of God—they are made perfect, but not immutable, and God wants voluntary obedience. Raphael then tells Adam and Eve about the fall of the angels due to Satan's envy of the announcement by God that He is begetting and anointing his Son to be Messiah and King. (By "begetting" Milton means exalting and appointing as Lord, rather than creating; however, somewhat unorthodoxly, Milton did apparently believe that God created the Son, but that this creation was before the Son himself then went on to create the angels.) Lucifer affects equality with God. He rouses his followers with talk of freedom and of refusal of God's monarchy. The good angel Abdiel asks him who shall dispute with God "points of liberty" (823). Satan claims that he and the rebel angels were "self-begot" and "self-raised" by their own "quickening power" (860–61). They will not bow to God, but will "try who is our equal." Abdiel sees Satan's fall determined and his defeat inevitable.

Book Six

Civil war now ensues in Heaven, with Michael and Gabriel leading God's cause. Satan and Abdiel battle first with words, Satan claiming that he is fighting for Liberty, against the sloth of servility of those who merely serve. Abdiel replies:

> This is servitude—
> To serve the unwise, or him who hath rebelled
> Against his worthier, as thine now serve thee,
> Thyself not free, but to thyself enthralled;
> Yet lewdly dar'st our ministering upbraid.
> Reign thou in Hell, thy kingdom . . . (178–83)

Their battle is then described in Homeric terms, and conflict rages all around, with neither side gaining an advantage. Millions are involved in the battle, and deeds of eternal fame are done. In the midst of the struggle, Michael addresses Satan as "Author of Evil, unknown till thy revolt / Unnamed in Heaven . . ." (262–63). Satan is wounded by Michael, but, though in pain, like all spirits he heals quickly enough. As night falls, the rebels are under pressure. They withdraw and Satan rallies his troops. They make a huge engine of war, and let it off on the second day in hope of victory. But Michael and the good angels uproot mountains, burying the devils' weapon. Both sides then fight with hills and mountains. On the third day, God sends his Son into the battle. Satan disdains flight, preferring "universal ruin" (797). In the final battle, he and his troops are chased by the Son, now a terrifying figure, beyond the wall of Heaven. They plunge into the abyss, where after nine days of falling they are enclosed in Hell, with the Son returning to his Father and Heaven in triumph. Raphael underlines to Adam the reward of disobedience.

Book Seven

Milton invokes Urania, the muse of astronomy, recalling his own blindness and the "evil days" on which he fell (referring, of course, to the difficult times he faced in 1660 with the Restoration of the Monarchy). Adam asks Raphael to describe the creation of this world after the fall of the angels. God first sought to repair the emptying of Heaven caused by the fall into Hell of the rebel angels. Raphael then embroiders the Genesis account of the six days of creation: first, out of Chaos and the Deep, God created Light; then, dividing the waters, the firmament; then dry land, with the waters forming the seas, and vegetation on the earth; then sun, moon, and stars; then living things (birds, fish, and fowl); then animals, creeping things, insects; and finally, at the end of the sixth day, Man, made in God's image, rational, upright, and free, praising God, and woman too, to multiply and fill the earth, holding dominion over it, but both warned off disobedience and the Tree of Knowledge. The seventh day is for rest and praise of the Creator. The angels who sing the praise also sing that "who seeks / To lessen thee, against his purpose, serves / To manifest the more thy might . . ." (612–15).

Book Eight

Eve, unlike Adam, is not so interested in speculation—from Adam's lip "not words alone pleased her" (57). But Adam questions Raphael as to why so large a universe is needed. Raphael replies that it is on earth that the otherwise barren light of the sun becomes virtuous and vigorous:

> Consider, first, that great,
> Or bright infers not excellence. The Earth,
> Though, in comparison of Heaven, so small,
> Nor glistering, may of solid good contain
> More plenty than the Sun that barren shines,
> Whose virtue on itself works no effect,
> But in the fruitful Earth; there first received
> His beams, unactive else, their vigour find.
> Yet not to Earth are those bright luminaries
> Officious, but to thee, Earth's habitant. (90–99)

So the sun, and by extension all the rest of the universe, are fulfilled only when their beams work on man, to produce a virtuous and conscious response to the grandeur of the universe, and hence of God—a very good response not just to Adam's question, but also to all those who would use the size and extent of the universe to insist that nothing of cosmic importance can be on this comparatively tiny earth. For the rest, though, Adam should leave high mysteries alone. Adam agrees, resolving to speak only of the useful, and recounts to Raphael his own first memories of God, the Garden, the Tree of Knowledge, and realization of his own solitude. God is pleased at this, for it is not good for Man to be alone. Adam sleeps, and in his dream he sees God creating Eve from his rib. He wakes, and she is there:

> To the nuptial bower
> I led her blushing like the Morn; all Heaven,
> And happy constellations, on that hour
> Shed their selectest influence; the Earth
> Gave signs of gratulation, and each hill;
> Joyous the birds; fresh gales and gentle airs
> Whispered it to the woods, and from their wings
> Flung rose, flung odours from the spicy shrub,
> Disporting, till the amorous bird of night
> Sung spousal, and bid hast the Evening-star
> On his hill-top to light the bridal lamp. (510–20)

"Here passion first I felt" (530), transporting him beyond all the other delights of nature, and also of reason: "All higher knowledge in her presence falls / Degraded." (551–52) Raphael points out that Adam shares carnality with the beasts. Adam replies that there is union of minds as well, and enquires whether the angels express love "by looks only" (616). Raphael says that the angels' embrace has no need of mixing flesh with flesh. He once more warns Adam about temptation, and after this long digression, lasting nearly four books, returns to Heaven.

Book Nine

At the start of Book Nine, Milton refers to Achilles' wrath, the rage of Turnus, the ire of Neptune and Juno, and the struggles of Odysseus and Aeneas, though his task is one of "higher argument" (42). Satan, bent on Man's destruction, after eight days' searching, has decided to be a serpent. In a great and pivotal soliloquy (99–178) he avers that if he is miserable, he will make others miserable too:

> . . . the more I see
> Pleasures around me, so much more I feel
> Torment within me, as from the hateful siege
> Of contraries; all good to me becomes
> Bane, and in Heaven much worse would be my state.

> But neither here seek I, no, nor in Heaven,
> To dwell, unless by mastering Heaven's Supreme;
> Nor hope to be myself less miserable
> By what I seek, but to make others such
> As I, though thereby worse to me redound.
> For only in destroying I find ease
> To my relentless thoughts. (119–30)

His only solace is in destruction and marring creation, and specifically Man, for whom God has created this magnificent world. He, who had once sat with the Godhead, is now "constrained into a beast, and mixed with bestial slime," in order to wreak his revenge. And if bitter revenge recoils on itself, so be it: "spite then with spite is best repaid." This speech, as Milton surely intends, puts into perspective the admiration of Satan of some of Milton's critics, who see only Satan's splendid defiance in the earlier books, but pass over the extent of his sheer malice in the later ones.

On the morning of the fatal day, Eve proposes to Adam that they divide their labor and work separately. Adam worries about them being easier to tempt if they are alone, but Eve thinks that this impugns her "faith sincere" (320), and Adam agrees to separate for the morning. The serpent finds Eve alone, and for a time her "heavenly form" (457) tempers his malice. But the hot hell within him burns, and his hate revives, obsessed as he is with "pleasure not for him ordained" (470). Raising himself up, he attracts her attention, telling her that it was eating the fruit which gave him both reason and speech and the knowledge of her unmatched beauty. He shows Eve the fruit, and argues that the Tree is harmless and God's motives suspect. God wants to keep his worshippers low and ignorant. Those who eat will be on a par with God, knowing both good and evil: what, in any case, is wrong with knowledge? Eve reflects that God's forbidding actually commends the Tree; in denying us the fruit, God is forbidding us to be good and wise. Moreover, what is death? Is death for us alone? The serpent has eaten, and is not dead. She plucks and eats:

> Earth felt the wound, and Nature from her seat,
> Sighing through all her works, gave signs of woe
> That all was lost. (782–84)

Eve, though, hymns the Tree and the wisdom it has brought her, resolving, for good or ill, to implicate Adam in her fate. She addresses Adam: having tasted, she has "dilated spirits, ampler heart / And growing up to Godhead" (876–77). Adam is horrified. Eve is now "defaced, deflowered, and now to death devote" (900). But he resolves to stay with her: "we are

266

one / One flesh; to lose thee were to lose myself" (958–59). Eve insists that the apple has augmented her life. With "female charm" she overcomes his resistance; "against his better knowledge, not deceived" (998), he eats. The earth trembles again.

> As with new wine intoxicated both
> They swim in mirth, and fancy that they feel
> Divinity within them breeding wings
> Wherewith to scorn the Earth. But that false fruit
> For other operation first displayed
> Carnal desire inflaming. He on Eve
> Began to cast lascivious eyes; she him
> All wantonly repaid; in lust they burn . . . (1008–15)

They take their fill of love, until wearied with amorous play, they sleep. But when they awake, they realize they have lost their innocence; they read in each other the signs of "foul concupiscence" (1078). They know Shame, and hide their genitals, contrasting with their earlier "first naked glory" (1115). Sensual appetite has usurped "sovran Reason" (1129–30). Recriminations begin. Adam says Eve should have listened to him and not gone off alone; Eve says he should have forced her to stay with him. Adam condemns her ingratitude and her deafness to his warnings, but blames himself for letting her go.

Book Ten

There is sadness in Heaven, but God reminds the angels that it was all foreseen (though not necessitated by Him). The Son is to judge, but He will temper justice with mercy. It is evening in Paradise. Adam and Eve hide from the Son. Adam blames Eve, but the Son asks "was she thy God?" (146). Eve blames the serpent. God curses the serpent, and pledges enmity between him and the Woman—and Mary, the second Eve. Women will have sorrow in childbirth, and Adam labor and death. The Son clothes the transgressors, and returns to Heaven to intercede for them. At the gates of Hell, Sin and Death take heart; they themselves will be henceforth inseparable. They build their bridge over the abyss joining Hell and Earth, and are greeted by Satan on the new great thoroughfare as he descends to Hell. Satan gives them dominion over Man, before entering Pandemonium. Satan is acclaimed there, boasting of his exploits over Man. But in an Ovidian metamorphosis, he and all the devils are changed into serpents hissing and hissed, forced to climb into trees and chew fruit of ash. Permitted by God, Sin and Death now ravage Paradise. The curse of God begins to take effect. Climates worsen. There is Discord among the beasts. Adam realizes that "increase and multiply" now means increase of travail and curses and woe. He fears a living death (788) and posterity's fate: but "why should all Mankind / For one man's fault, thus guiltless be condemned?" (822–23). But what proceeds from him is corrupt, and he "the source and spring of all corruption" (832–33). Prostrate on the ground, Adam calls on Death—but Death comes not at all. Divine justice will not be hurried. Adam curses Eve and her feminine nature and "female snares" (897). She begs for compassion and forgiveness, and Adam relents:

> . . . let us no more contend, nor blame
> Each other, blamed enough elsewhere, but strive
> In offices of love how we may lighten
> Each other's burden in our share of woe. (958–61)

Eve proposes childlessness. If chastity is impossible, then they should seek Death or, failing that, commit suicide. Adam says suicide will bring more punishment from God. God's plan, he says, is for our seed to bruise the serpent's head (1032). Meanwhile, our sentence—labor and pain in childbirth—is comparatively mild, compared to immediate dissolution. We can warm ourselves with fire, make comforts for our life, and make contribution to God. This they do.

Book Eleven

Like Deucalion and Pyrrha (Ovid, *Metamorphoses,* Book One, lines 313–415), Adam and Eve pray for the restoration of mankind. The Son intercedes for them, and the Father accepts, but they and the human race will be expelled from Paradise. Death will replace Happiness and Immortality as the "final remedy" (62) until the second life. Man now knows good and evil, which he did not know before; it should have been enough to know just good. Michael is sent to tell them their fate, but also of the new covenant. Adam and Eve (who is now called by Adam "Mother of all Mankind" (159)) believe their prayers have been answered and that they might continue to enjoy Paradise, but Michael tells them of the expulsion. They are devastated, fearing that they will lose the contact with the divine presence they enjoyed in Paradise, but Michael reminds them that God is omnipresent (336) and also that in their future troubles they will be compassed round "with goodness and paternal love" (353). Eve sleeps, and in a scene reminiscent of the prophecies in *The Aeneid,* Michael takes Adam up the hill of Paradise to show him the whole earth and the effects of his crime. He sees Cain and

Abel, and Death; also disease and despair—all as punishment. Adam despairs and Michael advocates temperance on the road to old age and living well as a remedy. Michael then shows Adam images of apparent industry, justice, peace, and good marriage—but these are in fact Cain's descendants, who are "unmindful of their Maker" (611). War, violence, the biblical giants, and manslaughter as "the highest pitch of human glory" (693–94) all follow; only Enoch is just; then appear scenes of carousing, corruption, and luxury, with the Flood and Noah following. Adam laments the evil he has caused, and his foreknowledge of it. Michael praises Noah and foretells the rainbow and God's covenant never to destroy the Earth again by flood.

Book Twelve

The second source of men starts peacefully, until Nimrod, the mighty hunter, builds Babel, and is punished by God with hubbub and confusion. Adam laments the attempt of this man to gain dominion over other men. Michael—in a reference to the English people's acceptance of the restoration of monarchy in 1660—discourses on rational liberty and the way it is undermined after the Fall by upstart passions and unworthy powers reigning over free reason:

> . . . true liberty
> Is lost, which always with right reason dwells
> Twinned, and from her hath no dividual being.
> Reason in man obscured, or not obeyed,
> Immediately inordinate desires
> And upstart passions catch the government
> From Reason, and to servitude reduce
> Man, till then free. (83–90)

After Noah, Ham and Canaan further pollute the human race (and slavery ensues). But then God calls Abraham the one faithful man, from whose seed and race will come the Great Deliverer who will bruise the Serpent's head. The narration continues through Isaac, Jacob, Joseph in Egypt, the Exodus of Moses and Aaron, Sinai, and the Law. Moses foretells of the Messiah and sets up the ark of the covenant. Adam asks why there are so many laws; Michael replies that because men are weak they will fail—so the Law "discovers" sin (290) but does not remove it, and thus prepares us for acceptance of grace and a better covenant. Michael briefly reviews Joshua, Judges, Kings, Prophets, David, Solomon and the temple, the Babylonian captivity and the return, and, finally, the Messiah. Adam is ecstatic, but Michael reveals the mechanism of salvation, not through a fight, but through suffering unto death, which is the fulfillment of the Law both "by obedience and by love, though love / Alone fulfil the Law" (403–404). Christ endures "thy" (Adam's) punishment. But He defeats Death and Sin and Satan, and rises, a salvation for all nations. After the last judgment and the World's dissolution, for the faithful, Paradise will be a far "happier place / Than this of Eden, and far happier days" (464–65). Adam raises the old Augustinian question: whether in view of this more wonderful second creation

> I should now repent me of sin
> By me done and occasioned, or rejoice
> Much more that much more good thereof shall spring. (474–76)

He also asks who will guide God's people after the Ascension of Christ into Heaven. Michael tells of the Spirit and the Church thereby set up; but this leads on to a Danteesque condemnation of the wolves who masquerade as teachers and use the Church to gain wealth and secular power. The Church and the World will go on corruptly until the conflagration of the second coming. Adam praises meekness as the means to the subversion of the worldly-strong and worldly-wise. Michael commends Adam for this insight, and to add to it good deeds and the virtues, above all Charity. That way Adam will possess a Paradise within, to compensate for the loss of this Paradise. He then tells Adam to waken Eve. In her sleep, despite the prospect of banishment and the loss she has brought about, she has found consolation and hope in her seed to come, the Promised Seed. They are expelled from Paradise, an angel now guarding it with a flaming brand:

> Some natural tears they dropped, but wiped them soon;
> The world was all before them, where to choose
> Their place of rest, and Providence their guide.
> They, hand in hand, with wandering steps and slow,
> Through Eden took their solitary way. (654–59)

Conclusion

There is no doubt that much in Milton and in *Paradise Lost* in particular makes uncomfortable reading today. Milton's world view is relentlessly and severely Christian, and in the main theologically orthodox, even dogmatic. No more than Dante does he appear to contest the notion of divine punishment, and he does not have the human generosity or sheer prodigality of invention we find in Dante, let alone the human interest. T. S. Eliot, indeed, in his second essay on Milton actually makes a virtue of the lack of any "affectionate observation of men and women" in Milton; had Adam and Eve been strongly delineated individuals, they could not stand, as they are intended to, as the prototypes for all of us, types of each man and each woman.

And it is not just lack of personality which critics such as Eliot have complained of in Milton. There is also the questionableness of much of the imagery. We have already mentioned the "darkness visible" of Hell and the flaming furnace emitting no light, an image impossible to visualize; but it is not just the images. As Eliot points out, at one moment in Book One we have the archfiend "chain'd on the burning lake" and at the next, without any authorial embarrassment or explanation, he is making his way to the shore ("forthwith upright he rears from off the pool / His mighty stature"). Such instances abound. But perhaps the indistinct, phantasmagoric quality of the writing could also be an asset. As Eliot remarks, having noted Milton's propensity for images of engineering and mechanics, "it seems that Milton is at his best in imagery suggestive of vast size, limitless space, abysmal depth, and light and darkness."[18] His very imprecision of visualization, together with the magnificence of his language, rolling on and on to ever greater heights and depths, could actually help him (and the reader here) to convey a sense of the sheer and overwhelming enormousness and enormity of what it is he wants to describe, both physical and moral.

Whether despite this lack of human interest or because of it, and whether because of or despite Milton's defective visualization of what he wants to describe, *Paradise Lost* is clearly of epic stature and grandeur, perhaps the only great epic in English literature, though unlike the epics of Homer and Virgil, *Paradise Lost* is in no sense a national epic. Many would follow Blake and Shelley in taking Satan to be the true hero of the work, the hero that even Milton, against his better judgment, is forced to admire. This view might be backed up beyond Milton's own text, by observing that in *Paradise Lost,* Milton the regicide and republican actually seems officially to be taking the side of absolute power, a power which would make any monarchy, however absolute, pale into insignificance. But is this really what Milton feels?

It might be worth recalling at the start that in *Paradise Lost,* Milton is no lover of license or rebellion for its own sake. See, for example, Abdiel's speech in Book Six, and even more Michael's disquisition on liberty in Book Twelve. Rebellion for Milton can be a sign of servitude, just as license in one's personal behavior may be a symptom of subjection to the tyranny of uncontrollable desire. Whether there are overtones of totalitarianism in Milton's doctrine of rational liberty is a question which might take us too far afield, but it is certainly worth observing that, for Milton, rational liberty is not a matter of doing what one wants, and it is particularly not a matter of rebelling against a wise or just ruler, whose edicts ought to be obeyed by free men, precisely because they are what reason would require.

There is no denying that in the opening of *Paradise Lost* Satan is attractive, particularly for an age which admires heroes who stand up against authority, and who do not give in even when all is lost. Milton may not have admired such people as much as we do, or even at all, but even from Milton's own point of view there is something compelling about Satan's swagger and about his cleverness when dealing with the rebel angels, to say nothing of his dauntless courage. But we have to remember that Satan represents temptation for Milton. This would not be psychologically or in any other way plausible were he—and it—not attractive, at least on the surface. So Milton had to make Satan attractive at first, or neither we nor the devils would ever be tempted by him. It is part of Milton's dramatic genius that we start to see other sides to Satan only later on. This is not only dramatically sound; it is convincing in a human sense too. All too often it is only later on that we begin to see the unpleasantness of cheats and rogues.

Blake and Shelley aside, once Satan leaves Hell, he is revealed as being deeply selfish, deeply self-centered, and deeply unpleasant and malicious. His challenge to God was motivated by personal pride, quite simply, but a pride which is prepared to drag countless others down with him. After his fall, he is full of malice in himself, wanting that others should suffer just because he has been punished. And there is nothing noble about his seduction of the all-too-weak and gullible Eve, particularly when Satan and we, the readers, know what the consequences will be. It is possible to argue about Milton's God, but there is little that can be said here which would improve a properly rounded estimate of Satan's character.

Part of the reason for the fascination with Satan is that he is undoubtedly the most interesting and well-drawn character in *Paradise Lost*. Adam and Eve are types, as we have already observed, rather than individuals, for all their initial beauty and innocence. And God, Father or Son, are hardly characters at all, perhaps because they suffer from none of the human limitations or defects of even the Olympian gods in Homer, let alone those of the human characters of the works we have been considering. Nor, it has to be said, does Milton's God have the mystical power of Dante's far more abstract but more religiously compelling vision, and nor is the prison of Hell envisioned as being part of the primal love of God as it is in Dante. If neither Satan, nor God, nor Adam, nor Eve can be considered to be the hero of *Paradise Lost,* perhaps the real hero is the language that Milton uses to scale his mountain, or even Milton himself in his attempt on heights hitherto unattempted.

Assuming that this is what he is trying to do deep down, does Milton justify the ways of God to men? No more than Saint Augustine does he explain where evil comes from in the first place (in Milton's case when it enters Satan). And for many readers of Milton, just as it is for readers of Augustine, the punishment of the whole human race through Adam and the punishment of the Son for our sins will remain a stumbling block. But that is only to say that Christianity itself is problematic, at least in its orthodox formulation. Maybe the things which Christianity is struggling to express are inexpressible without contradiction or tension. They may be valuable or even true for all of that, however. Certainly we might do well to take the thought of man's disobedience more seriously than we often do. We might also ponder on the Christian belief that, with the Fall, sin corrupts not just the sinner but also the natural world and our relation to it. Estranged from God and Paradise, we humans now seek only our own desires and satisfactions, henceforth to be victims of the harshness and sufferings visited on us by the now fallen natural world, stark in its brutality and rapaciousness (rather, indeed, as Darwin describes it). Against this, though, there is Milton's profound sense that the Fall may, through God's grace (however we may like to conceptualize grace), be the occasion of a better redemption, and necessary for it. Evil would be our good, then, though not in Satan's sense.

Here we can focus on one specific aspect of Milton's theology. Originally, in line with the Genesis myth (Book Five, 480 ff.), Adam has the power to name the beasts and the rest of creation, and to give sense and understanding to what he encounters in Paradise. It is as if at this point, language and understanding latch on to the world unproblematically and directly, and there is, as yet, no problem of the pandemonium of Babel in which there are many competing and conflicting and mutually untranslatable languages. Babel, indeed, is a result of the Fall of mankind.

However, when Satan, as the serpent, tempts Eve in Book Nine, the first thing which strikes her is that

> Language of Man [is] pronounced
> By tongue of brute, and human sense expressed! (553–54)

Satan explains that he is able to do this because he has eaten of the "goodly tree," the tree which gives knowledge of good and evil. Further, while she, Eve, knows the words "good" and "evil," she does not know what these words really mean. She learns that only when she exercises her freedom, and tastes of good and evil.

It is after that that Eve, like Satan, is able to use language to devious and rhetorical effect. Those who have tasted of good and evil can not only name, but can also persuade and speak creatively—for good or evil. The point here, surely, is that only those who have exercised their freedom, and who have moved away from rigid adherence to the divine command and to the mission of just defining and describing God's world, can actually be creative, again for good and evil. The cost of this increase in creativity and in imaginative power is the pandemonium of Hell and the mutual incomprehension implied in Babel. But the benefit is not just in the means of redemption (the Incarnation of Christ), but also in the increase in human power and creativity afforded by the possibility and actuality of freedom, including the sins which thereby come about. Milton's message seems to be that of Augustine: that the Fall is actually a good, because of the possibilities it brings about—for evil, to be sure, but for a greater good too. In this context, Satan and the Fall are not to be applauded for themselves, but they are to be seen as an essential part of the divine economy, by which mankind (or some of mankind) eventually rises to a state higher than that of Paradise, as symbolized by Adam's activity of merely naming things in accordance with the divine dispensation.

Through his poetry and his immense learning, Milton succeeds in giving the Christian story an epic shape and power which can stand some comparison with Virgil. It is, of course, the power of the vision which has his critics arguing to this day so fiercely about its true meaning and morality, even when few of them would admit to believing any of it.

Pascal
Pensées

Blaise Pascal (1623–62) was one of the greatest mathematicians of all time, but he is more widely known for his Pensées, *a collection of aphorisms and meditations—philosophical, psychological and theological—on the nature of human life. Following a profound mystical experience in 1654, Pascal had become convinced that we could never lift ourselves out of our corrupt and fallen state without the direct help of the grace of God. We could, though, prepare ourselves for the reception of grace by meditating on the vanity and ultimate hopelessness of our fallen existence, by practising religious rites, and by convincing ourselves of the existence of God by means of Pascal's famous wager (in which we decide to believe in God because the benefits of doing so far outweigh the gains from atheism, even if God does not exist). Theologically, Pascal was firmly in the tradition of Saint Augustine and was closely aligned with the Jansenists of his day, who espoused an uncompromising Augustinianism on the need for grace. But the power of Pascal's writing derives not from intellectual analysis, but from the depth of his psychological insights into our moral and intellectual infirmities, and also from his conviction of the living reality of God and of Jesus Christ: "The heart has its reasons which reason knows nothing of."*

B laise Pascal was born in the Auvergne in central France in 1623, and died in 1662 in Paris. Although often passed over in philosophical and literary histories, and less actually read than referred to, he is one of the greatest but also one of the most uncomfortable and unclassifiable geniuses our civilization has produced. Following the philosopher Descartes and figures from the Enlightenment such as Voltaire and Diderot, French thought has a reputation for clarity, optimism and brilliance. Pascal's writing is both clear and brilliant, but his aim is quite different from the thinkers of the Enlightenment, as we will see, and he is anything but optimistic about the powers of the human mind or spirit. The strength of his writing lies not in the brilliance of his insights—which is certainly there, and which makes Diderot, for example, seem shallow in comparison, and Voltaire frivolous—but above all in its intensely personal tone.

When we read Pascal we read the most intimate thoughts of the most passionate soul, whether we have the courage to follow him or not. But his passion is not that of a romantic dreamer or a solitary wanderer, such as might have appealed to Rousseau and the Romantics. Pascal's passion is a unique fusion of intellect and feeling, in which all is held taut in an almost mathematical vice, and transfigured. The resulting insights are impersonal, grimly so, cutting through subjective feeling to the bare essence of our condition. If we take Pascal's insights seriously, they will inevitably make each one of us deeply uncomfortable as to the superficial nature of so much of what we do, and ever more aware of our stratagems for hiding the truth from ourselves. In one way or another, much of what Pascal has shown us has become a permanent part of the moral landscape of the West.

Pascal's mother died when he was only three years old. With his two sisters (Gilberte and Jacqueline) Pascal was then brought up by his father, Étienne. He was always sickly, even as a child, and also a stranger to human affection and contact. Indeed, one of his *Pensées* (396/375) is explicitly directed at Gilberte. It warns her off attachments to human beings (her children, we are told); for, according to Pascal, human beings are not ultimate goals, and they do not have the means of satisfying the affection that others may direct at them; one is actually culpable if one encourages or allows others to be attached to one. Some readers will doubtless dismiss this thought in psychobiographical terms, but that does not confront the point Pascal is making.

By the age of twelve, Pascal's mathematical genius was already evident. He had worked out a large proportion of Euclid's geometry for himself. He was educated by Étienne at first, and went on to study under the distinguished philosopher and mathematician Marin Mersenne. Pascal's first work (*Essai sur les coniques*), written when he was only sixteen, was published in 1640, to be followed throughout the rest of his short life by pathbreaking investigations into topics as diverse as the calculating machine (which he invented in 1642), probability theory, geometry, number theory, and the vacuum (where he refuted Descartes' theoretical disproof by empirical testing, and in doing so also made far more precise our ideas on the falsifying of scientific hypotheses and on the weight of evidence in favor of successful hypotheses). Shortly before his death he made a major contribution to public transport, devising for the first time the idea of the omnibus (which he started in Paris, as a method of raising revenue for the poor).

But 1640 was significant for Pascal not only for his own first publication. It was also the year of publication of the posthumous study known as *Augustinus,* the work of the late Bishop of Ypres, Cornelius Jansen (or Jansenius). For most of the rest of his life, Pascal was to be caught up in the bitter controversies and struggles associated with the phenomenon known as Jansenism. Part political and part theological, Jansenism was a movement of strict religious practice but also a focus of opposition to the French monarchy and their spiritual advisors, the Jesuits. Ideologically, Jansenism was antihumanist, like Saint Augustine stressing original sin and the need for grace. It went against the casuistry of the Jesuits (who were criticized for finding excuses for the moral laxity of the rulers, in order, it was said, to promote the greater good). Jansenism also opposed the practice of frequent communion and the characteristically Counter Reformation and baroque spirituality of Saint François de Sales (whose teaching accommodated tolerance of human passions and celebrated sexuality within marriage). Above all, Jansenism stressed the inefficacy of human effort and good works unless elevated by divine grace. In his *Pensées,* Pascal may not have been a Jansenist in the strict sense, but, particularly on this last point, his moral, religious, and philosophical outlook was characterized by a Jansenist spirit.

In 1646, Pascal's family became Jansenist for all intents and purposes. After Étienne's death in 1651, Jacqueline became a nun at the convent of Port-Royal. Influenced first by the Abbé Saint-Cyran (an ally of Jansen) and later by Antoine Arnauld (two of whose sisters were nuns in the convent), Port-Royal had become the focus of Jansenist teaching and influence. At the start of this period, Pascal himself was already world-famous as a mathematician. At that time he was associating with a worldly, free-thinking set (the so-called "libertines"), who included among their number La Fontaine. But on the night of November 23, 1654 he had a searing spiritual experience, the "nuit de feu" (night of fire), the account of which he kept always sewn into his coat (*Pensées,* 913/711), and which changed his life. He went on retreat at Port-Royal, and henceforth identified himself with the defense of Port-Royal and with the Jansenist cause. The fortunes of the cause, however, went from bad to worse.

Also in 1654, the Pope (Innocent IV) condemned the "Five Propositions" supposedly to be found in *Augustinus.* In 1655, Arnauld was condemned by the Church and stripped of his doctorate at the Sorbonne. From 1656–57, Pascal wrote (anonymously) his *Lettres Provinciales,* supporting the Port-Royalists. While the *Lettres* have been taken ever since as a model of polemical writing, including by Voltaire himself, from Pascal's immediate perspective they did little good. His work was itself placed in the Index of Forbidden Books and the Jansenist movement as a whole was condemned by the Pope. In October 1661 Jacqueline died, and the next month the Port-Royal community capitulated to the Church authorities. In 1662 Pascal, now ill and broken, though still conducting scientific work, moved in with Gilberte, and himself submitted to the Pope. He died on August 19, 1662, leaving among other writings the notes which were to be published in 1670 as his *Pensées*.

Jansenism

The key point about Jansenism is an insistence on the powerlessness of man to save himself or even to improve morally without special grace from God. Without that, our own efforts can avail us nothing. This stark and pessimistic view has its immediate roots in Augustine and in Paul; more generally, it is part of the orthodox Christian doctrine of the Fall, as we saw it in Milton. However, as developed by the Jansenists and by Pascal, in its stress on the absolute helplessness of the human being unaided by grace, the doctrine is close enough to the Protestantism of Calvin to be viewed by the Catholic Church as heretical. Hence the condemnation by the Pope.

For the sake of completeness, we will give a little of the theological detail in what follows, but we should stress that the detail is not strictly necessary for understanding Pascal's general position.

The five propositions condemned by Pope Innocent IV were:

1. Some commandments of God are impossible to obey, even for those in a state of grace and making an effort. Specific divine grace is needed.
2. In a state of fallen nature, interior grace cannot be resisted.
3. In a state of fallen nature, in order to incur merit or guilt, it is not necessary to be free from all interior necessity. It is sufficient to be free from external constraint.
4. Pelagians or semi-Pelagians (those who think we can be saved by good works alone) are heretical because they believe that we can resist or yield to grace of our own free will.
5. It is semi-Pelagian to say that Christ died generally for all human beings.

It takes some effort to get one's head around these propositions, but their general direction is clear enough. Any good works that we do are not enough on their own to secure our salvation; we need, in addition, God's grace, a special gift from God, enabling us to turn to Him. In our fallen state, we also need God's grace to obey God's commands (a theme familiar already from Augustine's *Confessions*). God's grace, when and if it comes, cannot be resisted. But grace and the "interior necessity" which follows from it does not mean that, in what we do, we may not also incur either merit or guilt.

In fact, only the first of the five propositions is actually to be found in *Augustinus,* and much of the wrangling after the condemnation of 1654 was over whether one could be condemned for holding to beliefs one did not explicitly profess. The issue which really separated the Jansenists from their critics, though, was a deep one: was human nature, without grace, fundamentally perverted? For the Jansenists, self-love and ordinary psychological motivation (even of a beneficent kind) was normally taken to be an indication of the absence of grace and of true goodness. For them, even with grace, pure and disinterested love of God was very rare.

The Jansenists' critics saw their stress on the need for grace, and our powerlessness to resist it when it came, as close to the Protestantism and predestinationism of Calvin. For where, despite the claim of the third proposition, could human freedom be exercised if grace is irresistible? The answer seems to be that, irresistible as it is in one sense, grace is not enough in itself to stop us doing wrong (and hence incurring guilt). There is also the problem of those who are not given grace, and who therefore cannot be saved, but this is a problem for the orthodox just as much as for the Jansenists, as we saw in connection with Dante. However, more important than the minutiae of the Jansenist controversy and doctrines is the Jansenist spirit: an acute awareness of human imperfectibility and of our total reliance on grace from outside if we are to rise above our flawed condition. It is this awareness which permeates Pascal's analysis in the *Pensées;* or perhaps, less tendentiously, it is the insights Pascal offers as to the strict nature of our condition which might support a generally Jansenist orientation, by providing evidence of the need for divine grace for any sort of human progress.

Pensées

Pascal's *Pensées* (Thoughts) are notes and fragments left on his death. There have been many editions and reorderings, which creates problems for readers and also for referring to them. The numbers in this chapter refer to the numberings in the editions by Lafuma (which is that translated in the Penguin Classics by Alban Krailsheimer) and Le Guern (Gallimard, Paris, 1977). The Gallimard edition contains concordances to other editions.

As already remarked, *Pensées* is not strictly a Jansenist tract. Indeed, it is not a tract at all. It goes wider and deeper, and is in no sense a systematic treatise. And as well as philosophico-theological analysis it also contains a lot of biblical interpretation. Though critical for Pascal, in its support for his own election of his own brand of Christianity, the biblical analysis is likely to strike the modern reader as often spurious and beside the point. The modern reader may be wrong on the latter judgment. It was obviously not beside Pascal's own point. Nevertheless, little will be said here about these parts of the *Pensées*.

Basic Themes in the *Pensées*

For obvious reasons to do with their provenance and their editing, the *Pensées* can hardly be seen as developing an argument in an orderly fashion; and as a consequence of the work's unsystematic nature, it is highly repetitive. Maybe Pascal, had he ever come to edit the work himself, would not have eliminated the existential and meditative quality of the writing, or even its repetitiveness—after all, the truths that the *Pensées* contain are ones we have to assimilate by constant return to them, and seeing them in the light of our ever-changing experiences of the things he is meditating on. Whether he would have or not, though, and even as we have the text (in whatever ordering), certain fundamental contrasts shine through. These include:

> nature : grace
> the strength of human reason : the infirmity of human reason
> the vanity and diversion of much of human life : that which, in contrast, we really know—and seek to avoid
> sense : reason : heart (as we will see, a tripartite distinction)
> scepticism: and its overcoming
> the God of the philosophers : the God of Abraham, Isaac, and Jacob
> (the point here being that God is not something which can be reached by abstract philosophical reason, but is a living Being we experience, as Abraham experienced God in the burning bush)

Pascal's underlying contrast and pervasive theme is set out in 6/4:

> Misery of man without God : Happiness of man with God
> That nature is corrupt, (is shown) by nature itself : that there is a Redeemer, (is shown) by Scripture
> (All translations from *Pensées* are by the author.)

So right at the start it is clear that Scripture is important for Pascal, as it was for Augustine, with whom he has so many similarities. We may defend our inattention to the scriptural commentary of both authors by pointing out that in both cases, and especially in Pascal's case, what was critical in religious conversion and development was an experience of grace. Biblical study and meditation may have framed the experiences, and given them content; but on its own it was insufficient.

Pascal's thoroughgoing anti-Cartesianism is shown in 5/3, where he denies that a human seeking—or the use of the natural light of human reason—can solve our religious problems. What we need is faith, a gift from God, which is different from proof; in our hearts, belief, not knowledge (in the human sense). Descartes had postulated that we could refute skepticism and prove the existence of God by meditating philosophically, using the light of natural reason in our meditations. Pascal disagrees profoundly, and not just on the attainment of knowledge of God. For Pascal, skepticism of the sort that Descartes was concerned to refute cannot be effectively tackled by natural reason either.

There is indeed a deep contrast among philosophers on this point. Some believe—or hope—that philosophical skepticism about such things as physical objects, the self and scientific knowledge can be headed off by direct argument, by the light of natural reason as Descartes would have put it. Others, of whom Pascal, Hume, and Wittgenstein are notable examples, believe that arguments against skepticism are bound to be either circular or question-begging or both. I mention Hume and Wittgenstein here particularly, because they also think that we find a defense against skepticism not in reason or argument, but in what Hume calls our animal nature, Wittgenstein our forms of life, and Pascal the Machine: that is, in our unthought, instinctual and practical responses to the world and our fellows, which reveal that philosophical and other forms of skepticism are impossible to live by. (We cannot act, except on the assumption that there is a physical world separate from us, that we can gain knowledge of it, that our fellows are selves like ourselves, etc.) And, according to Pascal in 5/3, "la Machine" (glossed by one commentator as the psycho-physiological automatism of mankind) can also help to prepare us for faith. Like Augustine, Pascal believes that we have naturally certain instincts and desires which make us ready for faith. Proof, too, can be a useful instrument, building on the Machine and preparing us for faith (7/5 and 11/9).

La nuit de feu

What faith is, and how it comes, is shown in the *nuit de feu* account (913/711), in which among other things there is the contrast between the God of Abraham, Isaac, and Jacob, and the God of philosophers and scholars; and also the experience of Jesus Christ, and submission to Jesus Christ:

The year of grace, 1654.

Monday November 23rd, the day of Saint Clement, pope and martyr, and of others in the martyrology [the Catholic list of saints and martyrs of the Church].

The eve of Saint Chrysogonus, martyr and of others.

From around half past ten in the evening until around half-past midnight.

God of Abraham, God of Isaac, God of Jacob, not of philosophers and scholars.

Certainty, certainty, feeling, joy, peace.

God of Jesus Christ,

"My God and your God."

Your God will be my God.

Forgetfulness of the world and of everything, except God.

He is found only in the ways taught by the Evangelists.

Greatness of the human soul.

"O righteous Father, the world had not known thee, but I have known thee."

Joy, joy, joy, tears of joy.

I have separated myself from him.

"They have forsaken me, the fountain of living waters."

My God, will you leave me?

That I should not be separated from him eternally.

"And this is life eternal, that they might know thee, the only true God and Jesus Christ whom thou has sent."

Jesus Christ.

Jesus Christ.

I have separated myself from him, I have flown from him, renounced him, crucified him.

That I should never be separated from him.

He will be saved only through the ways taught by the Evangelists.

Total and gentle renunciation.

Total submission to Jesus Christ and to my (spiritual) director.

Eternal joy for one day of struggle on earth.

"I will not forget thy word." Amen.

(The phrases in quotation marks are scriptural quotations.)

This experience was what Pascal lived by for the rest of his life, and he interpreted it as the infusion of divine grace into his heart and soul. His account of it conditioned how he saw things, and everything he did henceforth. From it stemmed the attitudes and practices he developed in the *Pensées*.

Pascal's Wager

As already remarked, he did not believe that it was possible to prove the existence of God by pure reason. Even if there were a proof (which, contrary to Descartes and much Catholic tradition, he does not think there is), it would not put us in touch with God in a living way. It would take us only to the abstract God of the philosophers, and not to the living God who might save us through His grace. However, he did think that it was possible to prepare ourselves for the reception of grace, and also, for those who had it, to reinforce that experience subsequently. The method he had in mind is what has come to be known as Pascal's Wager (*Pensées,* 418–26/397 and footnotes).

The Wager is best seen as an exercise which prepares the way. Strictly speaking, we cannot prove or know God's nature, any more than we can know infinity. Rationally, faith is a folly (*stultitia*); we cannot decide whether God exists or not. In this state of rational indecision, we have to make some decision. What we should do is to wager. By wagering on God, we stand to gain infinitely and to lose nothing. If we wager the other way, not only do we stand to lose infinitely, but we will become unhappy and subject to our passions. Furthermore, rather than wasting our time in fruitlessly piling up proofs of God's existence, wagering on God and acting on this cures us by diminishing our passions. This will make us less rational, more natural, more mindless, more submissive, more Machine-like in Pascal's sense, enabling us to dampen down the passions, which are our big obstacles. In all this, Pascal sets great store by going through the motions of religious practice—praying, attending Mass, telling one's beads, sprinkling holy water—precisely so as to quieten the intellect and the passions, to put us into a state in which we will be able to receive divine grace, if it comes our way.

In a crucial addition to the Wager passage proper, after saying that it is the heart which knows God and not reason, Pascal adds:

> I say that the heart loves the universal being naturally and itself naturally, according to how it chooses, and from its choice it hardens itself against the one or the other.

So we are to use the Wager and our animal nature to wager on God so as to release the God-directed part of our nature and to clear reason for faith. Finally,

> It is only the Christian religion which makes men both happy and lovable together; living honestly with others in the world [*dans l'honnêteté*] we cannot be both happy and lovable at the same time.

We should note in connection with the Wager: 1) usually for Pascal, "reason" is what is supposed to separate us from the beasts, yet without faith, our reason leads us beastwards, to noxious pleasures, depravity, unhappiness; so we have in a sense to curb our reason so as to allow for faith; and 2) it is Christianity which is wagered on, because only Christianity plumbs human depravity *and* redeems it (back to the *nuit de feu*).

Our Condition

The analysis of what the Christian religion redeems us from is what Pascal is probably best known for. According to him:

> Man's condition.
> Inconstancy, boredom, anxiety. (24/22)

Immediately prior to this, he had written:

> Vanity of the sciences.
> The physical sciences will not console us for ignorance of morality in time of affliction, but knowledge of morality will always console me for ignorance of the physical sciences. (23/21)

From this uncompromising standpoint, Pascal sets about dissecting human vanity and susceptibility to illusion more generally. Our imagination constantly colors and falsifies everything. For example, a smooth and eloquent preacher will have more effect than a quirky one preaching the same message. Even a philosopher will feel frightened if he is walking over a precipice on a plank, even though he knows he should be perfectly safe (44/41). In these and countless similar cases, imagination overcomes reason, a point also illustrated in the discussion of Cleopatra's nose: if it had been slightly shorter—and her beauty compromised—the whole history of the world would have been different (413/392). No doubt in this case the noxious effects of love and human competitiveness are also lurking, and Pascal includes in his analysis of vanity the point used by Rousseau to base a whole philosophy: namely, that human vanity impels us endlessly and fruitlessly to seek to appear superior to others, who are then similarly enmeshed in an endless cycle of resentment and fruitless striving themselves.

From Pascal's analysis of our vanity, we can turn to his estimation of our intellectual powers. Human reason and our senses are two principles of truth and two sources of knowledge, yet, in Pascal's view, they are engaged in mutual deception and contradiction (45/41). (Here a relevant point would be Pascal's campaign against the rationalist Descartes' "rational" proof of the impossibility of the vacuum; Pascal thinks that both sense and reason have a place, but a limited place in the acquisition of knowledge.) Further, against dogmatism and rationalism, Pascal invokes the unassailable skeptical arguments to be found, for example, in his near-contemporary Montaigne. Pyrrhonian scepticism—that quietistic suspension of belief advocated by the ancient skeptics in the face of unassailable sceptical arguments—is true, Pascal says (691/585). We do not need here to rehearse the skeptical arguments, which Pascal does not in any case detail himself: it will be enough to point out that in attempting to justify the truth of any claim about the world, justifying reasons give out pretty quickly, leaving us with unsupported claims about the nature of the world and our knowledge of it (for example, that things really are as they appear to us, that the future will be like the past, that we really are free). What is interesting in Pascal at this point is not so much the skepticism itself, which he shares with many philosophers, including Montaigne and Hume, but his conclusions about what this reveals about us and our intellectual powers, and where he wishes skepticism to take us. Pascal does not want it to take us to the easygoing skepticism about religion of Montaigne or to the quiet irony of Hume, as we will see, but rather to a heartfelt commitment to a religion of fire.

Against skepticism, Pascal urges, we have our instinctive assurance that we are not dreaming, etc. (110/101 and 122/131)—but this does not amount to rational proof. (After all, even if we think we have a proof, we could just be dreaming it, or dreaming that we are carrying out tests to show we are awake.) We are a strange combination of greatness—ability to think—and of wretchedness—our thinking leading to impasses, and to the conclusion that we are wretched (114/105). In sum, the open war between skepticism and dogmatism leads to a standoff, dogmatism (asserting the world is as it appears, that we are not dreaming, etc.) being unprovable and skepticism unliveable (131/122). We are subjects full of natural error and contradiction, which can be eradicated only through grace and by following the heart. There is an interesting contrast here with Hume. Hume follows much of Pascal's scepticism, but goes on to say that "carelessness and inattention alone can afford us any remedy. For this reason, I rely entirely upon them"; and also that his skeptical humor vanishes only when he engages in diversion—dining, playing backgammon, making merry with his friends.[19] But for Pascal these are just the wrong weapons; what we really need is not diversion but grace, and only grace, even in our predicament over the inability rationally to answer the skeptics. Our lack of certainty is itself a sign of our depravity.

Further, the Humean search for diversion is itself a symptom of our fallenness and of our misery. Our contradictory and corrupted nature makes us so unhappy that we fall into an endless quest for diversion (136/126). The hustle and bustle and busyness with which rulers and officials surround themselves is actually what they are after, not the results of their activity. They want to do anything but think about themselves, attend to their own parlous condition. Being unable to stay quietly in one's room is the sole cause of man's unhappiness. Stuck between the infinitely big and the infinitely small, we can cope with neither. We can neither understand ourselves, nor find a firm footing over the abyss (199/185). Our only dignity lies in the fact that we are a reed, but a thinking reed. Nevertheless, when we think, "le silence éternel de ces espaces infinis m'effraie" (the eternal silence of these infinite spaces frightens me) (201/187). Our only comfort is that we must expect salvation by expecting nothing from ourselves (202/188). So the dignity which comes from our thinking is not fruitless speculation or science, but the realization of our baseness and the pious and steady hope that we might transcend our condition through grace.

As with Augustine, for Pascal true fulfillment is to be found only in God, that to which all our striving is really directed (148/138, cf. also 399/378). Stoicism and other philosophies which tell us to withdraw into ourselves are as false as those which tell us to look outside, for diversion: the solution is in God, both inside and outside us (407/386). The question, though, is how we should get to God, given our impotence, rational and moral, and the gap between our vileness and our divine aspiration (351/322). The answer is given by the Incarnation of Christ, which shows man the greatness of his wretchedness, given the greatness of the remedy required (352/333).

This takes us back to Pascal's tripartite psychology of sense, reason, heart. Heart (*coeur*), informed and infused with grace, can overcome our weakness; though to get there we have to accede to reason's last step, namely recognition that there are an infinite number of things beyond reason (188/177), and submission to the comfort from outside. And this means not metaphysical proof, but knowledge of God through Jesus Christ (189–90/178–79), recognizing both our own wretchedness and the Redeemer (449/419). Finally, in terms reminiscent of Augustine's *Confessions* (Book Seven, 18–19), in the passage entitled "At Port Royal" (149/139), especially in the sections entitled "Prosopopoeia" and "Incomprehensible," Pascal gives some indication of the state of mind in which conversion, faith, and grace might be offered (we are to imagine that the voice is that of Divine Wisdom):

> It is in vain, O men, that you seek within yourselves the remedy for
> your misery. All your reason can bring you only to the point at which
> you know that in yourselves you will find neither truth nor goodness.
> The philosophers have promised you these things, but they have not

been able to deliver . . . Your chief ills are the pride which withdraws you from God and concupiscence which attaches you to the earth. All that the philosophers have done is to entertain one or other of these ills. If they have given you God for an object, it has only been to exercise your pride, to make you think that you were like him and of a similar nature. And those who have seen the vanity of such pretension have thrown you over the other precipice in making you understand that your nature is like that of the beasts, leading you to seek your good in the lusts which are the domain of the animals. This is not the way to cure you of the injustices which these wise people haven't even recognised. I alone can make you understand what you are . . . Adam, Jesus Christ.

If you are united to God, it is through grace, not by nature.

If you are humbled, it is through penitence, not through nature . . .

God has desired to redeem men and to open salvation to those who seek it, but men have made themselves so unworthy that it is just that God refuses some, on account of their hardness of heart, what through his mercy he gives to others beyond what they have merited . . . but (so as not to compromise their freedom) he has tempered our knowledge of him, so that he has given signs which are visible to those who seek him, but not to those who do not.

There is enough light for those who desire only to see, and enough darkness for those of the contrary disposition.

Conclusion

It is hard to sum up Pascal or to come to a balanced judgment of him. His analysis of human vanity and weakness is unsurpassed, probably unsurpassable. Even those who are repelled by his religion will find it hard to deny the truth of much of what he says about our proneness to illusion and diversion, and also about our weaknesses intellectually and morally. We might like to pretend that skepticism is refutable and that human nature is basically good. But the greatest of Pascal's philosophical successors (Hume, Kant, Wittgenstein) have not managed to refute skepticism, but have sought rather to avoid its consequences; and history since Pascal's time has hardly improved a cool estimation of human nature. Maybe more can be said in favor of diversion than Pascal allows, as a cure for the ills of the mind; and maybe, despite the horrors of recent history, we do not live in quite such a hopeless plight as Pascal would have us believe. Maybe we are not quite as trapped in a machine in which there is nothing ultimately but guilt and despair—outside of divine intervention and grace.

Nevertheless, Pascal's philosophical successors have tended to address skepticism and other issues by abandoning his tripartite psychology of sense, reason, heart. Either heart falls out of the picture altogether, or it is interpreted in a naturalistic way, as animal belief (in Hume's terms) or as a matter of Wittgensteinian forms of life. With Pascal an entire philosophical era, which began with Socrates and the ancient Greeks, comes to an end: the era in which philosophy was seen as a royal road to faith or spiritual enlightenment. A new era now begins, that of the Enlightenment and of a rational enquiry into nature, and of the supremacy of a reason which has largely rejected heart and which is hostile to faith.

Having said all this, though, we can still question the accuracy of Pascal's account of human life. We can ask ourselves what it would be like to live without illusion in an unredeemed Pascalian world. Is our human world like that? There may be no better way to approach this question than by turning to a drama in which we find a terrifying vision of human misery remarkably close in mood and spirit to Pascal: Racine's *Phèdre*.

Racine
Phèdre

The great French dramatist Jean Racine (1639–99) was, like Pascal, close to the Jansenists. Phèdre, first produced in 1677, is on a classical theme: the incestuous love of Phèdre, Queen of Athens, for her stepson Hippolytus. Although there are all the trappings of a classical tragedy, and no Christian references in the play, Racine uses the tautness of his construction to create an atmosphere which could be described as Jansenist. For the portrait of Phèdre is of a woman who tries her best to escape her predicament, but cannot. She, like the rest of us, is powerless without divine grace. And, until the plot unravels with a sickening certainty, Racine's Phèdre has not actually done anything wrong. But in her conscience she is suffused with guilt and trapped, without hope of escape. What we see in Phèdre is a toxic concoction of conflicting personalities and overwhelming psychic drives in a stifling and claustrophobic atmosphere to which, in the absence of grace, death itself is the only logical or possible solution.

Jean Racine lived from 1639 until 1699. He had a Jansenist upbringing and education, but from 1660 until 1677 he became involved in the theater, writing a succession of plays, many of them tragedies based on classical themes. In 1677 he abandoned the theater for twelve years to take a position in the court of Louis XIV, which was itself becoming more puritanical, under the influence of Madame de Maintenon, Louis's mistress (and later his second wife). *Phaedra* (*Phèdre*) was the last play before Racine's withdrawal from the stage. It is suffused with guilt and oppressive, unresolved sexuality. It can be seen as part of a more general movement in French thought and life away from the exuberance, sensuality, and optimism of the baroque, and, for all its mythological trappings, back to a severity more Jansenist and Augustinian than classical, even though structurally *Phaedra* obeys the classical unities of form, the action taking place in a single location and over a single time. Racine's play also, as Aristotle demands of tragedy, arouses pity and terror.

There is no grace in *Phaedra,* no redemption. The individual without grace can do nothing. He (or she, in this case) is trapped by circumstances and a malicious fate, rather than as with Oedipus, say, or Antigone, an agent partially bringing about his or her tragic dilemma. In *Phaedra* there is no light at all, or even a sense, which one finds in Sophocles' *Antigone,* that things might have gone differently for Antigone in different circumstances. In Racine, predestination is total; the trap is closed from the start.

Voltaire—no lover of morbid religious sensibility or indeed of any type of religious feeling—called *Phaedra* "the masterpiece of the human mind." According to Racine himself, in his introduction, in *Phaedra* "the very thought of crime is regarded with as much horror as the crime itself." True, because the crime which is at the root of the whole tragedy (Phaedra's incest with her stepson Hippolytus) never actually takes place. Significantly, Racine here appears to depart from his classical models, Euripides and Seneca, where there is the accusation of a crime actually having been committed. What condemns Racine's Phaedra and what drives the action forward ineluctably is her inner state, nothing more than her desire for the crime, a state which horrifies her but which she can do nothing about, and which also drags down all the other characters with her, who are similarly impotent before forces they can do nothing about. For all its Jansenist context, in its hermetic and stifling psychodramatics *Phaedra* is a very modern play, more of an impossible hell of people trapped in mutually conflicting desires and hatreds than even that which Sartre tried to draw in *Huis Clos.* Or perhaps, as Pascal might have observed, *Phaedra* shows that the predicament of human beings without grace is as driven, as desperate, and as hopeless as the five propositions condemned by Innocent IV in 1654 would have it. In *Phaedra,* hell is not other people, as Sartre had it; much more, hell is ourselves. (Interestingly, on hearing Sartre's aphorism in the theater, T. S. Eliot is said to have whispered to a friend, "Hell is oneself," which is certainly Racinean.)

Before the play starts, Theseus has married Phaedra, bringing her to Athens from Crete, where he has killed the Minotaur. The Minotaur had been the issue of the obscene lust of Pasiphae (daughter of the sun, wife of King Minos of Crete and mother of Phaedra and Ariadne) for a bull. Hippolytus is Theseus's son from an earlier liaison with Antiope, the Queen of the Amazons. Phaedra, despite being married to Theseus and mother of other sons of Theseus, has an irresistible passion for Hippolytus.

The action of the play takes place in Troezen, a town in the Peloponnese some distance from Athens (where Theseus is king). Hippolytus has been exiled there by Phaedra, in order to have the object of her guilty passion taken away from her. Hippolytus himself is avoiding Aricia, who is also there and with whom he is in love, but whose six brothers had plotted against Theseus and had been put to death. Hippolytus, in other words, is in love with one of the enemies of his, and Theseus,' family. When the play starts, Phaedra too is in Troezen, having been brought there by Theseus. After having dispatched Phaedra to Troezen, Theseus has left Athens to help his friend Pirithous in his amorous quest for the Queen of Epirus, and possibly on amorous quests of his own. Theseus is, of course, a famous hero (though now approaching old age), and Hippolytus feels himself wholly in his father's shadow. When the play opens, Theseus has not been heard of for months and is believed to be dead.

Act One

Scene 1 opens with Hippolytus deciding to leave Troezen to search for Theseus, who has been missing for more than six months. Hippolytus laments what has happened since Phaedra arrived in Athens:

> That happy time has passed. Everything has changed
> Since the gods sent to these shores
> The daughter of Minos and Pasiphae. (33–35)
> (All translations from *Phèdre* are by the author.)

Theramenes, Hippolytus's mentor, tells him that Phaedra, who hates Hippolytus, is dying of some mysterious sickness. He asks Hippolytus if he, a hunter, is still "an implacable enemy of the laws of love" (59). Will he at last fall prey to Venus, whom, in his pride, he has disdained? Hippolytus contrasts his somewhat insignificant achievements with those of his heroic father, and eventually confesses his doomed love for Aricia, whom Theseus hates.

In Scene 2, Oenone, Phaedra's nurse, tells Hippolytus that Phaedra is close to death. Phaedra enters in Scene 3. She invokes the sun, her grandfather:

> Noble and brilliant founder of a sad family,
> You, whom my mother dared to boast as daughter,
> Who perhaps will blush at seeing my trouble,
> Sun, I come to see you for the last time . . .
> Where have I let my desires and my mind wander?
> I have lost it. The gods have seized it from me. (169–81)

Oenone tells her she must not think of death; she has a duty to her sons against Hippolytus. Phaedra says enigmatically that her hands are innocent, but not her heart. She cries out against the hatred of Venus for her mother (inflamed with lust for the bull), of Ariadne's fate (deserted by Theseus, whom she loved, on Naxos), and of Venus' hatred for her. She finally admits her unlawful love for Hippolytus. Hardly had she arrived in Athens as Theseus's bride when

> I felt my whole body freeze and burn,
> I recognised Venus and her dreaded fires
> And the unavoidable torments she inflicts on our blood . . .

She believed she could deflect her passion by her own efforts; she built

> a temple and offered sacrifices. But
> Even as my mouth invoked the name of the goddess
> I adored Hippolytus, and I saw him ceaselessly
> Even at the foot of the altars I was making smoke with sacrifice . . .
> (276–87)

She pretended outwardly to hate him, and banished him to Troezen, but then she herself was sent there by Theseus, and the wound re-opened:

> There is nothing but fire hidden in my veins,
> It is Venus, whole and entire, attached to her prey . . . (305–306)

She hates her passion and her life. If she had died she could have kept it hidden, but Oenone's tears have forced it out of her.

In Scene 4, Theseus's death is announced. The succession in Athens will be between Hippolytus, Phaedra's older son, and perhaps even Aricia. In Scene 5, Oenone tells Phaedra that Theseus's death has dissolved her bonds. She need no longer fear Hippolytus, but should join forces with him against Aricia. Phaedra determines to live.

Act Two

In Scene 1, Aricia, with her friend Ismene, muses on Theseus's death, and the rumor that he had descended into Hell with Pirithous, never to return. Aricia wonders if Hippolytus, who despises women, will be kinder to her than Theseus; Ismene tells her she suspects that Hippolytus loves Aricia. Aricia confesses that after her brothers' deaths she had been forbidden by law to marry (which was in accord with her own wishes), but that she now loves in

Hippolytus "his father's virtues, not his weaknesses" (442). She also loves his "generous pride," which has yet to bend beneath love's yoke. She would love to bring him down, a better prize than Theseus was for Phaedra, for that was a "homage offered to a thousand others" (447). But aren't these rash hopes? Won't his resistance be too strong?

In Scene 2, Hippolytus enters. He says he will restore Attica and Athens to Aricia, will keep Troezen himself and give Crete to Phaedra's son. Aricia, amazed, speaks of the earlier hatred between their lines; Hippolytus reveals his secret love for Aricia. His proud rebellion against love is over. For six months he has fought against himself:

> Present I follow you, absent I find you,
> In the depths of the forest, your image follows me.
> In the light of the day, in the shadows of the night,
> Everything brings back to my eyes the charms I avoid . . . (542–45)

All his manly sports are now forgotten, and she should not despise his ill-expressed desires.

Hippolytus is now summoned to see Phaedra; Aricia tells him to hear her speak at least, out of pity, even though she was his enemy (Scene 3). In Scene 4, Hippolytus tries to sail off; but he is intercepted by Phaedra (Scene 5), who speaks of her apparent enmity for Hippolytus, "but you could not read in the depths of my heart" (598). Hippolytus says that Theseus may not be dead. Phaedra speaks of the Theseus she once loved, not the worshipper of a thousand different objects, the one who would dishonour the bed of the god of the dead, but the faithful one, the one "with your carriage, your eyes, your voice, your noble modesty" (641–42). But what if Hippolytus rather than Theseus had been in the labyrinth . . . I, rather than Ariadne, would have led him into the labyrinth. In a great outburst, she professes her love for Hippolytus. She loves him, though she hates herself for it. The more she abused him and the more he hated her, the more she loved him, but not of her own volition. She calls on him to deliver the world of this monster; she bares her heart, imploring him to kill her with his sword. He refuses, and Phaedra grabs the sword herself. Oenone drags her away. Theramenes enters and finds Hippolytus in a state of shock (Scene 6). Theramenes tells him that in Athens, Phaedra's son is being declared king, but that there is also a rumor that Theseus is alive.

Act Three

In Scene 1, Phaedra is distraught and distracted at having revealed her secret and her shame to Hippolytus. Oenone tells her to act like a queen.

I, reign? Me, bring a state beneath my control
When my own feeble reason no longer rules me? (759–60)

Stiffened up by Oenone, though, she plans to win Hippolytus over with the offer of joint rule over Athens.

In Scene 2, Phaedra, alone, prays to Venus:

O thou! Who see the shame to which I have descended,
Implacable Venus, have I been confounded enough?
You could not inflict more cruelty on me.
Your triumph is perfect. All your strokes have hit home.
O cruel one, if you want a new triumph
Attack an enemy who is more rebellious against you.
Hippolytus is fleeing from you, and braving your anger
Has never bent the knee at your altar.
Your very name seems to offend his proud ears.
Goddess, avenge yourself, our causes are parallel,
Make him love . . . (813–23)

In Scene 3, Oenone announces that Theseus is on his way back. Phaedra's dilemma is compounded, now that Hippolytus knows. She thinks again of suicide, but is terrified for her children. Oenone schemes to denounce Hippolytus as having made advances to Phaedra, in the expectation that Theseus will then banish him. Phaedra agrees. Scenes 4, 5, and 6 follow very fast. Phaedra, in guilt, rejects Theseus's advances. Hippolytus asks to be permitted to leave Phaedra forever, never to see her again, and upbraids Theseus for bringing Phaedra and Aricia to Troezen. He pleads to be allowed to engage in adventures like his father before him. Theseus cannot understand the coolness of the welcome after his own adventures. He will ask Phaedra for the cause. Hippolytus is terrified that Phaedra will bring ruin on herself, but nevertheless resolves to tell Theseus of his innocent love for Aricia.

Act Four

In Scene 1, Oenone springs the trap. Theseus believes that Hippolytus drew his sword on Phaedra in order to have his way with her, and that Phaedra was silent in order to spare Theseus from knowing. In Scene 2, Theseus angrily confronts Hippolytus. He banishes him and calls on Neptune to revenge the wrong Hippolytus has done. Hippolytus is astonished that Phaedra has accused him. He protests his innocence and calls on his father to approve the respect which makes him keep his own mouth shut. He asks Theseus to remember his virtuousness and the inflexible rigor for which he is famous throughout Greece. Theseus tells him that he stands condemned by the very pride he has in his virtue, which leads Hippolytus to tell of his own forbidden love for Aricia. Theseus is outraged even further by what he takes to be a lie on the part of his son to exonerate himself. Hippolytus replies:

> My virtue may seem false to you and full of guile.
> In the bottom of her heart, Phaedra does me more justice. (1137–38)

Theseus is further enraged and throws Hippolytus out. In a short soliloquy (Scene 3), Theseus calls on Neptune to kill his son.

Phaedra enters (Scene 4). She begins by calling on Theseus to spare Hippolytus, but Theseus tells her that Neptune will avenge the crime Hippolytus did her. Phaedra is about to protest when Theseus reveals that Hippolytus has sworn that he actually loves Aricia. In a fit of jealousy (Scene 5), Phaedra resolves to stay silent before Theseus. In Scene 6, she tells Oenone what she has learned about Aricia and Hippolytus, upbraiding Oenone for not having told her earlier of their innocent love:

> They followed without remorse their amorous bent.
> For them each day dawned clear and serene.
> But I, spurned by the whole of nature,
> Hid myself by day, and fled the light.
> Death is the only God I can dare to implore. (1239–43)

Phaedra torments herself by thinking of their happiness, and in a crescendo of hate and desperation she calls for their destruction:

> I exude incest and deceit.
> My murderous hands ready to avenge me
> Burn to sink themselves in innocent blood.
> Wretch! And I still live? And I endure the sight
> Of the sacred sun from which I am descended?
> I have for a grandfather the father and the lord of the gods.
> The sky and the whole universe is full of my forebears.
> Where shall I hide myself? Let us flee into the hellish night.
> But what shall I say? My father holds the urn of doom.
> Fate, we are told, placed it in his ruthless hands.
> Minos in hell judges the pale humans.
> Ah! How his shade will tremble
> When he sees his daughter presented to his eyes,
> Forced to admit so many sins
> And crimes perhaps unknown in hell!

What, my father, will you say about this horrible sight?
I see your hand fall from the terrible urn,
I see you looking for a new torture,
You will yourself become the executioner of your own blood.
Forgive me. A cruel god has condemned your family.
See her vengeance in the fury of your daughter.
Alas! Of the frightful crime whose shame pursues me
My sad heart never received the fruit.
Pursued by misfortunes till my last breath
I end in the torment of a pain-filled life. (1270–94)

Oenone tells her mistress that she is simply caught up in love and the magic of fate, which she cannot resist, but Phaedra curses her for her meddling and plotting, which both made her see Hippolytus in the first place and then caused his death by her lie.

Act Five

In Scene 1, Aricia upbraids Hippolytus for not rebutting Phaedra's slander. Hippolytus replies that he refuses to cause his father shame, and that both he and Aricia should remain silent. Phaedra will eventually meet her fate. They should now flee together to get help against Phaedra from Argos and Sparta. Aricia says that they must be married first. Hippolytus wants to respect her honor, and proposes they go to an ancient shrine near his ancestors' burial place to celebrate their marriage. Theseus enters (Scene 2), and while Hippolytus goes, Aricia stays to mask his departure. In Scene 3, Aricia defends Hippolytus and his love for her before Theseus, but, in accordance with Hippolytus's wish, stops short of revealing the whole truth. Her demeanor, though, worries Theseus (Scene 4), who decides to recall Oenone for questioning. He is told (Scene 5) that Oenone has drowned herself; the Queen, meanwhile, is beginning to go mad, apparently seeking death. Theseus orders the recall of Hippolytus, and prays to Neptune to disregard his earlier prayer.

But it is all too late. In Scene 6, Theramenes tells Theseus that Hippolytus is already dead. As he drove his chariot out of Troezen along the coast, a great monster rose up from the sea. Hippolytus killed the monster, but a god maddened his horses. His chariot shattered and, entangled in the reins, he was dragged along in agony to the tombs where he was to meet Aricia. As he died in the arms of Theramenes, he asked that Aricia be shown gentleness by Theseus, should he ever know the truth. In the final scene, Theseus, by now despairing, is still disposed to think Hippolytus guilty of loving Phaedra. But at the very last, Phaedra herself admits that it was all a lie, that it was she who lusted after Hippolytus and Oenone who had engineered the plot. She herself is on the point of death, having taken poison. As she dies, Theseus prepares to give Hippolytus honorable burial and to receive Aricia as a daughter.

Conclusion

The most striking aspect of *Phaedra* is the tautness of its construction, and the unrelenting drive towards the dénouement. There is but one logic, one tempo, one tone, and one movement in the whole play. All this makes for an atmosphere which is utterly closed and claustrophobic, and entirely suited to the wider theme.

On the wider theme, it is notable that in her first big speech, in Act One, Phaedra recounts how she had tried to avoid the will of Venus by prayer and sacrifice, but to no avail. Good works without grace are ineffective, as the Jansenist doctrine would have it. She is trapped by Venus, as in their own ways are Hippolytus and Aricia, Hippolytus having also offended Venus earlier by his refusal of love. Phaedra is also a brilliant illustration of the Pascalian "thinking reed." She can think and she can agonize; she does think and she does agonize, but the only fruit is to increase her agony and impotence. She has the sort of conscience which the strict religious practice of the Jansenists would advocate, sensitive to the point of scrupulosity, but that in itself is not enough.

But perhaps the most puzzling thing about Phaedra's guilt and despair is that until she denounces Hippolytus to Theseus, she has not actually done anything wrong. She is anything but promiscuous or insensitive. Certainly she is not pleasure-loving or pleasure-seeking. What Phaedra does is mostly to attempt to avoid doing wrong; but, as with Oedipus, the determination of the gods is not to be set aside by human efforts. Our efforts to elude and outwit our destiny are unavailing; they conspire only to make that destiny the more inevitable.

Of course, dramatically speaking, we see here something of Racine's genius. Phaedra's attempts to escape her destiny might have succeeded had it not been for Theseus's impetuosity and anger, the rumor of his death and his return at the precise time that it happens, the revelation by Theseus to Phaedra of Hippolytus's love for Aricia, Hippolytus's proud virtue, Aricia's sense of honor and Oenone's low scheming—all these contingencies, as it were, coming together and intermeshing exactly as and when they do. Objectively speaking, the plot of *Phaedra* depends on a number of more or less improbable coincidences, but this is not how Racine makes us feel about the action, which seems rather to be driven by an inner logic and necessity.

The subject matter of *Phaedra* is not, of course, Christian. The gods are pagan. But if the pursuit of Phaedra by Venus can be seen as representing a kind of Augustinian situation of guilty sensuality without grace, the vision Phaedra has of being judged by Minos and her other ancestors in her great speech in Act Four is very similar to the promise or threat in the *Dies Irae* in the Christian liturgy that "everything hidden shall be made clear." There is no hiding place anywhere in the universe, and even one's most secret thoughts will be ruthlessly exposed and examined. It is this which obsesses Phaedra, and why not even death will be a relief from guilt and despair. And, as far as her actions are concerned, even though she is free at one level, in line with the Jansenist teaching, all her free actions conspire simply to lock her ever more tightly and inextricably into her predetermined fate.

We can, of course, read or see *Phaedra* without knowing about its Jansenist subtext, and still see it as a compelling drama. We can see it simply as the terrifying working out of a hopeless and doomed passion, making points of contact with familiar secular experience. To the extent that it remains true at that level, it shows that from a phenomenological point of view—from the point of view of experience, that is—the doctrines of the Jansenists and Pascal are not without grounding in our lives, however much we might dislike seeing ourselves as psychologically constrained and determined by forces we are unable to control or avoid.

Goethe
Faust

Johann Wolfgang von Goethe (1742–1832) was, for most of his life, the dominant figure in German literature, and for most of his life he worked on elements of his Faust. *Even aside from Goethe's own notorious inability to construct coherent works, then, we should not expect his* Faust *to be a unified or even performance. It is in all respects the absolute antithesis of Racine, and unlike Racine and most of our authors since Augustine, there is in Goethe little real sense of sin. What we do find in the sprawling canvas which is Goethe's* Faust *is Goethe's own sense of life as an organic, ever-changing, ever-creative, divinely-inspired process.*

Faust, Part One *contains the old Faust legend with which most of us are familiar: the desiccated and disillusioned medieval scholar who sells his soul to the devil (Mephistopheles) to acquire the experience he has been missing in his study. To this Goethe adds the poignant tale of Margareta (or Gretchen), the innocent girl whom Faust seduces, and who then is responsible for the deaths of both her mother and her baby. Imprisoned and awaiting execution, she is, however, redeemed from above, as Faust and Mephistopheles vanish from the scene, but she returns at the very end of the second part of the work to plead for Faust's own redemption when Mephistopheles attempts to take Faust's soul down to hell. Despite the Christian context of this last scene, Faust's redemption is hardly Christian in any orthodox sense. It is because Faust has striven that he is saved, not because he has repented. And indeed the Faust of* Part Two *is a striver, moving throughout the classical and medieval worlds, trying ever more audacious schemes, including counseling medieval emperors and helping them in their wars, reclaiming vast tracts of land from the sea and setting up utopian states for free people. But above all in* Part Two *there is the search for the eternal feminine, the source for Goethe of all life and creativity, as represented especially by Helen of Troy. And Faust finds her, not in Troy, but in Mistra, the medieval Sparta, where Faust himself appears as a Frankish knight. In a stunningly audacious fusion of the medieval and the classical, Goethe has taken us back to where we began, to the person of Helen herself, the cause of the Trojan War to be sure, but also the incarnation of the life force itself.*

Johann Wolfgang von Goethe was born in 1742 in Frankfurt. He studied law in Leipzig, but by the early 1770s he was the dominant figure in the German literary revival. *The Sufferings of the Young Werther* (1774) made him internationally famous as an early protagonist of the Romantic movement, with its study of a young man hopelessly and fatally in love. From that time on, he was a central literary and scientific figure, both in Germany and in Europe more generally, until his death in 1832. In 1775 he was called to the court at Weimar by the Duke (who ennobled him in 1782). He travelled to Italy in 1776–78, and the earlier Romanticism of Werther gave way to a classical phase, in which he worked closely with the poet and dramatist Friedrich Schiller, who died in 1805. Goethe wrote in all literary genres and styles, and assimilated influences and ideas from all over the world, including notably Persia and China. He also had profound, but unfashionable, scientific interests; anti-Newtonian, anti-mechanistic, organic, holistic, he was a leading figure in the reaction to the rationalism and reductivism of modern science.

Along with Goethe's varied and tumultuous gifts and personality unfortunately goes an almost complete inability to structure or contain or control anything. *Faust* itself has been described as "a hideous farrago, a staggering literary lumber room, in which no one has failed to stumble." That said, *Part One,* especially in the second half, does have speed and dramatic bite. And *Part Two* contains some of the most powerful visionary poetry ever written, as well as in perhaps more than one sense an incredible attempt to synthesize pagan, Christian, and Romantic thought, which is why we think it worth dwelling on here. In his work, every facet of his extraordinary personality continually burst forth, in what he called "organic form"; that is, in no form at all, if by form we mean the formal perfection and tautness of Racine. *Faust, Part Two,* especially, can be seen as expressing Goethe's own unbroken testimony to life itself—as one great, continuous, unending, ever-multiplying, ever-fructifying process, inherently unconfined, and inherently ungraspable, albeit at some deep level inherently unified, a great whole which is nature itself, a nature infused with divinity, to which our own consciousness is intimately attuned.

Faust, Part One

This contains most of what most people know of *Faust,* as prefigured in Marlowe's *Doctor Faustus* and in popular plays and legends, and, after Goethe, as taken up by the composers Schubert, Berlioz, Liszt, and Gounod, whose works were mainly based on the *Urfaust* material. Mahler, though, set the closing scene of *Faust, Part Two,* to which Liszt had also alluded in his *Faust Symphony,* as did Schumann in his fascinating but little-known *Scenes from Goethe's Faust,* in which he sets significant sections of both parts.

Mention of *Urfaust* takes us to a big problem. *Faust, Part One* has three distinct phases of development, and is not a wholly unified work:

> From 1772–75, possibly influenced by his affair with Fredericke Brion and certainly by the execution of Susanna Brandt in 1772 (for the murder of her child), and also by the *Sturm und Drang* (storm and stress) Romanticism which we find in *Werther,* Goethe worked on a (then) unpublished manuscript, known now as "*Urfaust*" (original *Faust*).

> From 1788–90, he added to *Urfaust,* and published the still incomplete result as *Faust, A Fragment* in 1790.

> Then intermittently, from 1797–1806 but mainly from 1797–1801, with Schiller's encouragement, Goethe worked on the text which we now have and which was eventually published as *Faust, Part One* in 1808.

Faust, Part One, then, is not a unity. It contains conflicting moods and themes, and even contradictions, especially regarding Faust's pact with the devil, which, until 1808 when *Faust, Part One* was published, had formed what subsequent scholars have referred to as the "great lacuna" in the *Fragment* (now lines 606–1769). These thousand or more lines do indeed fill a lacuna (or gap), as they contain, crucially, Faust's first long encounter with Mephistopheles, including his pact with the devil.

Urfaust, though, does contain much of the most characteristic and famous material, as already mentioned. This includes Faust's opening soliloquy and his conjuration of the Earth Spirit (354–517), the Faust-Wagner scene (518–605), Mephistopheles' taunting of the student and the long attack on academic study (1868–2050), the Auerbach tavern scene (2073–2336), and most of the Margareta/Gretchen scenes (2605–4614), excluding the Walpurgis material (which is from 1808). Thus Faust's gloom and the poignancy of the Gretchen story are at the heart of the piece, genetically and dramatically. Mephistopheles, added to in the *Fragment* stage, is fully realized only in the full version of 1808, though.

Throughout both parts of the work, Faust himself is a quester, a seeker, and a doer. In many ways the portrayal of Faust is Goethe's critique of philosophy and the contemplative life (though, as we will see, the most famous piece of anti-philosophy is uttered not by Faust himself, but by Mephistopheles, who has already revealed himself at that point as the spirit of eternal negation, which may imply a degree of distance on Goethe's part from the message). Although the Faust of *Part Two* is a somewhat different character from that of *Part One*, there is some continuity. In both parts, Faust the perpetual quester is on a journey. Like Odysseus, his condition is one of impermanence—indeed, necessarily so in Faust's case because, as we will discover, the point at which he rests content with where he is and what he has got, is the point at which he is doomed. If readers of *The Odyssey* have had problems with Odysseus's retirement in Ithaca, these are as nothing compared to the problems raised by the end of *Faust, Part Two,* which may look like a denial of everything that Faust—and Goethe—has stood for (and which, surely not coincidentally, was the source of some of Mahler's most bombastic and rhetorical music, in his Eighth Symphony—as if by sheer volume, in all senses, doubts could be quelled).

If there are parallels between Faust and Odysseus, there are also parallels between the pair of Faust and Mephistopheles and the pair of Dante and Virgil. In both cases, one member of the pair is guiding the other on a journey of exploration and self-exploration. In both cases the pair watch, and intervene to a greater or lesser extent, and move on. Dramatically and poetically, the pair function as a device to connect the audience with a plenitude of otherwise disconnected characters and events. But there are, of course, huge differences between the *Divine Comedy* and Goethe's *Faust,* of which the greatest is the attitude to Christianity, which brings us on to what may be the most formidable difficulty raised by *Faust.* In his *Faust,* Goethe not only uses a medieval legend with a Christian thematic structure (a man selling his soul to the devil), and, in developing the Gretchen story, goes on to add further Christian embellishments. He also—scandalously in the eyes of many—ultimately accords his hero what looks like a Christian redemption; this is scandalous because, in contrast to some of those redeemed in Dante, nothing in Goethe's hero's life or former attitudes has prepared him for any such thing. The scandal is as much dramatic and poetic as theological.

In Marlowe's *Doctor Faustus,* it will be recalled, Helen of Troy is magi-
cally summoned up. No doubt following this hint, in his treatment of Faust,
principally in *Part Two,* Goethe attempts his synthesis of the medieval and
the classical. In advance of Goethe's actual achievement, some might find
the attempt bordering on the absurd. No matter: flawed as the final result
remains, all of Goethe's considerable learning and powers of unification were
brought to bear to fuse the Faust story with the story of Helen of Troy (or
Sparta). Apart from anything else, Goethe brilliantly exploits the proximity
of classical Sparta to the great medieval city of Mistra to get Helen (literally) into bed with Faust, who has now been transmogrified into one of the
medieval northern knights who colonized the south of Greece en route to
the Fourth Crusade. As far as we in this book are concerned, Goethe has
returned us to our point of origin. But whether this imaginative sleight of
hand has really effected a thematic synthesis of Christian and classical is
altogether more problematic. At the very least, in Goethe we are clearly in
a wholly different atmosphere from that of Augustine or Milton or Pascal.
There is no sense of original sin in *Faust,* and, Faust's treatment of Gretchen
notwithstanding, not much of a sense of sin either. Nor is the somewhat
comic "Lord" in banter with Mephistopheles in Goethe's Prologue to *Faust*
much like Milton's God.

Scenes 1–3 of *Part One* are a Dedication, Prelude, and Prologue, all from
the 1808 version. (For ease of reference, we follow here the numbering of
scenes in David Luke's translation of *Faust* (Oxford University Press, 1987
and 1994).) In the Prologue, the Lord is more like an aristocratic ruler of
Goethe's own time than anything out of the Old Testament or Milton. In
a kind of parody of the Book of Job, the Lord challenges the devil Mephistopheles, whom he has summoned to court to report on mankind's fate, to
tempt Faust for a wager between the two spirits. Even at this point, the Lord
predicts Mephistopheles' ultimate failure, but the two part on comparatively
amicable terms. Significantly, though, for what eventually emerges, one of
the challenges the Lord throws down is for Mephistopheles to draw Faust
away from his "primal source"—which turns out to be the Earth Spirit, the
Spirit of Nature, a being closer to Goethe (and to Faust) than either "the
Lord" or Mephistopheles.

In Scene 4 the mood is quite different. It is night, and Faust, as the traditional scholar, is alone in his room, poring over his books. But he is in despair. All his learning and all his academic honors avail—and are—nothing
compared to Nature's power. But on seeing a mystic sign in one of his books,
he has an ecstatic vision of the inner workings of Nature, and of its endless
creativity, inspired by spirits forever moving through it, up, and down. Using a spell, he conjures up the mysterious and terrifying Spirit of the Earth,

who appears to him shrouded in flame. The Spirit sings of its ever-flowing, ever-changing essence, like an eternal sea, forever creating the living garment of the Godhead. But the Spirit is contemptuous towards Faust, telling him that Faust must find one whom he can understand, one closer to his own nature. As the Spirit leaves, Wagner, Faust's famulus or academic servant, enters. Faust tries, without success, to dissuade the pedantic Wagner from the scholar's life. Alone again, Faust despairs at his inability to hold the Earth Spirit. He is like a worm, stuck in the dust of his books. He contemplates suicide, but as he is about to drink the poison, he hears a chorus of angels singing of Easter. Faust is not a believer, but the song reminds him of his happier, younger days, when he still was pious. His tears flow. Earth holds him once more.

Scene 5 ("Outside the Town Wall") is a characteristic scene (from 1808) of the townspeople jollifying, carousing, and wenching in the country on Easter Day. Faust and Wagner observe proceedings, the one envious of the simple joy of the people and their freedom away from the town, the other dismissive. An old peasant remembers Faust's father's medical skill, but Faust is skeptical of the medical skill actually possessed by himself and his father—and of everything else as well. There are two souls in Faust, one earthly, clinging to its pleasures, the other wanting to soar above. Faust and Wagner are joined by a (diabolic) dog, a poodle.

In Scene 6 (from 1808), back alone in his study, Faust turns to the Greek gospel, to John 1:1: "In the beginning was the Word." But for Faust, in the beginning was the Deed; activity is the key to all. The poodle, meanwhile, continues to grow. With spirits outside the room singing of Faust's entrapment, Faust recites spells, designed to reveal the dog's true nature. Mephistopheles appears, as a wandering student; like Iago, like Milton's Satan, "I am the spirit who continually negates" (1338), and evil is his element. But something—this coarse world, indestructible, continually renewing itself—stands in his way. Faust raises the possibility of a pact between himself and the devils. Spirits enchant Faust, who falls asleep; but when he wakes, he wonders if it was all a dream. (Unless otherwise indicated, translation from *Faust* are by the author.)

In Scene 7 (still 1808 up to line 1769, *Fragment* 1770–1867, thereafter *Urfaust*), Mephistopheles reappears. Faust repeats his disillusion and curses everything, including all the usual pleasures and honors of life, and finally, hope, faith and, above all, patience. The spirits sing that he has destroyed "the beautiful world" (1609); but let Faust build it anew in his heart. Mephistopheles offers to be Faust's servant, against wages to be paid in the next world. Faust rejects the offer, reflecting on the transience of all human goods. He suggests his own wager. He will accept Mephistopheles' help, but if he is ever lulled into self-sufficiency, if he is ever deluded into saying of any moment "Linger on, you are so beautiful" ("Verweile doch, du bist so schön!"), then Mephistopheles can have him (1700). The point, of course, is that nothing is ever perfect or immutable, however wonderful, and only activity and change are worthwhile; it is the positive face of Faust's discontent with everything he has. The pact is sealed in Faust's blood. Now that the Earth Spirit has spurned him, and thought now disintegrates before him, he will give himself over to passion, sweetness, and sensuality; joy *and* suffering, the heights *and* the depths, will be tasted to the full in an onward rush of ever-changing experience. Faust leaves and Mephistopheles puts on his gown, singing of Faust's doom: to be dragged through every meaningless experience until he despairs of all—even without the pact, he would be lost. A student enters, and Mephistopheles, as Faust, in Goethean terms rubbishes logic, science, metaphysics, law, and medicine; learn instead to seize the girls! "Grey, dear friend, is all theory / And green the golden tree of life." In a nice touch, Mephistopheles signs the student's book with the words (in Latin): "You will be as God, knowing good and evil." Faust returns, and Mephistopheles plans his new way of living.

In Scene 8, the first port of call in Faust's new life is Auerbach's tavern in Leipzig, full of drunkenness and bawdy. Brander, one of the revelers, sings a vulgar song about a rat, which Mephistopheles caps with one about a flea. Mephistopheles conjures up quantities of wine. Amid more magic, a fight ensues. Faust and Mephistopheles vanish.

In Scene 9, Faust and Mephistopheles find themselves in a witch's kitchen amid a family of baboons. There is much medieval necromantic slapstick, in the midst of which Faust has a vision in a mirror of perfect female beauty. There is more knockabout, insults, and violence, in which Faust's vision of beauty turns to one of horror. Mephistopheles frightens the witch into giving him obeisance. Finally Faust is presented with a diabolic potion, which will make *any* woman seem like Helen to him.

The remainder of *Faust, Part One* is almost all devoted to the Margareta/Gretchen story, a story which was not in any of the old legends. It is tremendously fast and dramatic, and is virtually self-contained. During these scenes, Goethe refers to the girl throughout as either Margareta or Gretchen (the diminutive of Margareta), without much rhyme or reason.

In Scene 10, Faust tries to pick up the beautiful young Margareta in a street. She is virtuous, but is spirited, even cheeky. She brushes Faust off, but Faust is captivated. Mephistopheles explains she has just been to confession. They decide to use guile to effect the seduction.

In Scene 11, it is the evening and Margareta is in her room doing her hair. Faust and Mephistopheles enter secretly and Faust is profoundly moved by the beauty and innocence of it all. Mephistopheles, ever the cynic, hides a case of jewels in the cupboard. The intruders leave, and Margareta prepares for bed, singing a beautiful song about the ancient King of Thule, who was faithful to his dead wife until his own death. As she puts her clothes away she finds the jewels.

In Scene 12, Faust and Mephistopheles discover that Margareta's mother and the priest have taken the jewels, so Mephistopheles places another box in Margareta's room. In the next scene, Margareta is with her friend Martha, discussing the jewels. Mephistopheles enters and tries to seduce Martha by telling her that her husband has died as the result of syphilis contracted in Naples. She is interested, but wants more proof. Mephistopheles arranges for himself and Martha, and Faust and Margareta, to meet in the evening.

In Scene 14, Faust appears, still stricken with love for Margareta, with Mephistopheles yet more cynical. When the four protagonists meet in a garden (Scene 15), Mephistopheles and Martha pair off. Faust intrigues Margareta, but she is worried about not being intellectual. Faust replies that he values innocence and humility, Nature's highest gift. Margareta tells of her mother, brother, and dead sister. Is she to blame for responding to Faust? She picks a flower—"He loves me!" Faust and Margareta clasp hands, Martha and Mephistopheles looking on, and Margareta runs away from Faust. Faust chases her into a garden house (Scene 16). They embrace, and Margareta professes her love for Faust. Mephistopheles pulls Faust away, leaving Margareta to muse: "I'm only a poor ignorant child. I can't understand what he sees in me." (3215–16)

In Scene 17 (inserted at the *Fragment* stage), Faust is in a cave in the forest. In a monologue of high intensity, wonderfully realized in music by Berlioz, Faust invokes the Earth Spirit:

> Oh sublime Spirit! You have given me
> Given me all I asked for. From the fire
> You turned your face to me, and not in vain.
> You have given me Nature's splendour for my kingdom,
> And strength to grasp it with my heart. No mere
> Cold curious inspection was the privilege
> You granted me, but to gaze deep, as into
> The heart of a dear friend. Before my eyes,
> Opened by you, all living creatures move
> In sequence: in the quiet woods, the air,
> The water, now I recognise my brothers.
> And when the storm-struck forest roars and jars,
> When giant pines crash down, whose crushing fall

Tears neighbouring branches, neighbouring tree trunks with them,
And drones like hollow thunder through the hills:
Then, in this cavern's refuge, where you lead me,
You show me to myself, and my own heart's
Profound mysterious wonders are disclosed.
And when the pure moon lifts its soothing light
As I look skywards, then from rocky cliffs
And dewy thickets the ensilvered shapes
Of a lost world, hovering there before me,
Assuage the austere joy of my contemplation. (3217–39)
(Translation by David Luke (Oxford University Press, 1987).)

But for men, no joy is complete. The Spirit, for all his sublimity, and for all Faust's self-identification with nature, has, as we saw in Scene 4, added to all this a mocking companion, who has also fired his breast with passion for a beautiful woman's image (presumably the diabolic vision that Faust had in the witch's kitchen, rather than the flesh-and-blood Gretchen).

Into these pre-Coleridgean Coleridgean reflections, Mephistopheles enters. He mocks Faust's high feelings, which he says culminate simply in—sex. He should desist and reward Margareta for her love; she is desolate without him. But Faust, in a passage from *Urfaust,* portrays himself as a restless Byronic force, overwhelming her innocence and her sweet little world.

In Scene 18, we see the desolate and lonely Gretchen at her spinning wheel, lamenting the absence of Faust, in a song immortalized in 1814 in its setting by the seventeen-year-old Franz Schubert—a moment often somewhat romantically taken to mark the birth of the German song or lied ("Gretchen am Spinnrade," D.118):

My peace has gone,
My heart is heavy,
I find it never
And nevermore . . . (3374–78)

Scene 19 finds Faust and Margareta in the garden. They discuss religion: Faust's faith—and Goethe's. Does Faust believe in God? Who dares to name him? He believes in the eternal mystery filling his heart, call it happiness, heart, love, God—he has no name for it: "Feeling [of what?] is all there is" (3431–57). But this is not Christian, Margareta observes, and she worries about Mephistopheles too, who makes her blood freeze. In Faust's arms, though, she feels so good, and so warm, and so free. Faust gives her a potion to make her mother sleep through their future rendezvous. Mephistopheles appears, mocking Faust's infatuation.

In Scene 20, Gretchen and her friend Lieschen are at the well, discussing one Barbara, who has fallen. Gretchen muses on her own position: "but all that made me do it / God! It was so good! It was such love!" (3585–86). Gretchen's guilt begins to gnaw at her in Scene 21. She prays before the statue of the Mater Dolorosa: "Save me from shame and death" (3616).

In Scene 22, we see Valentine, Margareta's soldier brother, lurking outside the family house at night. He used to boast of Margareta's virtue, but now? He sees Faust and Mephistopheles coming to Margareta's door. Mephistopheles sings a ribald song about a girl losing her virginity: "She goes in a maiden, but no maiden returns." Faust fights and wounds Valentine. As Faust and Mephistopheles run off, Margareta comes out. Valentine curses her (she is a whore now), and then he dies.

The next scene (23) is in a cathedral, where there is a Requiem Mass for Margareta's mother, who has died from the sleeping potion that Faust provided. To the strains of the *Dies Irae,* Margareta is tormented by an Evil Spirit for her mother's death, for Valentine's, and also for her pregnancy. Overwhelmed by guilt and by the Evil Spirit, she faints.

In Scene 24, Faust and Mephistopheles go up into the Harz Mountains to celebrate a witches' Sabbath on Walpurgis Night. There is some fine nature poetry, some grotesque witches, some dancing and ribaldry, and also caricatures of various types, including an Enlightenment rationalist who is skeptical of the whole thing. No orgy actually takes place, despite some earlier hints to that effect, but Faust sees an apparition of Margareta, her neck encircled with scarlet thread, with which he is entranced. This scene is followed by the "Walpurgis Night Dream," a somewhat incongruous collection of irrelevant epigrams and poetical score-settling.

In Scene 26, we are on a heath in gloomy weather. Faust is in despair over Margareta's fate. He berates Mephistopheles, and insists on being taken to her. Through the night (Scene 27), Faust and Mephistopheles ride on black horses, past groups of witches performing rituals over the graves of executed criminals.

Scene 28 is set in a prison. Faust enters and finds Margareta distraught and half-mad. She sings, Ophelia-like. When she sees Faust, she first thinks he is the hangman. She wants to feed their (dead) baby, which she has killed. She then recognizes Faust and embraces him. Becoming lucid about her crime, she only wants to die and to be buried with her mother, brother, and baby. There is no hope for her, and she refuses to escape with Faust. As day dawns and the crowds gather around the prison, she says that what should have been her wedding day is the day of her execution. When Mephistopheles enters, Margareta is repelled. She asks for divine forgiveness. Mephistopheles says "She is condemned," but a Voice from above says "She is redeemed." As

Faust and Mephistopheles vanish, Margareta is heard from within her cell calling on Faust. In this scene, Gretchen achieves a moral stature and superiority achieved by no other character in either part of Goethe's *Faust,* but as we will see, this sense is not carried through by Goethe into the second part.

Faust, Part Two

Faust, Part Two was mostly written between 1825 and 1831, and published only in 1832, after Goethe's death.

Despite the fact that the numbering of the lines follows on from *Part One, Part Two* is not in any clear sense a continuation of *Part One,* as published in 1808. Indeed, it is often inconsistent with it, in mood, in theme, and in detail, although the Faust and Mephistopheles of *Part Two* do have some links with the figures who disappeared at the end of *Part One.* The quest for Helen of Troy, as in the old Faust legend, dominates much of *Part Two,* though Gretchen, as she is in *Part Two,* makes a crucial appearance right at the end, albeit as a somewhat angelic and fleshless "Penitent."

Thematically, there are links with the "Im Anfang war die Tat" (in the beginning was the Deed) passage of *Part One* (1239), and, of course, with Goethe's own lifelong belief in the potency of action, energy, creativity, and activity. The Faust of *Part Two* is above all active. Our essence is activity, and this continues even after death (and, in the case of the Homunculus, begins before birth). It is because of Faust's continual striving that he is ultimately saved (11936–37), despite his betrayal of Gretchen (who nevertheless intercedes for him, as "he whom I loved" (12073)). No doubt Goethe intended us, even in 1808, to take seriously the original wager (1699–1700), in which resting content with "the beautiful moment" is tantamount to perdition. Faust is tempted to precisely this reaction, and seems to envisage succumbing to it as he dies (11582), and in precisely the same terms as the contract was originally framed in line 1699 of *Part One.* And Mephistopheles claims victory in the same terms, insisting that there is now no avoiding the letter of the "blood-signed document" of *Part One,* line 1737 (11613). All this is in line with Goethe's pantheistic sense of eternal process and transformation and creation, a process which works within us and in all of Nature, and which we ourselves articulate and develop.

Faust, Part Two is about as un-Jansenist as one could imagine, in its lack of recognition of anything like original sin; in crucial respects, it is unChristian more generally as well. It is highly reminiscent of the serious aspects of Ovid and other classical authors, though filtered through Goethe's own vivid and, crucially, antimechanistic and nonmoralistic sense of the vibrancy both of Nature and of human action. In keeping with the character of its author, it is, on the face of it, an attempt to reconcile pagan and Christian themes, and also to integrate extreme sensitivity to Nature and its organic wholeness with human efforts to exploit Nature's power and fertility.

Despite (a few) attempts to put it on, and in contrast to *Part One, Faust, Part Two* is essentially unperformable; as it stands it is completely unintegrated, a kaleidoscopic medley of mood, of incident, of writing, and of theme.

Act One
(The enrichment of the Emperor; Helen's first appearance)

In Scene 1, the Prologue, Faust is asleep in a beautiful landscape. Shakespeare's Ariel brings him forgetfulness of the horrors he has experienced and perpetrated in *Part One*—principally, one assumes, the imprisonment, madness and execution of the pathetic Gretchen. Faust wakes and hymns the dawn and the revivifying power of Nature. But (with echoes of Platonism) the sun rising over the mountains is too powerful for us, and only its reflection in the waterfall cascading down the cliffs is fully available to us. (All this, by the way, is set to haunting and poetic music by Schumann—to such effect that, like Faust himself, we almost forget what he is waking up from. Gretchen has, to all intents and purposes, disappeared from view.)

In Scene 2, we are in the imperial palace at some indeterminate point in the medieval period. There is general disorder, along with efforts of the new wealth to displace the old. There is financial shortage and potential bankruptcy. Mephistopheles recommends to the Emperor extracting gold from the earth, which he says is buried everywhere and needs only to be discovered and released.

Scene 3 depicts a saucy masque at carnival time, with all kinds of characters, mythological and symbolic, and threats or promises of magic. Eventually a boy charioteer (Euphorion) appears, claiming to be both Plenty and Poetry. He leads on Plutus/Faust with a treasure chest, which becomes both a vat of gold and a fountain of fire, and the Miser/Mephistopheles, who can put gold only to vulgar use. The Emperor, disguised as Pan, seeking enlightenment, tries to grasp Faust's treasure, and gets burned. The fire threatens to engulf everything, but Plutus extinguishes it.

Scene 4 takes place in a pleasure garden, after the masque. Faust apologizes for the fire and Mephistopheles promises better times. The means and the gold promised in Scene 2 turn out to be paper money. (Vulgar) prosperity returns, along with bankers, usury, and moneychangers.

In Scene 5, the Emperor and the court have asked Faust to produce the ideal man and woman, Paris and Helen. Mephistopheles says that Faust himself will have to descend to the Earth Mothers of antiquity—the source of all living forms—because the classical is not his sphere. Initially terrified, Faust is encouraged by the thought that sensing awe and dread will move him in the depth of his being. He descends below the earth.

Scene 6 presents Mephistopheles helping some lovers or would-be lovers to achieve their goals—to his own chagrin.

In Scene 7, we are in the Emperor's great hall. Before the Emperor and the court, Faust, calling on the Mothers, conjures up first a somewhat effeminate Paris and then Helen, from the old Faust legend. Faust is overwhelmed by the Helen apparition. She kisses the beautiful Paris, who embraces her and seeks to carry her off. Faust intervenes, trying to seize the Helen apparition himself. There is an explosion and the spirits vanish. So ends the first quest for Helen.

Act Two
(Faust's second quest for Helen; the Homunculus)

In Scene 8, we return to Faust's old study, with Faust lying on his bed, unconscious after his first encounter with "Helen." Mephistopheles engages in more banter about the academic life and the desiccating effect of scholarship, first with Faust's current servant, and then with the student from Part One, who is now a graduate. He spouts the absurdities of idealistic philosophy, claiming that he himself has created the world, the sun, the moon, and all the beauties of the earth.

Scene 9. In a medieval laboratory we find Wagner, the servant from *Part One*, who is now himself a kind of alchemist-savant. By alchemical means, he has—though with unsuspected help from Mephistopheles—created a Homunculus. This is a kind of fetal brain or intelligence, floating in a retort; procreation, according to Wagner, now being out of fashion. The Homunculus wants to go to classical Greece. He sees the beautiful Leda, and the Swan, who is Zeus in disguise, flying down to nestle between her legs. (The result of this union is Helen herself and one of her brothers.) Compared to the dismal northern world of mists, monks, and knights, the groves and streams of ancient Greece are where there is true freedom and true beauty. The Homunculus persuades Mephistopheles to take him and the still unconscious Faust there, to effect Faust's recovery, leaving Wagner to his scholastic scholarship.

Scene 10 is entitled "Classical Walpurgis Night." It is a long and complicated scene in which the Homunculus pursues bodily existence (while also assuming a kind of tutelary role over the whole scene), Mephistopheles pursues various witches and monsters (who regularly insult him as a barbaric northerner), and Faust himself pursues psychic healing and Helen. It is all in the ambience of classical mythology (in which Goethe himself had found healing in his Italian journey of 1786–88).

The first half of the scene describes the journey undertaken by Faust himself. The setting for this journey is an ancient rite of passage or mystery cult celebrated every year in Pharsalia on the anniversary of Caesar's defeat of Pompey in Greece, a victory which led indirectly to the establishment of the Roman Empire. In the rite, the initiate, like Faust himself, descends into the underworld before rising reborn and reinvigorated. Faust travels from the medieval world and that of imperial Rome back into the Greece of Helen of Sparta and into the ancient underworld, to find both Helen and himself.

On being deposited by Mephistopheles and the Homunculus on the Pharsalian plain, Faust wakes:

> Where is she! But why ask! I should have known
> The soil her feet have trod, the sea
> That lapped against them; even enough for me
> This very air whose language was her own!
> Here by a miracle, here I am in Greece!
> At once I sensed the ground; what could release
> Me from my sleep but this fresh spirit's glow!
> And thus I stand: Antaeus was strengthened so,
> What wonders here in one place concentrate!
> This fiery labyrinth I will investigate. (7070–79)
> (Translation by David Luke (Oxford University Press, 1994).)

On his journey through the labyrinth into the underworld, Faust is passed on from one helper or guide to another: first the Sphinxes, then the Sirens, then the river god Peneus (surrounded by nymphs and swans, one of whom flies off on his secret mission), then the centaur Chiron on whom Faust rides across the Peneus (and who, to Faust's delight, tells of how the ten-year-old Helen also rode on his back when Chiron rescued her from abduction by bandits), and, finally, the sybil Manto who, as Virgil did for Dante, guides Faust into Hades or the underworld. For some inexplicable reason we never see Faust in the underworld, negotiating with Persephone, the Queen of Hades, for the release of Helen (as Goethe had originally planned), or indeed Faust arising from Hades with Helen. In Act Three, Helen is simply there, in Menelaus's palace in Sparta, without any further explanation.

With Faust gone into the underworld on his quest for Helen and sexual beauty, the focus for the rest of the scene then turns to the nature of creation itself and the Homunculus' quest for embodiment. First we see Seismos, the earthquake god, with his vision of violent Vulcanian activity throwing up mountains, together with the mining, metal-working, and forging of arms which this makes possible. After Mephistopheles has been taunted by the Lamiae, vampire-like creatures who assume attractive female form to snare their victims, the Homunculus expresses his desire to be born properly. This introduces a discussion on creation between Anaxagoras and Thales, two pre-Socratic philosophers, Anaxagoras seeing violent volcanic activity as the source of creation, while for Thales, the spokesman for the Neptunist point of view, everything is fundamentally water, and everything in the world that we experience arises from the gentle, patient work of water. After this discussion, Mephistopheles, finding a home at last in the classical world, teams up with the Phorcyads, who are three ancient, evil, ugly witches, daughters of Chaos (with one eye and one tooth between them).

The final section of the scene is presided over by Thales and the gods and spirits of water, as the Homunculus pursues his quest for human form. The ever-changing Proteus advises against any such thing: the flexibility of water-life is superior to the terrestrial, which is so easily broken. Nevertheless, assuming the shape of a dolphin, he allows the Homunculus to ride on his back. They see Nereus, the ancient god of the sea, and the beautiful Galatea, his daughter, riding on a chariot made of shells. Overcome by the beauty of it all, and moved by Eros, "that which begat everything" (8479), the Homunculus shatters the glass of his retort and disappears as flashes of light on the waves. He is about to begin what Thales had earlier described: the long, slow process of evolution, through thousand upon thousand forms, to reach at last the human state, all kept alive and sustained by the fructifying power of water.

Act Three
(Helen at Sparta and Mistra, and in Arcadia)

In Scene 11, Goethe attempts to recreate the mood and language of an Aeschylean tragedy, suffused with a sense of doom, foreboding, ancient guilt, and the implacable determination of the gods. Helen, with a chorus of captive Trojan women, is before the palace of Menelaus, awaiting the arrival of Menelaus—and her fate. Full of foreboding, she enters the palace which once she left with such lightness of spirit. The rooms are still and empty, apart from a veiled woman of monstrous aspect who bars her way to the bridal chamber. It is Phorcyas/Mephistopheles, who recalls her past and then foretells her future. She is to prepare a sacrifice for her husband, a sacrifice in which she herself is to be the victim, with her women hanged from the roof-beams; Menelaus will do the same to Helen as he did to Deiphobus, her last husband, at the fall of Troy, mutilating him horribly—for beauty cannot be shared—but there is a chance of safety if Helen and her women can betake themselves to the towers to the north of Sparta, newly built by invaders from the north. As Menelaus approaches, Helen agrees to follow Phorcyas into the medieval castle, which seems at first no less a prison to her and her women than had the Sparta that they had fled.

Scene 12. In the courtyard of the castle, Faust, as a medieval knight, welcomes Helen, while she reflects on her fate, which is to drive men to madness and war on account of her beauty. Faust has her seated on a throne, and treasure brought before her. He kneels before her and Helen prepares to give herself to him, but as they begin their amorous exchanges, Phorcyas warns of Menelaus's army seeking vengeance. Faust presents his commanders and troops who have already conquered most of Greece, and who will protect them from Menelaus. He then evokes the idealized Arcadia that he is offering Helen, for the two of them to settle in together in peace.

Scene 13 takes place in Goethe's Arcadia, a place reminiscent of a classical landscape of Titian or Poussin: jagged mountain ridges, ancient forests and wooded groves, rocky caverns, meadows, lakes and rivers, goats and sheep and cattle, and music too. Faust and Helen are living there with Euphorion, their youthful son, intended by Goethe as a portrait of Byron (who, of course, died in Greece, in the struggle against the Turks). Euphorion is a poet and a free spirit, scorning danger as he skips and dances with his girls over the mountains and their abysses and ravines. Helen and Faust fail to check him. Icarus-like, he rises in a trail of light—and falls dead, revealed as Byron. In her grief, Helen vanishes back to Hades, committing both herself and Euphorion to the arms of Persephone. Helen's clothes drift upwards into the clouds, Faust with them. The enchantment is ended, but the girls of the chorus do not follow her. They become spirits of Nature and its fruits, including Dionysus and his revels, all of which they hymn in a four-part chorus. Phorcyas stands revealed as Mephistopheles.

Act Four
(The Emperor's War)

In Scene 14, Faust steps out of his cloud and out of the classical world on to a high mountain peak. He is inspired by the mountain solitude and the depths below him. In the cloud he sees the form of a giant, godlike woman, like Juno, Leda, and Helen. As it drifts away towards the icy summits, another cloud shapes itself above him:

> Does joy delude me, or do I see
> That first, that long-lost, dearest treasure of my youth?

They rise to view, those riches of my deepest heart,
That leapt so lightly in the early dawn of love;
That first look, quickly sensed and hardly understood:
No precious jewel could have outshone it, had I held
It fast. Oh lovely growth, oh spiritual form!
Still undissolving, it floats skywards, on and up,
And draws my best and utmost soul to follow it. (10058–66)
(Translation by David Luke (Oxford University Press, 1994).)

Into this reverie on what will later be called the eternal feminine, Mephistopheles breaks with Vulcanian thoughts on the energy underlying the mountains and on how Faust should build himself a grand pleasure city. Faust, ever the Neptunist, thinks of exploiting the "purposeless power and untamed element" of the sea (10229) and of curbing its force. But the Emperor is in trouble, with a priest-inspired insurrection and a rival for his throne. Faust and Mephistopheles will help him, so that Faust will be rewarded with his own lands on which to enact his plans for the sea.

In Scene 15, Faust, down from the mountains, joins the Emperor, who is being mocked by his rival (partly for the pleasure-loving regime that he instituted as a result of the invention of paper money in Act One). In a reference to the old Faust legend, Faust presents himself as an ambassador from a Roman sorcerer whose life the Emperor had once saved. The battle is fought in the mountains, with Mephistopheles summoning up warriors and ancient powers from the mountains. By means of magic, Mephistopheles gets rid of the rival emperor, relishing the mutual destruction, comparing it to the ancient and meaningless quarrels of the Guelphs and Ghibellines.

In Scene 16, restored to power and occupying his rival's tent, the Emperor begins dishing out honors and positions to the four princes who supposedly helped him in the war. He also has to give a huge fortune, including the gift of a priory, to the Lord Chancellor Archbishop, officially as penance for having been helped by Satan. The Archbishop returns twice, asking for more each time, and including the revenue from the land that Faust is to reclaim on the coast. The Emperor reflects that he might just as well have given the whole empire away in one go.

Act Five
(Faust's old age and redemption)

Scene 17 takes place in open country, where Faust, as a vassal of the Emperor, has achieved his project of land reclamation. Zeus appears as a wanderer revisiting the now-aged Baucis and Philemon (from Ovid's *Metamorphoses*,

Book Eight). They explain how Faust has tamed the seas and reclaimed the land, building villages and a port. But he wants their house and their trees too, as well as all he has already got. They toll their chapel bell as the sun goes down.

In Scene 18, Faust, now an old man, is in a palace surrounded by a large ornamental park with a long straight canal. He is infuriated with the chapel, its bell, and the ungeometrical nature of the hut of Philemon and Baucis. As a ship unloads riches from far-off lands, Faust decrees that the old couple must give way to his "masterpiece of the human spirit" (11248). Mephistopheles and three mighty men go off to enact Faust's desire.

In Scene 19, in the middle of the night, Lynceus the watchman sees Philemon's hut and grove burning, and laments. "Regrettably," Mephistopheles and his henchmen had to use a bit of force. Philemon and Baucis died of fright, and their visitor was killed when he tried to help. Faust, beset with misgivings, sees something moving in the shadows.

Scene 20. It is Midnight. Want, Debt, Need, and Care, as four grey women, come to haunt Faust, intimating death. But only Care remains. Does he know her? Faust: "I have only run through the world. / I grabbed by the hair each passing pleasure" (11433–34). But there is no salvation in eternity. He still has much to do and experience, and the courage to go ever further; now, he says, as a man alone and without magic. At the very end, then, Faust implicity rejects Mephistopheles, and he also refuses to recognize Care or submit to her regime. She breathes on him, blinding him, but Faust remains courageous and defiant. His workmen will set to work again.

In the forecourt of the palace (Scene 21), Mephistopheles and a gang of Lemurs come to claim Faust. They are digging his grave, not, as the blinded Faust believes, at work on another of Faust's projects. He speaks of his last great enterprise, to clear a swamp to produce an inland paradise, a living space for millions, a free people on a free land; but he contemplates then sitting back and saying to that moment, "Linger on, you are so beautiful" (11582). Mephistopheles pounces. He has Faust, and Faust dies: "All is fulfilled" (11594).

Scene 22. As Faust is prepared for burial, Mephistopheles claims his due. He will show the dead Faust the "blood-signed document" of the wager. Hell opens to receive Faust, but angels descend from above, scattering heavenly roses. The devils descend back into hell and Mephistopheles, distracted and titillated by the boy-angels, is betrayed by his lust. This allows the angels to command the space around Faust. They soar upwards, carrying with them Faust's "immortal part." Mephistopheles is left to rue his loss.

Scene 23 shows mountain gorges, with holy anchorites settled in the caves in the mountainside. (This scene, with some cuts, was set by Mahler as the colossal second and final movement of his Eighth Symphony.) The fathers sing of nature and of the ecstasy and the releasing energy of everlasting love. The spirits of boys who died young make their way to heaven. Angels in the upper atmosphere carry Faust's immortal part. The noble spirit is redeemed from evil: "He who is ever striving / Him can we save" (11936–37). But Faust still needs purification. After a prayer from Doctor Marianus, the highest of the fathers, the Virgin Mary appears as Mater Gloriosa. The three penitent women from the gospels intercede for Gretchen, who in turn, as a penitent herself, intercedes for Faust: "he whom I early loved, now undarkened, he comes back to me" (12073–75). He is purified, dazzled by the new day into which he steps. The Mystic Chorus sings:

> All that is passing
> Is but an image;
> What lies beyond us
> Here becomes definite.
> What cannot be described
> Here can be reached.
> The eternal feminine
> Draws us on high. (12104–11)

Conclusion

The parallels of the last scene with Dante are obvious, but so are the differences. Gretchen is no Beatrice. There is hardly a sense of sin, or of man's disobedience, first or otherwise. There is a quest and a salvation, but it is driven by energy and the transformative power of life and Nature; and the eternal feminine which draws us on and spurs us to creative activity (and in the case of the Homunculus, to embodiment itself) is symbolized as much by Helen, Galatea, Aphrodite, and Margareta/Gretchen as by the Mater Gloriosa and the other Marys of the Gospel. Goethe's ambition in *Faust, Part Two* was, late in his long life, to express his own vision of the mystery of life and of human experience by melding his vast sensitivity to classical and Christian/medieval mythology into a single epic poem. The result defies classification and even interpretation, but in its own energy, inventiveness and poetry, it nevertheless shows something of that which cannot be encompassed in any one dogmatic framework or language.

There is, of course, an obvious problem about Faust's redemption, in that, in contrast to Augustine or to Pascal, say, Faust himself has shown little sign at any point that he needs redeeming. Indeed, we are to believe that his

memories of the Gretchen episode—for which he certainly does need forgiveness—have all been wiped away at the start of *Part Two,* in a somewhat
blasphemous parallel with Dante stepping into the River Lethe in *Purgatorio.* Nor does he show remorse for the deaths of Philemon and Baucis. It is
not his penitence, of which there is none to speak of, which saves him, but
his endless readiness to strive. In any case, does he really need saving? Arguably—and Goethe surely meant us to see this—Mephistopheles, for all his
legalism about the blood-signed document, has not actually won the wager,
for Faust never uttered the fatal words himself: he merely speculated that he
might do so at some time in the future. But, even aside from all this, there is
an even deeper problem with Faust's "Christian" redemption.

It is that, in his encounter with Care, Faust not only abjures magic and
Mephistopheles. In what is perhaps his only—or certainly his most impressive—piece of moral development, Faust professes the courage to be on his
own and to do on his own. In an echo of Luther's "Here I stand, I can do no
other," Goethe's Faust reveals a profoundly un-Christian sense of courage
and self-sufficiency:

> I would stand before Nature! Before you, a man alone.
> That would be worth the effort, to be a man! (11406–407)

Not that this humanism of Goethe is exactly classical either. We cannot
imagine Achilles or Odysseus or Aeneas professing their pride in being men.
Proud they were, but they had too keen a sense of the gods, of fate, of the
conditions of life which were not of their choosing, of missions not chosen,
to think that there was anything firm enough to sustain an attitude of pride
in the human condition in itself.

Here we touch on what for many will be a problem with Goethe's Faust.
He is a great builder, a regimenter, and an enforcer of people and of Nature.
When in his final speech he proclaims that he will be creating a race of free
people, their freedom depends absolutely on the taming and exploitation of
Nature, specifically on the holding back of the sea and doubtless also the
harnessing of its energy for human purposes. It is, of course, precisely this
instrumentalist attitude to Nature which has come to be known as Faustian, the seeing of Nature as something to be tamed, and as a resource to
satisfy human needs. And, we might ask, what is so wrong with contemplation, with "Verweile doch, du bist so schön"? Isn't this attitude—that of
letting Nature and all else simply be—a more profound, more sublime, more
mystical attitude to Nature and to the world than Faust's endless working,
striving, and exploiting? In Faust's activity and in the premise of the wager,
Faust—and Goethe—show themselves as children of the Enlightenment,
maybe in Goethe's case somewhat inconsistently and unwittingly, for it can

look like a violation of the very Nature that Goethe worships. And in this context, we should recall that Faust had been condemned because he looked as if he had stopped striving, but was redeemed because he was one who had striven. From one point of view, it looks as if striving—and land reclamation—is all.

Striving, though, is not all for Goethe or for Faust, and at a deep level even the Mephistopheles pact is something of a sideshow. For the more profoundly Goethean attitude to Nature is shown in the depiction of the Earth Spirit and of Faust's mountaintop meditations, in which he communes with that Spirit: Nature as elemental force, part of us and we a part of it, bearing us, sustaining us, destroying us, in an endless cycle of creativity, far more potent and awe-inspiring than anything like a temporary bit of Dutch land-reclamation or (from Goethe's point of view) than the God of the chapbook and inventory of salvation:

> Birth and grave,
> An eternal sea,
> An ever changing weaving,
> Ever burning life,
> So I create at the rushing loom of time
> The living garment of the Godhead. (504–509)

And even when Faust abjures his magic when confronted by Care, what he wants is, as a man, to stand face-to-face with Nature, the same Nature that he invokes from the mountaintop as the Great Spirit who has given him all. And we could recall that the "Lord," pale as he is in comparison with the Earth Spirit, in his opening dialogue with Mephistopheles at one point challenges the devil to take "this spirit" (Faust) away from the "very source of his life"; and the source is assuredly not God or Mephistopheles. It is Nature and the Earth Spirit.

It is in this context that we are to see both the thousand upon thousand forms of evolution and the eternal feminine. For us human beings, for all the awe-inspiring forces of the mountains and the storms and the sea, the most personal image and actualization of Nature's creative power, and perhaps the most potent too, is the female form: rising up from the sea in her shell, like Galatea/Venus; like Helen in Arcadia; and also like Margareta/Gretchen in her room and in the summer house. At the end of the classical Walpurgis Night, as the Homunculus shatters into the sea, we are told that Eros is the cause of all. This is the eternal feminine which draws us on, and whose sense Goethe captures in his hauntingly beautiful evocation of the classical Arcadia in which Faust and Helen and Euphorion momentarily disport themselves.

It is easy, too easy, to point to the inconsistencies of time, place, mood, and theme in Goethe's *Faust,* and really beside the point. No one would want to argue that in the two parts, and over the sixty or so years he worked on it, Goethe actually reconciled the medieval/Gothic/Christian with the classical. Even if Helen does come to Mistra, her ambience and the air she breathes is actually the pastoral Arcadia of the poets of ancient Greece and Rome. For all Goethe's efforts, Mephistopheles cannot really find a home in that world; nor, for all her moral superiority at the end of *Part One* (which is almost wholly overlooked in *Part Two*), is poor little Gretchen anything but a simpleton before the sensuality of Leda and the swan, the tragic beauty of Helen, and the Botticelli-like vision of Galatea. *Faust, Part One* is dramatically compelling, and an endless inspiration to the northern imagination. By comparison, *Part Two* is sprawling, discursive, and at times obsessive in its treatment of themes as diverse as the invention of money, the disputes between the Vulcanists and the Neptunists, the nature of empire, and the exploitation of nature. And it is not easy to accept, let alone justify, Faust's— and Goethe's—shameful forgetfulness of Gretchen between the two parts. In compensation, though, in its poetry *Part Two* conjures up many of the aged Goethe's most powerful evocations of nature, and above all that generous and sunlit sense of the beauty of the south and of classical landscape and myth which he himself had acquired as he moved from his early Romantic and Germanic preoccupations into his poetic maturity.

Epilogue

Our survey of great books has taken us from Homer, in the mists of European pre-history, to the firmly historical figure of Goethe in the nineteenth century. There is in a sense a nice symmetry about this, because we have gone from Homer's Helen of Troy, with whom it all began, to Goethe's Helen of Sparta, the same figure refracted through so much history and legend and through Goethe's own synthesizing genius. Of course, neither Helen nor great books stopped in 1831. Helen herself has featured with more or less profundity (and often with less) in countless literary works since, to say nothing of operas, films, and plays. And, to speak of only the European nineteenth-century post-Goethe, great books have surely been written by many writers, including Tolstoy, Dostoyevsky, Balzac, Flaubert, Dickens, and George Eliot, to name only novelists.

There is, though, some rationale for stopping where we have. For—with some notable exceptions, particularly in poetry—nineteenth- and twentieth-century literature does not presuppose in the reader a detailed knowledge of the Greek and Roman classics, in the same way that Milton does in *Paradise Lost,* say, or as Goethe does in the second part of *Faust.* A certain type of difficulty which the modern reader will experience in reading many of the works we have considered here will just not arise when he or she reads *Great Expectations,* or *War and Peace,* or *Crime and Punishment,* or the novels of Thomas Hardy, or Henry James, or from the twentieth century, Hemingway, or Scott Fitzgerald, or Saul Bellow, or Betjeman, or Larkin. And even in modernist poetry—the great receptacle in our age for classical reference—the difficulty arises as much from a deliberate cultivation of a hermetic style, quite foreign to Virgil, say, or Dante, as from the classical references themselves.

The difficulty we face in reading many of the great books we have discussed is comparatively straightforward. It is not that their authors are putting deliberate difficulties or obscurities in our path, as a sort of metaphor

321

for our own fragmented mind and culture, as were twentieth-century writers such as Pound, Eliot, and Joyce. The difficulty we face, to put it crudely, is simple ignorance in our age of the myths of Greece and Rome, and, for the later works we have considered, of the Bible as well. There is no need to apologize for having spent so much time in this book on the classics of ancient Greece, for their study is not just an education in itself; they simply are the soil from which Western art and literature have sprung. Yet, for reasons we cannot consider here, and to our collective shame, for the vast majority today they remain a closed book—which part of the point of this book is to open a little.

Apart from the pleasure and instruction to be gained from reading Homer, Virgil, Dante, Milton, and the rest, a knowledge of the great books considered here will throw light on many modern works. There are, of course, those which refer explicitly to the ancient classics—the poetry of Pound and T. S. Eliot and George Seferis, Joyce's *Ulysses,* and so on. But over and above that, the themes of the great books are perennial in our culture (and maybe in others too): war and peace, homecoming, guilt and redemption, revenge and justice, family love (and hate) and public duty, sexual love and lust and all the emotions connected with them, Dionysiac passion and civilized restraint, thought as opposed to action, ideals and reality, the dialogue between the noble and the common man, the picaresque in dialectic with the aristocratic, and the journey of the human spirit in this world and to the other.

There is more than a little to be gained by encountering these themes in the hands of writers universally admitted to be great, but whose presuppositions are not those of our age. One way into one of the contrasts between ourselves and most of the writers we have considered might be to focus on the way in which the power and conception of reverence and of a sacred order not of human making operates in their works: in Homer, certainly, in Greek tragedy and Plato, in Virgil and even in Ovid, in Augustine and Pascal, in Dante and Milton, in Shakespeare and to a degree even in Chaucer (as, for all the ribaldry, simply unquestioned), in Racine (almost by the absence of God), and in Goethe with his tremendous sense of the power and creativity of the Earth Spirit.

It is not that men are better in these works than they are today; but their lives and sensibilities are conditioned by a potent sense of subordination to a reality we have not chosen and to powers greater than us—by a sense of what the philosopher Santayana called piety. Of course, there are differences between the powers and orders involved, depending on the works. To adapt Ruskin, for the Greeks the gods were those of Wisdom and Power (and of a wisdom and power unsentimental and unconcerned with the feelings of humanity); for the medieval and Christian, the God was of Judgment and Consolation (and of consolation only because He was also the God of judgment, who could thereby meaningfully bestow love and mercy on his disobedient creation); and for those affected by the Renaissance, the gods were those of pride and beauty and nature (discernible in different ways in our selection in Shakespeare and in Goethe).

Following on from the power of—and reverence for—the gods displayed therein, we find in most of our great books human characters of heroic stature: Achilles, Hector, Odysseus, Agamemnon, Oedipus, Antigone, Aeneas, Dido, Hamlet, Henry V, Phèdre, Faust; or pilgrims in a realm of religious grandeur and awe, such as Augustine, Dante, and Pascal, and maybe even Chaucer and his companions on the road to Canterbury; or anti-heroes, whose anti-heroism derives much of its shape and force from a context of ideals of greatness and reverence: Falstaff, Don Quixote, and Milton's Satan. In our democratic age, the heroic is deeply anachronistic, so much so that we could hardly recreate a Don Quixote for our time, for there is nothing now remotely analogous to knightly chivalry to contrast him with, let alone a Miltonic Satan raging against the injustice of an omnipotent deity, for among contemporary writers there is scarcely any sense of such a god to rebel against. Even Falstaff is a lord of misrule against an unquestioned background of rule, the antithesis of the kingly Henry IV and the temptation to which the heir apparent so willingly succumbs—but only for a time before he is called back to his divinely sanctioned vocation of kingship, for which, as he tells us, he has to suffer the suppression of ordinary feelings and joys.

We have said enough in this book already to underline the distance in belief, in sensibility and in vision between us today and the classical and Christian writers whose works we have been considering. The distance is not completely unbridgeable. As we have emphasized, there is continuity too, and their visions are those which have directly and indirectly formed our own. But we do nothing by pretending that there is not distance, as happens so often in contemporary approaches to the classics. Instead of visions from which we might learn something old and something important, in approaching the classics all too often we simply refract ourselves and our own prejudices back from the myths of the past.

We will consider two recent examples taken more or less at random, but which can stand for a host of other similar cases. In the 2004 film version of *Troy*, leaving aside a host of gratuitous alterations to the story, Agamemnon, far from being the (flawed) eagle and leader of men of whom Homer and Plato speak, becomes a contemporary politician; Odysseus hardly the commanding figure we know from Homer, but just the ubiquitous fixer and spin-doctor; and in two startling anachronisms of interpretation, Briseis is portrayed as a gutsy liberated female, and Hector a new man role model; and, worst of all, aside from an embarrassingly improbable Thetis, there are no gods at all—as if Homer and the Greeks make any sense at all without the gods, and without that sense of interconnectedness of the divine, the human and the animal of which George Seferis wrote so illuminatingly. Then in English National Opera's production of Berlioz's *Trojans* (which was intended by Berlioz as the culmination of a lifetime of homage to Virgil) we find almost every Virgilian connotation almost deliberately wiped out: Aeneas—according to Virgil, like "the Lord Apollo in the spring," with his hair bound "in fronded laurel, braided in gold," walking "with sunlit grace upon him," this son of Venus—is portrayed here as a shaven-headed punk; Dido herself—Sidonian Dido, Queen of Carthage, a leader and inspiration to her people, a truly regal figure clothed in gold and scarlet, according to Virgil— on the stage in a business suit, as if she was on her way to a board meeting to set targets and adumbrate outcomes; the cave in which the lovers consummate their love (to some of Berlioz's most magical music), opened by Primal Earth herself and Nuptial Juno, and attended by torches of lightning and nymphs crying from the mountaintops, according to Virgil (and Berlioz), here a trap door in the middle of a bare stage; and the Trojans themselves boorish mercenaries, carrying not the gods of Troy but the impedimenta of modern warfare (as if, on entering what we thought was to be a representation of Carthage, we needed to be reminded of Iraq).

We profess to be shocked at Garrick's alterations to *Romeo and Juliet* and to *King Lear*, at Victorian bowdlerizations of Shakespeare, and congratulate ourselves on being beyond all that sort of stuff; but I can see very little difference between these aberrations and what English National Opera did to *The Trojans* or Hollywood did to *The Iliad,* and what countless other opera directors, theatrical producers, and filmmakers routinely do to the works of the past. Far from swimming in the lake of antique poetry, as Berlioz himself said he hoped to do in composing his opera, or even leading the audience to its shore, they appear to see their role as to shallow out the lake altogether so that any paddling we might do in it conforms to the dictates of contemporary mental health and safety.

In response to what I have so far said, it might be replied that the history of literature is, in part, a history of the reworking of old themes in the light of new mentalities. Indeed, as we hope to have brought out in this book, Homeric themes and their continual reworking run like a golden thread through much of our culture: the tragedies of Aeschylus and Sophocles, *The Aeneid,* Shakespeare's *Troilus and Cressida* (no gods there!), Racine's tragedies, Goethe's *Faust,* Berlioz's *Trojans* itself, Joyce's *Ulysses,* etc. In this context we should surely draw a distinction between a distorted production of an antique work and an attempt to revivify an old myth for a modern audience. The film of *Troy* is thus vindicated where ENO's *Trojans* stands condemned.

We might accept part of this reply. There is indeed something far worse about a self-conscious and deliberate distortion of the spirit of an existing work than a harmless variation on an old theme. But there is still a question as to the light or otherwise that the new variation throws on the old theme (and, frankly, does anyone think that *Ulysses* throws light on *The Odyssey*, rather than Homer's *Odyssey* being needed to make sense of Joyce's labyrinthine obfuscations?), and also as to the extent to which the new variation adds to or subtracts from the original. I suppose that nothing could actually add to *The Iliad* or even to *The Odyssey*. Compared to the exuberant directness of Homer and his sheer joy in storytelling, Virgil's attempt to synthesize both epics and to vindicate Troy and Rome will appear self-conscious, even if in Virgil's own way *The Aeneid* has furnished our collective mind with its own enduring images and poetry, and continues to do so.

It is doubtful that the film *Troy* will ever do that, because of its utterly commonplace mentality, but the real criticism of it is that by its very verisimilitude of setting and costume it misleads people into thinking that they have been given Homer. It proclaims itself as having being "inspired" by Homer. At best it is a colossal lost opportunity and at worst it is as misleading as setting Wagner's *Ring* in a nineteenth-century factory, or with the gods of Valhalla as 1930s gangsters or the Gibichung court as a bunch of Nazis. It is a domestication of something which should resist domestication, a testament to our own parochiality of mind (or at least of the parochiality of the director, as we saw in the production of *The Trojans*), and it sabotages its potential. Perhaps, to show that what we are complaining about here does not infect only the theater and popular culture, we should say that the way Plato is usually taught in British universities (though not, we hope, discussed here) is just as parochial as Petersen's film of *Troy,* for those doing the teaching nine times out of ten simply ignore the mythology and mysticism which permeates all Plato's thought, as if these things were too naïve and embarrassing even to notice.

Revisionist directors and producers will say—as do many contemporary teachers of literature—that the reason we have to revise the obvious intentions of earlier authors and composers is because we have to make difficult and alien texts relevant to the needs and interests of potential audiences of today. They will also claim that in their resettings they are clearing away the gratuitous accretions and misplaced reverence which have become attached to these texts over the centuries and making them relevant to our own time, in much in the same way as cleaners treat old paintings, restoring them to a pristine and original freshness. Actually this is not an analogy which helps their case. The history of the restoration of old paintings and buildings has been as much a history of how succeeding ages have imposed their own aesthetic on works of the past, and in so doing have all too often contributed to the destruction of what they claim to be restoring.

But, one wonders, why do we want relevance anyway? It is, of course, as close to dogma as anything in current cultural and educational practice that all material has to be made relevant to the needs, interests, and backgrounds of today's audiences, readers, and pupils. This dogma is all of a piece with the Whiggish presumption that our society and our mentality is the prism through which the past and other eras should and must be viewed. But it is just that, dogma and presumption.

In fact, "relevance" is just as likely to dampen interest and enthusiasm as to inspire them. This is in part because of the fruitful complexity and density of works like *The Aeneid* or *Paradise Lost,* to say nothing of the wealth of critical literature about the great works of the past. In this critical literature we see the contribution of some of the most reflective minds of the past to the understanding of the literature of the past, which itself becomes part of the weight of the meaning of those works. All this helps to explain why at school able pupils, at least, often actually prefer studying Milton or Shakespeare or Donne to the contemporary writers of works of fiction and poetry who increasingly appear on their examination syllabi. The incidentals of plot aside, contemporary authors and books tell them what they know (or think they know) already, and there is little of any great interest to say about them, or certainly little of any great interest that has been said about them.

By contrast, it is not difficult to inspire interest in the languages and images of *Paradise Lost,* say, and once interest has been inspired, the great lake of antique poetry is before one. To attempt to pretend that *Paradise Lost* has immediate or obvious connections with the life (or simulacrum of life) which is portrayed in *EastEnders* or *Coronation Street,* or that such material might provide a way in to it, is condescending to all involved. A critical point about contemporary productions of this sort is that in their quest for a certain sort of "realism" there is a relentless determination to show life in its most brutal, sentimental, demeaning, and vulgar light. They present the audience with a vision of life which (in Ruskin's terms) can "neither see anything beautiful around it, not anything virtuous above it," precluding just that element of reverence which characterizes most of the great books of the past. To deny or obscure the elevated ambition and achievement of these works in the name of contemporary realism or relevance is, as Matthew Arnold put it, not the way of culture; according to Arnold, "culture does not try to teach down to the level of inferior classes," nor does it "try to win them with ready-made judgments and watchwords."[20] It is, of course, partly because Milton is not "ready-made," trotting out the clichés of the day like a television soap, that he can still speak to us today, as his great learned, poetic, and religious sensibility wrestles—and maybe all too obviously and uncomfortably and unsuccessfully wrestles—with the most profound of themes.

At a deep level, no doubt Milton does speak to the condition of those portrayed in *EastEnders,* as indeed he speaks to the rest of us; but that the characters in *EastEnders* would recognize their predicament as having anything to do with "man's first disobedience"—or indeed with human disobedience at all—is inconceivable. It is inconceivable precisely because in contemporary prejudice, as reflected in the popular culture of our time (and no doubt itself deeply permeated by the Romanticism of Rousseau), there is no logical space for the thought that our lives might be tainted by disobedience of the sort that Milton and, in their different ways, Saint Augustine and Dante and Pascal, and also Aeschylus and Sophocles and Euripides and Plato were all obsessed by.

In fact, contra Rousseau and his myriad followers both high and low, there is a strong case for thinking that mankind is naturally disobedient. Original sin, even as we try to ignore it, is part of our condition, even if not necessarily in the way Milton describes; also redemption of the sort hinted at by Augustine and Dante and Milton may be an ever-present possibility, though again not necessarily in the way they adumbrate. But even for those unable or unwilling to see the world in this way, there is no denying that the notions of disobedience, original sin, and redemption have been deeply influential in Western consciousness, and indirectly at least still are. As Nietzsche recognized more clearly than most, and even as our most progressive thinkers strive to avoid the implications of the point, our whole morality and sensibility—our predicament, if you like—continues to be informed by concepts and feelings which really make sense only if we recognize their Greek and Christian roots. We should include here the otherwise philosophically baffling notions of justice, human rights, equality, and colonial guilt, which play so large a role in our politics and popular culture, but which make little sense except if we see ourselves as children of God, before whom we are all equal. (We are not all equal in any other way; nor, for all the deluge of books and articles on the subject, has any other way so far been satisfactorily excogitated for grounding universal human rights.) In the sense that it takes us back to the mythology which spawned these concepts and feelings, *Paradise Lost* throws light on our predicament, but only if we take it on its own terms. We have to swim in its lake and begin to understand how it might be to live and move and have one's being in such a mentality.

In their own way, so do the *Divine Comedy, The Oresteia,* and *The Iliad* throw light on what we are today, for, to continue the theme of disobedience, the notion of disobedience to God or the gods, and the continuing effects of that disobedience, is ever-present in Greek epic and tragedy, as well as in Christian thought. To take but one example, which we have already considered, the destruction of Troy itself is a colossal offense to man and to the gods, and was seen by the Greeks as such, as was the brutal deed which launched the Greeks on their way, and which proved ten years later to be Agamemnon's nemesis; none of Greek thought and literature can be understood without understanding that their greatest mythological triumph was also a great offense, and recognized by them to be an offense, polluting all involved—and their descendants, who in a sense benefited from this primal crime. Simone Weil put the point about hidden continuity between the Greeks and ourselves on such matters as primal guilt by talking of "intimations of Christianity" among the ancient Greeks. We might just as well put the same point by speaking of echoes of ancient Greece in Christianity.

So, what I am saying, to put the matter programmatically, is that to benefit from antique poetry we have to let it speak as it is. We have to submit ourselves to the works, bend ourselves to them. We do not ask ourselves what impression they make on us, or how we feel about them—before we have studied them in and for themselves. Even less should we get pupils into the habit of asking themselves how they would feel if they were Hector, say, or Dido, or getting them to transpose Hector and Dido into a twenty-first-century context; this would be of a piece with thinking that history can be done by getting pupils with a pristine and untroubled twenty-first-century mentality to say what an agony aunt might have said to Lady Macbeth (an actual example from a recent public exam in England); or how they themselves might have felt had they been a slave in ancient Athens or in the trenches of the Somme or in the Crusades. For whatever our pupils might think they would have felt in these situations or as these personae, without an education which distances them from the prejudices of their own time, it would not be how the historical agents or literary characters of earlier times felt.

What matters is that we ask the poets and their characters what it is they have to tell us, striving as far as we can to hear what, across the centuries, they have to say to us. Then, and only then, is our response to the point, and our response must be to them and to what they say, not to some modernized version of them. Then and only then will the response be part of a genuine conversation through the ages, and not a self-enclosed dialogue whose only voices are those of our own time.

There is, though, a question of ability. Is the lake of antique poetry for readers of all abilities? Some have certainly thought so, including Simone Weil, who wrote, simply but uncompromisingly, about Sophocles' *Antigone* for French factory workers. In Saul Bellow's *The Dean's December* we are told that only the savage poetry of *Macbeth* could touch the souls of children from the Chicago ghetto, surrounded as they were with poverty and violence, so as "to rival the attractions of narcotics, the magnetism of TV, the excitements of sex, or the ecstasies of destruction."[21]

One would like to think so. But there are dangers here, too, in the agenda of inclusiveness. Should we simply assume that art is for all, when we do not know who are included in the all, and when, in conversations of this type, "all" is likely to signify people en masse, people as reflected in the mirror of the mass media, people without any of the education in antique poetry and the rest that they would need in order to come to any sort of appreciation of it? The ambition and hope of a book such as this is that it will go some way to including those let down by their education in the worlds of "great books."

There is a hard path to be trodden here. As followers of Arnold we must not track down to the masses. The masses must be offered the best, unadulterated, and also treated as individuals with their own individual potential and viewpoint, and not just as representatives of some sociologically defined group. But in the confidence that we are offering the best, we must not be deflected when, as will inevitably happen, "the public" in its collectivist voice, or in the persons of those purporting to speak on its behalf, rejects the best as elitist or as too difficult or as just irrelevant.

The poet Kathleen Raine once said this: "Suppose human society to be a pyramid whose base is everyone's due, and whose apex is the highest attainable human excellence. Somewhere between base and apex we must each find our place; but never must the standards of excellence be lost or corrupted, for to realize the highest excellence is perhaps the task of our race in the economy of the universe. Those who give expression, whether in knowledge or in moral or aesthetic beauty, to the highest things, are giving to the world patterns of a perfection to which all must strive, which is latent in all. Through the creations of the few we all live, somewhat, in Genji's court, in Plato's Academy, in Mme Verdurin's salon."[22]

I have to say that I have my doubts about living in the Verdurin salon itself, as opposed to inhabiting the comedy and irony of Proust's matchless description of it, but Raine's underlying intuition I do share. We have to aspire to the highest things, to the extent that we can. As teachers, particularly of literature, our most important task—and the one for which ultimately we will most be thanked—is to open eyes and feelings to those highest things.

It will be obvious from what I have said that I believe there is value in the world and in some works of art, objectively speaking; and that even if it needs a human sensibility to perceive the value in (say) *The Iliad,* and *The Iliad* is a human creation, nevertheless that it is valuable is not just a projection of their own feelings on the part of those who perceive it. What they perceive, its meaning and its value (to the extent that it is valuable), is there, whether particular individuals perceive it or not. To the extent that people do not perceive it, they are diminished. Good art, says Iris Murdoch, "thought of as symbolic force rather than statement provides a stirring image of a pure transcendent value, a steadily visible enduring higher good, and perhaps provides for many people, in an unreligious age without prayer and sacraments, their clearest experience of something grasped as separate and precious and beneficial and held quietly, and unpossessively in the attention."

Think, I would suggest, of *The Tempest*, of *Phèdre*, of the *Divine Comedy*, of *Antigone*. This is at least part of the reason for swimming in the lake of antique poetry, and part of the reason for us submitting ourselves to it. And in the confrontation with the other thing and its value, hinted at in our earlier remarks about piety and the sacred order, for a time the grip on us of what Murdoch calls the soft fat ego is loosened. This is the most fundamental reason why in approaching great art the route should not be through our own ego, nor through our own prejudices and those of our time, as refracted through our own unchallenged and unrefined feelings and self-awareness. Of course, as Iris Murdoch also emphasized, there is also plenty of art which is not great, and which simply feeds the soft fat ego with wish-fulfillment, and flatters its view of the world; so, instructed by our experience of the best, we must learn to discriminate, and, as occasion arises, pass this discrimination on.

But, bad and mediocre art aside, in the contemplation of good art we let the thing and its value speak for itself. We value it in and for itself. To adapt a striking image of the poet Hölderlin, in our contemplation of it, a great work of art is like a rock against which the wave of our sentimentality is scattered. In its presence we cease to be the center of our world, and the structure of our feelings and sensibility is reformed. In a sense, that a work of art precisely does not stem from or reflect the surfaces of our existing needs, interests, and cultural background is in its favor. It may be something which can work on us, rather than the other way round.

Part of what I want to say is hinted at in Rilke's First *Duino Elegy:*

> Beauty's nothing
> but beginning of Terror we're just still able to bear,
> and why we adore it so is because it serenely
> disdains to destroy us
> So, the thing is there, apart from us, impermeable and still, impervious
> to us, yet so attractive to us, and attractive in part because it has no
> need of us. And yet, and yet;

Rilke goes on:

> Many a star
> was waiting for you to perceive it. Many a wave
> would rise in the past towards you; or else, perhaps,
> as you went by an open window, a violin
> would be utterly giving itself. All this was commission.
> But were you equal to it?
> (Translation by J. B. Leishman and Stephen Spender (Chatto & Windus/Hogarth Press, 1963).)

Our imaginative response to beauty is part of the divine economy of the world. But our response must be one of giving, rather than of taking, of letting be, rather than of grasping, of letting go of ourselves rather than of wrapping the thing up in the rags of our needs, interests, and backgrounds. As Rilke says in "Archaic Torso of Apollo" (of 1908) of the "intact stone" torso, which is all that is left of the kouros, it gives light like a star, prompting the command: "You must change your living." Many of the works discussed here will in their own individual ways prompt such a response.

The metaphysical view underlying what is being urged here is unfashionable. The fashionable view is that when we apply aesthetic and moral predicates to things, be they works of art or natural objects, what we are really doing is expressing our feelings, feelings which we then project on the things. Further, the human world, the world in which things are endowed with human meaning, is something which we add to the world—and add without ultimate warrant in the nature of things.

It is this view which is attacked by C. S. Lewis in the first chapter of *The Abolition of Man*,[24] in which Lewis analyzes the views of the writers of a school literature textbook. The writers, whom he calls Gaius and Titius, say that when Coleridge talks about the travelers at a waterfall, one of whom calls it "sublime" and the other "pretty," and Coleridge agrees with the one and disagrees with the other, he is himself confused. For when the man calls the waterfall sublime, he is not saying anything about the waterfall, but only about his own feelings. According to Gaius and Titius, that he is saying something objective, and about which Coleridge can disagree, is an illusion ever-present in our language: "We appear to be saying something very important about something: and actually we are only saying something about our own feelings."

As Lewis point out, the view of Gaius and Titius flies in the face of the age-old conviction that even to inanimate nature, and certainly in our responses to moral good and aesthetic beauty more generally, certain responses are more appropriate than others. This conviction, Lewis adds, underlies all the great philosophies and religions of the past. I would add that, far from being a confusion, the age-old conviction is actually the only one which makes any sense of our language and behavior. So many of our judgments, moral and aesthetic, make sense only on the assumption that the world itself (and not just the human world) is infused with a value in itself beyond anything we humans have projected on to it. Nevertheless, Lewis spoke in vain, at least as far as many modern critics are concerned, who write as if in discussing beauty and other aesthetic properties, all you can talk about are the responses we have to what we see or experience.

Thus Robert Macfarlane in *Mountains of the Mind* says that "when we look at a landscape, we do not see what is there, but largely what we think is there. We attribute qualities to a landscape which it does not intrinsically possess—savageness, for example, or bleakness—and we value it accordingly. We read landscapes . . . The way people behave towards mountains has little or nothing to do with the actual objects of rock and ice themselves. Mountains are only contingencies of geology . . ." And apart from their geology, all the rest of what we think about them has been "imagined" into existence by human beings down the centuries.[25]

In support of this view, Macfarlane quotes Byron's Childe Harold staring down into the waters of Lac Leman: "to me, / High mountains are a feeling." This is very misleading. What the Childe actually says is:

> I live not in myself, but I become
> Portion of that around me, and to me,
> High mountains are a feeling, but the hum
> Of human cities a torture; I can see
> Nothing to loathe in nature, save to be
> A link reluctant in a fleshly chain,
> Class'd among creatures, when the soul can flee,
> And with the sky, the peak, the heaving plain
> Of ocean, or the stars, mingle, and not in vain.

And a couple of stanzas further on, he asks:

> Are not the mountains, waves, and skies, a part
> Of me and of my soul, as I of them?

What Byron is saying is that, far from his feeling about the mountains being a projection that he reads into them, he and they are part of a unifying, quasi-pantheistic Goethean process in which he achieves his higher vocation in fleeing to them and mingling his feelings with theirs and with what their nature summons forth from him. The sky, the mountains, and the ocean's heaving plains are chemistry, geology, biology, but they are more than that; and that more we can respond to, and in so responding, we complete one turn of the Rilkean (or is it Hegelian?) circle in which we are formed by these things through progressively rendering their spirit and meaning articulate and conscious.

Against a perspective of objective value in the world, at least in part summoned up in human perception of and activity in that world, but really there nevertheless to be summoned up by us, I would conclude by saying this.

The lake of antique poetry, like the archaic torso, is one way in which we get in touch with and articulate the value in the world, or possibly out of the world, precisely because the works we have been considering are not just powerful and beautiful in themselves, but assume an order beyond their and our making. And here we return to a crucial difference between much modern literature and art and the great classical and Christian classics we have been considering here. In the classics we have been looking at the assumption that there is an order to which we respond. We may make that order articulate, but in responding we respond to values and meanings which are there. We disclose what may not have been seen before, but which is there to be disclosed. We interpret and name, as Adam did in Paradise; but even if, before Adam did his work, things were not experienced and named in quite that human way, his interpreting and naming was within an objective order, set up by God, and constrained by it. Babel happened when men in their pride sought transcendence of the divine order, when we sought to become creators and arbiters of value ourselves.

We live in an age when god is dead, or supposed to be dead, in which we as humans project value on to an otherwise valueless world; we invent values where there were none without us, and we interpret to satisfy our needs, not in a quest to uncover what is there in some sense without us. Since the mid-nineteenth century much (though not all) art and literature has been premised on that assumption and has been a deliberate attempt to articulate a vision of a world without god or gods, and of value and values as no more than a human creation or projection. We, but not our forebears, are in the situation of Babel. In this situation art becomes, not an insight into truth, but an avoidance of a truth too deadening and terrible to contemplate, a diversion in Pascal's sense. By contrast, in their being rooted in a sacred order, and in their premise of a symbolic order shared by their audiences, the great books we have been considering may be as foreign to us as individuals as their spirit is foreign to our age. But even if god is dead, there is something to be gained from knowing from the inside, as it were, what it might have been like to live in a world filled with the presence of god or gods, for we still live in the hollowed-out shell of such a world.

There is perhaps a paradox here, for, as just remarked, the backgrounds of belief against which these books were written presupposed a settled value and order of things not of human making. Yet they are all works of human making, as much fictions as anything written today in the belief that human fictions and creations are all there is. In our age, as we have just said, we are brought up to believe that any values we have are values that we ourselves have created. We believe that we invent right and wrong (to paraphrase the title of a highly influential philosophy text). In our art and culture we reverence human creativity above all else, and (like Macfarlane and Lewis's Gaius and Titius) we see ourselves in a universe with no ultimate meaning or direction other than what we give it.

Yet—and this is the potential paradox—what we have in our selection of works from *The Iliad* to *Faust* are productions of human imagination, and in many ways theatrical and contrived and idiosyncratic creations, as much as any work of twentieth-century deconstruction, as at least some of our authors playfully recognize. For all that they bear witness to orders supposed to be beyond human imagination. But—to soften the paradox a little—it might be that entry into imaginative expressions of worlds of faith and sacred order, such as some of those we have been considering here, might give us today the most accessible route into those worlds. But they will do this for us only, of course, to the extent that we take them on their own terms, as so close to us but also as so far from us.

References

References to Secondary Texts Quoted or Referred To:

1. David Hume, "Of the Standard of Taste," 1757.
2. George Seferis, *A Poet's Journal: Days of 1945–51* (Harvard: Belnap Press, 1974), 49.
3. Matthew Arnold, "The Choice of Subjects in Poetry," the Preface to his *Poems* of 1853.
4. Simone Weil, "*The Iliad*, Poem of Might," in her *Intimations of Christianity Among the Ancient Greeks* (London: Routledge and Kegan Paul, 1957).
5. Friedrich Nietzsche, *The Birth of Tragedy out of the Spirit of Music,* 1871.
6. I. F. Stone, *The Trial of Socrates* (London: Jonathan Cape, 1988).
7. Hermann Broch, *The Death of Virgil,* originally published in 1945 in both English and German.
8. Friedrich Schiller, "On Naive and Sentimental Poetry," 1795.
9. Hector Berlioz, letter to his sister Adèle Suat, June 22, 1856 (quoted in David Cairns, *Berlioz: Servitude and Greatness 1832–1869* (London: Penguin Books, 2000), 606.
10. In *Selected Prose of T. S. Eliot,* edited by Frank Kermode (London: Faber and Faber, 1975), 123.
11. Ted Hughes, *Tales from Ovid* (London: Faber and Faber, 1997), ix.
12. Thomas Carlyle, "The Hero as Poet," lecture 3 of *On Heroes, Hero-Worship and the Heroic in History,* originally delivered in 1840.
13. In *Selected Prose of T. S. Eliot,* as in note 10, 220.
14. In Simone Weil, "Are We Struggling for Justice?," *Philosophical Investigations,* Vol. 10, No. 1, January 1987.
15. Jorge Luis Borges, "Everything and Nothing," in his *Labyrinths,* (Harmondsworth: Penguin Books, 1970), 284–85.
16. William Empson, *Milton's God,* (London: Chatto and Windus, 1961), 251. Blake's judgment is in "The Marriage of Heaven and Hell" (1793)

and Shelley's in "Essay on the Devil and Devils" (1819) and in "A Defence of Poetry" (1821).

17. Sir Philip Sidney, *Defence of Poesie,* written c. 1580–81, published 1595.

18. T. S. Eliot, "Milton II" (1947), in *The Selected Prose of T. S. Eliot,* as in note 10, 269–70.

19. David Hume, *Treatise of Human Nature,* 1739, I.iv.2 and I.iv.7.

20. Matthew Arnold, *Culture and Anarchy,* 1869 (New York: Chelsea House, 1969), 31.

21. Saul Bellow, *The Dean's December* (London: Secker and Warburg, 1982), 187.

22. Kathleen Raine, *Autobiographies* (London: Skoob Books, 1991), 123.

23. Iris Murdoch, *The Fire and the Sun* (Oxford University Press, 1977), 76–77.

24. C. S. Lewis, *The Abolition of Man* (Oxford University Press, 1943).

25. Robert Macfarlane, *Mountains of the Mind* (London: Granta Books, 2004), 18–19.

Acknowledgments

The author and publisher wish to thank the following for their permission to reprint copyright material:

R. M. Rilke, *Duino Elegies,* trans. J. B. Leishman and Stephen Spender (London: Chatto & Windus/Hogarth Press, 1963). Reprinted by permission of The Random House Group Ltd.

G. Seferis, *Collected Poems, 1924–1955,* trans. Edmund Keeley and Philip Sherrod (London: Jonathan Cape, 1969). Reprinted by permission of Princeton University Press.

Augustine, *Against the Academicians* and *The Teacher,* trans. Peter King (Indianapolis: Hackett Publishing Company, Inc., 1995). Reprinted by permission of the publisher. All rights reserved.

J. W. von Goethe, *Faust Part One,* trans. David Luke (Oxford: Oxford University Press, 1987) and *Faust Part Two,* trans. David Luke (Oxford: Oxford University Press, 1994). Reprinted by permission of the publisher.

Augustine, *Confessions,* trans. R. S. Pine-Coffin (London: Penguin Books, 1961). Reprinted by permission of the publisher.

Sophocles, *The Theban Plays,* trans. E. F. Watling (London: Penguin Books, 1947). Reprinted by permission of the publisher.

Cervantes, *Don Quixote,* trans. John Rutherford, (London: Penguin Books, 2000). Reprinted by permission of the publisher.

B. Williams, "The Women of Trachis: Fiction, Pessimism, Ethics" in *The Greeks and Us: Essays in Honor of Arthur W. H. Adkins,* edited by R. B. Louden and P. Schollmeier (Chicago: University of Chicago Press, 1993). Reprinted by permission of the publisher.

Every effort has been made to contact copyright holders for other extracts contained in this book.

Index

Note: the following authors—Homer, Aeschylus, Sophocles, Euripides, Plato, Virgil, Ovid, St Augustine, Dante, Chaucer, Shakespeare, Cervantes, Milton, Pascal, Racine and Goethe—have not been indexed, as they occur passim. This applies also to characters—such as Don Quixote, Henry V, Hamlet, Phèdre, and Faust—who are eponymous to their works.

Index

Byblis, 113
Byron, Lord, 307, 314, 332

C

Cacciaguida, 133, 164–65
Cadmus, 48–49, 61–66
Caesar, *see* Julius Caesar
Cain and Abel, 268–69
Caiphas, 144
Calchas, 5
Callisto, 109, 156
Calvin, John, 278–79
Camilla, 91, 95–100, 137
Cana, marriage feast of, 152, 155
Canaan, 269
Capet, Hugh, 154
Capetian dynasty, 154
Carlyle, Thomas, 170, 173
Carthage, 79–87, 90, 98, 101, 117, 121–25, 228, 324
Cassandra, 15–17, 26, 40–43, 84–85, 110
Cassius, 79, 147
catharsis, concept of, 48
cathedrals, 171, 180
Catholic Church, 278
Cecilia, Saint, 191
Celestine V, Pope, 136–37
centaurs, 66, 105, 140
Cerberus, 89, 139
Ceres, *see also* Demeter, 85, 234, 237
Chaos, 257, 260, 264, 313
Charlemagne, 161, 165
Charles of Anjou, 151, 154
Charon, 88–89, 137
Charybdis, 27, 86
chauvinism, 198
Chiron, 140, 312
chivalry, 193, 243–44, 247, 251–52, 323
Choephori, the, 43
Chorus, role of the, 34
Christ, *see* Jesus Christ
Christian(s), 121, 145, 158–59, 167, 175, 242
  beliefs, 214, 227, 273
  Church, 117, 122
  doctrine, 117, 278
  message, 80
  mythology, 317

martyrs, 191
themes, 125, 302, 310
thought, 117, 171, 175, 328
tradition, 172
virtues, 1
Cicero, 121, 129, 137, 185
Cicones, the, 25
Circe, 25–27, 91
civil war, 45, 57, 71, 79, 154, 256, 263
civilization, fragility of, 46, 61, 66, 99, 199
Claribel, 229, 231–32, 236
Cleopatra, 92, 98, 137, 284
clergy, 150. 178–79
Clouds, The (Aristophanes), 72, 76
Clytemnestra, 5, 36–44, 187
Cocytus, River, 88, 141,
Coleridge, Samuel Taylor, 215–16, 228, 331
Constantine, Emperor, 143, 158, 165
Contra Academicos (St Augustine), 130
conversion, religious, 118–19, 123–25, 126, 128–29, 281, 286
Corinth, 49–50
Corneille, Pierre, 197
Coronation Street, 326
Counter-Reformation, 277
courtly love, 134, 241, 243
Creation, 103, 106, 127, 175–76
Crécy, Battle of, 203
Cretan labyrinth, 110
Crete, 5, 27, 75, 77, 85, 141, 156, 290, 293
Crime and Punishment (Dostoyevsky), 321
Crito (Plato), 70, 74, 77
Crucifixion, the, 143
Crusades, the, 328
Cupid, 84, 107, 234
Cyclops, 22, 25, 66, 83, 86
Cymbeline (Shakespeare), 228

D

Damascus, 119
damned, the, 135–37, 139, 141, 146, 173–74, 176, 258
Daniel, 155, 186
Daphne, 107
Darwin, Charles, 273
De Casibus Virorum Illustrum (Boccaccio), 185
De Genesi ad Litteram (St Augustine), 130

341

H

I

Index

About the Author

Anthony O'Hear is Professor of Philosophy at the University of Buckingham, Director of the Royal Institute of Philosophy, and Editor of the journal Philosophy. He is the author of many books and articles on philosophy, including *Karl Popper* (1980), *The Element of Fire* (1988), *Beyond Evolution* (1997), *Philosophy in the New Century* (2001), *After Progress* (1999), and *Plato's Children* (2006). His journalism has featured particularly in the *Daily Telegraph*, the *Daily Mail,* and the *Express,* and he has often contributed to BBC Radio 4's *Today* program and Radio 3's *Nightwaves*.